The Name Book

The Ultimate Book of Names

REVISED EDITION

By Pierre Le Rouzic
Foreword by Rodney Charles

The ultimate book of names.
An invaluable resource for new parents.
This remarkable volume reaches beyond the ancestry of
names and reveals how names define our personality.

By Pierre Le Rouzic

Souvenir Press

First published in France under the title
Un Prenom pour la vie by Editions Albin Michel S.A., Paris.
English translation first published in the USA in 1982
by Bantam Books. Republished in 1989 by The Sound Name, Inc.,
and in 1994 by Sunstar Publishing Ltd.

First British edition published 1995 by
Souvenir Press Ltd.,
43 Great Russell Street, London WC1B 3PA

ISBN 0 285 63296 5

Printed in Great Britain by
The Guernsey Press Co. Ltd., Guernsey, Channel Islands.

FOREWORD

How can I begin to explain the importance of a name? I recall being greatly impressed with Pierre Le Rouzic when he explained how repeated exposure to sounds (names) effects the way we behave. Some sounds, like fingernails against a blackboard, make us cringe and shiver through our spine. While others, like the playful giggles of a baby, make us feel like everything in the universe is harmonious. Imagine being saddled with a name that made us cringe every time it was spoken. Or on the other hand, imagine a name that filled us with confidence and clarity of character.

The miracle of names and the subtle influences they invoke is made clear by examples from the Old and New Testament of the Bible. Moses mentions that Abram changed his name to Abraham by God's direction and became both the father and leader of the nation of Jews. Further, his wife Sarai remained barren until, by God's endorsement, she changed her name to Sarah and became abundantly fruitful, despite the fact that she had passed the age of childbearing.

Saul actively rallied forces against the new Christian cult, but when transformed by a miracle, he changed his name to Paul and ascended to become the most successful and prolific disciple of Christ. And Christ changed Simon's name to Peter, when he chose him to be the first pope.

Names are vitally important to the extent that they can benefit or disorder our lives with their influence. It is worth our while to understand the appropriateness of naming and Pierre Le Rouzic has made this easy by sharing his fifty years of study in his masterpiece, *The Name Book*.

— Rodney Charles
Author of *Every Day A Miracle Happens*

CONTENTS

Part I

What's in a Name

CHAPTER 1

NAMES

If any one thing is universal, it is a name. At every place and at every time, everyone has received a name. Names brand us with distinctive marks that separate us from the the rest of the herd and, at the same time, make us a part of it.

Strange as this may seem, your name contains a characterological message of paramount importance whose secret code is worth knowing. A name, either yours or mine, is like a computer chip, whose wealth of information needs to be explored to understand its full potential.

This gives us pause for reflection on the extraordinary distillation of our personalities into these few syllables that will be repeated, thousands, or hundreds of thousands of times, during our lives, starting with mother's first tender whisper as we lay sleeping in our cribs.

Our family name is our identity card, but our first name is our own. In the intimacy of our family and friends or in the heat of love's passion it distinguishes us. It is our personal theme, our personal melody, a voice which, on the telephone, invokes a world of feeling and associations: "Hello, this is Dominique . . ."

Is it not strange that our name, which lasts throughout our lifetime, is chosen for us almost at random? Astronomical sums of time and money are spent choosing the best brand name for laundry detergents, yet when it comes to naming a child, we follow current trends, family traditions, the whims of our near and dear ones, or even less sound methods!

THE "CAPITAL NAME"

A name is a reservoir of energy, and this makes good sense, because the constant repetition of these syllables creates a "harmony" which significantly influences our individuality. It acts like a lever that pries up just a few of the infinite possibilities contained within ourselves. How many of these possibilities are uncovered is directly dependent upon the name.

Names contain secret vibrations we are unaware of, yet which exist nonetheless—just as we cannot detect the sound from an ultrasonic whistle that a dog hears with no difficulty. If we admit the existence of these vibrations, which are clearly different for each name, it is not difficult to image that they can resonate with something inside us and trigger specific reactions, according to the name we bear. This is to say that a name can influence our behavior and personality and to a certain extent our destiny as well. This helps us to understand what seems almost unbelievable—that a name can bear a direct influence on people.

It is therefore not immaterial if a child is named Henry instead of Michael. Obviously a sound does not "create" our character—rather it accentuates the basic tendencies or reacts with them in such a way that if another name were chosen, the same psychological traits would not be displayed.

CAT TEST

The story I am about to tell you does not pretend to be a scientific procedure, and I leave it with you only to create a better sense of the significant influence that a name bears on it's owner.

A few years ago we tried the following experiment.

We selected two tiny kittens from a particularly prolific litter and "baptized" them, if you could call it that, with the names Maurice and Robert.

For two years our "subjects" were called by these names, until at last it seemed our experiment had proceeded far enough. We invited veterinarians, psychologists, and psychiatrists to evaluate their behavior. The result of their evaluations was surprising. With due respect, Maurice the Cat behaved like a two-footed Maurice—introverted, emotional, timid, impressionable, delicate, etc. Robert the Tomcat, an unrestrained rascal, was covered with scars. He was short tempered, spat like a panther, was constantly in motion and a real firecracker.

Proof? No. Amusing or revealing coincidences, perhaps. In any case it is clear to me, after experiences with thousands of people, that the phonetic hue of names assists in molding one's character.

If you take the trouble to review your friends, family members or colleagues who have the same name, you will certainly be surprised by the characterological similarities.

CHARACTEROLOGY

Characterology concerns itself with character types. And character types are determined by the way we respond or react to the world. We all react differently and it is this which distinguishes one person from another. Investigations in these areas have led us to conclude that individuals who share the same name show undeniable resemblances.

To further our research, we have attempted to identify the elements that should be weighed in the selection of a name and the risks involved in foisting on a child an unusual name, a curious diminutive, or a compound name. We also maintain that the role of the mother in the selection of a name is paramount. Further, we have attempted to show that each name has a specific sonority and is associated with a specific color, which is nothing other than a wave frequency, albeit on another scale. Awareness of these elements can help us to understand the mystery of harmonies and discords in relationships with family and friends and help us to see the unexplained attractions, as well as incompatibilities, between a person and his profession.

The reader should understand, however, that this book does not purport to announce any absolute truths. It will satisfy the author's ambitions if it has provoked some thought on the challenge of selecting a name and the importance of choosing the right one.

———————

CHAPTER 2

CHOOSING A NAME

If it is true that a name serves to define our individuality and reveal our psychic make-up, and if it is true that it can condition the the character of a child to whom it is attributed, it is even more imperative that it be chosen with particular care. It is necessary, for example, to resolutely avoid unusual names that are hard to pronounce, or those that make puns of questionable taste when combined with the family name (it is more common than you may think). It is equally important to be cautious with compound names that are "weak" because they are too artificial, and names that, because of their uniqueness or strangeness, are a handicap to those burdened with them.

I can recall a young girl whose unusual name was the source of a series of minor ailments because the taunts of her playmates made her feel left out. The child's cure came about only after she was persuaded that her name was pretty even though it was uncommon.

Likewise, parents should guard against the temptation to name their offspring after political figures, movie stars, entertainers, or TV heroes. Such names are quickly outdated and sometimes unkindly date their bearers.

Also to be avoided are diminutives that destroy the true potential of a name and sow the seeds for a disturbing division of personalities. Take, for example, young John who in the warmth and security of his own home is called Jackie by his parents and big sister. But then he goes to school. In this harder, colder, somewhat hostile environment, he is addressed by the name John. Thus he is left to speak from two different sides. Do you see the danger?

ROLE OF THE MOTHER

For nine months the mother bears a child who transforms her life on a physical level by the tiniest imperceptible movement and on a psychological level by inspiring a loving desire to speak to him.

Strangely, the more this tiny being multiplies in a cellular fashion and "originates" himself, or personalizes himself, the more the mother needs to communicate to her child, to establish an ineffable bond between herself and her child. Physiologists do not officially recognize this psychological bonding but it is well know to medical practitioners. Midwives encourage this subtle communication.

Thus, it is the child that makes his mother feel the force of his presence, the resonance of his vibration, and in some way communicates to her what his name should be. Oh, to be sure, he doesn't call her on the telephone and say "I am called David; take it for granted!" Rather it is like a deep intuition that the mother perceives as the child sends her clues that are barely discernable but are constantly repeated.

Resting quietly in the mid-afternoon, between about 2 and 3 p.m., the mother should listen to the little one, and try out the names that rise in her mind to assess the suitability. This is a little like humming a song in the shower, when suddenly a note can make the whole room resound in vibrations. In this way she will begin her loving conversation with her baby.

"SPEAK TO ME MOMMY..."

Here are some astonishing lines by Dr. A.A. Tomatis from his book, *The Uterine Night*, published by Stock Publications in 1981:

"I have continued to be perplexed by the reaction of every newborn child, from the first hours of his life, to the pronunciation of his name by his mother, toward whom he leans as if to rejoin her, as if to relive that exceptionally unique, harmonious relationship, that he had known formerly in the womb. He is only responsive to the voice of his mother. The rest do not interest him. If anyone other than his mother pronounces his name, it evokes no reaction on his part."

What more can be said, except that the "signal" or sound of the mothers voice must have been heard by her baby, proving to her that her message of welcome helped to cross over the frightening "wall" of life.

A LITTLE HISTORY...

Names have always had a magical dimension among primitive peoples. A name empowered it's owner and invoked certain energies to him. To possess a name was far from being common place, as they were reserved for a select number of the initiated.

In Jewish history, the Hebrews used only one name derived from a special event associated with the birth of the child. Only later did children receive three names. The Greeks also used only one name, though the son's name was followed by the father's. In Rome the names used were hereditary, within families and without much variation; there were hardly twenty altogether.

With the triumphant growth of Christianity, names began to be chosen from among its martyrs. From the 5th to the 10th centuries, Christian names were used exclusively. From the 11th to the 15th century a surname, which passed from father to son, was added and became the family name (Carpenter, Smith, Baker, etc.). From the 16th century onward, with the birth of civil status, it became obligatory for baptismal names to be associated with a family name, and the name, as we understand it today, underwent its final stage of evolution. During the period of the French revolution, saint's names were forsaken for names from ancient history so that Brutus, Caton and Scaevola multiplied. Then names were drawn from nature: animals, plants, and inanimate beings. This practice was prohibited near the end of the Revolution and there was a return to the calendar saints.

TODAY'S CHOICES

Choices for today's names tend to be paired indiscriminantly, without regard for first and last name compatibility. But names fit together just like words. The rarer the word, the more restricted its audience. While we all understand words like, eat, drink and sleep, the more refined our vocabulary becomes the fewer the number of people who understand us, until at the extreme limit an audience exists of only a handful of specialists. At this level a name loses its impact due to its uncommon usage. If I whistle the melody from "Bridge on the River Kwai," everyone would recognize it. But if I were to hum the third movement of the Quartet in F Minor by Paul Hindemith, only a few informed music-lovers would recognize it.

In France, or more specifically Brittany, parents may be imprisoned for daring to name their offspring Morgane or Gwena! Such is the way of the world.

———————

CHAPTER 3

THE COLOR OF NAMES

SIMPLE NAMES

It is commonly understood that specific wave lengths are assigned to the colors of the spectrum, going from the shortest wave length, violet, to red, the longest. For a physicist, both color and sound are seen to be nothing other than vibratory phenomena.

A name is simply a sound or a series of sounds, combined by vowels and consonants, which necessarily testify to the existence of specific sound vibrations. Therefore, it is not surprising that these vibrations can be associated with colors.

Colors also have a characterological significance. Hues of color are associated with personality characteristics and it is therefore possible to determine that Joseph is red, Mary is blue, John is yellow, etc.

Names can be assigned to six basic color groups— three primary (red, yellow and blue) and three secondary (orange, green and violet). Clearly there is nothing arbitrary about this classification. It is the product of long and arduous investigation into the characteristic resonances of names.

At the end of this chapter there is a list of all the pilot names with their characterological colors to help make this concept as clear as possible.

I will explain in detail the correspondence between different groups of pilot names and the various colors. Let it be clear, however, that relating Gerard to orange, for example, in no way implies that orange is the favorite color of the name Gerard or one of its associated names.

Following is a table showing the correspondence of colors with various qualities, which will help clarify their vibrational significance on the level of body (existence), soul (feeling), and spirit (creation).

Color	Body	Soul	Spirit
Red	Anger	Passion	Domination
Orange	Feelings	Love-passion	Seduction
Yellow	Will	Radiance	Intelligence
Green	Mental	Intuition	Imagination
Blue	Vitality	Pure love	Spirituality
Violet	Subconscious	Unconscious	Awarenesss

COMPOUND NAMES

Having established that there are three primary colors (blue, yellow and red), the three secondary or compound colors (violet, green and orange), come into play. You can probably guess what I am about to say: a yellow name, like John, coupled with a red one, like Michael, gives an orange compound name: John Michael. Bravo!

Anne plus Mary gives a pretty blue since both are of the same color. Perfect! However, things start to get complicated when you juxtapose a primary color such as yellow with a secondary color like green. Yellow plus green results in a washed out color that weakens the influence of the two single names. It may even get worse. If one associates a violet name with a green one, as in "Henry-Victor," the outcome is a dark indefinable color which gives an unconvincing radiance to the personality.

No one is questioning your freedom to choose names as you wish—that is your business—I am simply trying to caution you against undesirable mixtures, because as a characterologist, the coupling of names is not an innocent affair. In characterology, as in other sciences such as chemistry for example, one cannot do just anything. One must avoid "neutral" or "explosive" combinations. In other words, it may be harmful to your child's future to create a compound name at random or based on your sense of humor.

And one last piece of advice. If one of the two sounds in a compound name troubles you, don't hesitate: simply drop it. It is better to be called Peter and feel good about it than to be called Louis-Peter and continue the annoyance of being saddled with a second name that is not peddling fast enough.

———————

TABLE OF COLORS

No.	Name	Color	No.	Name	Color
01	Agnes	green	41	Genevieve	red
02	Albert	blue	42	George	yellow
03	Alfred	violet	43	Gerard	orange
04	Alphonse	violet	44	Guy	violet
05	Andrea	orange	45	Helen	yellow
06	Andrew	red	46	Henrietta	red
07	Anne	blue	47	Henry	violet
08	Anthony	yellow	48	Hugh	violet
09	Antoinette	red	49	Jacqueline	blue
10	Baptiste	yellow	50	James	red
11	Barnaby	green	51	Jeanne	yellow
12	Bartholomew	blue	52	John	yellow
13	Bernard	violet	53	Joseph	red
14	Bertha	orange	54	Leon	green
15	Camille	yellow	55	Louis	red
16	Catherine	red	56	Louise	green
17	Cecilia	blue	57	Lucien	orange
18	Charles	red	58	Madeline	violet
19	Christine	green	59	Marcel	orange
20	Christopher	blue	60	Margaret	green
21	Claire	green	61	Martha	blue
22	Claude	orange	62	Mary	blue
23	Claudia	red	63	Maurice	violet
24	Clement	red	64	Michael	red
25	Colette	blue	65	Paul	red
26	Daniel	yellow	66	Peter	yellow
27	Danielle	violet	67	Philip	green
28	Denise	yellow	68	Raymond	blue
29	Dennis	orange	69	Robert	red
30	Dominic	green	70	Stephen	green
31	Dominique	yellow	71	Theresa	orange
32	Edmund	violet	72	Thomas	blue
33	Edward	red	73	Victor	green
34	Elizabeth	orange	74	Vincent	red
35	Emil	blue	75	Virginia	violet
36	Eugenia	blue	76	William	green
37	Felix	orange	77	Yves	orange
38	Frances	red	78	Yvette	blue
39	Frank	blue	79	Yvonne	blue
40	Gabriel	blue			

CHAPTER 4

NAME CHANGES

THE "WRONGLY NAMED"...

We must be cautious not to add to the lengthy list of boys and girls who are unhappy with their present names and have only one desire: to change it. And it is relatively easy to discover whether a child has been well named or not. In the course of a casual conversation, while the child is in an adjoining room, ask someone who is a stranger to the family to pronounce the name without raising their voice. If the child responds to the name, chances are it is well-suited. But it is also possible that the child will not respond at all. This is because he unconsciously refuses to hear it and his deafness has created a "psychological deafness" in him. He doesn't want to hear his name pronounced so he doesn't hear it. Often the consequences of this can be serious and you should seriously consider changing the child's name.

There is also a problem associated with foreign names. There is nothing to stop you from naming your child Sasha or Pierre, but there should be a reason for your choice. It should not be just a passing fancy, and the name should be harmonious with your family name. If you are descended from Russian forefathers and have Pavlov as your surname, you can name your offspring Tatiana or Dmitri without hesitation. But are you sure Vladimir Martinez will feel very happy?

CHANGING NAMES

A change of name is a serious affair, and should

never be treated lightly. One out of every fifty people will change their name in their lifetime.

The most common explanation for a name change is the belief that one's name is strange. Fashions very often make a name appear out of date, but how many times have we thought that a name is gone forever, only to discover its re-emergence in popularity again. In reality, the name that seems strange is, nine times out of ten, simply ill-adapted to the person bearing it. It simply does not fit because it does not resonate with the deep vibration of the person's being.

A person may dream of changing his name to that of a hero in in a novel, a favorite actor or a friend, but without due consideration the consequences could be considerable.

As we have seen, our name is our personal reference point, a summation of who we are. Since it is the sound to which we are familiar and recognize instantly, any change would imply a break with the past, a fresh start, a new beginning with a different orientation and the acquirement of new capabilities. These few letters that form a sound which has been repeated to us a thousand times, sharing joy or bringing us back in line, or persuading or threatening us, cannot be suddenly replaced by other letters forming another word, without having a profound influence on our behavior.

SOME FAMOUS EXAMPLES...

In religion

The most famous name change, and the most profound, is unquestionably that of the founder of the Christian Church; after a solemn profession of faith, Jesus changed Simon's name to Cephas, or Peter. adding: "On this rock I will build my church," thus designating the apostle as the future leader of Christianity. Christ felt it necessary to rebaptize Simon in order to confer on him this new authority for his supreme mission. It is significant that since that time not a single pope has been named Peter.

It is, however, notable that the pope changes his name as part of the election by the Conclave of Cardinals. He assumes an added dimension; the authority with which he is invested distinguishes him from the rest of the clergy. In effect, assuming the role of spiritual guide of millions of believers, the office of this exceptional personage overtakes his human identity. He undergoes a kind of rebirth, like monks who change their names after having taken their vow to begin a new life devoted to God.

In time of war

During the last world war, army resistance fighters changed their names when they went underground. Initially this was strictly for security reasons. But then a curious phenomena took place: some of these patriots, faced with great risk which required enormous courage, self-sacrifice and responsibility, acquired a new self-knowledge and took on a new personality. When the war was over, often they retained their resistance identity. Their civilian life no longer reflected the name they assumed in battle. This change often became the cause of severe personality disorders, some of which were highly dramatic cases.

On stage

Actors, both on and off the screen, are, by virtue of their profession, called upon over and over again to assume the role of many different personalities and to literally live, for a period of time, their destinies, hopes and fears. For this reason they are susceptible to a kind of instability in their own personalities. They often change their first and last names without due consideration, thinking only in terms of its euphony or commercial appeal, or simply yielding to the fashion of adopting a foreign name. It is a dangerous habit and can, as we have mentioned lead to psychological disorders. On the other hand when an actor has been wrongly named from birth, or resents his first or last name, it becomes a handicap, and the change of name may be highly beneficial. Such is the case of Simone Roussel, who says that in becoming Michele Morgan she had the feeling of being transformed, liberated from her past, and of truly beginning a new career.

In politics

Even politics confirms this principle. We couldn't possibly enumerate all the name changes that have paved the way to success for the political leaders. Lenin was born Vladimir Ilitch Oulianov, and Stalin was born Iossif Vissarionovitch Djougarchvili. It is easy to understand the reason for these name changes.

———————————

CHAPTER 5

CHARACTEROLOGY OF NAMES

THE WHEEL OF CHARACTER

A "wheel of character" will help us to understand names more intimately. This diagram will tell you more in a single glance than any lengthy discourse I could provide. It shows a circular "charactergram" divided into "24 hours". Curiously it resembles an ancient Italian clock whose face was similarly divided and in which a single hand was used to mark the hour. This little hand took a day and a night to make a complete revolution.

These 24 hourly divisions correspond in reality to two dozen psychological parameters which sketch the outline of a person's personality in such a way as to give a real characterological "imprint":

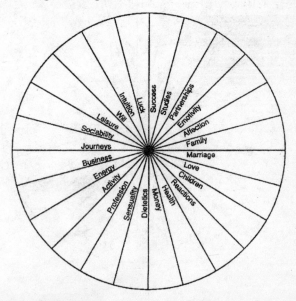

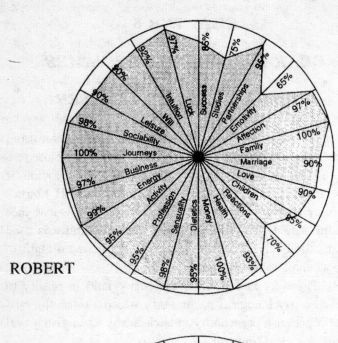

ROBERT

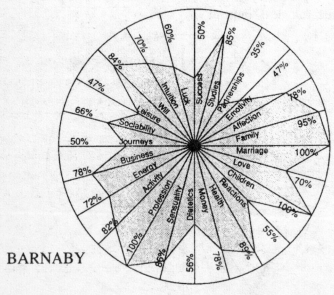

BARNABY

To illustrate this idea, I have chosen two names with opposing characteristics, Robert and Barnaby. The first, occupies a majority of the area and manifests a great expansiveness, while the other timidly creeps out of its shell.

You can imagine how interesting it is to compare similar diagrams between couples, parents and children, employers and employees, etc. Thus you have before your eyes a "cut out" of the two names and can see how exciting it is to put the charactergrams of an entire family side by side.

A TALKING CHARACTERGRAM

Refer to the charactergrams for Robert and Barnaby on the previous page and try to determine their characters. Please note that each of our "wheels" are divisible into four sectors, each with six parameters:

Will	Emotivity	Reactions	Activity
Intuition	Affections	Health	Energy
Luck	Family	Money	Business
Success	Marriage	Dietetics	Journeys
Studies	Love	Sensuality	Sociability
Partnerships	Children	Profession	Leisure

The 24 parameters do not appear to conform to the same set of rules. More precisely, I mean to say that the percentages used to define a person's character are not comparable. For example: a man with a sensuality of 70% possesses only modest virility, while a masculine emotivity of 70% opens the door to all kinds of emotional instability. This latter percentage, applied to a feminine character, will cause no trouble. This is why it is necessary to reconcile the gender with the percentage (see following page).

CHARACTERGRAM PERCENTAGES

PARAMETER	FEMININE			MASCULINE		
	Weak	Mod.	Strong	Weak	Mod.	Strong
Will	00–35	35–70	70–90	00–50	50–75	75–95
Intuition	00–40	40–60	60–100	00–30	30–50	50–100
Luck	00–35	35–55	55–100	00–50	50–70	70–100
Success	00–50	50–70	70–100	00–55	55–75	75–100
Studies	00–60	60–75	75–100	00–60	60–75	75–100
Partnerships	00–25	25–55	55–100	00–40	40–80	80–100
Emotivity	00–30	30–45	45–70	00–20	20–40	40–55
Affections	00–50	50–80	80–100	00–40	40–75	75–100
Family	00–60	60–85	85–100	00–50	50–75	75–100
Marriage	00–45	45–70	70–100	00–35	35–60	60–100
Love	00–40	40–75	75–100	00–30	30–65	65–100
Children	00–50	50–80	80–100	00–45	45–70	70–100
Reactivity	00–20	20–40	40–75	00–25	25–40	40–65
Health	00–50	50–80	80–100	00–50	50–80	80–100
Money	00–35	35–65	65–100	00–50	50–70	70–100
Dietetics	00–40	40–75	75–100	00–45	45–80	80–100
Sensuality	00–50	50–75	75–100	00–50	50–80	80–100
Profession	00–35	35–65	65–100	00–50	50–80	80–100
Activity	00–50	50–75	75–100	00–50	50–80	80–100
Dynamism	00–40	40–65	65–100	00–50	50–80	80–100
Business	00–30	30–55	55–100	00–60	60–85	85–100
Journeys	00–40	40–60	60–100	00–55	55–75	75–100
Sociability	00–40	40–75	75–100	00–50	50–80	80–100
Leisure	00–60	60–90	90–100	00–55	55–85	85–100

Also, it should be mentioned that the significance of each exceeds 60% for men and 75% for women. Beyond this, it leaves an open door for all kinds of disturbances.

NAMES AND CORRESPONDENCES

To fully understand my system of characterological evaluation, I ask you to examine the six columns of correspondences found in the table at the end of this chapter. They are arranged in groups of three.

1. The three astro-characterological indications:

(a) the element

(b) the sign—this is a way of giving life to a personality, as each sign has a well defined behavior.

(c) the color of the names.

None of this bears any relation to the date of birth of the person considered and is only given to better define the subject's profile.

2. The three totemic indications, which merit a detailed explanation:

(a) animal

(b) plant

(c) mineral

"TOTEMS"

The word "totem" is intended to refer to the correspondences between names, minerals, plants, and animals. In fact, I am one who believes that everything on earth is interconnected and there are no watertight compartments between the various kingdoms of creation.

Without dwelling much on parallels and forced comparisons, let me point out that many ancient traditions maintain that every human ever born has his reflection, or double, in the mineral, plant and animal kingdoms. Even the Bible is full of this kind of symbolic reference, where a pure woman is a dove, peace an olive branch, a crafty man a snake in the grass, love a rose, etc.

The word "totem" evokes the images of the American Indians with their fabulous names representing a true synthesis of the bearer's personality. Who could forget the legendary Sitting Bull, Silver Cloud, or the famous Crazy Horse? It would be easy to dismiss all this were it not for psychoanalysis—especially that practiced by the Swiss psychologist Karl Gustav Jung— which demonstrates the persistence of archetypal representations in the collective unconscious.

By including this table of correspondences I intend to emphasize some rather interesting characterological similarities. Thus associating the name Charles by analogy with the elephant as its animal, the willow as its plant, and iron as its mineral, represents the image of strength and wisdom (the elephant), contemplation and melancholy (the willow), and the hardness of life and decisions (iron), which are the essential constituents of this type of individual.

I assure you that you will learn more about the personality of your little Danielle, and those with the same name, by understanding the totems violet and the robin, which represent humility and, paradoxically, a certain pretentiousness.

Now I sincerely feel that we have travelled far enough together, so you are free to explore on your own the marvelous world of names. That magical forest where, on the trunk of every tree, every mother, the lovers of the world and all the men and women who have lived on this earth have carved a name for a lifetime.

TABLE OF CORRESPONDENCES

No.	Pilot Name	Element Animal	Mineral Sign	Plant Color
1	Agnes	Air Messenger pigeon	Lead crystal Libra	Tobacco Green
2	Albert	Air Sea horse	Ruby Aquarius	Digitalis Blue
3	Alfred	Air Adder	Gold Gemini	Hazelnut tree Violet
4	Alphonse	Water Octopus	Brass Scorpio	Elder tree Violet
5	Andrea	Air Fox	Agate Gemini	Hyacinth Orange
6	Andrew	Fire Peacock	Radium Aries	Almond tree Red
7	Anne	Water Lynx	Diamond Scorpio	Myrtle Blue
8	Anthony	Earth Marabout	Hematite Capricorn	Garlic Yellow
9	Antoinette	Water Duck	Serpentine Cancer	Absinth Red
10	Baptiste	Water Jaguar	Nickel Cancer	Fig tree Yellow
11	Barnaby	Water Pike	Chrysolite Pisces	Wild cherry tree Green
12	Bartholomew	Fire Salmon	Bismuth Leo	Poplar Blue
13	Bernard	Fire Cuckoo	Salt Aries	Mulberry tree Violet
14	Bertha	Air Boa	Topaz Aquarius	Virgin's vine Orange
15	Camille	Earth Antelope	Sodium Capricorn	Leek Yellow
16	Catherine	Fire Swan	Zircon Leo	Strawberry Red
17	Cecilia	Fire Squirrel	Amethyst Sagittarius	Carrot Blue
18	Charles	Fire Elephant	Iron Sagittarius	Weeping willow Red
19	Christine	Earth Toad	Granite Virgo	Gentian Green
20	Christopher	Fire Elk	Amber Aries	Chestnut Blue

TABLE OF CORRESPONDENCES (cont.)

No.	Pilot Name	Element Animal	Mineral Sign	Plant Color
21	Claire	Air Swallow	Clay Libra	Cedar tree Green
22	Claude	Air Gazelle	Flint Gemini	Spindle tree Orange
23	Claudia	Air Giraffe	Titanium Libra	Thyme Red
24	Clement	Water Heron	Aquamarine Scorpio	Eucalyptus Red
25	Colette	Air Mouse	Manganese Libra	Flax Blue
26	Daniel	Water Whale	Arsenic Pisces	Holly Yellow
27	Danielle	Air Robin	Limestone Aquarius	Violet Violet
28	Denise	Earth Locust	Slate Virgo	Manila hemp Yellow
29	Dennis	Earth Night hawk	Malachite Virgo	Vervain Orange
30	Dominic	Air Titmouse	Red lead Aquarius	Plane tree Green
31	Dominique	Water Golden carp	Garnet Pisces	Heather Yellow
32	Edmund	Air Badger	Silver Aquarius	Rush Violet
33	Edward	Water Seal	Jasper Scorpio	Maize Red
34	Elizabeth	Air Weasel	Copper Aquarius	Laurel rose Orange
35	Emil	Water Crab	Tourmaline Cancer	Lilac Blue
36	Eugenia	Fire Hippopotamus	Tungsten Aries	Hawthorne Blue
37	Felix	Air Tuna	Opal Aquarius	Beech tree Orange
38	Frances	Earth Sole	Seleniate Capricorn	Fern Red
39	Frank	Air Cock & Albatross	Chrome Gemini	Lemon tree Blue
40	Gabriel	Water Horse	Mercury Cancer	Nettle Blue

No.	Pilot Name	Element Animal	Mineral Sign	Plant Color
41	Genevieve	Earth Leopard	Quartz Taurus	Pear tree Red
42	George	Fire Bison	Uranium Aries	Olive tree Yellow
43	Gerard	Earth Zebu ox	Lapis lazuli Taurus	Honeysuckle Orange
44	Guy	Air Sea gull	Platinum Gemini	Aspen Violet
45	Helen	Air Codfish	Jade Gemini	Orchid Yellow
46	Henrietta	Air Reindeer	Sapphire Libra	Grapevine Red
47	Henry	Earth Mountain goat	Alabaster Capricorn	Orange tree Violet
48	Hugh	Earth Cobra	Turquoise Capricorn	Ivy Violet
49	Jacqueline	Fire Magpie	Tin Aries	Rose bush Blue
50	James	Fire Stag	Carbuncle Aries	Box-wood tree Red
51	Jeanne	Fire Termite	Crystal Leo	Broom shrub Yellow
52	John	Fire Dolphin	Porphyry Aries	Truffle Yellow
53	Joseph	Fire Turtle dove	Antimony Sagittarius	Chestnut tree Red
54	Leon	Air Sable	Calcium Libra	Apple tree Green
55	Louis	Water Nightingale	Sardonyx Cancer	Wheat Red
56	Louise	Earth Kangaroo	Sun stone Virgo	Lavender Green
57	Lucien	Fire Camel	Bronze Leo	Pine tree Orange
58	Madeline	Air Rooster	Meteorite Libra	Mistletoe Violet
59	Marcel	Fire Mink	Molybdenum Sagittarius	Ash tree Orange
60	Margaret	Water Trout	Chalcedony Pisces	Maple tree Green

No.	Pilot Name	Element Animal	Mineral Sign	Plant Color
61	Martha	Fire Lark	Jet Sagittarius	Tulip Blue
62	Mary	Earth Dove	Emerald Virgo	Lily Blue
63	Maurice	Fire Condor	Cornelian Sagittarius	Birch tree Violet
64	Michael	Earth Tiger	Sulphur Virgo	Elm tree Red
65	Paul	Fire Beaver	Sandstone Sagittarius	Hemlock Red
66	Peter	Fire Ram	Cobalt Aries	Oak tree Yellow
67	Philip	Fire Ibis	Aluminum Leo	Acacia Green
68	Raymond	Earth Ox	Bromine Taurus	Hemp Blue
69	Robert	Earth Panther	Moonstone Capricorn	Walnut tree Red
70	Stephen	Fire Vampire	Beryl Aries	Laurel Green
71	Theresa	Air Doe	Marble Aquarius	Linden tree Orange
72	Thomas	Air Python	Onyx Aquarius	Juniper tree Blue
73	Victor	Earth Cricket	Silica Virgo	Thistle Green
74	Vincent	Earth Deer	Lead Taurus	Cypress tree Red
75	Virginia	Water Lizard	Obsidian Cancer	Lily of the valley Violet
76	William	Earth Wild boar	Basalt Capricorn	Yew tree Green
77	Yves	Earth Ladybug	Zinc Taurus	Wild rose Orange
78	Yvette	Fire Cicada	Coral Leo	Cherry tree Blue
79	Yvonne	Air Hedgehog	Pitchblende Libra	Valerian Blue

CHAPTER 6

PILOT NAMES

There are 79 names, or categories, that act as the "heads of the family" over the other 9,000 names listed in the index at the back of this book. Unfortunately it has not been possible to create as many charactergrams as names. That would be an undertaking of enormous proportion—more than 20,000 pages! Instead, I have grouped together all those names whose diagram was strikingly similar to one of the basic 79 categories or character groups.

"But," you may say, "why the number 79? Why is it a significant number? Why not 50, 80, or 100?" The answer to this must be somewhat abridged as it would take an entire book to explain the hows and whys of these distinctions.

Quite simply, according to ancient tradition there has always been a finite number of fundamental possibilities. There are thus only 79 "models" which reproduce themselves at every level of creation. Thus, in these "cosmic pigeonholes" we can put all types of faces, the names of every town in the world and all the different varieties of plants, animals, minerals and names.

LARGE FAMILIES

We have classified under the heading "Associated Names" all those names that are similar in character to the principal Pilot name with which it is associated. But mark well that these "associated names" are not poor relatives sheltered under the roof of a rich cousin. The differences—in theory and practice—are tiny and do not change the essential psychological portrait of each of them.

In this way Helen (Name Portrait 45) gathers under

its wing more than 80 feminine names having the same essential characteristics: Barbara, Blanche, Douce, Gail, Nelly, etc. Mary, (Name Portrait 62) collects nearly 210 affiliates, from Beatrice to Zita, by way of Eve, Grace, Muriel, Veronica, etc.

Above all pay little attention to the phonetic similarity of sounds and look closely in the characterological resonances which I have determined in more than 50 years of research.

Test them all from your own experience remembering that one out of every ten persons could be wrongly named and therefore not recognize himself in his name portrait.

Thus begins the exciting game of looking for the name that truly corresponds to your temperament. A very useful game, I believe.

Part II

Name Portraits

Name Portrait 1

Charming Enchantress

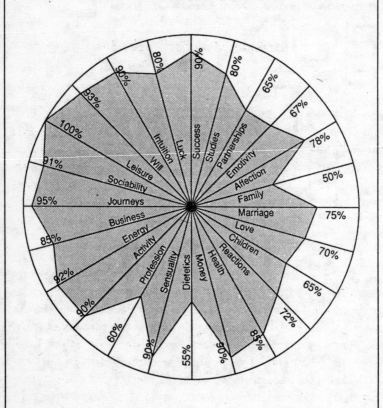

Element : Air

Mineral : Lead crystal

Animal : Messenger pigeon

Plant : Tobacco

Sign : Libra

Color : Green

Personality Type:

Charming Enchantress

(Associated names – page 36)

BASIC CHARACTER

You tend to be high-strung, intensely emotional, and sometimes supersensitive. Your nature is restless, flighty, fast moving, and sometimes capricious. Communication is intrinsic to your nature as is your need for self-expression. However, there are times when you are outspoken and talk before you think. Your communicative mentality is associated with the carrier pigeon, your special animal totem.

YOUR PSYCHOLOGY

Despite your charm, you're not that easy to get close to, and that is mostly because of your mood swings. You can go from the heights of excitation to the depths of despair in record time. But luckily, your down periods never last long. In general, you enjoy a lot of attention. However, at the same time you're capable of giving out the same concern to others. Although you have an expansive, outgoing personality, emotionally you are an introvert who enjoys long periods of time alone. Your outward self-confidence sometimes masks deep-seated insecurities. At the same time, your will is strong and your determination powerful.

HOW YOU ACT AND REACT IN THE WORLD

You tend to be fantasy-prone and easily enthralled by unusual experiences. At times your flighty and capricious behavior conceals a wish to escape. Discipline and structure are essential for your productivity. At work, you resent supervision and take it as an invasion of your privacy.

YOUR DEEP INTUITIVE PERSONALITY

You are astonishingly intuitive which adds to your attractiveness. However, at the same time you can appear distant and flighty. Essentially, you are as evanescent as smoke. It is not surprising that the tobacco plant is your plant totem. Not only are you elusive, but you are also highly changeable—both in terms of how you think and how you feel.

YOUR INTELLIGENCE

Your mind is explosive, your energy prodigious. You have the ability to synthesize ideas in record time. Your intelligence is both vast and comprehensive. However, because you're so impatient, you tend to be poor at details. An intense curiosity consumes you and when you are studying something you love, the results are spectacular. However, discipline should be developed at a very early age to help you master the subjects you snub out of disinterest. You have a very quick mind, a fertile imagination and are so adaptable that you can adjust to almost anything.

Because monotony makes you miserable you are best suited in a vital profession that is both dynamic and exciting. You could be anything from a flight attendant, to a writer, to a public relations person. However, whatever career you ultimately choose, you have to feel that it excites you far more than it confines you.

YOUR EMOTIONAL NATURE

Emotionally you are moody, changeable, and prone to swing between extremes. At times you are tempted to use your bad moods to control those around you. You surround yourself with friends among whom you spread yourself thin. Not only is your personality complex and contradictory, but you seem to be attracted to that quality in other people. Failure makes you despair, but because nothing keeps you down for long, you're soon off and running in a new direction. Although you embrace high standards of behavior, at times your capriciousness can create havoc to those around you. When it comes to loving, you are hasty, impulsive, and whimsical. Because you are so fantasy-oriented, there is often a great gap between your idea of a person and what that person really represents. Security is essential to your sense of well-being. What you must work to develop is a sense of stability.

YOUR HEALTH AND VITALITY

While your health is generally good, you tend to be accident-prone due to impulsiveness. Broken bones and kidney ailments are your nemesis. Because you are so mentally energetic, you rarely get enough sleep and have a tendency to indulge in all sorts of stimulants. Balance, order, and a calm regime would prove to be greatly beneficial.

THE SOCIAL YOU

You are enticing, delicious, and disarmingly attractive. Your personality literally lights up the world. You are outgoing, fun to be with and you love constant excitement, being the center of attention, and always a lot of change. Because you are so restless, you love to change houses, friends, and habits every few months or even minutes. When you really want something, your willpower is overwhelming. On the other hand, you have a hard time disciplining yourself to do the things that disinterest you. You change your mind and your emotions according to circumstances. However, although your behavior can be extremely trying, your personality is so irresistible that you always come out the winner.

NamePortrait
1
Associated Names

Aggie
Agna
Agnella
Agnes
Ana
Anastasia
Anastasie
Annis
Anstace
Anstance
Anstice
Cameo
Edwige
Etiennette
Fern
Filberta
Filberte
Filbertha
Filberthe
Filida
Filipa
Filippa
Filis
Fillida
Fillis
Hedwig
Hedwige

Ines
Inez
Iris
Lavender
Lavvie
Leocadie
Leopolda
Leopoldina
Leopoldine
Nara
Narda
Nessa
Nessie
Nessy
Nesta
Neysa
Nokomis
Nova
Novia
Oana
Perdita
Phil
Philberta
Philbertha
Philberthe
Philiberte
Philippa

Philippine
Philis
Phillida
Phillie
Phillipa
Phillippa
Phillis
Phylis
Phyllida
Phyllis
Pippa
Riva
Sacha
Signa
Sil
Silva
Silvana
Silvia
Silvie
Stacey
Stacia
Stacy
Stefa
Steffie
Stepha
Stephana
Stephane

Stephanette
Stephania
Stephanie
Stephena
Stephenia
Stephenie
Stevana
Stevania
Stevena
Stevenia
Stevie
Syl
Sylva
Sylvana
Sylvette
Sylvia
Sylviane
Sylvie
Tempesta
Tempeste
Ynes
Ynez
Zilva
Zilvia

Name Portrait 2

Keeper of a Secret World

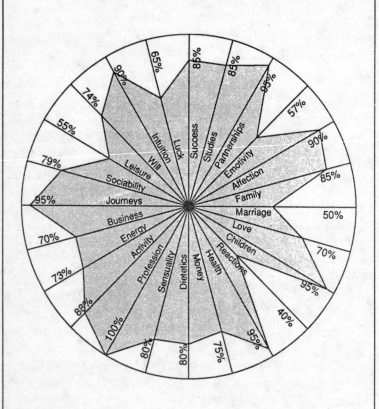

Element : Air   **Plant** : Digitalis

Mineral : Ruby   **Sign** : Aquarius

Animal : Sea horse   **Color** : Blue

Personality Type:

Keeper of a Secret World

(Associated names – page 42)

BASIC CHARACTER

You are both cerebral and sentimental and the duality appears constantly in your behavior. Although on the surface you may appear cool and controlled, underneath you are totally tuned in to the emotional side of a situation. Your outward calm comes from the fact that you hold in your fears, worries, and deeper feelings. Psychologically, you resemble your animal totem, the sea horse, since this animal can go from sleeping peacefully among the ocean currents to becoming quite unexpectedly aroused. Likewise, your personality range runs from open emotional display to secrecy and withdrawal.

YOUR PSYCHOLOGY

Even though you are warm and affectionate, you can also be moody and standoffish. You tend to be jealous and possessive, although you'll seldom show it. Your mind is highly intuitive and your profound understanding of people and situations is far beyond the norm. Emotionally, you are complex and sometimes contradictory, and sexually, your deeper feelings can be easily cut off. You tend to change your beliefs as you do your friendships and the people you keep around you. Because of your deep inner reserve, you are often difficult to understand. A nagging indecisiveness negatively affects your will and sometimes interferes with your ability to assertively satisfy your desires.

HOW YOU ACT AND REACT IN THE WORLD

Although you are introverted and appear to be uninvolved, you observe everything around you with depth and clarity. Long before you make your moves, you have everything thought out in advance. When you finally do act, it's with a dynamic energy that others find quite convincing.

YOUR DEEP INTUITIVE PERSONALITY

You tend to use your intuitive abilities more as a self-protective device than as a means of developing your potential. Often you use the duality of your nature to your advantage and play from whichever side seems to offer most.

YOUR INTELLIGENCE

You have an energetic mind and a highly adaptable intelligence. Your attention span is focused and your interests selective. At times you can become passionately interested in certain subjects to the exclusion of all. However, the kinds of things that interest you most usually have a practical value. You excel in areas involving technical ability, such as electricity, electronics, and aeronautical engineering. In addition, you are an organized researcher who can handle several projects at the same time. Because of your understanding of people and ability to communicate persuasively, you could also excel in sales.

YOUR EMOTIONAL NATURE

Often you allow external situations to affect your moods as well as your quality of thinking. At the same time, you see things too subjectively which causes you to become obsessed and insecure. At times this tendency may make you worrisome and cause you to doubt yourself.

Your sexuality reflects the most mysterious part of your nature. Sex can be a sort of refuge from disturbing feelings and an escape into the passionate side of yourself that you find most pleasurable.

Once you feel secure in an emotional situation, you're capable of being deeply committed. Your obstacle in the act of loving is that it's so difficult for you to reveal your deeper feelings.

YOUR HEALTH AND VITALITY

Although your vitality is good, you tend to tire easily. Often you don't allow yourself the proper rest and relaxation that your body really requires. Because you have a tendency toward stimulants and larger than life experiences, you often lower your resistance to diseases. Especially susceptible areas are the eyes and the bronchial tubes.

THE SOCIAL YOU

Your charming public personality masks your moodiness and behavioral inconsistencies. You especially enjoy being in the center of things, carried along by the intensity around you. You obtain a special pleasure from "the good life" that your clever abilities create quite naturally. However, because you are torn between outside involvements and a craving for solitude, your greatest success will most likely come at a later age.

———————

NamePortrait
2
Associated Names

Adelin	Colbert	Gilby	Oro
Ailbert	Colvert	Griff	Osbert
Alban	Culbert	Griffin	Oz
Alben	Dalbert	Griffith	Ozzie
Albert	Delbert	Gruffyd	Renfrew
Albin	Doogan	Halbert	Rufus
Aldabert	Dougan	Hephzibah	Shanley
Alder	Dugan	Lindell	Tobe
Alva	Dunc	Lindley	Tobias
Alvah	Duncan	Linley	Tobit
Alvar	Edbert	Norm	Toby
Aubert	Elbert	Norman	Walden
Aubin	Ethelbert	Normand	Waldo
Bert	Eugene	Normie	Waldron
Bertie	Gene	Norris	Walford
Berty	Gilbey	Obert	Walfred

Name Portrait 3

Unassuming Achiever

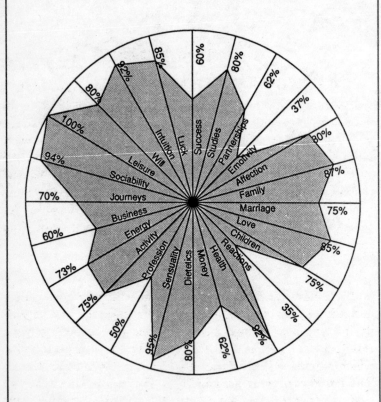

Element : Air   **Plant** : Hazelnut tree
Mineral : Gold   **Sign** : Gemini
Animal : Adder   **Color** : Violet

Personality Type:

Unassuming Achiever

(Associated names – page 48)

BASIC CHARACTER

Although you're not exactly a fireball, it has to do more with a diffidence than an underlying indifference. At times your sentimental nature can slow you down and perhaps even interfere with your performance. However, like the spirit of your animal totem, the adder, a certain amount of rest and relaxation is requisite to your optimum functioning. Your personality is polite, well-mannered, sensitive, and aware. At the same time your emotions are subdued and it's not that easy to know what you're really feeling.

YOUR PSYCHOLOGY

You have an intensely private side to your personality and a highly fertile imagination. Your emotions can be easily influenced by people and situations who appeal to your sensitivities. There is a protective quality to your personality which expresses itself quite often in a willingness to please. The paradox of your personality is that while a part of you desires the security of a conventional existence, another part would like to be free to take flight. However, at the same time, you are highly capable of grounding yourself in an intense dedication to an activity, person, or a cause. An underlying anxiety limits your own appreciation of your performance. Yet, on the outside, your personality remains cool and dignified. You are practical in dealing with each step of life as you encounter it. And although you may occasionally experience setbacks, your spirit is resilient and nothing ever gets you down for long.

HOW YOU ACT AND REACT IN THE WORLD

Your emotions are strong and so are your affections. However, at the same time, due to your self-consciousness, you are reluctant to express them. Ultimately, this conflict can bring about a good deal of frustration for both yourself and others. People have a problem realizing that you are often far different than your surface appears.

YOUR DEEP INTUITIVE PERSONALITY

You are extraordinarily intuitive and can see beyond the surface with ease. Little surprises you since you believe that almost anything is possible. But an occasional melancholy mood may momentarily get you off guard. Because your insights into people are so profound, you can be highly effective when it comes to influencing others. Your deep emotional understanding, along with your strong degree of sensitivity, can also bring you much success in your relations with women.

YOUR INTELLIGENCE

You are highly intelligent and can evaluate a situation at a glance. You have an alert mind, a remarkable memory, and you enjoy the learning side of experience. However, at the same time, you have the mind of a daydreamer which can drift off in midstream. Therefore, mental discipline and follow-through should be developed and mastered for those subjects that especially bore you. Your initial reaction to any situation is always thoughtful and evaluative. Only upon careful consideration do you come to an operative conclusion. Because you are so insecure and sensitive to failure, you are likely to withhold your opinion until you are assured it is correct.

Careerwise, you are drawn to literature and can be a talented writer or journalist. However, it is likely that you excel in mathematics and could also find teaching attractive. Business, law, bookkeeping, and the world of finance are additional areas which you could find particularly suitable to your personality.

YOUR EMOTIONAL NATURE

Because you feel awkward revealing the deeper nature of yourself, it takes you a long time to open up to another person. The first prerequisite is that you have to feel familiarity and trust. Romantically speaking, your feelings toward a woman are defined by what you think of her. As a friend, you can be counted on in a crisis and have a sense of loyalty that is limitless. Sexually speaking, your feelings are deeply tied to your emotions. At times you can be more than a trifle unrealistic. When you are deeply involved, you can become too accepting and should develop a sense of detachment to keep your emotions in perspective.

YOUR HEALTH AND VITALITY

You have an overworked mind and often an exhausted nervous system. Other areas to watch out for are digestion, circulation, and your glands. Generally, your health tends to be good, although you often feel that you suffer from a lack of sleep.

THE SOCIAL YOU

While you're not exactly adverse to socializing in large groups, you by far prefer meaningful quiet talk to a lot of empty chitchat. Therefore, you are usually just as happy to stay at home. You have a great chance of success in the material world and can function quite efficiently in your own business. Likewise, you're a delegative boss who stays on top of your employees—even if your business requires you to be elsewhere.

NamePortrait
3
Associated Names

Aelfred	Gordy	Nevins	Rutley
Ailfrid	Hagan	Newman	Sewald
Al	Hagen	Niven	Sewall
Alf	Haggan	Nivens	Seward
Alfie	Haggen	Norbert	Sewell
Alfred	Hayden	Olaf	Siwald
Alfy	Haydon	Olar	Skelton
Amhlaoibt	Lach	Olen	Smith
Beach	Lache	Olin	Theron
Beacher	Lachlan	Pickford	Wirt
Beech	Leif	Pitney	Wirth
Beecher	Link	Prentice	Witt
Fane	Lombard	Ritter	Witter
Gordan	Lunn	Rogatien	Xenos
Gorden	Major	Rothwell	Zedekia
Gordie	Muir	Ruck	Zedekiah
Gordon	Nevin	Ruskin	

Name Portrait 4

The Grasper

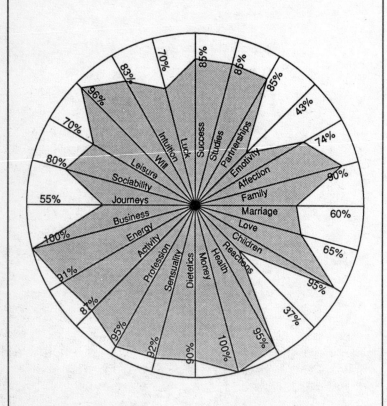

Element : Water   **Plant** : Elder tree

Mineral : Brass   **Sign** : Scorpio

Animal : Octopus   **Color** : Violet

Personality Type:

The Grasper

(Associated names – page 54)

BASIC CHARACTER

Although you have an intense emotional nature, you keep your feelings very much under control. Most of the time you sublimate your volatile temper into action plans which enable you to accomplish your desires. You have a reflective, manipulative mentality which gives you the ability to get what you want more quickly than most people. Like your totem animal, the octopus, you are tenacious in grabbing onto whatever it is that you desire. In both your business and personal life you are organized and efficient. Essentially, there are two aspects to your personality—the one that you show to the world and the one that you tend to hide.

YOUR PSYCHOLOGY

You're a go-getter who wants to attain as much power and influence as possible, and at times you may take on too much. However, your will is so strong that you would never admit to being overwhelmed. Emotionally speaking you keep your feelings hidden and no one can be certain of your real motives. You tend to control those around you with your probing mind and exceptional memory. Negative qualities are your need to be right and your self-assured stubbornness that borders on arrogance.

HOW YOU ACT AND REACT IN THE WORLD

Your personality is like a Molotov cocktail that could go off at any time. In extremes you can be tyrannical and will go very far to get your way. Your need to assert your power in a situation usually sets the tone of all of your personal interactions. As a boss, you can be difficult, demanding, and determined to have your way. Usually you express your anger through a stinging sarcasm that slays your opponent while it diminishes your own vulnerability.

YOUR DEEP INTUITIVE PERSONALITY

You are both intuitive and imaginative and know how to make these qualities serve you. Your shining personality defines your personal power while it adds to your professional success. You can make dreams come true and life luminescent with possibility.

YOUR INTELLIGENCE

You have a pragmatic intelligence and a good deal of human insight. With ease, you can manipulate situations to your advantage and can therefore be an awesome enemy when crossed. Because your mind is both fertile and resourceful, you would make an excellent inventor, researcher, engineer, or technician, especially in the area of atomic research or oil. Government is another area where you would especially shine.

YOUR EMOTIONAL NATURE

You tend to find it easier to manipulate than to express your emotions freely and are capable of putting romantic considerations in the background to accomplish an immediate goal. Your moral standards can be somewhat ruthless when it comes to the pursuit of your desires. Essentially you tend to be more mental than emotional and find the give-and-take of relationships something of a strain. Because you are so strongly sexual, your emotions are deeply tied to your erotic needs. You can easily be enslaved by your sensuality and overly indulgent in all areas of sensual pursuit.

YOUR HEALTH AND VITALITY

Your health tends to be good and your energy superb. However, problem areas are intestines, eyes, and migraine headaches—all relating back to your nerves. For optimum health, stimulants should be avoided and special attention should be paid to not overstraining the stomach.

THE SOCIAL YOU

Utility plays an important role in your social life. Essentially you are most interested in friends who can either further your career or enhance your social status. Your approach to your social relationships is as goal-oriented as your involvement in your career. In both, you enjoy long-lasting success. However, you must also keep in mind that the heights of such a success can sometimes also lead to a fall.

———————

NamePortrait
4
Associated Names

Alfonse	Beamer	Les	Selig
Alfonso	Berenger	Lesley	Seton
Alonso	Berg	Leslie	Shandy
Alonzo	Berger	Manvil	Sheehan
Alphonse	Bergess	Manville	Sheldon
Alphonsin	Berk	Mercer	Shelton
Alphonso	Burford	Milford	Sholto
Alphonsus	Burg	Millford	Stillman
Andeol	Burgess	Quemby	Stilman
Anse	Burke	Quenby	Stoke
Ansel	Camden	Quimby	Tilden
Ansell	Frick	Quinby	Tilton
Anselm	Hansel	Renshaw	Trowbridge
Anselme	Ingemar	Seaton	Udell
Anshelm	Ingmar	Seetin	
Beaman	Keith	Seeton	

Name Portrait 5

Blithe Performer

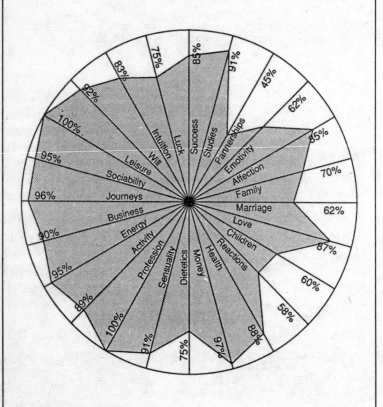

Element : Air   **Plant** : Hyacinth

Mineral : Agate   **Sign** : Gemini

Animal : Fox   **Color** : Orange

Personality Type:

Blithe Performer

(Associated names – page 60)

BASIC CHARACTER

You are exciting and unpredictable, emotionally complex and occasionally prone to extremes. Like your animal totem, the fox, your mind is both shrewd and clever. Your sense of irony makes you fond of fooling those around you and somewhat prone to playing practical jokes.

YOUR PSYCHOLOGY

You have an extroverted personality and a deepseated need to attract attention. Therefore, you tend to dress and behave in a way that will be noticed. Your mind is curious; your memory, exceptional. Essentially, you live your life with ease, get along well with a lot of people, and work out day-to-day problems with little difficulty.

HOW YOU ACT AND REACT IN THE WORLD

You are highly emotional, occasionally volatile, and sometimes control situations by your personal reactions to them. Although little actually escapes your awareness, you're not that easy to see into. Not only are you clever at concealing your intentions, you're also protective of the privacy of your own little world.

YOUR DEEP INTUITIVE PERSONALITY

Under your surface charm, you're a person in search of self-understanding. Often you are afraid of your own feelings and of showing that vulnerable side of yourself. Because you want the world to see you only as a smiling winner, you conceal your feelings and create a facade. The more that you integrate your inner and outer personalities, the more your intuitions will take on their own life.

YOUR INTELLIGENCE

Your mind is quick and spontaneous but somewhat scattered. Your memory is astonishingly retentive and your perceptions profound enough for you to pigeonhole another person's vulnerability. Both mentally and physically you have more energy than you tend to utilize and often waste it performing for other people. Because you so enjoy seeing your self-image reflected back to you, you could make either a successful actress or singer. At the same time foreign languages, travel, and people-oriented professions also appeal to you. Therefore, you would be comfortable being anything from a translator to an airline stewardess to a public relations consultant.

YOUR EMOTIONAL NATURE

On the surface, you are gregarious and effusive, friendly to all but open to very few. Underneath your insouciant facade lies a serious being who is both difficult to understand and bursting with the joy of living. Emotionally speaking, you are an impulsive risk taker who is capable of cultivating many superficial friendships which you don't necessarily follow up on. Essentially, your behavior can be inconsistent and your emotions complicated. Basically you want to be liked for yourself. But the problem is that you're not entirely sure what that is and this can cause difficulties, especially in your sex life.

YOUR HEALTH AND VITALITY

Your physical health is a function of your emotions. Therefore, when your spirits are high, your health is at its best. However, when your moods dip down, so does your vitality. In general, your constitution is strong and your body athletic. Your recuperative ability tends to be exceptional. Yet a potential problem area is your lungs.

THE SOCIAL YOU

Because your personality so needs a public, you usually manage to create one. Therefore, you are most often active, gregarious, and found in the center of things. Not only do you have a strong willpower that gets you what you want, but you have a streak of luck as well that helps you keep it.

———————

NamePortrait
5
Associated Names

Aindrea	Edrea	Majesta	Patty
Andi	Fealty	Maxene	Peony
Andre	Flo	Maxie	Reba
Andrea	Flor	Maxima	Rebeca
Andreana	Flora	Maxine	Rebecca
Andree	Florance	Megan	Rebeka
Andria	Flore	Meghan	Rebekah
Andriana	Florence	Nitya	Rebekka
Andy	Florencia	Nordica	Riba
Aphrodite	Florentia	Nordika	Riva
Arnalda	Floria	Odessa	Saxona
Aura	Florinda	Ozora	Sidra
Aure	Florine	Pat	Sidria
Aurea	Floris	Patience	Yedda
Auria	Florrie	Patienza	Yetta
Beckie	Florry	Patrice	Zilla
Becky	Flossie	Patricia	Zillah
Bekky	Flower	Patrizia	Zinia
Dorek	Galiana	Patsy	Zinnia
Eadrea	Galiena	Patti	
Edra	Kim	Pattie	

NamePortrait 6
The Reigning Presence

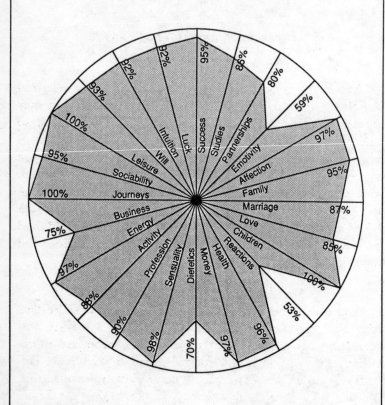

Element : Fire   **Plant** : Almond tree

Mineral : Radium   **Sign** : Aries

Animal : Peacock   **Color** : Red

Personality Type:

The Reigning Presence

(Associated names – page 66)

BASIC CHARACTER

You have strong, sometimes unmanageable emotions and a tendency towards irritability. Although at times you may appear to be lackadaisical, in point of fact, you are waiting to make the right move. When you finally do, you're capable of driving yourself hard to attain your desires. As a result, you usually enjoy a sort of success that is lasting and substantial. Your nature is adventurous, independent, and proud. Like your plant totem, the almond tree, your shell has to be broken before anyone can really get to know you. From childhood on, your potential is high for achieving your most serious and sought-after endeavors.

YOUR PSYCHOLOGY

You are a person of both spontaneous action and reflection. Perhaps because of this, you maintain a private personal life while another part of you seeks public exposure. Although your mind is not easily persuaded, your more vulnerable emotional nature can be somewhat impressionable. You possess a strongly developed will power that can sometimes turn to stubbornness. That is why you feel a natural tendency to create your own private kingdom from which you reign as the sole authority.

HOW YOU ACT AND REACT IN THE WORLD

Although you possess strong emotions, you still have an objectivity which contributes to your sense of justice. You

63

also have a burning desire to set the world on fire and will play a variety of roles to do it. Your inherent self-confidence and need for challenge spur you on. You tend to do best at what truly interests you. Otherwise, your attention becomes distracted and your performance compromised.

YOUR DEEP INTUITIVE PERSONALITY

You are highly intuitive and have swift, penetrating insights. Another significant part of your personality is your intelligence and charm.

YOUR INTELLIGENCE

You are exceptionally intelligent and can swiftly sift the importance of larger issues from a morass of minor details. Your memory excels for the sort of things that make an emotional impression. And because you are so inquisitive, you are likely to undertake new experiences and regard them as exciting adventures. However, because you tend to be weak in mastering routine matters, you need to develop both prudence and discipline. When you really want something, you can be rather single-minded, and it seems that you want a lot of things a lot of the time. The most profound part of you demands authority which you usually command from your earliest years.

In terms of career, you would do well in technical or scientific areas, specifically in such roles as engineer, industrialist, chemist, soldier, or agronomist. However, whatever you ultimately decide to do, your dedication to your work helps you adapt quickly and succeed rapidly.

YOUR EMOTIONAL NATURE

On a very deep level you want others to love you and approve of you and tell you so. Only when that need is satisfied, can you feel a deep measure of affection. Underneath your cool exterior, you are intense, passionate, but often domineering when in love. At the same time, you have a very independent nature and a desire to go your own way. You tend to be a target for the "femme fatale" imbued with a dazzling dose of charm and beauty. At an early age, you're aware of the pleasures of romantic love and naturally expect the best that life can give you.

YOUR HEALTH AND VITALITY

You have a strong vitality and an excellent resistance to disease. Your problem area is too little sleep and a tendency to digestive problems. Your teeth could also benefit from close attention to regular checkups.

THE SOCIAL YOU

Because you love to be surrounded by people, you are an exciting and accommodating host. You tend to favor such activities as huge picnics, surprise parties, and romantic walks in the country. Throughout your adult years, something of the child remains. And that precious part of you takes you ever anew toward a wider variety of activities.

NamePortrait
6
Associated Names

Aindreas	Cyrenaica	Fiora	Scoville
Anders	Cyriaque	Fiorenza	Somerville
Andie	Cyril	Florentine	Sommerville
Andir	Cyrill	Fuller	Sorrel
Andre	Cyrille	Halsey	Sorrell
Andreas	Cyrus	Halsy	Sven
Andrew	Dandie	Harcourt	Ted
Andrien	Dandy	Laird	Teddie
Andy	Derek	Newall	Teddy
Aylworth	Derk	Newel	Tedrick
Beaufort	Derrick	Newell	Theodore
Bonar	Dirk	Price	Theodoric
Bonaz	Dore	Rhodes	Theodorick
Broderic	Drew	Ros	Theon
Broderick	Druon	Rosco	Tucker
Brodrick	Fanny	Roscoe	Tudor
Chatham	Feodor	Roz	Tupper
Cyr	Feodore	Savile	Walby
Cyrano	Fielding	Saville	Wordsworth

Name Portrait 7

The Seeker of Experience

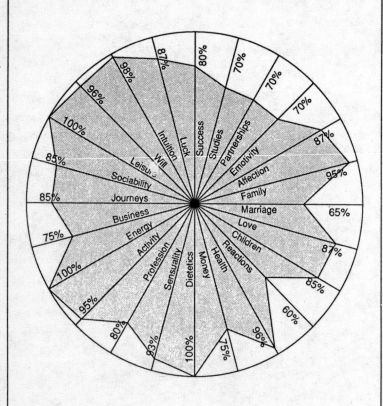

Element : Water   **Plant** : Myrtle
Mineral : Diamond   **Sign** : Scorpio
Animal : Lynx   **Color** : Blue

Personality Type:

The Seeker of Experience

(Associated names – page 72)

BASIC CHARACTER

You are exciting and insouciant, highly emotional and very much alive. You tend to be curious about everything around you. Yet, at the same time, you have a deep, contemplative nature that can eventually make you very wise.

YOUR PSYCHOLOGY

Although you tend to live within a very private world, you are very alert to everything around you. You have a remarkable memory, a highly developed imagination and an active interest in a plethora of things. Emotionally, you tend to be subjective and see the world as an extension of your psyche. At times you can be self-serving, impatient, and determined to have everything exactly the way you want it. Because you have such a charming way of appearing self-confident, you usually get it.

HOW YOU ACT AND REACT IN THE WORLD

At times you can tyrannically blame others for your own shortcomings. You have a rebellious nature that is opposed to restriction and convention. You are proud, vain, and prone to emotional outbursts when your desires are countered. At the same time you are the ardent supporter of a cause and a self-righteous believer in what you consider progress. At times you appear consumed with life and in a perpetual state of motion, and because your tenacious nature never allows you to give up, you usually emerge on top.

YOUR DEEP INTUITIVE PERSONALITY

You have a finely tuned prescient sense, which, combined with your charm, can easily magnetize members of the opposite sex. Just like your animal totem, the lynx, you contemplate and carefully measure circumstance. You have eyes that see all, leading to the uncanny insights of a witchy nature. However, you would do well to develop your objectivity. Otherwise, your thinking could become unbalanced.

YOUR INTELLIGENCE

You possess both an analytical and perspicacious mind which sees and senses everything. Your ideal is the arts and a career such as an actress, singer, sculptress, etc. However, you're also suited for a more concrete profession such as medicine, engineering, and even politics. With your commanding self-confidence and sense of intrigue, you could even end up in the Senate!

YOUR EMOTIONAL NATURE

You tend to be possessive and have an all-or-nothing personality. Essentially, your need to claim ownership is an outgrowth of your craving for appreciation. You find it difficult to reveal your deeper emotions and often fall victim to the dictates of your pride. Hidden under your defensive behavior is an exciting sensuality that can be extremely evocative, and when you fall in love you feel all!

YOUR HEALTH AND VITALITY

Quite often you are more concerned with the health of others than with your own physical well-being. Weak areas to watch out for are the eyes and the digestive tract. Too many late nights on the town can also wear down your body's resistance to diseases. Finally, because your bones tend to be brittle, you should take special care to avoid accidents.

THE SOCIAL YOU

While you can be the most faithful of friends, you're exceptionally careful about whom you let close to you. As an acquaintance, you maintain an affable distance; yet only as a close friend do you allow yourself to become involved. When it comes to romance, your feelings are often changeable and occasionally capricious. It is not unlikely that in an entire lifetime you may have more than one husband. At all times your ability to begin anew retards your fear of unhappy endings. Like an exuberant, insatiable child, you embrace as many exciting people and experiences as life will allow you.

———————

Associated Names

Alberta	Anitra	Coral	Esta
Albertina	Ann	Corale	Estella
Albertine	Anna	Coralie	Estelle
Alex	Annabel	Coraline	Estrelita
Alexa	Annabella	Corella	Estrella
Alexandra	Annabelle	Corett	Ethel
Alexandria	Annabla	Coretta	Ethelda
Alexandrina	Annable	Corette	Etheldred
Alexandrine	Annaliese	Corie	Etheldrede
Alexia	Anne	Corin	Ethelinda
Alexine	Anneliese	Corina	Etheline
Alexis	Annetta	Corinna	Etheljean
Alix	Annette	Corinne	Ethelred
Alla	Annie	Corissa	Ethered
Allie	Annona	Corisse	Ethyl
Amalia	Annora	Correna	Ethylyn
Amalie	Annys	Corrie	Favor
Amalinda	Anona	Corrina	Favora
Amealia	Anora	Doanna	Filantha
Amelea	Anouchka	Eada	Frodis
Amelia	Anouck	Elberta	Frond
Amelie	Aubane	Elbertine	Fronde
Amelinda	Bella	Electra	Garda
Amelinde	Belle	Emelie	Gemma
Ameline	Berta	Emelina	Gemmel
Amelita	Berte	Emeline	Gerda
Ana	Bertie	Emilia	Guenna
Anabel	Blossom	Emilie	Gwen
Anais	Cora	Emilienne	Gwenda
Anemone	Corabella	Emily	Gwendolen
Anita	Corabelle	Emmeline	Gwendolene

Associated Names (cont.)

Gwendoline	Ite	Nona	Sandi
Gwendolyn	Lexie	Nonnie	Sandie
Gwendolyne	Lexine	Nydia	Sandra
Gwennie	Lisa	Orva	Sandrine
Gwyn	Mel	Perfecta	Sandy
Gwyneth	Melisa	Philantha	Solange
Gwynne	Melissa	Philanthe	Sondra
Haidee	Mell	Piper	Star
Hana	Mellie	Pris	Starr
Hanna	Mill	Prisca	Stella
Hannah	Millie	Priscilla	Stelle
Helice	Nan	Prisilla	Strella
Helixa	Nana	Prissie	Tania
Ida	Nancy	Psyche	Tanya
Idalia	Nanete	Rox	Tatiana
Idalina	Nanetta	Roxana	Tatienne
Idaline	Nanette	Roxane	Titania
Idalle	Nanine	Roxanna	Tory
Idelea	Nanna	Roxanne	Vignette
Idelia	Nanon	Roxie	Wendy
Idella	Neala	Roxina	Xanthe
Idelle	Neale	Roxine	Xaviera
Ila	Nina	Roxy	Xaviere
Ilda	Ninette	Sancha	Zandra
Ilde	Ninon	Sanchia	
Ita	Nita	Sancia	

Name Portrait 8

The Thinker

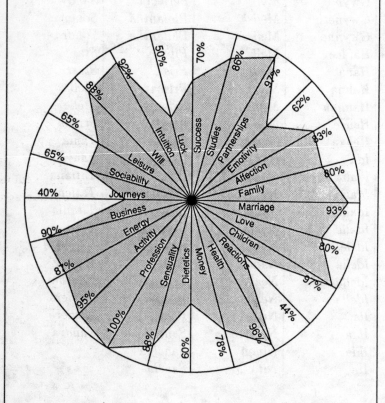

Element : Earth   **Plant** : Garlic
Mineral : Hematite   **Sign** : Capricorn
Animal : Marabout   **Color** : Yellow

Personality Type:

The Thinker

(Associated names – page 78)

BASIC CHARACTER

You are quiet and reflective, sensitive and diffident. You survey the world from a quiet, thoughtful place. Your mind is ruminative and your personality dreamy. Your proclivity is to think things out carefully before committing to a course of action. Although your emotions are strong, you efface them with your mental thought processes. The result is that you can be a rather difficult person to get to know.

YOUR PSYCHOLOGY

You find your inner world far more important than the outer world. Therefore, you can easily become withdrawn. Not only are you closed about your feelings, at times you willfully conceal them. Essentially, you are far more silent than self-expressive and your self-confidence suffers from your excessive self-examination. However, when you do make a decision, you become dedicated to its execution and make up for your timidity with a great deal of tenacity.

HOW YOU ACT AND REACT IN THE WORLD

There are moments when your emotions can make you weaken, and deep inside you feel very much confused. During such times you tend to retreat from the scene in an attempt to sort out the situation. Although you are difficult to get to know, with friends you are devoted and reliable. Such personal emotions often provide motivations for a variety of life decisions, including your career.

YOUR DEEP INTUITIVE PERSONALITY

You tend to be highly intuitive and trust your inner voice. You are also imaginative and creative. The problem is that you don't trust yourself to communicate the workings of your inner mind. Therefore, you're prone to remain silent about your most private feelings.

YOUR INTELLIGENCE

You have a profound intelligence which is not particularly adept at details. Rather, yours is a mind much more concerned with both meaning and depth. For that reason, the study of philosophy suits you as does anything dealing with psychology or medicine. Even in areas like engineering, finance, farming, or electronics, you possess the potential for considerable success. Finally, as a writer, artist, or musician, you could find fame due to your original in-depth way of looking at the world.

YOUR EMOTIONAL NATURE

You tend to hold things inside and hang onto disappointments long after they're over. Emotionally you are cautious, self-protective, and possessive in instances in which your deeper feelings are touched. From time to time a moodiness overtakes you and you seek refuge from the infringing world. Because you're far more shy and sentimental than aggressively sexual, you're basically uncomfortable in the role of predator. A romantic setting with a low risk factor is far more to your making since you loathe feeling vulnerable in any situation. Because you are so reticent in showing your feelings, often others are unaware of your needs. The conflict between your self-protective defenses and your need for deep emotional connection is one that is profound and overshadows your life.

8

YOUR HEALTH AND VITALITY

While you possess tremendous energy and an extraordinary vitality, despite your desires to the contrary, you still do need your sleep. Potential weak areas are kidneys and the eyes. Due to excessive eyestrain, headaches could be a problem.

THE SOCIAL YOU

You are not the most intensely social person and prefer small gatherings to large groups of people. Since serious conversation is particularly to your liking, you're usually most free and easy with friends. A warm situation offering stimulating conversation makes you happier than any glamorous fete. Basically, you're a serious person who needs few external props for a sense of wellbeing and a lot of emotional reassurance with a sense of purpose.

———————————

NamePortrait
8
Associated Names

Abbe	Arlen	Hartleigh	Ozzie
Abbot	Arley	Hartley	Roald
Abbott	Arlie	Hiatt	Rowley
Abel	Arly	Hyatt	Rus
Abelard	Boot	Ichabod	Russ
Abott	Boote	Kent	Russel
Airleas	Booth	Kime	Russell
Albern	Boothe	Lathrop	Russet
Amadee	Both	Lem	Rust
Anntoin	Fabe	Lemmie	Rusty
Anstice	Fabian	Lemuel	Saber
Anstiss	Fabien	Lindsay	Saxe
Anthony	Fulbert	Lindsey	Saxon
Antoine	Harden	Linsay	Sigurd
Anton	Harl	Linsey	Spangler
Antonin	Harlan	Maloney	Swann
Antonio	Harland	Merton	Tailor
Antony	Harleigh	Os	Taylor
Aristide	Harley	Oscar	Tino
Aristodemus	Harlon	Oskar	Tony
Aristotle	Harly	Ossie	
Arlay	Hart	Oz	

Name Portrait 9

Romantic Dreamer

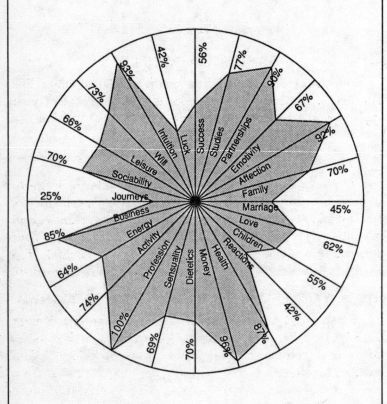

Element : Water   **Plant** : Absinth

Mineral : Serpentine   **Sign** : Cancer

Animal : Duck   **Color** : Red

Personality Type:

Romantic Dreamer

(Associated names – page 84)

BASIC CHARACTER

You are a dreamer with a richly developed inner life. You loathe routine, love the more ethereal aspects of your existence, and would probably be happiest on an island in paradise, getting lost in the beauty.

YOUR PSYCHOLOGY

You have an evanescent nature and an intense desire to create a dream world. Essentially, your escapist nature incites you to avoid responsibilities, overlook unpleasant realities and "forget" everything you don't prefer to think about. Your personality is introverted and your imagination fanciful. You are like a flower child adrift in the middle of a sunlit meadow.

HOW YOU ACT AND REACT IN THE WORLD

Because you tend to be secretive about the joys of your inner world, you're not easy to get close to. Your mind moves in a world of chimerical visions and technicolor fantasies. Therefore, you find it more satisfying to retreat from life than to interact with it. Coming down to earth to endure the banal routine is a challenge that you don't particularly feel suited for. Essentially your poetic soul would rather drift and dream in solitude like your animal totem, the duck.

YOUR DEEP INTUITIVE PERSONALITY

You are extraordinarily intuitive to the point of being psychic. It is likely that you have precognitive dreams and an ability to both remember and interpret their meaning. However, because your mind is so receptive to psychic influences you should protect yourself from excessive stimulation.

YOUR INTELLIGENCE

You have a highly imaginative sort of mind that has little interest in the real world. For this reason, you are best suited to work in an undemanding atmosphere. Places such as museums and libraries are definitely appealing as is any kind of work which will allow you to retreat within your head. Because of your tendency toward timidity, you often fail to impress your intelligence upon the outside. Ideally your romantic nature is most comfortable living in a fairy castle where you have nothing to do but dream away the hours while you watch the stars.

YOUR EMOTIONAL NATURE

While you have an extraordinary need for love, your nature often makes it difficult for you to experience it. Often you distance yourself from feeling vulnerable by creating and projecting cynical attitudes. Because you tend to escape behind self-protective defenses you can make yourself inaccessible to the experience of loving. Likewise, your excessive romanticism makes you both fantasy oriented and somewhat fearful about sex. Essentially, you are far more comfortable thinking than feeling, which both frustrates and complicates your emotional needs. In many ways you are an enigma unto yourself, wavering among your emotional contradictions.

YOUR HEALTH AND VITALITY

Most of your potential maladies have their base in your emotions. Therefore, attention should be given to relaxing your mind. Plenty of sleep plus a healthy diet is not only of salubrious benefit but absolutely essential. Regular exercise and especially hiking will increase your energy and all around sense of well-being.

THE SOCIAL YOU

Although you possess both charm and personal appeal, you still have to be pushed to socialize. Often shyness and a tendency toward self-effacement retard your potential for total enjoyment. A better balance should be cultivated between your inner and outer life to allow you a more expansive experience of living.

———————————

NamePortrait
9
Associated Names

Airleas	Arlie	Ericka	Netty
Anthonia	Arlina	Erika	Odelet
Antoinette	Arline	Herleva	Odelette
Antoinietta	Arlyne	Imogen	Orenda
Antoni	Calvina	Imogene	Prima
Antonia	Cerealia	Imogine	Sireen
Antonietta	Cerelia	Ireta	Sirena
Antonina	Cerelie	Irete	Sirene
Arlana	Cerellia	Iretta	Tansy
Arleen	Ceryl	Irette	Toinette
Arlen	Cirila	Lena	Toinon
Arlena	Cirilla	Lene	Toni
Arlene	Cyrilla	Lona	Tonia
Arletta	Emogene	Netta	Tulsi
Arlette	Erica	Nettie	

Name Portrait 10

The Energized Crusader

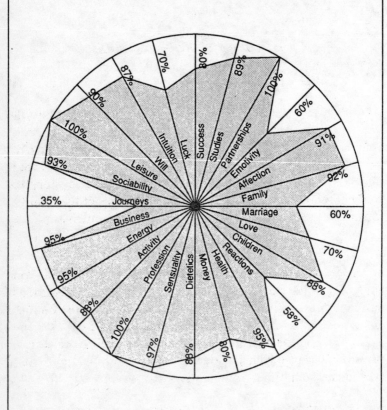

Element : Water

Mineral : Nickel

Animal : Jaguar

Plant : Fig tree

Sign : Cancer

Color : Yellow

10

Personality Type:

The Energized Crusader

(Associated names – page 90)

BASIC CHARACTER

Associated with the sound of your name is a secret knowledge of the world. Even your plant totem, the fig tree, symbolizes knowledge and discovery. Your personality tends to be nervous and emotional, and your reactions are so rapid that your animal totem is the jaguar. There is a mystery to your character that is difficult to define because of the duality of your nature which is both reflective and impulsive.

YOUR PSYCHOLOGY

You are both an introvert and an extrovert. While you enjoy a rich inner life, at the same time you have a gregarious outgoing personality that is both compassionate and communicative. You are a deeply caring person who is open to the world and concerned about the affairs and feelings of others. However, because your personality can be both obstinate and tyrannical, sometimes your motives are misunderstood.

HOW YOU ACT AND REACT IN THE WORLD

Your emotions are strong, and your temper can be volatile. However, at the same time you are a loyal, trustworthy friend who demands the same in return. You have a probing, skeptical mind that tears away at the surface in order to envision what lies beyond. In any problem situation you're at your best when you withdraw from the world to consider perspectives and possibilities. Essentially you are a man of ideas which you prefer to be carried out by someone else. Not only could you be a formidable politician but also a successful psychologist.

YOUR DEEP INTUITIVE PERSONALITY

Your intuitive vision is one of clarity and scope. Your perceptions are both lucid and far-seeing. In addition you have a remarkable power of persuasion that is reinforced by both your magnetism and imagination.

YOUR INTELLIGENCE

Your mind is both receptive and analytic. With ease, you can envision the core of a complex situation and remember the details with remarkable recall. Because you have such an insatiable curiosity, you are most likely an omnivorous reader who conquers many subjects simultaneously. Your high energy level can lead you to take on too much or to carry things too far. And your extraordinary self-confidence can leave others with the impression that you are a man with a mission.

YOUR EMOTIONAL NATURE

You are both highly responsive and easily aroused. Therefore, you can be both the impassioned defender of the underdog and the person committed to a religious, social, or political issue. Because you have a deep-seated need for closeness, your behavior can be considered controlling and possessive. However, in actuality, this has less to do with your need to own than with your tendency toward emotional extremes. You have a strong sexuality which you sometimes sublimate into some intensely embraced cause. However, excessive frustration can bring on a strain that will force you to confront the destructive effects of your self-escapism.

YOUR HEALTH AND VITALITY

You have a powerful vitality and capacity for physical

endurance. Even in childhood, you've experienced a strong resistance to disease. However, should you choose to abuse your remarkable health, potential problem areas could be the respiratory and circulatory systems. Also, due to your incredible energy and intensity, you are somewhat accident prone.

THE SOCIAL YOU

Your social life can suffer from your tendency to be startlingly direct. Most people would prefer a more diplomatic approach and may wish that you try to mince your words. Your rigid moral codes can make you difficult, demanding, and uncompromising. Still, you know exactly what you want and what you have to do to get it. Because of that, you usually succeed in everything you seriously undertake, from attaining materialistic goals to attracting the most desirable people to your side.

———————————

NamePortrait
10
Associated Names

Anatol	Calvert	Lysander	Northcliff
Anatole	Campbell	Mat	Northcliffe
Arch	Cornal	Mata	Northrop
Archard	Cornall	Mathew	Northrup
Archer	Corneille	Mathias	Nortrop
Archerd	Cornel	Mathieu	Nortrup
Archibald	Cornelius	Matt	Rawlins
Archie	Cornell	Matthew	Rawson
Archimbald	Cornille	Matthias	Rover
Archy	Donatien	Matthieu	Ryan
Balbo	Donato	Mattias	Rycroft
Baptist	Fidel	Mattie	Sandy
Baptiste	Fidele	Matty	Troy
Baptistin	Fidelio	Neal	Vasili
Barclay	Fiske	Neale	Vasilis
Baron	Fitch	Neall	Vasily
Barron	Floyd	Nee	Vassili
Basil	Gaud	Neil	Vassilis
Basile	Gilleasbuig	Neill	Vassily
Basilio	Haddan	Nial	Vassy
Basilius	Hadden	Niall	Wace
Bay	Haddon	Niel	Wylie
Bayard	Hyacinthe	Niels	Zephyrin
Berkeley	Lenaic	Niles	
Berkley	Lloyd	Nils	

Name Portrait 11

Unpredictable Individualist

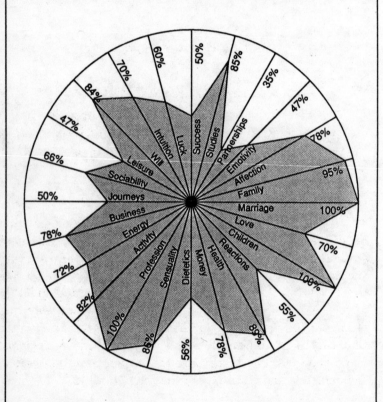

Element : Water

Mineral : Chrysolite

Animal : Pike

Plant : Wild cherry tree

Sign : Pisces

Color : Green

Personality Type:

Unpredictable Individualist

(Associated names – page 96)

BASIC CHARACTER

At times it almost seems like you're two people. One is quick and direct while the other is convoluted and acerbic. Like your animal totem, the pike, your personality has a bite and a sting that lingers long after you.

YOUR PSYCHOLOGY

You tend to prefer your own company to that of other people. At times your preference for the inner life can make you quite withdrawn. Yet your remote facade masks a contradictory nature that is emotionally inconsistent and sometimes volatile. Your mind is impressionable and quick to anger. And when someone strikes you the wrong way, you strike out in retaliation. You have a strong need for freedom that can be at times selfish and idiosyncratic. A principal nemesis in your life is learning to accommodate yourself to the demands and restraints of the outside world.

HOW YOU ACT AND REACT IN THE WORLD

You tend to be changeable and flighty, anxious and insecure. Often the self-confidence that you summon is only a facade. The more fearful you become, the greater your changeability. A deep-seated fear of failure haunts your inner reaches. Therefore, a career that you feel comfortable in is crucial to your sense of well-being. When you feel out of sync with your situation, you are especially vulnerable to psychosomatic disorders.

YOUR DEEP INTUITIVE PERSONALITY

Because you adhere to a rational approach to life, you tend to repress your intuitive faculties. Logic supersedes incandescent inspiration and your superior imagination is kept tightly under control. Although your personality is generally considered attractive, your hairtrigger temper can be both disruptive and destructive.

YOUR INTELLIGENCE

You have an analytic mind and a tremendous capacity for detail. However, at times this can reach an extreme concern with the picayune. At the same time you have an impressive memory and a vital curiosity. Even though you need to be provoked to action, your mind is an imposing force that must be reckoned with.

YOUR EMOTIONAL NATURE

Your emotions are both complicated and unpredictable. Often you suffer from mood swings that make it difficult for others to understand you. Emotionally you tend toward extremes and can get caught up in progressive movements and causes. Although your sensuality is intense, it often tends to be detached from your emotions. Your body is often the battleground between your mind and your emotions. At the same time you tend to be a possessive person inclined to embrace a double standard.

YOUR HEALTH AND VITALITY

Because your nervous system is somewhat fragile, you should avoid stimulants and excessive overwork. Your health tends to be dependent on the state of your emotions. Therefore, you feel best physically when your life has some semblance of serenity. A good deal of rest and relaxation should be included in your routine. Also, avoid smoking since another potential problem area is the lungs.

THE SOCIAL YOU

You can be unreliable in your dealings with others. On certain days you desire to be completely alone and then on other days you'd like to entertain the entire world. Your desires and decisions are often at the whim of circumstances. You can ruin your opportunities through caprice if you're not careful. In brief, your name is not an easy one to bear until you learn how to transcend your lower self.

————————

NamePortrait
11
Associated Names

Alric
Barnaba
Barnabas
Barnabe
Barnaby
Barnet
Barnett
Barney
Barny
Beathan
Beatie
Beattie
Beatty
Beaty

Ben
Benjamin
Benjy
Bennie
Benny
Benoni
Benson
Bert
Bourn
Bourne
Burn
Burnaby
Burne
Byrne

Candide
Cicero
Fergie
Fergus
Galmier
Harbert
Harbin
Hebert
Herb
Herbert
Herbie
Hoibeard
Hoireabard
Jason

Lamar
Nairn
Nobel
Noble
Nolan
Onesime
Orrick
Rudd
Shepley
Tarleton
Ulric
Ulrich
Vachel

Name Portrait 12

Fiery Protagonist

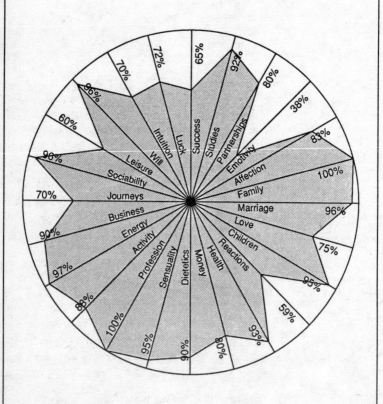

Element : Fire   **Plant** : Poplar

Mineral : Bismuth   **Sign** : Leo

Animal : Salmon   **Color** : Blue

Personality Type:

Fiery Protagonist

(Associated names – page 103)

BASIC CHARACTER

By nature, you possess a will of iron and the pride to go with it. You tend to be driven—a man who will resist the winds and the tides to get to where you are going. Freedom is important to you. The worst situation you can find yourself in is one that hampers or restricts your enviable energy in any way. This drive for freedom is what keeps you going; without what you see as your liberty, you can become nervous and irritable and your own worst enemy. You are quick to act— as long as it's your way—and can know fulfillment only when your actions come to fruit in the world.

YOUR PSYCHOLOGY

Because you are so outgoing and sure of yourself, you often attract people to your ideas and ways. You can walk into a room and draw others like a magnet—unless you're in one of your bad moods, in which case people are bound to think of you as arrogant. Though your self-confidence and will can work wonders in the world, they can get in your way, especially when someone else does not agree with you; for if anyone knows it all, you do. You must be able to project your energies, and this results in two things. First, you have the capacity to bring about great works, especially works that have to do with protest and reform. Second, and less happily, you tend to be a bit too subjective in the way you view people and things. This goes hand in hand with a certain amount of possessiveness and inability to understand that you may not always be correct. But like your plant totem, the proud poplar, you are equipped both to resist the wind, and, when it becomes too strong, to bend with it.

HOW YOU ACT AND REACT IN THE WORLD

You need discipline and structure for your energy, lest it is frittered away on useless endeavors. The spirit of the rebel is close to you, which is probably why your reactions to other people and to situations fluctuate so often. It is not that you are a changeable person; however, you may not be channeling your energies in ways that bring about the results you want. You are probably something of the adventurer; at least you seem so to others. But what you are actually doing is trying to keep your space—and it had better be wide enough for you. You are given to such work as labor union activity, job foreman, or engineering—those sorts of occupations that allow you not only to express yourself, but which will show results. Journalism in the tradition of Mencken, Woodward, and Bernstein, has always been another career option for you. You are a man of action, and very probably would be the first out there to man the barricades—as long as it was you who thought of putting them up in the first place. Though you do not always take easily to discipline and structure, they are absolutely essential to your productivity in the world, in order to keep your very strong actions and reactions aimed at a goal.

YOUR DEEP INTUITIVE PERSONALITY

When you take the time to listen, your "inner voice" is your best guide. But most often you are just plain too busy to rely very much on your intuition, even when you know that the direction that you've taken yourself is dead wrong. You must apply great effort to calm yourself, and to overcome the nervous energy that accumulates in idle moments, to commune with your intuitive side.

YOUR INTELLIGENCE

You are very quick-witted, able to take in and understand the many facets of a problem or a task at once. This, combined with your prodigious memory and an almost insatiable intellectual curiosity makes you something of a heady person. Your superior intelligence and your high energy, however, need channeling; for though your comprehensive mind allows you to come to decisions far more rapidly than most people, your intense energy can cause you to make mistakes in this area.

YOUR EMOTIONAL NATURE

Deep within, you have a great need for admiration, encouragement, and attention from your loved ones. People may not realize it when they encounter you on the job, but you have a deep store of hidden tenderness, which you are willing to give to the right person. The "right person" will have to agree with you and understand your superiority complex. Still, you are flexible in your responses to other people and though you may not appear very expressive of your personal needs, they are obvious to the few who make up your inner circle. When you express yourself sexually—and you probably began doing so at an astonishingly early age—you are intense. But not necessarily faithful. You enjoy whatever is new, and if you give in to your wanderlust, you will find yourself with a long line of essentially satisfying, if fiery, lovers. Like your totem animal, the salmon, you are moving, always, through new experiences and encounters, but always in the direction of what you regard as home. On the way, you will find love and tenderness, but fury and irritation as well.

YOUR HEALTH AND VITALITY

You are one of the lucky few in that you have a strong vitality despite your excesses. You like to eat at odd times, and you are given to drinking too much alcohol and coffee. As long as you direct your energies, taking up some sport for instance, you can avoid accidents. But, Bartholomew, remember that you are on the accident-prone list, so be a bit more cautious in your daily regimen, and look before you leap.

THE SOCIAL YOU

Though just about everyone finds you an exciting and even awesome character, you have very few whom you count as close friends. They are most likely extraordinary people, and your friendships with them are deep and penetrating. Your special crowd are bolder than most, and recognize your great wit and charm. You can have a mesmerizing effect on people of weaker character than you, and may have a string of "followers" just waiting word from you. As you grow older, your social life becomes more sedate, but until then, you find your society off the beaten track, in adventure, and from unusual situations. You have little patience with others, especially with those who do not understand that you are Number One, so the friends you do make along the way most often defer to you.

_____

NamePortrait
12
Associated Names

Adalwine	Barthol	Fitzgerald	Kazimir
Alden	Bartholome	Flann	King
Aldin	Bartholomew	Garold	Kingsley
Aldwin	Bartie	Gearalt	Kingston
Aldwyn	Bartley	Ger	Kingswell
Alvan	Bartolome	Gerald	Kinsey
Alvin	Bat	Geraud	Lance
Alwin	Baudoin	Gereld	Lancelot
Alwyn	Baudouin	Gerrald	Lancey
Amable	Baudric	Gerry	Lancilot
Aubrey	Bert	Gery	Launce
Aubry	Berthold	Giraud	Launcelot
Audwin	Berthoud	Halliwell	Marmaduke
Aylmer	Bertie	Heath	Octave
Aylwin	Bertold	Heathcliff	Octavian
Baldric	Casimir	Heathcliffe	Octavien
Baldrick	Cass	Jer	Octavius
Balduin	Cassie	Jerald	Octavus
Baldwin	Cassy	Jereld	Orion
Bardo	Duke	Jerold	Presley
Bardrick	Edel	Jerrold	Rogan
Barret	Edelie	Jerry	Rutherford
Barrett	Elden	Joe	Spark
Bart	Eldin	Joel	Tavey
Bartel	Elmer	Joey	Tedmond
Barth	Elvin	Josse	
Barthelemy	Elwin	Josselin	
Barthelmey	Epiphane	Kasimir	

Name Portrait 13

First Crusader

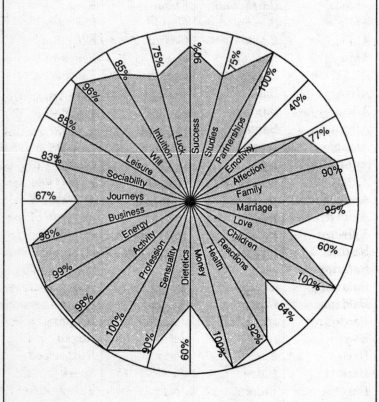

Element : Fire   **Plant** : Mulberry tree

Mineral : Salt   **Sign**   : Aries

Animal   : Cuckoo   **Color** : Violet

Personality Type:

First Crusader

(Associated names – page 109)

BASIC CHARACTER

You are energetic and creative, driven both from without and from within to change the world around you. Your lofty principles and your sense of social justice urges you into action to change a situation which you see as misguided or wrong-headed. Consistency and a high regard for duty are two of your strongest points in all you do, and yet, you are a man of extremes. You have the capacity to be either a saint or a demon, and you know it. This gives you a sort of flexibility, at least the appearance of it, for you are well-centered and therefore able to be at home in any situation, as long as you are active in it. Your animal totem, the peregrinating cuckoo, is a fine symbol of this capacity. In all, you are a harbinger of the future, able to make changes in the world according to your deep regard for principles and "the proper way."

YOUR PSYCHOLOGY

You are a natural extrovert, but despite your outward-going disposition, you are not always the warmest of people. This comes from a tendency that you often succumb to, of believing that only you know the answer. It's a kind of superiority complex which is difficult to deal with, since most times, you probably are right. Because you possess a powerful will, you tend to get by at times on sheer willpower, which can be emotionally draining and cause you to lose your perspective. You like to be in control, and do not take well to criticism, though eventually, you can be persuaded of the correctness of other points of view. Your astonishingly keen sense of egalitarianism—being able to see the injustices around you—tends to get you into situations that can provoke your sizzling hot temper if you feel you cannot control and change them; and you sometimes tend to speak before you think when dealing with such circumstances.

HOW YOU ACT AND REACT IN THE WORLD

Very likely, you leap, feet first, into your work, your friendships, your love affairs. If there is a cause for reform, you are right in there, most likely leading the march—and it's the march you planned. You don't lead any one else's! You like to be first, and if you are, your high level of energy draws others after you like the mulberry tree, your plant totem, draws the moth. You are always pushing yourself, no matter what it is you're involved in, to get results. You would make an excellent technician, writer, or scientist, though it's probably politics or religious leadership which attracts you the most, for you must be able to make changes. You are ready to sacrifice everything for your ideals and the success of your projects.

YOUR DEEP INTUITIVE PERSONALITY

When you listen to your inner voice, you become inspired, and your intuition is the source of much of your energy. However, it is rather inconsistent—ebbing and flowing like the tides. But when it flows, and you are listening, it provokes you with remarkable acuity, and the ability to solve any problem with lightning speed.

YOUR INTELLIGENCE

You go right to the details of any matter. Your well-organized, analytical mind gives you the ability to solve the most baffling problems with no delay. You are a born builder, with an uncanny memory and a powerful mastery of the language. Those attributes, along with your consuming curiosity, make for a firm and strong intellect.

YOUR EMOTIONAL NATURE

The faithful friend or lover, the true and solid husband, you give much of yourself to those close to you, and demand much in return. Love for you should be binding and based on equality and justice. Though you do not need an overactive sex life, you do need to be loved and understood. Though you are not the jealous sort, you are possessive, but only in order to establish a firm relationship where you can give of yourself. Your egalitarianism, carried into emotional relationships, forbids you to show any sort of favoritism to your children; and it also probably prevents you from being a Casanova or a Don Juan.

YOUR HEALTH AND VITALITY

You have a naturally strong constitution and good health, but your intense activity sometimes causes you to overlook your diet. Good nutrition is important for you, if you are to maintain that incredible level of energy at which you're usually moving. Fresh air can be especially restorative to your health at those times when you have abused it. You must also be careful to avoid accidents as you are a bit prone to them.

THE SOCIAL YOU

With your close friends you are true blue; but you simply will not waste your time with anyone who lacks resolve or spirit. Lukewarm and inconsistent people are anathema to you. Though at times you tend to be dominating with people, it is usually "for their own good," as you might put it yourself. You accept certain social conventions and attend social gatherings when you have to—that is, when you see that it is the right or dutiful thing to do, but as a rule, the casual, meaningless "social do" is not at all your thing. There has to be a purpose in all you do, and this includes gatherings with your friends. You are an organizer, so it wouldn't be surprising if most of your social life is built around your philanthropic and reformist interests.

————————

NamePortrait
13
Associated Names

Aineislis	Burkett	Hartwell	Quasimodo
Art	Burnard	Hartwill	Race
Artair	Chase	Harwell	Radleigh
Arthur	Egmont	Harwill	Radley
Artie	Fillmore	Horace	Redley
Artur	Filmer	Horatio	Ridley
Artus	Filmore	Horatius	Romaric
Aurthur	Fin	Kipp	Stan
Barnard	Findlay	Leander	Stanislas
Barnet	Findley	Lee	Stanislaus
Barnett	Finlay	Leggett	Stanislav
Barney	Finley	Leggitt	Stanleigh
Barny	Finn	Liggett	Stanley
Bearnard	Gavan	Ludlow	Stanly
Berk	Gaven	Maddock	Stanmore
Berke	Gavin	Maddox	Stanton
Bern	Gawain	Madoc	Stanway
Bernard	Gawaine	Madock	Stanwick
Bernardin	Gawen	Madog	Stanwood
Bernhard	Gawin	Moe	Tab
Bernie	Greagoir	Moise	Tabb
Berny	Greg	Mos	Tabby
Birk	Gregg	Mose	Theobald
Birke	Gregoire	Moses	Thibaud
Bonne	Gregor	Mosie	Thibaut
Boone	Gregory	Moss	Tibal
Boris	Greiogair	Nev	Tibbald
Bourke	Halstead	Nevil	Tibble
Bud	Halsted	Nevile	Tiobaid
Budd	Harper	Neville	Tiobald
Burk	Hart	Pompey	Tybalt

Associated Names (cont.)

| Whitaker | Yule | Yuli |
| Whittaker | Yules | |

Name Portrait 14

Intriguing Seductress

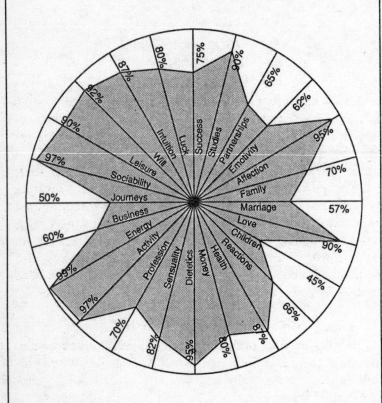

Element : Air

Mineral : Topaz

Animal : Boa

Plant : Virgin's vine

Sign : Aquarius

Color : Orange

Personality Type:

Intriguing Seductress

(Associated names – page 116)

BASIC CHARACTER

Lively and affectionate, you are able to enwrap people with your irresistible charm and engaging sense of humor. There is something of the actress in you that urges you onward into more and more activities and dramatic involvements. You are the last to withdraw from an intrigue; indeed, you often create situations that cast you in the center role as the *prima mobile* of love and attachment. Your totem animal is the enfolding, embracing boa—you surround others with your good humor and affection, and there is positively no way to resist you. Your plant totem, the virgin's vine, is also a symbol of your propensity for such attachments, as well as for the effervescence and essential purity of your motives.

YOUR PSYCHOLOGY

In spite of your outwardness and natural extroversion, there is a deeper, serious side to you, which you do not always reveal. Occasionally, this leads to a tendency to contradict your better judgment, for it is important to you that your bright and social charm always be out there in front. Because you are subjective by nature, you tend to see things only as they relate to you; and there is propensity in you towards indiscretions and impulsiveness which you are constantly battling.

Still in all, your charm and grace see you through most of life's situations. You possess a remarkably strong will. Occasionally, however, you may be troubled by anxiety due to your habit of undertaking too many things at once. Meditation and reflection are not your cup of tea but would be helpful in order to prevent the anxieties that grow from your impulsiveness and high level of activity.

HOW YOU ACT AND REACT IN THE WORLD

You want to take on anything and all. Your loquaciousness gets you involved in a lot of lengthy conversations about what is going on in your life. But it certainly isn't all talk. You do as much as you say you are going to do. Very early on, you probably made your career choice—and it is an important decision for you. But because you are decisive, it was rather simple—except that it isn't just one career. You are inclined to choose at least two pursuits. You could be at the same time a competent nurse or doctor and have an established career on the stage or in films. Or perhaps as an effective and engaging teacher in the daytime, and as a member of the symphony at night. Because of your sense of intrigue, you would also make a good, if big-hearted, spy.

YOUR DEEP INTUITIVE PERSONALITY

You have an uncanny intuition, which gives you your great perspicacity. This is the source of your many subjective truths, and it lends you the ability to judge people accurately. It is also the source of much that is attractive about you, the well of your seduction.

YOUR INTELLIGENCE

You have an holistic intellect. Unlike the analytic mind, you see a problem at once, and never mind about the details that go into it. You are especially good at remembering situations that have emotional significance. It is as if you carry paintings around in your mind and understand the importance and placement of each in the gallery of your life.

YOUR EMOTIONAL NATURE

You need to love. In fact, it seems as if you are happier loving than being loved. There is a strong element of possessiveness about you, but it is rarely negative or jealous. Rather, your sense of possessiveness is nurturing. You are at your best when your beloved is totally seduced by your intriguing charm. Your sexual encounters are another expression of this sort of possessiveness. Most likely, you are often the first one to make a move in even the most casual of encounters. On the other hand, you are not at all a casual lover; you are intense and active in all your emotional relationships.

YOUR HEALTH AND VITALITY

With your surprisingly robust vitality and good resistance to serious illness, it is a bit perplexing that you can be afflicted with minor illnesses—colds, headaches, and upset stomach. Your weak spots are your intestines and circulatory system. It is important that you get enough outdoor exercise. Perhaps a regular athletic regime would keep you at your healthy best.

THE SOCIAL YOU

What would you do without people? You have an active social life, and if people don't come to you, you go out and get them. You are a charming talker, a great storyteller, and people are seduced by the marvelous tales you weave. At times, you can be downright aggressive socially. When you get it in mind to have a party, everyone can be sure of a fabulous time. It's as if you will it to happen. There's bound to be a touch of intrigue in everything you do, but that is part of your charm and natural attractiveness, and it contributes greatly to your good fortune and success.

———

NamePortrait
14
Associated Names

Alba	Berthilde	Debbie	Melisande
Albane	Bertie	Debby	Melisenda
Amanda	Bertilda	Debora	Melisende
Amandine	Bertilde	Deborah	Mellicent
Amaris	Bertille	Debra	Mellie
Amaryllis	Bertina	Decima	Melloney
Armela	Bertrande	Delfine	Mellony
Ashwina	Berty	Delia	Melly
Ashwine	Bren	Delphine	Meloney
Atalaya	Brenda	Elfie	Milia
Atalia	Brenna	Elva	Milicent
Atalya	Cailin	Elvia	Milisent
Athalea	Ceara	Elvie	Milissent
Athalia	Clothilda	Elvina	Milli
Athalie	Clothilde	Fayme	Millicent
Athie	Clotilda	Kimberley	Millie
Attie	Clotilde	Kimberly	Milly
Aura	Coleen	Malan	Norna
Aurea	Colene	Malinda	Nyssa
Aurel	Coline	Manda	Opal
Aurelia	Colleen	Mandie	Opalina
Aurelie	Colline	Mandy	Opaline
Aurie	Colly	Mel	Ora
Aurora	Colomba	Melan	Orabel
Bastienne	Colombe	Melane	Orabella
Berdine	Colombina	Melania	Orabelle
Bert	Columba	Melanie	Oralia
Berta	Columbia	Melany	Oralie
Bertha	Columbine	Melicent	Oriana
Berthe	Dagmar	Melinda	Orianna
Berthilda	Deb	Melisanda	Orianne

Associated Names (cont.)

Oriel	Paloma	Pilar
Orpah	Palometa	Rudella
Palma	Palomita	Rudelle

Name Portrait 15

Quiet Sensualist

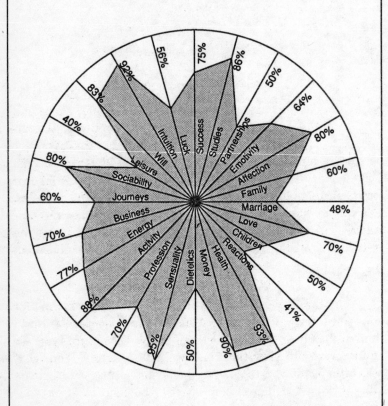

Element : Earth   **Plant** : Leek

Mineral : Sodium   **Sign** : Capricorn

Animal : Antelope   **Color** : Yellow

Personality Type:

Quiet Sensualist

(Associated names – page 122)

BASIC CHARACTER

Although you are active and very emotional, there is a great timidity about you. Like your totem animal, the antelope, you are ready to take flight in an instant. You are sensitive—sometimes painfully so—and usually tense. On the other hand, like your plant totem, the leek, which is known for its medicinal qualities to soothe and relax the muscles, you can be calm and tender under the right quiet circumstances. You like to keep both feet on the ground, despite your highly strung nature, and your rich, deep imagination.

YOUR PSYCHOLOGY

Your timidity can cause you some serious problems, for you tend to run away from a situation, and only later stop to think about it or evaluate it in any way. By nature, you are an introvert and view the world very subjectively. Your shyness often leads you to escapist behavior, and that often eats away at your fragile self-confidence. You tend to allow your emotions to dominate your life. Self-discipline does not come easily to you, but by developing it, you can overcome most of your "flight" reactions to unusual or threatening situations.

HOW YOU ACT AND REACT IN THE WORLD

Once you decide that sticking around is better than running away, you become stimulated by a variety of intellectual and manual activities. Usually, your actions are very effective. You get things done, but are keenly sensitive to failure. There are, essentially, two completely different types of careers open to you. One encompasses law, journalism, or teaching; and the other, farming, business, and the trades. You take great pride in your work when your emotions free you enough to apply yourself fully to the job. You are also very sensitive to any forces of opposition around you; competition on the job is simply not your thing. You are at your best when you can work quietly and bring your marvelous imagination into play with no criticism from others.

YOUR DEEP INTUITIVE PERSONALITY

It's in your lively intuition that your charm is born. With both a fertile imagination and a deep sense of foresight, you are irresistibly attractive in the most basic sense.

YOUR INTELLIGENCE

You have a rapid, analytic, and meticulous intellect. Your curiosity is finely tuned and your memory is prodigious. However, your emotions often get in the way of your concentration and must be held in check (if that's possible) when you are working on problems and decisions that call your analytic powers into play.

YOUR EMOTIONAL NATURE

Here is where most of your energies go. Your affections are intense and passionate, though often your sexuality is stronger than your feelings. In fact, you tend to repress your true feelings about someone—though not always your sexual attraction—until you are sure of her loyalty and commitment. You have a tendency to flee from emotionally ambiguous situations, but once you are assured of someone's loyalty, and can make your own moral and emotional commitment, you are a tender and sensitive lover. Of course, you are a sensualist par excellence, and this means not only that you are a refined and marvelous lover, but that you enjoy all the good things of life, intensely and completely.

YOUR HEALTH AND VITALITY

Usually, you enjoy excellent health, but you must avoid mental exhaustion. Though you are resistant to fatigue, you must have plenty of sleep, relaxation, and a balanced diet. Be sure to avoid using stimulants of any kind. You are susceptible to viral diseases; your weak point is your nervous system.

THE SOCIAL YOU

Your best social time is with a few solid friends whom you trust. But even in a large crowd, you are very sociable. You don't like your social life to be dominating, however, for it is important to you to be able to get away from it all, and spend considerable time with your own reflections. When you are around other people, you have a calming effect on them, as long as you have your own timidity under control. You enjoy good fortune, and much of your success comes from good luck. Good luck for you means being able to enjoy the sensual pleasures, and for you they are many.

NamePortrait
15
Associated Names

Armand	DeArmand	Hareford	Marty
Armin	DeArmond	Harford	Mathurin
Armond	Dixon	Henleigh	Noll
Armyn	Ferd	Henley	Nollie
Ben	Ferdie	Hereford	Nolly
Bendix	Ferdinand	Herford	Oliver
Benedic	Ferdy	Hernando	Olivier
Benedick	Fernand	Hilliard	Ollie
Benedict	Fernando	Hillier	Osborn
Benedix	Forest	Hillyer	Osborne
Bengt	Forester	Ingraham	Osbourn
Benito	Forrest	Ingram	Osbourne
Bennet	Forrester	Kean	Osburn
Bennett	Forrie	Keane	Osburne
Benny	Forster	Lovel	Osmar
Benoit	Foss	Lovell	Rudyard
Benot	Foster	Lowell	Stedman
Blaise	Guin	Mart	Teague
Blase	Gwyn	Marten	Tully
Blayze	Gwynn	Martie	Weldon
Blaze	Handley	Martin	Welton
Camille	Hanley	Marton	

Name Portrait 16

Stately Beauty

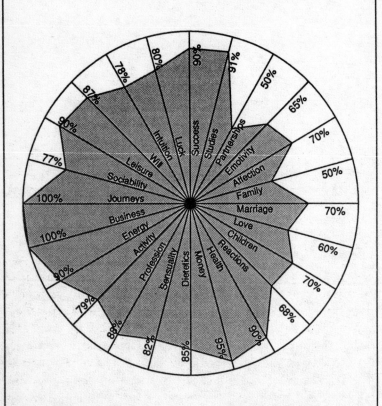

Element : Fire   **Plant** : Strawberry
Mineral : Zircon   **Sign** : Leo
Animal : Swan   **Color** : Red

Personality Type:

Stately Beauty

(Associated names – page 128)

BASIC CHARACTER

You are very emotional, rather assertive, and your life is most likely filled with its share of turbulence. You have rapid reactions, and cannot remain calm. But there is another side to you as well, which is best typified by your animal totem, the swan—a loftiness, which is supported by your unflappable faith in your own intelligence. You are incisive and curious, and you need a calm, disciplined, and orderly life.

YOUR PSYCHOLOGY

Because you are more introverted than extroverted, and have a tendency to be subjective, you often judge other people harshly, or else tend to be too domineering in your relations with others. Deep down, you are nervous, high-strung, and a bit tormented about what others think of you. But rather than ever admit this, or ever display your worry or inner strife, you tend to become disdainful or haughty, and to withdraw with an air of disgust. You can be quite wrathful, however, and have a habit of letting loose with some caustic barbs if you feel insulted. The demands you make on yourself are often very much like the demands you make on other people.

HOW YOU ACT AND REACT IN THE WORLD

You react more strongly than you act; often, once you've begun something, you lose interest and don't follow through.

Still, you are never daunted by an undertaking, and rely on your intelligence to see you through. You are at your best if your activities are useful and somewhat indispensable to others. Very likely, you pursue two different careers at once, or else have a hobby that is as important to you as your career. You would make an excellent journalist, a good businesswoman, or an effective public relations executive or politician. Very possibly, your life will be filled with travel. You have an innate sense of intrigue, which helps you to adapt easily to numerous situations and environments.

YOUR DEEP INTUITIVE PERSONALITY

Your intuition is based on your reflections, which, like your totem plant, the strawberry, stays close to the soil and grows prodigiously. Though you do not often heed it, you do have a fine intuitive sense, and might possibly be attracted to astrology and clairvoyance.

YOUR INTELLIGENCE

First, it is important to point out that your intellect is very important in your life; you simply assume that you are intelligent, and everything else follows naturally. You are essentially analytic, able to solve problems by focusing on the details and fine points. You memory is excellent; and you have a fine curiosity.

YOUR EMOTIONAL NATURE

Although your emotions are very strong, and indeed influence much of your activity and reactions, you are not very easy to get close to. You tend not to trust someone right away, and much time and persuasion will have to go under the bridge before you are confident in your lovers. Still, you tend to be emotionally impulsive at times, and to get involved in short-term, stormy affairs. You are possessive in your relationships, above all else. Though you wouldn't come out and say "my man," that's what you believe. You can be jealous or vindictive if your feelings have been toyed with or hurt. You tend to idealize your lover—the man of your life—and keep terribly high standards which every man must meet, and if he doesn't, he'll meet your arched disdain. You often conceal your strong sexuality under a facade of indifference until you are sure there are no hidden thorns to prick your pride. Once you are confident in your lover, you are able to let go and share an enriching emotional and sexual life.

YOUR HEALTH AND VITALITY

Your vitality is good, but your health is uncertain. It is influenced by your psychological states. You have a very fragile nervous system, and need a well-balanced routine. You become over-tired easily, and need lots of sleep. You also can benefit from regular diversions and entertainment. Be careful of stimulants and depressants, as you have a tendency to use them to excess.

THE SOCIAL YOU

You find traditional entertainment more enjoyable than impromptu parties and gatherings. You are at your best among a circle of trusted friends. You can be very sensitive to other people, and the next moment, want to be the center of attention. Still, there is a grace and loftiness about you which draws others to you. You do not care for timid people, as you yourself are rather aggressive in your social relations, assured by your own beauty and intelligence. You can pass unhesitatingly from the office to the boudoir, and much of your social life probably revolves around your career.

NamePortrait
16
Associated Names

Agave	Catriona	Gina	Kora
Althea	Caty	Kasmira	Luvena
Althee	Concepcion	Kate	Napaea
Altheta	Conceptia	Katel	Napea
Althita	Conception	Katerine	Napia
Audie	Concha	Kateryn	Raina
Audrey	Conchita	Kath	Raine
Audrie	Corona	Katharina	Rayna
Audry	Coronie	Katharine	Regan
Beril	Dee	Katherina	Regina
Berri	Docila	Katherine	Regine
Berrie	Doreen	Katheryn	Reina
Berry	Dorene	Kathie	Reine
Beryl	Dori	Kathleen	Rejane
Beryle	Dorie	Kathlene	Rina
Bev	Dorinda	Kathryn	Rioghnach
Beverley	Dorine	Kathy	Sergine
Beverlie	Dory	Katia	Simona
Beverly	Ekaterina	Katie	Simone
Caitlin	Fausta	Katrin	Simonetta
Caitrin	Faustina	Katrina	Simonette
Casmira	Faustine	Katrine	Teddie
Catalina	Feadora	Katryn	Teodora
Caterina	Feadore	Katty	Teodore
Catharina	Fedora	Katy	Thea
Catharine	Fedore	Kay	Theadora
Catherine	Feodora	Kaye	Theadosia
Cathie	Feodore	Ketti	Theda
Cathleen	Fulvia	Ketty	Theo
Cathy	Gena	Kit	Theodora
Catia	Gervaise	Kitty	Theodore

128

Associated Names (cont.)

| Theodosia | Wandie | Wenda | Wendy |
| Wanda | Wandis | Wendeline | |

Name Portrait 17

Agile Gatherer

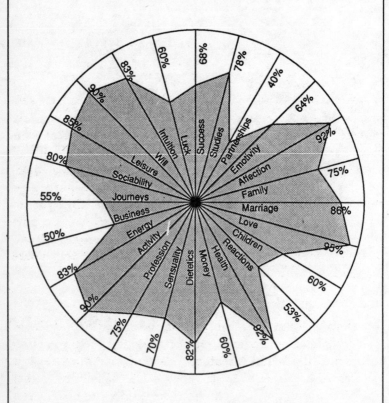

Element : Fire

Mineral : Amethyst

Animal : Squirrel

Plant : Carrot

Sign : Sagittarius

Color : Blue

Personality Type:

Agile Gatherer

(Associated names – page 134)

BASIC CHARACTER

With your emotional nature as strong as it is, it's surprising that you can be as patient and objective as you are. Instead of giving way to whims, you are likely to direct your enormous activity toward productive ends. You do like a sense of security, so, like your totem animal, the busy squirrel, you go about with a firm if not always obvious purpose— to gather whatever you need to be comfortable. Still you do have a taste for adventure, but any adventures you do pursue are well thought out ahead of time. You are patient and unselfish, willing to forego your impulses in order to prepare for the future.

YOUR PSYCHOLOGY

Despite your dynamism, you can be quite timid at times. You're an introvert at heart, and often withdraw to your own secure nest if you feel threatened. One of your worst fears is the fear of betrayal. Another is your fear of failure. Either one of these may also incite your formidable temper, draw you out of your introversion, and lead you into quite impetuous actions. Your will power is strong, especially when you are involved in a project. You can draw deep from your will to bring things about—like your plant totem, the carrot, symbol of your urge to accumulate and use underground reserves which are surprisingly solid and strong compared to the plant's delicate leaves.

HOW YOU ACT AND REACT IN THE WORLD

You have a highly developed sense of antagonism and like demanding professions that have a bit of danger to them. You're not at all happy unless you're involved in some project which you've planned out thoroughly. Because of your natural unselfishness, you are always ready to lend a friend a hand when need be, and can work well with others—as long as there is some dynamic tension among the team. You begin to think about career choices early, and once you start working, you're a conscientious achiever. The risky jobs are your forte. It wouldn't be surprising if you were an airplane pilot or sky diver, a stuntwoman, or a scuba diver. It's as if you can discover your true worth only through action, and the better if the job is at least a bit perilous.

YOUR DEEP INTUITIVE PERSONALITY

Among the most powerful of your natural assets is your astonishing intuition. You are able to anticipate events, and frequently you might have startling visions. This deep, inner side of you gives you considerable help in your life.

YOUR INTELLIGENCE

You have a very active mind with a keen critical sense and a prodigious memory. Your intellect is essentially analytic; your ability to focus on details, combined with your strong intuition, gives you a fearsome perspicacity of the world and events around you.

YOUR EMOTIONAL NATURE

Far be it from you to lead a tempestuous love life, at least openly. But your affections are deep, even if you do keep them veiled under a quiet reserve. Most likely, you have one permanent, faithful lover to whom you are strongly attached. You do not readily express your sexuality, partly out of fear of being cheated, and partly out of natural timidity. Until you are secure with one lover, you hold your sensuality in check and lead a rather secretive emotional life.

YOUR HEALTH AND VITALITY

Although you have a great vitality and resist fatigue very well, you are prone to mental exhaustion. Because you sometimes tend to be impetuous, you expose yourself to accidents. A regular regimen and a certain amount of care should be taken for you to maintain good health. Your weak spot is your liver. Also, you are susceptible to bacterial infections.

THE SOCIAL YOU

If someone were to drop in unexpectedly to dinner, you would probably have a hard time of it getting a sincere welcome across, even if the wine he brought were Chateau Lafitte '37. It would make you feel violated, to have your nest so obtrusively invaded. Although you do like the company of other people, you prefer to keep your social life planned out, and just don't take well to the impromptu gathering. You have a flair for discerning insincerity in other people, so you stay with your trusted friends; and in your own circle, you are a marvelous and charming companion and friend. Because career is so important to you, you probably make friends at the job, and much of your social life undoubtedly revolves around business associates. Though your home life is important to you, you would never become a thorough homebody at the expense of your job.

NamePortrait
17
Associated Names

Apolline	Eliette	Joselen	Salome
Ariel	Eloise	Joselene	Salomi
Ariela	Elyette	Joselin	Salvia
Ariella	Fac	Joseline	Salvina
Arielle	Fae	Joselyn	Shari
Candra	Fay	Joselyne	Sharon
Candre	Fayanne	Josilen	Sharri
Cece	Faye	Josilene	Sharry
Cecelia	Fayette	Josilin	Sheela
Cecil	Helyette	Josiline	Sheelah
Cecile	Hortense	Josilyn	Sheila
Cecilia	Hortensia	Josilyne	Shelia
Cecily	Huberta	Joslin	Sheliah
Cele	Huberte	Josline	Sheri
Celia	Hubertha	Josseline	Sherry
Chandra	Huberthe	Joy	Sheryl
Chandre	Jess	Joyce	Shir
Cicely	Jessica	Joycelin	Shirl
Cici	Jessie	Joycelyn	Shirlee
Cicily	Jessy	Joyous	Shirleen
Cicy	Jocelin	Lila	Shirlene
Cid	Joceline	Love	Shirley
Cieci	Jocelyn	Lyn	Shirlie
Ciecy	Jocelyne	Lynne	Sileas
Ciel	Joice	Maelle	Sis
Cissie	Joicelin	Nolwenn	Sisile
Cyci	Joicelyn	Ofelia	Sisle
Dalila	Jolie	Ofilia	Sisley
Delila	Joscelin	Ophelia	Sissie
Delilah	Josceline	Orna	Sissy
Doria	Joscelyn	Phelia	
Eliane	Joscelyne	Saloma	

134

Name Portrait 18

Tenacious Champion

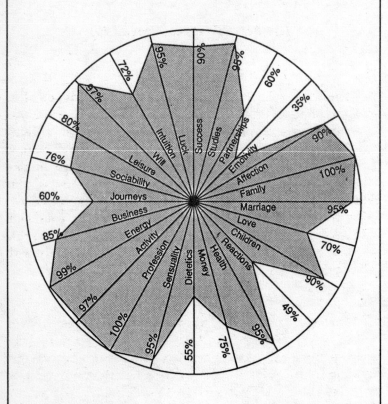

Element : Fire   **Plant** : Weeping willow

Mineral : Iron   **Sign** : Sagittarius

Animal : Elephant   **Color** : Red

Personality Type:

Tenacious Champion

(Associated names – page 140)

BASIC CHARACTER

You are so solid and have such self-control, that you often give the impression that you're immobile. But in truth, you can outdistance anyone; once you're set in motion, nothing can stop you while you move onward toward your well-defined goals. It's not surprising, then, that your special animal totem is the elephant. There is an even balance among your activity, your energy, and your will. It makes you a leader— effective and efficient in all you do. You act on your high and solid principles, usually toward practical ends. You're a bit of a loner, however, and do not communicate easily with other people, except through your actions.

YOUR PSYCHOLOGY

You're a "holder," and where you hold things is "in their place." Your emotions are kept so firmly in place by your overwhelming will, that at times it might seem that you are downright icy. But in fact, you are just terribly occupied with your own goals; sometimes too occupied. You are essentially an introvert and view things subjectively. You are not easily moved by the plights of other people, and tend to look down on others' weaknesses, sometimes holding them in scorn. But you need some sort of opposition in order to be at your best, and this is the cause of much of your apparently unsympathetic nature. There is another side of you which you rarely show, and that is a deep, implacable melancholy, an

137

almost existential sadness, symbolized by your plant totem, the sturdy yet weeping willow.

HOW YOU ACT AND REACT IN THE WORLD

Most of all, you cannot do without a goal. Everything you do is directed toward an end, and all your activity is intense and leaves its mark on those around you. It would not be surprising if you had a drawerful of diplomas and degrees, which you collected on your way to become a leader in your profession. You may be attracted by business or industry, or else by the military, the legal profession, or even religion. As long as your career promises that you can teach your fellow man that life is a struggle, and success comes about by combat, you are happy. You are ecstatic if your job takes you to a position of authority and leadership.

YOUR DEEP INTUITIVE PERSONALITY

"Either it works or it doesn't": that is your motto in life, and it applies to the manner in which you heed your inner perceptions. They are there; your intuitive voice is strong, but you can get along well without it if it's not forwarding your aims.

YOUR INTELLIGENCE

Although you're not a great talker and not interested in the least in impressing people with your intelligence, you do have a powerful intellect. Your mind is both holistic and analytic, a rare and formidable combination, because you can see things as a whole, grasping the complete picture at once, and you can sort out and analyze the minutest detail. Your brilliant intellect, however, is often under the control of your strong will, and in order for you to use your astonishing intellectual insights to best advantage, you have to learn to loosen up a bit and abandon yourself to your mind.

YOUR EMOTIONAL NATURE

You are no Casanova, but there is a touch of Don Juan about you. Though you do have deep emotions, you rarely express them—your will, again, holding things in check. But you do have a strong sexual appetite, which you are more likely to express than your feelings. You enjoy the sensual pleasures—good food, good drink, good sex—but are not dominated by them. Heaven forbid such weakness! And you double up on the control when it comes to your feelings. Your reserve and introversion when it comes to love makes it difficult to get close to you. But once someone is able to negotiate a way into your heart, you are a devoted and pleasing lover.

YOUR HEALTH AND VITALITY

Ordinarily, your health is good, but because you are so driven, you tend to tax your health. Your weak spots lie in your bones and liver. You should avoid alcohol and try to maintain a steady regimen of nutrition and exercise.

THE SOCIAL YOU

You are not the sort of person who maintains a rigorous social schedule. In fact, you would do just as well without being encumbered with a lot of purposeless activity and idle get-togethers. When you do take time to relax, you like to be around strong people and are at your social best if there's a bit of tension in the air. Small social gatherings with your colleagues, for instance, would be your most frequent social outing. Your luck is good, and appears to be better than it actually is; as in any realm of life, you succeed by dint of your steady, hard work.

———————

NamePortrait
18
Associated Names

Adler	Charles	Felton	Kerr
Amos	Charleton	Fenton	Kerry
Ardolf	Charley	Freeman	Key
Ardolph	Charlie	Gallard	Klaus
Armstrong	Charlton	Galor	Knox
Balthasar	Charly	Gaspar	Lander
Balthazar	Chas	Gaspard	Landers
Bishop	Chuck	Gasper	Landor
Borg	Claus	Gayler	Launder
Bromley	Col	Gaylord	Lawton
Cailean	Colan	Haldan	Leicester
Carl	Colby	Haldane	Lester
Carleton	Cole	Halden	Lunt
Carlile	Coleman	Halfdan	Malcolm
Carlin	Colin	Havelock	Mallory
Carling	Colley	Havlock	Malo
Carlisle	Collin	Holden	Marland
Carlo	Colman	Jasper	Marley
Carlos	Corcoran	Jeremiah	Marlow
Carlton	Corguoran	Jeremias	Marlowe
Carlyle	Corquoran	Jeremie	Marly
Carlysle	Delling	Jeremy	Monro
Carol	Dempsey	Jerry	Monroe
Carollan	Demsey	Jethro	Munro
Carr	Dermot	Kane	Munroe
Carrol	Donoghue	Karl	Neacail
Carroll	Dorby	Karol	Neree
Cary	Dow	Karr	Nichol
Caspar	Durward	Kaspar	Nicholas
Casper	Emry	Kasper	Nicholl
Charlemagne	Fairfax	Kermit	Nick

Associated Names (cont.)

Nickie	Read	Snowden	Twain
Nicky	Reade	Stafford	Walworth
Nicodemus	Reading	Stamford	Walwyn
Nicol	Redding	Stanford	Warmond
Nicolas	Redford	Starr	Warmund
Nigel	Redvers	Sterling	Waverley
Nik	Reed	Stiles	Waverly
Nikita	Reede	Stirling	Whitlock
Nikki	Reeve	Styles	Winslow
Nikky	Reid	Tearlach	Winston
Niles	Remington	Tearle	Winter
Pickworth	Rochester	Templeton	Winthrop
Quennel	Rooney	Thatch	Winton
Radford	Rowney	Thatcher	Witton
Radvers	Ruan	Thorp	Yeoman
Ralegh	Rufford	Thorpe	Zupeika
Raleigh	Saul	Tracey	Zuriel
Rawleigh	Sereno	Tracy	
Rawley	Sherman	Turpin	

Name Portrait 19

Winsome Watcher

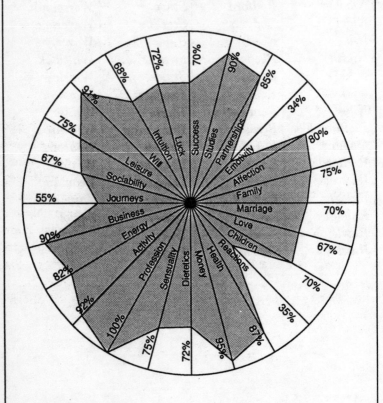

Element : Earth   **Plant** : Gentian

Mineral : Granite   **Sign** : Virgo

Animal : Toad   **Color** : Green

Personality Type:

Winsome Watcher

(Associated names – page 146)

BASIC CHARACTER

Quiet and watchful, you act only after you've given things considerable thought, and then you act with resolution. You are precise and methodical in all you do, and even when you're active, there is a reserve about you. It sometimes might seem to others that you waste a lot of time, or that you are a dreamer, but you're not. Your feet are firmly on the ground, even when you're silently observing things. Your animal totem is the unobtrusive yet alert toad, who fades into the background where he keeps a keen vantage point on his surroundings. With your sense of propriety and your basic unselfishness, you possess an enduring and subdued charm which draws others to you.

YOUR PSYCHOLOGY

Your natural reticence can sometimes lead to painful shyness and timidity; and because you are more inclined to give than to take, you can feel anxiety when it seems as if others are taking advantage of your good will. You have trouble developing your self-confidence and may be inclined to abandon projects before they are finished. Image is important to you, and if your self-image is severely threatened, you'll jump out of the shadows and lose your temper—only to hop right back, out of the way, and resume your silent, peaceful life.

HOW YOU ACT AND REACT IN THE WORLD

You organize your activities carefully and cautiously, and tend to avoid taking risks. So it might seem surprising that you become so involved in your work or your studies. In fact, you take refuge in your activities, and have a tendency to let your work consume you. You are attracted to fields which demand a lot of precision and attention, and could pursue a successful career in the classics, in finance, in diplomacy, or in technology. You would make an outstanding research scientist, engineer, technician, or teacher. You're dedicated to your work, and fit in well with a team. At times, you can abandon a project which you've begun so carefully, out of your timidity or because you lose confidence in it. But in general, you are thorough in your work. At those rare times when you do feel thwarted, you probably do not react very strongly to any opposition, but simply let events take their course, going with the flow.

YOUR DEEP INTUITIVE PERSONALITY

Although your intuitive side is deep, you rarely let it loose. Rather than relying on a momentary inspiration, you will proceed cautiously, reining in your intuitive impulses, or else pondering them at length.

YOUR INTELLIGENCE

You have an analytic mind and are able to search out the details of any problem or situation patiently, until all the pieces fit together logically. Your good memory and healthy curiosity enhance your acute intellect, and though you do not leap into discussions with your insights, when you do speak, it is with careful precision.

YOUR EMOTIONAL NATURE

Boisterous displays of affection irritate you no end. You will not have your sense of propriety violated by a strong come-on, anymore than you would pursue someone openly.

144

You tend to go out of your way to avoid emotional upsets, and consider talk about your emotional and sex life to be utterly tasteless. Your own secretiveness about your feelings, however, veils a soft tenderness and an unselfish willingness to love and be loved. Like your totem plant, the gentian, with its lovely, delicate flowers and its strong root that is used as a tonic, your feelings are as delicate as they are soothing.

YOUR HEALTH AND VITALITY

In order to keep your health, you need to lead a subdued life, interspersing reasonable outdoor exercise with a good diet and plenty of rest and relaxation. Early in life, you are susceptible to troubles of the lymph system, and later, you have to watch out for calcium deficiency and viral infections. You are inclined to overtax your system with hard work and must be careful not to overestimate your physical limitations.

THE SOCIAL YOU

Your respect for the obligations of friendship is strong, and you are an excellent companion—cooperative, tenacious, and faithful. Still, as delightful as your company is, you rarely entertain just for the sake of entertaining. You like social events that are well-organized, and prefer the company of a few select friends to a big bash. You tend to be rather conventional in your amusements, observing the well-established traditions more than the avant-garde. You would make an excellent, just mother and could be the head of a large family.

NamePortrait
19
Associated Names

Benigma	Christilla	Esmeralda	Sonya
Benigna	Christina	Esmeralde	Sophia
Calista	Christine	Felda	Sophie
Calisto	Christy	Kallista	Sophy
Callista	Chryseis	Kallisto	Tama
Celandine	Chrystal	Kristabel	Tamara
Celandon	Chrystod	Kristabella	Tammie
Cesarine	Crisela	Kristabelle	Tammy
Chris	Crissie	Leoma	Tina
Chriselda	Crissy	Nyx	Ulrica
Chrissie	Cristal	Ola	Ulrika
Chrissy	Cristina	Persephone	Vic
Christabel	Crysta	Ronda	Vick
Christabella	Crystal	Rhonda	Vicki
Christabelle	Daphne	Rica	Victoire
Christel	Domita	Sadhbh	Victoria
Christelle	Domitille	Sadhbha	Victorie
Christian	Emerald	Sofia	Victorine
Christiana	Emerant	Sofie	Vitoria
Christiane	Emeraude	Sonia	Vittoria
Christie	Esme	Sonja	

Name Portrait 20

Torch-Bearer

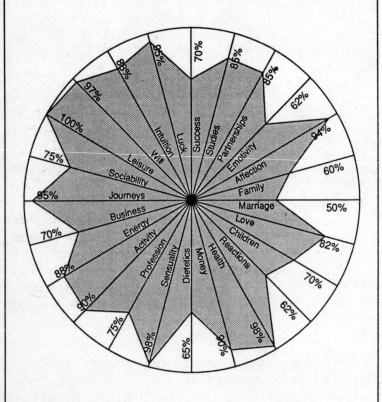

Element : Fire   **Plant** : Chestnut
Mineral : Amber   **Sign** : Aries
Animal : Elk   **Color**: Blue

Personality Type:

Torch-Bearer

(Associated names – page 152)

BASIC CHARACTER

You want to know the "whys" of life, and your prodigious, sometimes impulsive activity is always leading you on to find them. But you're a traveler; you need to see the world in order to understand it. And you are a man with a mission; you are drawn to lead in causes and to win. This is where you get the meaning in your life which is so important to you. Because you are very emotional by nature, you view your mission personally: "I am the one upon whom this mission depends and I will win." Your totem animal, the stately yet impulsive elk, is a fine symbol of the way your emotional nature is expressed—against a certain coolness which often restrains you from becoming explosive and hence, ineffectual.

YOUR PSYCHOLOGY

Although you are primarily an extrovert and receptive to others, you can become introverted when you need to withdraw and reflect. This dualism can cause some anxiety at times. You need an audience and you need understanding and love, but your inner-directed emotions sometimes put people off. Your plant totem, the chestnut, appears similarly inaccessible, sheathed in a thorny outer shell which guards its rich inner fruit. You can be very impatient with others, and you do not accept failure graciously, but tend to mull it over. Still, you have a well-developed self-confidence and a will that drives you to excel in your many pursuits, even if your perfectionism does sometimes get in the way.

HOW YOU ACT AND REACT IN THE WORLD

You are most often charming and act with an air of authority. Your work has to give meaning to your life, and through your intelligently conducted enterprises, with your combination of good luck and hard work, you are very likely to find both meaning and success. You are a dedicated, dutiful worker, stable and enlightened. You use your lust for life to make changes in the world, but in your own sphere, you do not adjust to change all that easily. For this reason, you have to take care that the profession you choose is the one you will stay with, as changing courses in mid-life might be upsetting to you. You are attracted to a career in medicine and would make an eminent doctor, surgeon, or gynecologist. You could also choose to become a teacher, an explorer, or a researcher.

YOUR DEEP INTUITIVE PERSONALITY

Your intuition is remarkable, providing you with clear insights and authority. It is here where your charm resides and, often, the more complex facets of your personality.

YOUR INTELLIGENCE

With your reliable and refined intellect, you crave learning and understanding. Your mind is holistic—which means that you do not analyze every detail, but tend to perceive problems and events in their total outline. Undoubtedly, you were intellectually precocious as a child. Your curiosity is intense and often incisive, and your memory excellent. You are at your best when you are facing things squarely, without idle frills.

YOUR EMOTIONAL NATURE

Passionate, somewhat paternalistic, and most certainly precocious, you love and hate with equal force. Though you will wait a while before you express your feelings, once you do, it's no denying them. Very often, you act possessively, and you are inclined to fits of explosive jealousy. Sexually, you are an excellent and pleasing lover—but you must be "numero uno" in any affair, and you'll put up a powerful fight to stay that way. A softer side of the same tendency is your paternalism, your inclination to protect and reassure your lover. Naturally, you want to excel emotionally and sexually, as you want to do in everything else.

YOUR HEALTH AND VITALITY

Fortunately for someone as involved in the world as you are, you have a wonderful vitality, excellent health, and you can resist fatigue rather easily. Still, you do benefit from outdoor exercise such as long walks. Enough sleep and a regular diet will also help you to combat mental stress to which you are prone. You must avoid heavy smoking and too much alcohol; your weak point is your liver.

THE SOCIAL YOU

You would not like to find yourself in the position of choosing between work and pleasure, for although you enjoy the good things of life and are always looking for excitement, your work comes first, automatically. You have too many other things to do besides taking part in idle entertainment. But you are good and stimulating company, with an easy and natural charm. You have a strong sense of friendship, and you choose your friends carefully. In all, you believe in causes and in people—not so that you can have a good time hanging out, but because you have a mission in life which is very personal: to make everything excellent.

NamePortrait
20
Associated Names

Altman	Derby	Kris	Slaven
Annan	Dryden	Kriss	Slavin
Ansley	Duane	Maitland	Sleven
Apollos	Dwayne	Mead	Slevin
Aries	Edwald	Medwin	Sol
Axton	Fortunat	Merrill	Solamon
Bailey	Fortune	Merritt	Sollie
Baillie	Garnet	Miner	Solly
Baily	Garnett	Minor	Soloman
Barton	Gilchrist	Moore	Solomon
Bayley	Gilecriosd	More	Solon
Blyth	Gillecirosd	Myron	Storr
Blythe	Glanvil	Nestor	Tilford
Brand	Glanville	Norton	Toft
Brandon	Goddard	Orson	Trent
Buko	Guenole	Pelham	Urson
Byron	Gwenola	Quent	Vailintin
Carney	Harv	Quentin	Valente
Carny	Harve	Quintin	Valentin
Cassidy	Harvey	Quinton	Valentine
Chris	Herv	Renan	Valentino
Christie	Herve	Ring	Valiant
Christophe	Hervey	Ronan	Weddell
Christopher	Javier	Salomon	Wolfe
Christos	Kester	Serle	Xavier
Darby	Kit	Shizuo	Xerxes

Name Portrait 21

Scintillating Star

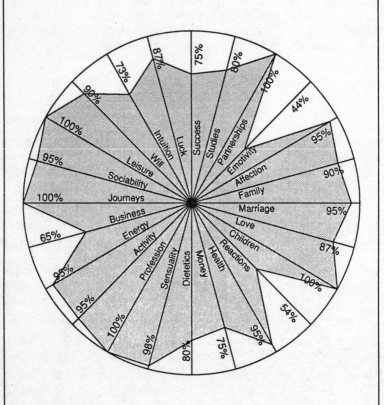

Element : Air   **Plant** : Cedar tree

Mineral : Clay   **Sign** : Libra

Animal : Swallow   **Color** : Green

Personality Type:

Scintillating Star

(Associated names – page 158)

BASIC CHARACTER

From the time you were a young child, you were in motion. You have a bounding spirit and must give life its full expression in endless activity. Like the migratory swallow, your animal totem, you love to travel and are always looking for an excuse to fly off to some new and exciting place. Yet, in spite of the astonishing pace you impose on yourself, you can emerge with admirable coolness and calm. What distinguishes you is your resourcefulness; you are able to come up with solutions to any problem in a moment's time.

YOUR PSYCHOLOGY

You are always in the sun, never in the shadow. You like to affirm yourself by overcoming problems and obstacles, and can throw yourself into the fray on a whim. Along with this tendency is your inclination to take on too many things at once. When you're not busy, you can become anxious, frustrated, even explosively angry. You have a very strong will, and are confident of the absolute truth in everything you do or say. In fact, you tend to deal in absolutes, especially when you're engaged in a bout of self-analysis, which you are prone to do rather often. At times, you can become a bit self-interested and inclined to look down at people who are not as energetically involved in the world as you are.

HOW YOU ACT AND REACT IN THE WORLD

Despite your occasional burst of snobbery, you are responsive to people and have a very strong sense of friendship. You enjoy being surrounded by a band of happy, bright friends. Failure hardly affects you at all, and you rarely restrain yourself from any activity. You are an avid learner, who learns best from experience. You possess an incredible amount of energy and apply it to moving about, traveling through the world, and picking up insights into life and different cultures. At times you may be disorderly—picking up at a moment's notice and disappearing on a new adventure—but you bring joy wherever you go. You tend to be clever with your hands: your gestures are clear and precise. Among possible career choices are media reporter and public relations official. Your attitude toward your work, however, depends a lot on the specific tasks involved. If they're not exciting or engaging enough, you could well pick up and leave, not only to a new job, but to a new country as well.

YOUR DEEP INTUITIVE PERSONALITY

You are just too outer-directed to spend much time heeding your inner voice; you put much more faith in your observations of the world than in your intuition. The mountains of the world, and not the caverns of the mind, are your source of inspiration. Still, your intuitive personality is the source of much of your charm and your capacity to bring joy to those around you.

YOUR INTELLIGENCE

You have a broad-ranging mind and can synthesize information easily. This gives you a capacity for deep wisdom; it is not surprising that your totem plant is the cedar, symbol of depth and wisdom. You think quickly, inspired by people and events of the world.

YOUR EMOTIONAL NATURE

There is something devilishly ravishing about your way with love. Much of your energies are expended in your

156

sensual life. You are always ready to fall in love, and it seems that your open, big-hearted nature could love everyone you meet. But you're actually in search of the love you need—and you need a lot. You're probably asking your lovers every other day not only if they love you, but how much. And if there's a new possible lover on the horizon, you'll find a way to entice him into your circle. If he doesn't come willingly, you'll come up with a way to command his affections, even if it means sowing a little emotional disorder. Once he's responded, you'll delight him with sensual pleasures of the first and highest order.

YOUR HEALTH AND VITALITY

With such a turbulent life, you are fortunate to have as much vitality and resistance as you do. But you are inclined to overindulge yourself in food and drink, and must be wary of becoming overweight. You are especially susceptible to cellulitis. And though you hate going to bed early, you need plenty of sleep.

THE SOCIAL YOU

Planned or spur of the moment, you love a party, and when you throw a bash, it's one that people remember for a long time. You adore surprises and, of course, long vacations to dispel some of the orderliness of life's normal routines. You love your many friends and your family intensely, if a little flightily, and although other people have a hard time keeping up with you, your social life is a success and a constant source of pleasure to you.

NamePortrait
21
Associated Names

Adora	Clarabella	Crispina	Musetta
Adorabella	Clarabelle	Crispine	Musette
Adoree	Claramae	Ellice	Musidora
Adorna	Claramay	Ellis	Nissie
Anju	Clare	Flavia	Nissy
Ara	Clarence	Flavie	Nixie
Augusta	Claresta	Flavienne	Olimpie
Auguste	Clareta	Gaea	Olympe
Augustina	Clarette	Gaia	Olympia
Augustine	Claribel	Gillette	Olympie
Austine	Clarice	Gussie	Platona
Chlarimonda	Clarimond	Gusta	Rindi
Chlarimonde	Clarimonda	Hilaire	Rindy
Chlarinda	Clarimonde	Hilaria	Sophronia
Chlaris	Clarinda	Hilary	Tim
Chlorinda	Clarine	Jobina	Timmie
Chloris	Clariss	Jobyna	Timmy
Clair	Clarissa	Justina	Timothea
Claire	Clarisse	Justine	Tina
Clairette	Clarista	Klara	Tuesday
Clar	Clarrie	Metis	Varina
Clara	Clorinda	Metys	

Name Portrait 22

Nimble Leaper

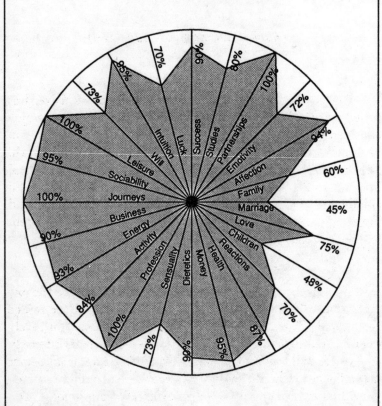

Element : Air

Mineral : Flint

Animal : Gazelle

Plant : Spindle tree

Sign : Gemini

Color : Orange

Personality Type:

Nimble Leaper

(Associated names – page 164)

BASIC CHARACTER

You have strong emotions and an artistic, sensitive, but proud nature. There is a duality in your character, which can resolve itself either in a constant nervous anxiety or in an inner awareness which can become a source of strength. On the one hand, you are attracted to a domestic, practical life, as typified by your plant totem, the fruitful and useful spindle tree. On the other hand, you are enterprising, and have a fierce need for independence, like the free-spirited, leaping gazelle, your animal totem.

YOUR PSYCHOLOGY

Most likely, the independent side of your nature is the one you show to the world; and your retreating need for refuge remains a private part of your personality which you rarely exhibit. Though you need your privacy—sometimes intensely so—you are also a bit of an actor. You like to ham it up before an audience. Nervous anxiety as a result of a conflict between your dual nature can lead you to overreact emotionally. You don't have a lot of willpower and it's difficult for you to keep your impulses down. You can be short-tempered, and your ill humor, if provoked, can show itself with your ironic or snidely insolent statements. Failure affects you awfully; then you tend to withdraw and hang around the house, licking your wounds until the gazelle in you takes to the field again—which it inevitably does.

HOW YOU ACT AND REACT IN THE WORLD

You have to learn to develop structure and discipline, for you just don't have it naturally. Circumstances determine what you do in the world, more than any reflective thought. But you adjust with great ease to different situations, and can shift from great enthusiasm over something to complete indifference. You enjoy meeting people and learning from them, more than you do plumbing books for understanding. Anything having to do with fantasy or luxury attracts you. Your creative imagination might lead you to a career in fashion design, entertainment, or music. You could be a talented singer or dancer as well. Still, career preparations present a problem for you, since you often wait for the vicissitudes of fate to make up your mind for you. But once you have chosen what it is you'll do, you can be resourceful beyond your own wildest imagination.

YOUR DEEP INTUITIVE PERSONALITY

Even though it might be embarrassing to you, you have a powerful intuition. You're able to "psych out" situations and people easily with your imposing intuitive gifts. It's your inner self which helps you adjust so easily to the often rapidly changing circumstances of your life.

YOUR INTELLIGENCE

Your intellect is quick, flexible, and analytic. Your mind is very active; your memory, excellent. You can focus in on the fine points of a problem and put them all together with astonishing speed. And you probably are doing that rather often, as your curiosity is insatiable.

YOUR EMOTIONAL NATURE

Here, again, that duality comes into play. The nest or freedom? If everything is not going so well in your life, you'll opt for the security of a steady love life. But when all is well, you're out on a new sexual adventure. But wherever you are, you resent being told about your lovers' past loves, because you tend to assume you're being compared to someone else. You need to be understood, and you'll take the opportunity to explain yourself.

YOUR HEALTH AND VITALITY

Although your health is only average, you have a lot of vitality. You need balance in your life, or your health can suffer. This means a combination of exercise and relaxation, and a nutritious diet. You tend to overindulge in sweets. Your weaknesses lie in your heart, lungs, and nerves.

THE SOCIAL YOU

You are captivating, socially, with your theatrical ways. You mix well with people, and give everyone a good time. There's a bit of inconsistency in your social life, which comes from your needs both to be out there in front of everyone and your occasional need to withdraw into a private space. You do well at large gatherings when you're feeling well, and prefer a quiet time with a few close associates at those other, introverted moments. You have hundreds of friends, it seems, but not all of them are welcome into your personal retreats— only those who understand you and have exhibited patience with your changeability. In all, your fortune is good, and you are charming, interesting company.

———————

NamePortrait
22
Associated Names

Ascot	Delwin	Kinnard	Ridpath
Ascott	Delwyn	Laban	Rodman
Asher	Driscol	Lang	Rodmond
Atwater	Driscoll	Leith	Rodmund
Banning	Farnley	Leverton	Rodwell
Barthram	Fernley	Locke	Roper
Bartram	Garland	Lundy	Rugby
Beavais	Garton	Magee	Ryman
Bert	Garvey	Mandel	Salton
Bertin	Garvie	Mendel	Sedgeley
Bertram	Gib	Muguet	Sedgequick
Bertramd	Gibb	Murdoch	Sedgley
Bertrand	Gibson	Murdock	Sedgwick
Bevis	Gil	Murtagh	Shattuck
Blagden	Gilbert	Park	Stanberry
Claud	Gilibeirt	Parke	Stanbury
Claude	Gill	Parker	Sutton
Claudian	Gilleabart	Pascal	Trigg
Claudius	Gillie	Penley	Unwin
Clovis	Gower	Penn	Urbain
Cluny	Griswold	Penrod	Urban
Conlan	Hamar	Phelan	Vern
Conlin	Hammar	Phelps	Verner
Conlon	Hutton	Ranger	Verney
Crandall	Innocent	Redpath	Vernon
Crandell	Judah	Reece	Walmond
Cranley	Judd	Rhys	Walmund
Danby	Kinnaird	Rice	Yates

Name Portrait 23

Woman of Secret Fire

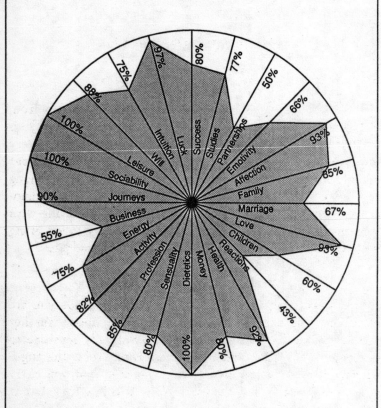

Element : Air   **Plant** : Thyme

Mineral : Titanium   **Sign** : Libra

Animal : Giraffe   **Color** : Red

Personality Type:

Woman of Secret Fire

(Associated names – page 170)

BASIC CHARACTER

You are an intensely emotional and sentimental person, but your easy-going good naturedness acts to balance your feelings and lends you a charming, sparky side. Love is very important in your life, and in its name, you're always out looking for new experiences and adventures. You are among the lucky few who never seem to lose their essential innocence. Cynicism is unknown to you; you approach life with a pleasant ingenuousness which makes you easy to get along with and open to all manner of situations and people.

YOUR PSYCHOLOGY

As easy-going as you are on the outside, inside you are often fiery and explosive, plagued by doubts about whether you are acting in the right way. You are keenly sensitive to criticism of any kind, and though you rarely show the anger which criticism evokes in you, the chance is that you carry it around, silently and secretly. Your will is strong but it fluctuates; you do not always pursue your aims to the end, especially if a love problem gets in your way.

HOW YOU ACT AND REACT IN THE WORLD

Like your totem animal, the giraffe, you tend toward a certain detachment, standing above things and watching with a tender indulgence as events unfold beneath you. This is not to say that you are aloof or distant, for you are by nature an extrovert; but in your own activities, you preserve a distance and changeability. You are likely to change careers more than once, and have a lot of concern over your career. You tend to specialize, and the more specialized your job is, the more likely you are to succeed professionally. You are drawn to the luxury trades: cosmetics, hair dressing, and fashion.

YOUR DEEP INTUITIVE PERSONALITY

Your quiet intuition is discreetly attractive. Like your plant totem, thyme, it lends you an elusive and fragile quality—perfume carried on the wind, refreshing and pure.

YOUR INTELLIGENCE

When you approach a problem, you focus on the details, bringing your keenly analytic intellect to bear. Abstractions and large philosophical ideas are not your forte; rather, you tend to be practical and to use your intelligence toward visible ends. Your memory is excellent and reliable.

YOUR EMOTIONAL NATURE

Love is where you find your self-worth and meaning. You are affectionate in the extreme, and need to have your affections returned. Without love and tenderness, you begin to feel abandoned to cruel fate, and as a consequence, you're always in search of emotional adventure. Because you are so sensual, your sex life is enviably active. But at times, you confuse sexuality with love and physical affections with heartfelt devotion.

YOUR HEALTH AND VITALITY

Your health is good, but you have a tendency to wear it down with exhausting activities. When you're run down, you are prone to slight fevers. Your weak area is your respiratory system, especially the lungs; smoking should be on your taboo list.

THE SOCIAL YOU

When you are in a sociable mood, you can go all night, from dinner to party to dance floor. You are charming company, and expend a lot of your energies making friends and entertaining people. The unusual and exciting new setting is like a stimulant to you, bringing out your effervescence and wit. At times, you overdo it, and find yourself having to recover from an exhausting weekend of partying. In all, your fortune is excellent, and success comes to you suddenly, often on the tails of a great love affair.

———————

NamePortrait

23

Associated Names

Aleyde	*Daria*	*Gleda*	*Paulie*
Arabela	*Demeter*	*Gwladys*	*Paulina*
Arabella	*Demetria*	*Gwyladys*	*Pauline*
Arabelle	*Dickie*	*Hermia*	*Paulita*
Araminta	*Dicky*	*Hermina*	*Ricarda*
Arbel	*Emina*	*Hermine*	*Richarda*
Arbelia	*Erma*	*Herminia*	*Richarde*
Arbelie	*Erme*	*Herminie*	*Ricky*
Armina	*Ermina*	*Hermione*	*Serena*
Armine	*Ermine*	*Hildegarde*	*Toussainte*
Arminia	*Erminia*	*Irma*	*Vi*
Bel	*Erminie*	*Irme*	*Viola*
Bella	*Fenella*	*Irmina*	*Violaine*
Belle	*Finella*	*Irmine*	*Violante*
Claude	*Flanna*	*Paola*	*Violet*
Claudette	*Glad*	*Paula*	*Violetta*
Claudia	*Gladdie*	*Paule*	*Violette*
Claudie	*Gladine*	*Pauletta*	*Volanda*
Claudina	*Gladis*	*Paulette*	*Yolanthe*
Claudine	*Gladys*	*Pauli*	

Name Portrait 24

Zealous Knight

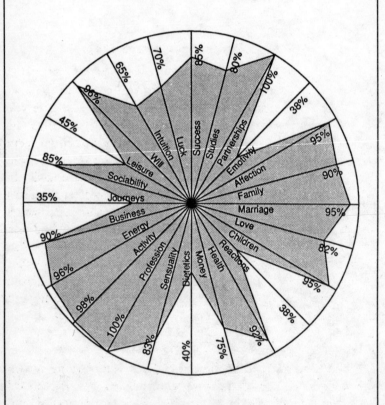

Element : Water   **Plant** : Eucalyptus
Mineral : Aquamarine   **Sign** : Scorpio
Animal : Heron   **Color** : Red

Personality Type:

Zealous Knight

(Associated names – page 176)

BASIC CHARACTER

Your acute sense of justice and missionary zeal give you the soul of a knight errant, ready to bare your sword to the indignations which mankind must suffer. Yet, you often seem more like a warrior of the impossible, driven by ideals so high, that eons will have to pass before they can be realized. In the meantime, you'll make yourself heard with enthusiasm and conviction. You have a well-defined moral code which guides you, whether you are acting or speaking out, and you are an adventurous sort who views each move as a step in a greater mission. You're a thinking man who makes other people think in new ways. Your animal totem, the heron, symbolizes your character well; it is the bird of morning and the generation of new life.

YOUR PSYCHOLOGY

If it seems at times that yours is a voice crying out in the wilderness, that's due to your natural propensity toward both introversion and extroversion. You go on whims, and then retreat into depression. Your tendencies toward fanatic zeal can leave you both belligerent and excitable. You can be both aggressive and timid. One moment, you're ready to fly to the rescue of Dulciana—and the next, you're withdrawing into the hermitage to contemplate her awful fate. There is no doubt that you're a man of extremes. But the extremes can find an exquisitely sensitive balance, as long as you do not feel as if you are in competition. In other words, you require those moments of contemplation in order to come to an inner accord. Your will is strong and effective, emerging suddenly to meet a task or a call; and though you are quick to anger, you are able to control your temperament with your sense of justice and by sheer will power.

HOW YOU ACT AND REACT IN THE WORLD

You are always involved in something—if not work, then a crusade against injustice. You would make an excellent union activist, lawyer, legislator, or public relations consultant. Any profession or activity which allows you to express your keen sense of social morality is attractive to you. Much of your activity, as well as the reasons you react to situations, is based on a deep-seated romanticism. You tend to avoid competitive situations—unless, of course, you are competing with a sinister force—and in the name of putting an end to rivalries, you can become a political agitator of the first order.

YOUR DEEP INTUITIVE PERSONALITY

Though you are highly imaginative, you do not tend to put much faith in your intuition. And, often, when you are obeying the urgent commands of your heart, you believe it is reason that is compelling you. In short, though you do not admit very often to the dictates of your intuition, it is strong and influential in your life.

YOUR INTELLIGENCE

Very early on, your intellect matured and took the form in which it operates today. Though you rely upon reason, you have a very synthetic—holistic—intelligence, which allows you to glide over details and discern the main lines of force in any problem or situation. Your judgment is excellent; you have a reliable, solid memory, and an active curiosity.

YOUR EMOTIONAL NATURE

You need to be loved and can become extremely sentimental, especially where ideals are concerned. Your emotional life is quite tied to your ideals, and you tend to imagine the perfect, perfectly just lover. You can be moved to tears by people or events and you tend to want to help your beloved out of real or imagined travails. Because you always seem to be on some quest, your sex life can become unusually complicated and complex; you tend to be more the giver than the getter in any sensual encounter.

YOUR HEALTH AND VITALITY

The eucalyptus is a sturdy plant with some astounding medicinal powers, and it is no surprise that it is your totem plant, for you enjoy a remarkable health and have marvelous recuperatory powers. You do need a lot of sleep to sustain you, and athletic activity to calm you. Your weaknesses lie in your lungs, heart, and kidneys.

THE SOCIAL YOU

Though your social life is rather far-flung, your social sensibilities tend to be delicate. Much of it revolves around your social and political convictions, and it is likely that you will join various fraternal groups. You can be most entertaining and generous in social encounters, and tend always to want to do some good for other people. You avoid manipulators and superficial people and favor those who share your peculiar sensitivities and fervor.

NamePortrait
24
Associated Names

Arcadius	Donald	Linden	Riley
Arcady	Donn	Lindon	Rylan
Balfour	Donnall	Linton	Ryland
Bradford	Donnell	Lisle	Ryle
Canwall	Donnie	Lyall	Ryley
Carson	Donny	Lyel	Sennett
Carvey	Drury	Lyle	Speed
Carvy	Edelmar	Lyndon	Squire
Cathmor	Fitz	Marden	Stroud
Clem	Haig	Marsden	Thorburn
Clemence	Hawley	Marsdon	Thornburn
Clemens	Hogan	Mason	Torburn
Clement	Horton	Morse	Toussaint
Clemmy	Joliet	Orval	Townley
Clim	Jule	Osmond	Townly
Con	Jules	Osmund	Trumble
Conal	Julian	Palmer	Uriah
Conan	Julie	Peregrine	Urias
Conant	Julien	Perry	Uriel
Conn	Julius	Primael	Vianney
Connaire	Junius	Quinn	Wentworth
Connall	Kynan	Rafferty	Westcott
Connel	Kyne	Ransom	Wilton
Connor	Liall	Redwald	Zared
Don	Lind	Redwall	
Donal	Lindberg	Reilly	

Name Portrait 25

Exciting Coquette

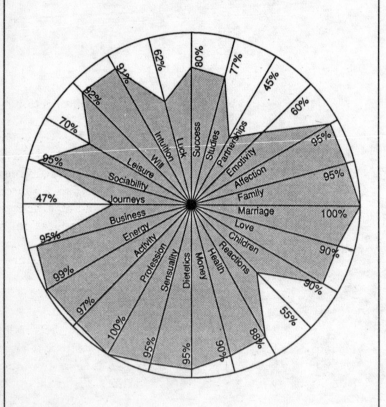

Element : Air
Mineral : Manganese
Animal : Mouse

Plant : Flax
Sign : Libra
Color : Blue

Personality Type:

Exciting Coquette

(Associated names – page 182)

BASIC CHARACTER

Both your emotions and your will spur you to action, and once you are in action, you cannot hold still. You are imaginative and charming, and you enjoy comfort and beauty, even though your passionate and impulsive nature often disrupts the subtle charm which you've created for your environment. In general, you have sound judgment, based on a powerful intellect; and in spite of your often unpredictable behavior, you tend to achieve your goals by a quiet application, not unlike the mouse, your totem animal. Your totem plant is the flax—a delicately lovely plant which nonetheless has its utilitarian function.

YOUR PSYCHOLOGY

If anyone misjudges you as mousy or plain, he's in for a big surprise, for you can be singularly incisive in your acerbic wit and your often repressed anger can turn into a vindictive attack. All your life, you have trouble controlling your emotions and tend to be highly critical of others. Your impassioned temper does not always show itself immediately, but waits in the shadow with its grudge, ready to wreak revenge at the most opportune moment. Still, such reactions have their positive side: you are always ready to fight on, no matter how keen your disappointments. And you are capable of overturning your normal lifestyle and embarking on a new adventure if life's frustrations become too great.

HOW YOU ACT AND REACT IN THE WORLD

You have to be engaged in challenging, exciting projects. You live at an intensely active level, and your good moral foundation lends you the faithfulness and devotion to projects which you need to see you through. You can be totally committed to your work, and there is no task too big for you. You are exceedingly generous and can handle yourself well in problem situations. Among your dreamed-about projects are restoration work, building, and antique collecting. If you do not pursue one of those areas as a career, it's likely that you'll take up one or the other as a hobby. The trades involving fashion or interior design, to which your good tastes might be applied, are possible career choices. You would also make a fine public relations consultant, a popular society writer, or a flight attendant. You tend to adjust well to change, and are very successful in persuading other people to your outlook.

YOUR DEEP INTUITIVE PERSONALITY

Your intuitive powers are astounding, enabling you to size up people at a glance. This is the source of much of your attractiveness and self-confidence in the world.

YOUR INTELLIGENCE

Your intellect is supple, ironic, and analytic, and it allows you to observe the smallest detail of any situation. Most likely, the situations which are most attractive to you are those in which you are involved, and your memory for those is astonishingly acute. Despite your tendency toward intellectual egoism, however, your wit is sometimes outward going, and when it is, you are capable of outstanding intellectual achievements.

YOUR EMOTIONAL NATURE

You need friends and companionship, and tend to be somewhat possessive in your emotional attachments. Your charm can become self-serving, and your strong, demanding sensuality, a means of possessive seduction. But in all, you are affectionate without being effusive, and there is something deliciously nymph-like in your sexuality, which your many lovers find impossible to resist.

YOUR HEALTH AND VITALITY

Even though you tend to overlook your health, your vitality is good and up to the demands which you place on yourself. You cannot function well without enough sleep, and need a balanced diet. You are prone to frequent headaches and must stay away from alcohol, as your weak area is in your kidneys. Your lungs are also somewhat sensitive, and you are sensitive to chills.

THE SOCIAL YOU

At heart, you are a social being, delighted to be able to entertain, as long as you can do it in your own way. Tradition means nothing to you when it comes to trying to dazzle people with a new wardrobe or lifestyle. Still, you are able to put everyone at his ease, and to bring people together and to resolve all the conflicts among them. You are a model wife, and when your domestic situation is calm, you are able to exude that calmness to your guests. You enjoy enviably good fortune, and your success is more likely to come from your attractiveness than from any prolonged effort.

———————

NamePortrait
25
Associated Names

Coletta	Geraldine	Lethia	Pammie
Colette	Gerhardine	Lethita	Pammy
Colinette	Gerry	Leticia	Reseda
Collete	Giralda	Letitia	Tiffanie
Collette	Godgifu	Letizia	Tiffy
Cosetta	Godiva	Lettia	Tiphaine
Cosette	Ina	Lettice	Tish
Cosima	Jeraldine	Lettie	Tita
Cosina	Jeroldine	Letty	Triphena
Fiona	Jerri	Lida	Triphenia
Fionn	Jerry	Liddy	Tryphaena
Gabbie	Joachima	Lidia	Tryphena
Gabriel	Joakima	Lidie	Tryphenia
Gabriela	Laetitia	Lydia	Typhena
Gabriele	Landa	Lydiane	Viridiana
Gabriella	Lara	Lydie	Viridis
Gabrielle	Larissa	Pam	Wallace
Gaby	Leithia	Pamela	Wallie
Geralda	Leta	Pamelina	Wallis
Geraldina	Letha	Pamella	Wally

Name Portrait 26

Tranquil Prophet

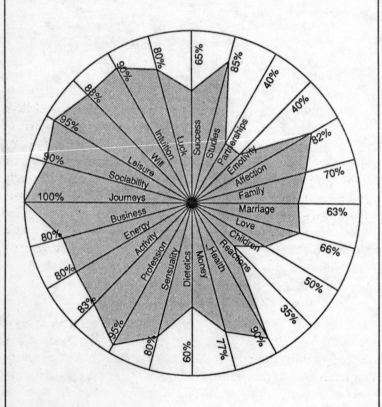

Element : Water   **Plant** : Holly

Mineral : Arsenic   **Sign** : Pisces

Animal : Whale   **Color** : Yellow

Personality Type:

Tranquil Prophet

(Associated names – page 188)

BASIC CHARACTER

No matter how turbulent your life becomes, you always have a ready smile and a cool calmness about you which is at once inspiring and relaxing. You are highly imaginative and generous to a fault. Your patience is enduring, and you are faithful and affectionate to your loved ones. Although you may run into a lot of minor problems in life, you remain untroubled on the surface, much like your totem animal, the whale, symbol of concealment and containment. You don't like to bother other people with your woes; it goes against your remarkably high morality and sensitive aesthetics.

YOUR PSYCHOLOGY

In general, you are well-balanced; your will and energy are equal to each other, and your emotions and reactions are similarly subdued. You are an introvert, and your introversion tends to a slight timidity. You tend to take refuge in your own inner world. You are highly sensitive to the opinions of others and can be selfishly jealous about friendships and affections. Yet, you refuse to get riled about anything and take your reactions deep within yourself, to ponder and mull over them there, rather than showing your anger or frustration. You have a sound will but it is subject to fluctuations; at times, it seems to evaporate, and at others, it is there, forcing you into action.

HOW YOU ACT AND REACT IN THE WORLD

You are efficient but never hasty. You are inclined to pursue more than one goal at a time, and this diversification tends to give you reassurance and self-confidence. Because you possess a highly creative imagination and can adjust easily to change, you are drawn to the arts. You enjoy work that gives you the freedom to read and write. Still, there is something essentially pragmatic about you; that, and your inclination to do two things at once might lead you to becoming a medical doctor and a painter, a writer and a lawyer. You are also attracted to professions involving the natural sciences and the theater. You are extremely sensitive to failure and can be influenced by powerful personalities.

YOUR DEEP INTUITIVE PERSONALITY

Your intuition is not only a powerful force in your life, but you seem always to be listening to it for guidance. You're extremely uncomfortable if events force you to go against your instincts, which are the source of your own good judgment and so much of your ineffable charm.

YOUR INTELLIGENCE

Your intellect is analytic and profound. You can pursue an intellectual problem to the end, keeping track of minute details with patience and the awareness of where each might fit in the final picture. Because you have such a sharp imagination, you're often able to jump ahead of logic and make assumptions and presumptions with astonishing speed and accuracy.

YOUR EMOTIONAL NATURE

Although you are very affectionate when the time is right, you tend to be discreet about your emotions. There are times when you simply cannot see where love fits into your life, and have trouble expressing your emotions. You're a bit embarrassed by flowery shows of love, to the point of being repelled by such forwardness. By the same measure, a lot of talk about your sexuality can either anger you or send you plunging to the depths of your own private world. You are a coolly attractive person, like your plant totem, the holly, with hidden prickles if someone should try to force herself on you too abruptly. Often, the sensual license of the modern world is repugnant to your sensibilities, especially where faithfulness is concerned. You are inclined to be monogamous, attentive to the needs of your spouse and family, even if you do sometimes give the impression that you are aloof from them.

YOUR HEALTH AND VITALITY

You need a balanced diet and outdoor athletics, especially swimming or perhaps volleyball at the beach. Your vitality is good, but you tend to lead a disorderly life and so abuse it. Most likely, you recover rather slowly from illnesses which are due, nine times out of ten, to the chaos of your diet and lifestyle in general. Keep a watch over your mouth and teeth.

THE SOCIAL YOU

With such exquisite sensitivity to people, it is natural that you have a refined social life. You need to go out and be seen, to let your tranquility flow into other people. And when you do, you go in style, usually impeccably dressed and with a touch of ceremony. Your own parties, at which you play the engaging host, are both entertaining and refined. You enjoy tradition more than the avant-garde; your parties reflect this with a discreet elegance and propriety which must be observed. In general, your many talents bring you success and admiration, and your acute sensitivities, the insight into people and events, without which you cannot live happily.

NamePortrait

26

Associated Names

Adair	Bret	Ernest	Lambert
Adar	Brett	Ernie	Loring
Aethelard	Busby	Ernst	Marsh
Aethelhard	Cartland	Erny	Marshall
Alard	Cawley	Esra	Orestes
Allard	Culley	Ethan	Prior
Anwell	Cully	Ethelard	Pryor
Anwyl	Dacey	Ez	Quigley
Anwyll	Dacy	Ezra	Ransford
Arden	Dan	Hall	Rearden
Ardin	Dana	Hallam	Reardon
Ashlin	Dane	Halley	Riordan
Aswin	Daniel	Holt	Selby
Aswine	Daniell	Hulbard	Stanfield
Athelhard	Danielle	Hulbert	Starling
Aylward	Danny	Hulburd	Swinton
Belden	Darnell	Hulburt	Thayer
Beldon	Darrel	Hunt	Tomkin
Benton	Darrell	Hunter	Tomlin
Beres	Darryl	Hurlbert	Travers
Beresford	Daryl	Jabez	Travis
Birley	Deepak	Kemble	Tredway
Birney	Dunmore	Kim	Warburton
Boas	Dunn	Kimball	Winwald
Boase	Dunton	Kimbell	Winward
Boaz	Egbert	Kimble	

Name Portrait 27
Courier of Springtime

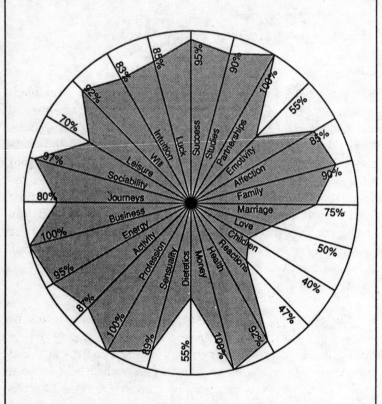

Element : Air
Mineral : Limestone
Animal : Robin

Plant : Violet
Sign : Aquarius
Color : Violet

Personality Type:

Courier of Springtime

(Associated names – page 195)

BASIC CHARACTER

You have a double nature, best described by your plant totem, the subdued and discreet violet, and your own animal totem, the robin redbreast, so noticeable in the springtime. Though you would be perfectly happy to remain in the background, people cannot help but take notice of you, with your quiet, soothing charm. You have a sincere need to be noticed, though your violet side often compels you to disappear from time to time. Still, because you have a strong will, you are bound for success in the world; you are able to persevere (quietly) at any task and, when the results of your work bring attention your way, you are able to receive it graciously.

YOUR PSYCHOLOGY

Possessing, as you do, a dual nature, you may often be plagued with self-doubts: "Am I really good enough?" or "What am I doing here, anyway? Where's the door?" But take heart, for you cannot fail to find satisfaction in your work and among a close circle of trusted friends. There is an innocence about you which draws others to you; and a subtlety in your actions—a natural grace—that tells others they can trust you with a secret. Often, you find that you rely upon your will to get you through a situation. Even at those times when you feel the urge to withdraw and fold in on yourself, you know you can trust your will to see you through. You may not like parties and such, but are able to summon up your charm and bright, springtime personality to overcome your shyness.

HOW YOU ACT AND REACT IN THE WORLD

The last thing in the world you'll ever do is to scream and yell and make a fuss over anything. There seems to be a halo of tranquility about you, and this helps you enormously in establishing business and social contacts. You enjoy work that has to do with communications: radio, television, public relations—but you are at your best when you are doing the behind-the-scenes jobs. People might believe you have no ambition, but we know that this is not true. Rather, you are a quiet achiever. You take advantage of a good situation, and continue to rise on the success ladder. In fact, you might have invented women's liberation when it comes to the job. You also possess a love of children, which could make you a successful pediatrician or teacher.

YOUR DEEP INTUITIVE PERSONALITY

Your natural innocence and grace keep you very much in touch with your intuition. You have the ability to act quickly on your "inner voice," and often follow it more closely than you do any advice you get from others.

YOUR INTELLIGENCE

Very quickly, you can see the whole of things. Yours is what is called a synthetic intelligence, and it is dependent on both your astonishing reason and your deep intuition. You are an efficient thinker, one who wastes little time figuring things out. It is very easy for you to express things verbally, but on occasion, especially when you are hit by an inspiration, you might talk before you think things through. Your occasional talkative bent probably developed early in life. It's quite natural for you, and hardly ever do you use your gifts of verbal expression to stun people with your brilliance—as your intelligence is without guile—but just out of habit.

YOUR EMOTIONAL NATURE

You are honest, if somewhat sentimental, about your emotional ties; you expect and are able to ask for fidelity from your lover or husband. Though you tend to be traditional where relationships are concerned, you do not confuse sexuality with motherhood; in fact, though you do love little children, you probably won't ever be mother of the year. This is, in part, because of a certain possessiveness you have which can lead to difficulty in granting your child independence. And it is in part due to those self-doubts which can crop up from time to time, making you wonder whether you are doing the right thing by your family.

In attachments which do not cleave to tradition, you may feel unwanted or unloved, or else feel indecision. Still, you are a sensitive and sensual woman who can give and receive great satisfaction, as long as you keep your self doubts under control and do not withdraw into yourself if a problem arises in your relationships.

YOUR HEALTH AND VITALITY

You have a good constitution, though you tend to use too many stimulants at times, either to keep going at a job, or to lose weight. Yes, there is a natural tendency to gain weight. Your metabolism is a bit fragile, so be careful of those "quickie" diets. If you have any health problems at all, they will show themselves in your circulatory system, or in the knees. Winter sports are not your natural cup of tea; you're better off sitting by the fire on a cold winter night than out there on the ski slopes.

THE SOCIAL YOU

There's no doubt about it—people enjoy your company. You are always ready to serve, and make an excellent hostess. Your grace and charm draw people to you, and you always seem to have an interesting story to tell. You're a good listener as well. This combination delights your guests and friends and makes your home a place where everyone is happy to come to. Unlike so many other people who are successful in their careers, you have an uncanny ability to suppress any jealousy that anyone might feel toward you. Perhaps that is because you would rather vanish into thin air than upstage somebody. Then, too, your love of tradition and ability to put others at their ease makes a joyous impression on people. Others hold you in high regard—and this is, in your own discreet way, very important to your social well-being. The only thing you do find distasteful is loud, abrasive behavior, and you tend to avoid it at all costs. One way to avoid it, as you've no doubt discovered, is to keep your social life very close to home and under your control. The wide public eye is not one of your favorite things, and if you find yourself in the limelight too often, your violet side may well shrink from the stage.

NamePortrait
27
Associated Names

Aelfreda	Danella	Elga	Neva
Alfie	Danelle	Elva	Nevada
Alfreda	Dania	Eustacia	Pansy
Allie	Danica	Eustacie	Sadira
Alva	Daniela	Freda	Secunda
Alvina	Danielea	Guyonne	Stacey
Alvine	Danielle	Hebernia	Stacia
Atalanta	Danitza	Hiberna	Stacy
Atalante	Delta	Kayla	Thalassa
Atlanta	Elfreda	Kelosia	Valda
Casta	Elfreida	Kineta	Vina
Caste	Elfrida	Merdyce	Walda
Celosia	Elfried	Mertice	Welda
Cynara	Elfrieda	Mertyce	

Name Portrait 28

Bringer of Unity and Joy

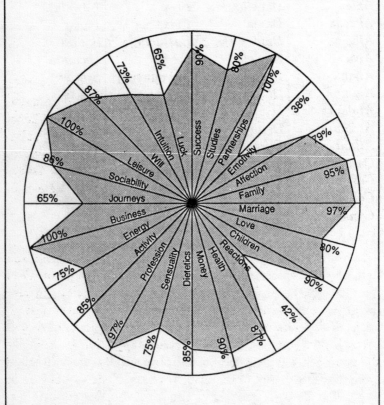

Element : Earth   **Plant** : Manila hemp
Mineral : Slate   **Sign** : Virgo
Animal : Locust   **Color** : Yellow

Personality Type:

Bringer of Unity and Joy

(Associated names – page 201)

BASIC CHARACTER

Patience and organization are the keynotes of your nature. You will never do anything prematurely and are almost unable to act with imprecision. There is an underlying calmness and self-confidence about you, and like the cricket of the hearth, your totem animal, your soothing song is always heard, often long before you make your presence known in other ways.

YOUR PSYCHOLOGY

Your natural patience can be both your best friend and one of your worst enemies. It gives you the time you need to sort out the problems that confront you, but it can also result in your waiting until the last minute to make a decision. You tend to withdraw from the world, and to view it from inside your secure hearth very subjectively. You like to approach people head-on and are usually very direct in your comments and observations, which tends to get you in trouble since your remarks at times lean to the wittily caustic. It is important that you do not allow your natural bent to "lay back" to interfere with your activities in the world, lest you become frustrated in belated attempts to make your mark in the world and find yourself seeking refuge in a tendency toward introversion. You have an even, powerful will which, when applied along with your natural discretion, can overcome your oft-felt need to withdraw into yourself.

HOW YOU ACT AND REACT IN THE WORLD

Like the locust, you don't like to show yourself, and when you do, you act in measured and controlled ways. More than most, you look before you leap—and very often you simply look. But once you are out there and doing, you persevere with admirable discipline and structure. Like your totem plant, the Manila hemp, you excel in rigorous service. You make an enviable administrator; a profession in management and business is perfect for you. There is a dedication, a nearly divine sense of loyalty to your profession which makes you a valued employee and employer. Because of your acute attention to detail, you are well-suited for a vocation in the sciences as well—in many of the professions, in short, which until recently were open only to men. Usually, you will act pragmatically, assessing a situation before approaching it, which makes you a fine decision-maker both on the job and at home.

YOUR DEEP INTUITIVE PERSONALITY

Though you have a strong intuition, you scarcely ever rely upon it. Your "inner voice" is often slow to announce itself to you—hence, your profound patience. However, with reflection and meditation, you are able to heed and use this hidden side of yourself to your best benefit, as it does enhance your relations with the outside world.

YOUR INTELLIGENCE

You are at your best when you are able to analyze a situation or a problem. To understand the whole of anything, you simply must understand the parts—details first. On occasion, especially when you reflect too long on the myriad details, you might not see the forest for the trees, but ultimately, you figure everything out. You have an astonishing memory for facts and minutiae, and your curiosity keeps you alert and aware.

YOUR EMOTIONAL NATURE

Once you open yourself, you are capable of great affection. But you are not at all the sentimental sort of woman who wears her heart on her sleeve. Emotionally, you tend toward secretiveness. Talking about your love life is distasteful to you, though it is important that you are truly loved. Inside, you are something of a volcano of passion, and the right person can tap that fire within. Essentially, you are honest and principled in your relations with others, and may tend to rely upon convention to express your feelings. Love and sex are very closely allied in your relationships; you are not, by nature, well suited to an open-marriage sort of arrangement or to very much experimentation with sexuality. Yours is, overall, an emotionally cautious nature.

YOUR HEALTH AND VITALITY

You have always had an excellent vitality; because of your caution and care, you take good care of yourself. However, you are prone to slight anxiety attacks and possible stomach problems, especially if you are not minding your eating habits. Simple outdoor activities which will give you the benefit of fresh air and nutrient sunshine are necessary for continued good health; and meditation or yoga will help prevent those anxieties caused on the job.

THE SOCIAL YOU

While you won't be dancing around with a lampshade on your head, you are a lot of fun at the office party. It's your camaraderie with the people you work with that sets you apart socially—your fellow workers turn to you and often rely upon you socially. Outside your professional ties, you have a close circle of friends, and they are people who have been able to draw you out and to bear with your occasional sardonic humor. People admire your steady values, and, whether you like it or not, you draw others to you by virtue of the aura of calm which you cannot help but exude. Though you would often just like to be left alone to sit in a corner and watch the party go by, others are bound to come to you and make you participate. These are moments when your often needle-sharp wit can be set to puncturing the swollen egos around you—a tendency which you are forever trying to control. And control it ultimately you do, with a gentle humor that your friends find entertaining and often enlightening.

NamePortrait
28
Associated Names

Adelfia	Denys	Hyacinthe	Phedra
Adelpha	Dextra	Hyacinthia	Phedre
Adelphe	Dixey	Jacenta	Quinta
Adelphia	Dixie	Jacinda	Quintina
Aidan	Dixil	Jacinth	Rafaela
Aiden	Dixy	Jacintha	Rafaella
Alura	Donalda	Jacinthe	Raphaela
Argenta	Edana	Jacinthia	Raphaelle
Argente	Eida	Jackie	Tallie
Argentia	Eidann	Lark	Tallu
Bena	Fabia	Linnea	Tallula
Bronwen	Fabiana	Ludella	Tallulah
Brucie	Fabianna	Mercredi	Tally
Clymene	Fabienne	Neola	Undine
Cynthis	Giacinta	Neoma	Vashti
Dacia	Hermance	Olinda	Zabrina
Denice	Hyacinth	Peppi	
Denise	Hyacintha	Phaidra	

Name Portrait 29

Squire to Mystery

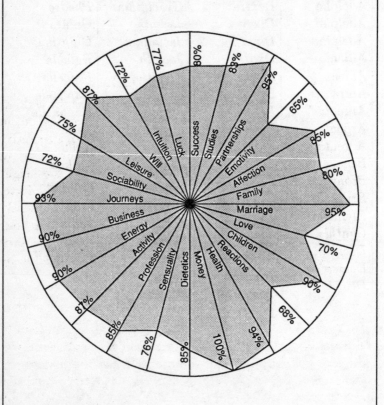

Element : Earth   **Plant** : Vervain

Mineral : Malachite   **Sign** : Virgo

Animal : Night hawk   **Color** : Orange

Personality Type:

Squire to Mystery

(Associated names – page 207)

BASIC CHARACTER

Your totem plant, the fine-leaved vervain, has throughout history held a special place in occult rituals, in religion, in the healing arts. Like its symbolic nature, you are a secretive sort of man, at once imaginative and serious. Your ability to adapt to changing situations is remarkable, as is the height to which your emotions can soar. But mystery is your forte, and it is rare indeed when you let on to anyone precisely what it is you are thinking, inventing, or feeling. Like your totem animal, the nighthawk, you are guided by your own inner signals, and into paths not immediately discernible by the rest of the world.

YOUR PSYCHOLOGY

Your ego is as sensitive as the vervain leaf, so you tend to be withdrawn, something of an introvert. It is only your own doubts—and not those of people around you—that makes you a taciturn man; and it isn't always true that you would like to be known as a man of few words, for when the situation is right and you can be confident that your insights will be understood, you have much to say. Indeed, you go about most of the time sure of your mission in life. There is a conflict between your desire to be willful and dominate any scene and your fear that you might not be up to it after all. Hence, you aren't very quick to act on your own judgment and are not at all open to criticism, good or bad. Yet, you are driven by your keen sense of purpose, and it is this which will see you through, time and again.

HOW YOU ACT AND REACT IN THE WORLD

As a man with a mission in life, you must be involved in work that lends meaning to your world. You spend long hours working or studying, often late into the night. Fortunately, you are naturally well-disciplined, with your own structure which, though it is not always the same as the structure of the status quo, works well for you. A career in medicine or technology, as a doctor or engineer, would suit you fine. It is a simple matter for you to hit upon amazing discoveries with the slimmest details to go on. In friendship as in love, you are an almost formidably serious person—giving yourself to another is not to be taken lightly at all. Hand in hand with this is your often explosive reaction to other people; you appear to be a contrary sort of fellow—at first quiet, mysterious, but if provoked, your protective cloak drops and you speak your mind clearly and forcefully.

YOUR DEEP INTUITIVE PERSONALITY

If someone were to ask you about your intuition, you would probably deny having any. Yet, you are gifted with strong and profoundly forceful intuitive powers, which reveals itself in your imagination and fantasy, as well as in your dreams. You do not rely on your intuition in achieving your goals as much as you could, and it is rare that you will unveil this side of yourself to anyone but your most beloved and trusted companions. Allowing your intuition its play is a constant struggle for you, and one that, paradoxically perhaps, provokes you with your dynamism and energy.

YOUR INTELLIGENCE

Your memory and your curiosity are your two most reliable tools in this realm; your memory is well ordered and reaches far back in your experience. Your curiosity is almost insatiable; it leads you to new challenges and discoveries. You usually comprehend a problem or situation at a glance, and this comes from your strong intuitive powers; but you prefer to approach things rationally. The two modes, of course, can work together; as we said above, it is important for you to synthesize the two, to know when to call upon your intuition and when to apply your rationalistic powers.

YOUR EMOTIONAL NATURE

When you fall in love, it will be forever—and when you fall out of love, that will be forever too. Another paradox in your nature, at least on the surface. You absolutely must have the feeling of trust and trustedness from your friends and loved ones before you will commit your emotions to a relationship. You are easily hurt or slighted, often by a casual remark from someone, often because it seems you are not taken seriously. So you do have a tendency to be quite guarded and often withdrawn emotionally. Yet, the same remark that might send you running off to a missionary hospital in the wilderness can make you explode in indignation and fury. You equate love with possession, and possession with security; yet your passion can be a consuming fire and ignite the hearts of those around you, as well. Actually, it can go either way—outward, to flame a lifelong love relationship, or inward, to fire a romantic mysticism.

YOUR HEALTH AND VITALITY

As long as you do not overwork yourself and remember to eat a balanced diet, you will remain in excellent health. Your natural vitality is extraordinarily good. Your only real weak spot is your stomach, hence your need to watch your diet. It is also important for you to be wary of accidents, for you have a susceptibility to bone injury.

THE SOCIAL YOU

A surprise birthday party is undoubtedly one of your worst nightmares. You simply are not a gadabout. At those parties to which you do drag yourself, you will likely be found off in an easy chair in the corner, watching the goings-on, or back in the library or the record collection, perusing the titles. You prefer the company (after yourself) of close family and a few trusted friends to whom you can speak confidently and without fear of being misunderstood. You are a timid soul in the face of crowds—and yet (paradoxically again) you appear to others to be a strong, silent type, which you are, to your loyal circle.

———————

NamePortrait
29
Associated Names

Alpin	Denison	Ferreol	Peverill
Arnall	Dennie	Firman	Raoul
Ashburn	Dennis	Firmin	Raul
Avenall	Dennison	Hallward	Riddock
Avenel	Denny	Halward	Roarke
Avenell	Deny	Hermes	Rorke
Averel	Denys	Honorat	Rourke
Averell	Denzil	Honore	Ruark
Averil	Dion	Honorin	Santo
Averill	Elvera	Karney	Santon
Avery	Elvira	Kekuni	Shelley
Barric	Elvire	Kemp	Storm
Brawley	Farand	Linford	Titus
Cadman	Farant	Manning	Tynam
Cadogan	Farnam	Pacome	Tynan
Delmar	Farrand	Peveral	Zelig
Delmer	Ferand	Peverall	Zelotes
Den	Ferant	Peverel	Zenas
Denby	Ferrand	Peverell	
Denis	Ferrant	Peveril	

Name Portrait 30

Harbinger of Hope

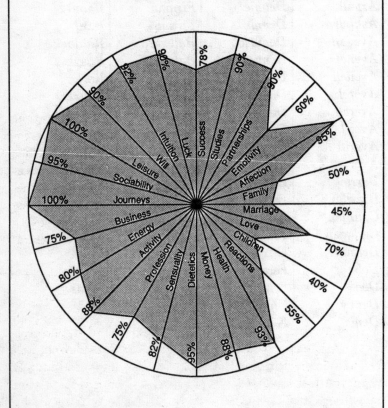

Element : Air
Mineral : Red lead
Animal : Titmouse

Plant : Plane tree
Sign : Aquarius
Color : Green

Personality Type:

Harbinger of Hope

(Associated names – page 213)

BASIC CHARACTER

Among the first trees to bud and leave in the springtime is the plane tree, your plant totem; and since time immemorial, the quick and active titmouse, your animal totem, has been the first bird of springtime, announcing rebirth and resurrection. In your essential transcendence of the mundane, along with your communicativeness, you are a natural messenger. There is an irrepressible spontaneity about you, a dynamism that is impossible to resist. You will be heard; you must be heard.

YOUR PSYCHOLOGY

Though you are gregarious and intense, an extrovert of the highest order, you have a tendency toward hypersensitivity. Frequently, you fall into a downward moodswing and feel unhappy with your lot in life. This happens, usually when you feel thwarted in your need to communicate your perceptions and insights to others. It can also happen as a consequence of falling under the influence of too many other people or ideas. Now, this latter is ironic as it is in your nature to be an influential person, and usually you do know just where you stand. But because you are so open, you risk a sort of enthrallment by transcendental ideas or other powerful personalities. As long as you can enjoy your extroversion, you can avoid these mood swings.

HOW YOU ACT AND REACT IN THE WORLD

You must be active, and you must be active in communal activities for your life to have its greatest meaning. Archeology, aviation, or teaching in an alternative school are among the professions you are suited for. It is important that you have an effect on your environment, and you are most likely to have the best effect through unusual experiences and unorthodox vocations. Though your perceptions of the world and of all that happens are not the same as everyone else's, people can learn much from you, for you are, at heart, an objective man, able to discuss the most bizarre, inflammatory subjects straightforwardly and unflinchingly. Your intensity transforms into a magnetism that makes others want to hear what you have to say. You are not a fanatic about anything, and your ease with communicating your ideas makes even the strangest things you have to say sound obvious and simple. You do tend to surround yourself with people whom you can influence, however, and for this reason your life work should be amenable both to your communicative abilities and to your need to influence. Thwarted, you tend to flee society, regroup your thoughts, and either run off to some new exotic place, or return to the former one, re-armed with new, supporting experiences for your point of view.

YOUR DEEP INTUITIVE PERSONALITY

When you were a child, people very likely called you a dreamer. And a dreamer, in a way, you remain all your life. For dreams are the doorway to intuition, and yours is wide open. You are possessed of a profound and strong "inner voice," which you follow and heed for inspiration and deep understanding. It is here that your perceptions arise, and as long as the door does not close—and you do not tarry always in your dreams—you will be able to apply your deeper insights to your active, daily life with fruitful results.

YOUR INTELLIGENCE

You have an holistic intelligence, in that you see a problem, a task, a situation all at once. Yours is not the analytic

HARBINGER OF HOPE

30

mind that worries over details; indeed, you often skip right over them, which often leads to chagrin later on. There is a lack of mental discipline in your approach to things, for you depend so much on that quick, intuitive grasp of the whole. However, you most likely find that, as you are communicating an idea, you are at the same time thinking it out aloud. You don't hatch ideas or solutions to problems—they just come out. Your memory is very good, and your intellectual energy prodigious, which, under the right circumstances, can overcome your shortfalls on the analytic side.

YOUR EMOTIONAL NATURE

If anyone has ever given more than he receives, it is you; you throw yourself into involvements, which again hearkens back to your natural communicativeness. When you love, you are communicating with your heart, your body, your mind. You love; and you need to be loved, for your heart, body, and mind. But it cannot be an ordinary kind of love; its expression, as the expressions of your many friendships, must transcend this mere earth. Ecstasy, not simple passion, is the height for which you reach. Without emotional commitments of this nature, you can be a most explosive fellow. Your sex life is undoubtedly rather complicated, as it is another arena for the new and unusual experiences which are so important to your overall well-being. It is very probable that your sex and/or love life have led to experiences that can only be described as mystical.

YOUR HEALTH AND VITALITY

Despite a good vitality, you often feel physically ill. Sometimes your ailments have physical causes—not taking care of your basic diet, not keeping to a healthy regimen of proper sleep and exercise. Sometimes you suffer from psychosomatic ailments as a consequence of thwarted emotional or psychological needs. Bone problems, especially in youth, may trouble you; and you are prone to appendicitis and intestinal problems.

THE SOCIAL YOU

Since the days of ancient Greece, your totem plant, the plane tree, has been cultivated in the crowded cities and thrives in the midst of noise, activity, and movement. Like it, you are a sociable man, most at home in an urban setting. You can charm a crowd and mesmerize a close cirle of friends. You draw people to you by the sheer force of your magnetism, and are at your best in communion with other people. You would never think of dining out alone; companions are extremely important to you. When you marry and rear a family, you tend to devote your extraordinary energies to them, as you once did to your many friends. As long as you are the energetic center, you are Mr. Society himself. And as long as you are heard and understood, people will see you as living on a higher plane than the ordinary extrovert.

———————————

NamePortrait
30
Associated Names

Al	Dearborn	Juste	Roy
Aleron	Derwin	Justin	Sawyer
Alison	Dido	Justinien	Shanahan
Allie	Dom	Justis	Si
Almo	Domingo	Justus	Silas
Alston	Dominic	Ladd	Silvan
Arnatt	Dominy	Laddie	Silvanus
Arnett	Eachan	Larson	Silvere
Arnot	Eacheann	Lee	Silvester
Arnott	Forbes	Leroy	Silvestre
Atwell	Garman	Lincoln	Sylvain
Bax	Garmon	Malachi	Sylvan
Baxter	Garmond	Malachie	Sylvere
Beavan	Garmund	Nic	Sylvester
Beaven	Hanford	Nick	Sylvestre
Bevan	Hilaire	Nickie	Tim
Beven	Hilarion	Nicky	Timmie
Birch	Hilary	Rad	Timmy
Birk	Hillary	Radbert	Timothy
Birket	Hillery	Radborne	Tiomoid
Birkett	Hudson	Radbourn	Valeau
Birkey	Isham	Radbourne	
Burch	Jagger	Redbourn	
Calhoun	Just	Redbourne	

Name Portrait 31
Silent Achiever

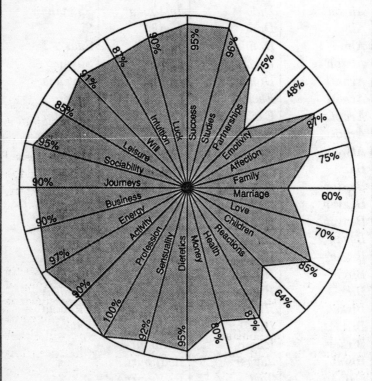

Element : Water   **Plant** : Heather
Mineral : Garnet   **Sign** : Pisces
Animal : Golden carp   **Color**: Yellow

Personality Type:

Silent Achiever

(Associated names – page 219)

BASIC CHARACTER

You are an active, sensitive woman for whom success comes easily. Communication is necessary to you, but it is expressed more by what you do than by what you say. There is a refinement in your sensibilities, which was best expressed by Izaak Walton when he wrote of your totem animal, the golden carp, "The Carp is the Queen of the River; a stately, a good, a very subtle fish."

YOUR PSYCHOLOGY

You are an extrovert with a great deal of self-possession and a natural tendency to dominate a situation or a group of people. Your extroversion does not show itself in gregarious chatter, but in actions. You love a cause and will devote yourself body and soul, but are not at all the sort who will either participate in or put up with sloganeering or idle, pointless discussions. You are easily turned off to people, and, though you are hesitant to show it, are capable of turning people off or away from you. Some deep-seated insecurities cause you to cling to other people too, not unlike your totem plant, the delicate-blossomed, twining heather. So there is something of a conflict in your psyche between turning away from people whom you find contrary to your sensibilities and clinging to people no matter what. But your naturally powerful will can be tapped to overcome this conflict.

HOW YOU ACT AND REACT IN THE WORLD

Though you appear on the outside to be a thoughtful and cautious person, you often act rather cavalierly; once you have decided on a course of action, you follow it, and let the chips fall where they may. In your quests in life, you leave no stone unturned. Frustrated, you explode, but your frustrations are likely to be few, for you are always active, and if something or someone stands in your way you will probably discuss it, win, and go on your upward way. Despite your apparent stubbornness to remain unthwarted in your activity, you are a generous person to those you meet along the way—in fact, you're likely something of a spendthrift when it comes to giving of your possessions. Your main concern is a choice of career, and it must be something that involves risk—better still, if you are the boss or your own boss. You are well-suited for a career in speculative business or real estate, in advertising or in the beauty industry. It also may well be that you have artistic talents, such as painting or sculpting. With your firm opinions and drive, you have fewer problems than most who possess the amount of professional drive which you do, and are known as one who gets things done.

YOUR DEEP INTUITIVE PERSONALITY

You possess a sharp intuition and you use it, honing it more keenly as you go along in life. You probably rely on your dreams and imagination in your daily life far more than most people do, and you know you can rely on them. The vision, the sudden revelation, are no strangers to you, so you never allow yourself to become drowned in fantasy or overwhelmed by your inner world, but rather enlist it to work for you in the outer world.

YOUR INTELLIGENCE

With so strong an intuitive nature, it goes almost without saying that your intelligence is synthetic—that is, you comprehend the total picture at once instead of piecing it together detail by detail. Intellectually, you are a rather awesome character, though you use your intellect in action rather than words. Your energy is awesome, though it sometimes takes a bit of willpower to make it work toward solving a problem, especially if a solution can be produced only by attending to details. You have a keen memory and an alert curiosity.

YOUR EMOTIONAL NATURE

Perhaps it is because your emotions are so strong that you keep them partially concealed. You have a feeling that you should not express yourself much in this realm, and out of fear that others will not understand you, you hold yourself back. Still, you have many close and trusted friends, though your behavior toward them is often a bit like a roller-coaster. When you do express your emotions, you show them with a fiery intensity, a passion that nears the ecstatic. You are discreet, but are bound to have numerous liaisons and sexual experiences, not all of which are orthodox. You can get a kick out of any sensual pleasure—good food, good wine, good art, or a good old-fashioned dance. Deep down, you know you would have been right at home in Caesar's Rome, emotionally anyway.

YOUR HEALTH AND VITALITY

Your vitality is excellent, but you have a tendency to abuse it. Your health is in general, then, adequate. You must be careful of overwork and over-exercise and to balance your diet. You are nature-bound to keep irregular hours and eat at odd times, so special attention should be paid to your nutrition and to the need for enough sleep. You think you have the strength of a horse, but you will find yourself under anxiety by pushing too hard. Your weak physical points are your intestines and your genitals.

THE SOCIAL YOU

Despite occasional swings into bad temper, you have a remarkable understanding of people which, when combined with your astute intuitive powers, makes you an infinitely attractive hostess. People love to come to your parties because you entertain graciously; you know how to put guests at ease and are able to tell what a person's interests are very quickly. Friends and family are important to you, and you rely upon them; and one of the things you rely upon them for is a granting of your independence. You have a sixth sense in making advantageous business and social connections, and you seem to have plain good luck when it comes to business and society. That, with your gracious charm and strong, extroverted will, spells a brilliant and, very likely, successful life.

_____

NamePortrait
31
Associated Names

Adah	Anatola	Carmacita	Donatienne
Ailie	Anatolia	Carmen	Donna
Aisleen	Anatolie	Carmencita	Elisa
Aislinn	Axelle	Carmia	Elissa
Alcina	Baptista	Carmina	Eolande
Aleece	Baptiste	Carmine	Eusebie
Aletha	Baptistine	Carmita	Farica
Alethe	Basilia	Charmain	Federica
Alethea	Batista	Charmaine	Fidela
Alette	Battista	Charmian	Fidele
Alice	Bebhinn	Charmiom	Fidelia
Alicea	Beda	Charmion	Freda
Alicia	Benedetta	Corliss	Freddie
Alie	Benedicta	Corlissa	Freddy
Aliette	Benedicte	Darel	Fredericka
Alisa	Benedikta	Darelle	Frederika
Aliss	Benita	Darleen	Frederique
Alissa	Bennie	Darlene	Freida
Alithia	Benoite	Darline	Frerika
Alla	Bevin	Darrelle	Frerike
Allie	Binnie	Darry	Frida
Allis	Cam	Daryl	Frieda
Allison	Camelia	Dixie	Friederik
Allson	Camella	Domenica	Friedie
Ally	Camellia	Domina	Fritzi
Allys	Camile	Dominga	Gaudeline
Alta	Camilla	Domingue	Germain
Alyce	Camille	Dominica	Germaine
Alys	Carliss	Dominique	Gildas
Alysa	Carlissa	Dona	Golda
Alyssa	Carma	Donata	Goldie

Associated Names (cont.)

Halfreida	Luna	Romelle	Vesta
Halfrida	Luneta	Romola	Viola
Halfrieda	Lunetta	Salima	Violante
Hallie	Marelda	Salina	Violetta
Haracia	Marella	Scarlet	Violette
Horacia	Marta	Scarlett	Yolanda
Horatia	Martina	Scarletta	Yolande
Iola	Martine	Solenne	Yolanthe
Iolanthe	Meara	Soline	Zena
Iole	Millie	Solvig	Zenaida
Ivy	Milly	Sunny	Zenda
Jinx	Obelia	Sydel	Zenia
Lemuela	Olive	Sydelle	Zenina
Lemuella	Olivette	Thora	Zenna
Lissie	Olivia	Thorberta	Zennie
Lisy	Ollie	Thorberte	Zenobia
Livi	Olva	Thorbertha	Zenorbie
Livia	Pallas	Tibelda	Zephyr
Livie	Reva	Tilly	Zephyrine
Livvi	Romella	Tina	

Name Portrait 32

Quietude in the Tempest

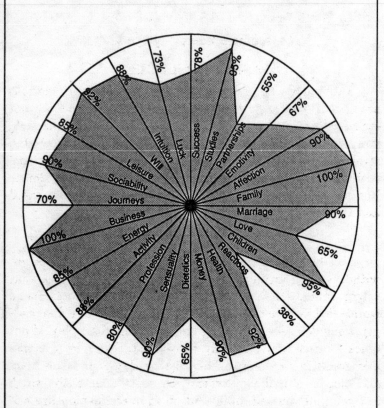

Element : Air   **Plant** : Rush
Mineral : Silver   **Sign** : Aquarius
Animal : Badger   **Color** : Violet

Personality Type:

Quietude in the Tempest

(Associated names – page 227)

BASIC CHARACTER

Though you are a man of sentiments and your emotions are strong, you are an inward sort of person who does not express your feelings readily. Like your plant totem, the rush, you will bend rather than resist when the wind grows too strong. Comfort, quiet, and security are dear to you, and with them, you exude a strong peacefulness and confidence. You possess an exquisite sensitivity to your own quiet world and the capacity to defend it against all intruders.

YOUR PSYCHOLOGY

You have a tendency for a certain stand-offishness, for withdrawing from the world into your private self. Like your totem animal, the badger, yours is mainly a subterranean world—solitary and hidden from view. But like the badger, your defenses are strong and will come into play, if not quickly, when you feel truly threatened. Your introversion may result in an almost callous disregard of your fellow man, and this is a tendency which you must constantly watch lest you find yourself totally cut off from companionship and friendship, which are also important to you. You need understanding, and must put forth an extra effort to participate in groups and express yourself.

HOW YOU ACT AND REACT IN THE WORLD

You enjoy having friends, as long as friendship does not demand a commitment from you or any sort of responsibility for other people. You prefer to work in a profession that demands little in the way of commitment as well, and have probably encountered some difficulty in making up your mind just what you want to do in life. Because it is not easy for you to get out of yourself and participate fully in the world around you, you often find that you are acting on a feeling or intuition too late; and since failure is so abhorrent to you, this causes frustration and, though seldom, the rise of your formidable temper. A profession midway between management and labor—the civil service, wholesaling and distributing, or administration—fits your temperament very well and allows your naturally meticulous side to blossom. A career as a surgeon or dentist is also a possibility. You must work at establishing discipline and structure in order to be productive in the outside world, and to stay out of your fantasy life as much as possible.

YOUR DEEP INTUITIVE PERSONALITY

This is where you dwell—in your exceptional intuition. You tend to depend upon it too much, in fact. "I feel like this," or, "I don't feel like that," are probably common remarks for you. Still, this naturally strong and well-developed side of you is also the wellspring of your attractiveness and charm; and as long as you do not hide yourself away in it, you can rely upon your intuition for inspiration and direction.

YOUR INTELLIGENCE

Unlike most people with a strong intuitive nature, you possess an analytic intellect, reinforced by your strong imagination. You focus on details on the one hand, but on the other your imagination can take those details and whirl them back into your fantasies rather than making them work on the outside world. This is a function, very much, of a certain intellectual timidity—or a hesitation to express your intellect, which is entirely unfounded, for your mind is quick. You have a remarkable memory for facts and will tap this in making decisions or solving a problem.

YOUR EMOTIONAL NATURE

You are a man of the heart, keenly sensitive and affectionate and very easily touched emotionally. Along with your open, delicate emotions goes a poignantly refined sensuality. Women do not call you a "great lover," but rather, an exquisite lover. And yet, you can be quick of temper; this is part of your natural dualism. Your tenderness can easily be turned into anger, even rage if you are provoked emotionally, and the sensitive, sensual man can become closed, enraged, even violently protective. But you are never possessive; it is not jealousy which can set you off, for in general you have a hard time believing that what you have really belongs to you anyway. It is caused, more likely, by a feeling that you might be robbed of your calm and your peace, which can inspire a negative reaction, emotionally. Still, overall, your emotional life is on an even keel.

YOUR HEALTH AND VITALITY

Though you tire easily, you have a lot of vigor. You are not a man of action, hence you are prone to exhaustion and need a lot of sleep. You have likely found that you benefit from vacations at the beach and from sitting in the sun. Be careful not to take stimulants; you are at your best when you are "laid back," and should not try to change that artificially. Your weak points physically are your nervous system and your genitals.

THE SOCIAL YOU

Throughout your life, you charm those around you with confidence and goodwill. You enjoy being surrounded by people, even if they do not possess the qualities you look for in true and fast friends. When you are with your family, you are most comfortable; your sense of family and close family ties are highly evolved, though at times, in your search for peace within the family circle, you tend to make many concessions in order to be assured of calm and security. You seem to be a well of good luck in the world—though often you rely too strongly on Dame Fortune in your dealings with other people. In the end, your social and professional success comes from your own efforts and out of the structure you have provided for yourself.

———————————

NamePortrait
32
Associated Names

Adon	Cory	Eustace	Miles
Ambroise	Covell	Eustache	Myles
Ambros	Covill	Gallagher	Ned
Ambrose	Cromwell	Giffard	Nero
Ambrosius	Derward	Gifferd	Orel
Ange	Dillon	Gifford	Placide
Angelo	Don	Gilroy	Privat
Arpad	Donahue	Hadley	Shaw
Arvad	Donat	Hearst	Siddell
Atley	Donn	Holles	Sinclair
Balder	Duff	Hollis	St. Claire
Baldhere	Eamon	Hurst	Thurstan
Baldur	Eamonn	Juvenal	Thurston
Barlow	Ed	Kerrin	Verall
Bowen	Eddie	Kerry	Verill
Brush	Eddy	Kieran	Verrall
Buck	Edme	Kieren	Verrell
Buckley	Edmond	Kieron	Verrill
Calder	Edmund	Maixent	Wycliff
Corey	Emrys	Mayfield	

Name Portrait 33

Conquering King

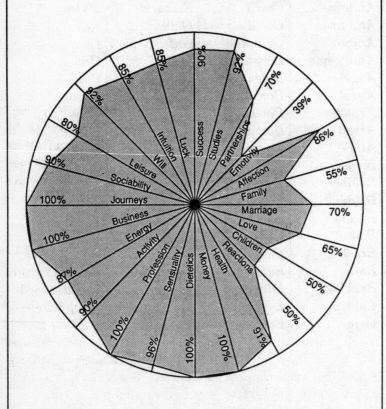

Element : Water   **Plant** : Maize

Mineral : Jasper   **Sign** : Scorpio

Animal : Seal   **Color** : Red

Personality Type:

Conquering King

(Associated names – page 233)

BASIC CHARACTER

Principled and determined, you are a man of strong character, the master of your fate. You are guided in your life by an urge to succeed and a first-rate will; and like your totem animal, the seal, you are able to enlist both your natural passivity (associated with water) and your firm and active resolve (associated with earth) to get to where you are headed.

YOUR PSYCHOLOGY

Though other people might find that it's impossible to predict how you are going to react, you yourself know precisely which side of your nature—passive or impassioned—you will enlist to attain your goals. You have a precise self-image, which you do not always show to the outside world; what others see is a casualness or an unshakable coolness which can transmute itself into passion and great activity, depending upon which is suitable for your aims. You possess an astonishing self-confidence and are well-motivated.

HOW YOU ACT AND REACT IN THE WORLD

You have a remarkably good attitude toward your profession or vocation; and more likely than not you have turned down jobs—or have found yourself uncomfortably explosive in jobs—when you were not given enough information about them: who you are working for; precisely what your task is;

why you have to do this or that. You must know where you stand and the purpose of your endeavors. You are assertive and able to resolve a discussion quickly. Rare is the person who can win an argument with you. Although you can be explosive in your reactions at times, you are better known for your incisiveness and ability to make decisions quickly. For this reason, a profession in the judiciary, or as a progressive legislator or industrialist is right for you. You would also make an excellent doctor or a dedicated soldier or officer in the military. You are an effective leader for social change and have potential as a revolutionary leader.

YOUR DEEP INTUITIVE PERSONALITY

One of the most attractive things about you is your strong and reliable intuition. It is this deep, inner part of you which is, unfailingly, your best guide. Because your intuition is so well-structured, you can rely upon it in assessing situations and in deciding which of your "faces" is appropriate in dealings outside yourself.

YOUR INTELLIGENCE

Yours is an astonishingly well-balanced mind, both analytic and holistic. You are able to comprehend something in its entirety as well as by its details. This is an intriguing ability, and of much benefit to you in your profession and in your personal life. You also draw on your fine memory; and your well-organized curiosity enhances your astounding intellect. It is important to point out here that your intellectual balance is almost always attuned to whatever task is in front of you; that is, you rarely ever find yourself spending more time or energy on a problem than is necessary, and it is this capacity which provides for your talent for making a decision quickly and efficiently.

YOUR EMOTIONAL NATURE

There is a certain restraint in the way you express yourself emotionally. Perhaps it is better to call it nuance, for your emotions are broad and deep, but you prefer to show yourself with refinement, and rather traditionally. You always seem to have your antennae out, feeling out other people's emotions, not only toward you, but toward themselves. Hence, you are quick to understand another's emotional state, and as quick to react appropriately and sensitively. Your passion is intense at times, and can take you both inward, toward an enlightened mysticism, and outward, into a deep, affectionate, and mutually respectful relationship. You probably flabbergasted your parents with some very early sexual experiences, but your sexual maturity is, or was, genuinely precocious. Very early on, you became a refined sensualist, and as an adult are more the epicure than the bohemian. You are faithful to your loved ones, and exhibit at once an intense love and a passionate calm.

YOUR HEALTH AND VITALITY

Generally, you have a remarkable vigor, and your daily regimen, like the rest of your life, is fitted and balanced to your nature. The only problems that might develop would be blood pressure and digestion troubles. As long as you balance your exercise and diet—as you are wont to do, in any case—your naturally good health will remain so.

THE SOCIAL YOU

The richness of your character is open to the world; you show a great deal of self-confidence in dealing with other people, though at times, you tend to become, shall we say, a bit too militaristic in your social dealings. A night out with the boys might end up seeming, to the boys at least, like they've just been through exercises with the sergeant. You do have a deep appreciation for social hierarchies, and you must know precisely where you stand therein. But even if you find you are standing at the bottom you will not be dismayed, for you know you are, if not today then tomorrow, the head honcho. You enjoy, first and foremost, the traditional sort of social gathering, and, from your well-established and ordered home, you entertain with great dignity and ceremony. The best of everything will be served, of course—no California Sparkly for your guests! The expense and care with which you conduct your social life is generally not a burden for you, for you usually have few problems attaining success in business. In accord with your plant totem, maize, which is a symbol for productivity and prosperity, you apply your determination and will, as well as your many talents, to solid, firmly-based achievement.

———————

NamePortrait
33
Associated Names

Al	Edson	Hilton	Rigby
Alberic	Eduard	Hylton	Rigg
Algernon	Edvard	Kerwin	Royce
Algie	Edward	Kirwin	Royd
Algy	Edwin	Logan	Roydon
Alton	Emmet	Marc	Sam
Arvin	Emmett	Marcius	Sammy
Brigham	Emmit	Marco	Sampson
Burnell	Emmot	Marcus	Samson
Casey	Emmy	Mark	Sansom
Cian	Falkner	Marston	Sim
Darton	Faulkener	Ned	Simpson
Demos	Faulkner	Neddie	Simson
Derran	Fowler	Neddy	Teddy
Derrin	Gamaliel	Oakes	Thor
Dunley	Granger	Oakley	Tor
Ed	Guthnie	Oakly	Venceslas
Edd	Guthrie	Okeley	Washington
Eddie	Guthry	Okely	Wenceslas
Eddy	Haslett	Paine	Wenceslaus
Edison	Haslitt	Payne	
Edlin	Hazlett	Perth	
Edouard	Hazlitt	Renfred	

Name Portrait 34

Intriguing Empress

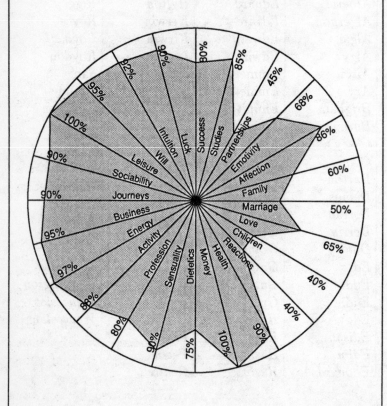

Element : Air   **Plant** : Laurel rose
Mineral : Copper   **Sign** : Aquarius
Animal : Weasel   **Color** : Orange

Personality Type:

Intriguing Empress

(*Associated names – page 238*)

BASIC CHARACTER

You have a fine sensitivity, combined with a reassuring calmness. This lends you an outward majesty of carriage and at the same time an inward ability to adapt marvelously to the most extreme events. Like your totem plant, the laurel, there is an ineffable triumph in all you do. Though seldom a bustle of activity, you take measured steps, depending upon your will and your intuition for surety and guidance.

YOUR PSYCHOLOGY

Essentially you are an introvert and not that easy to understand, though it is important to you that others understand you. Rarely will you tell what you are thinking, not so much out of a sense of insecurity as guile. Not unlike the wily weasel, your totem animal, you present a sleek exterior, gliding smoothly along; but you can be tenacious, even ferocious. You tend to be a bit narcissistic at times and can spend too much time acting out a role rather than actually going about the business of securing firm accomplishments. Though you are willful, your well-organized will is kept concealed, which leads to a tendency to mount personal intrigues of the highest order. Although it is your secretiveness which contributes to your regal bearing, this tendency should be guarded against, as you might find yourself retreating too often into your own private world instead of taking part in the world around you and thereby developing your vast potentials.

HOW YOU ACT AND REACT IN THE WORLD

Even though you possess great confidence in your rising star, you have to prod yourself to get things done. Seeing a project through to the fruitful end often is a problem for you. Still, you are effective once you do act. You like to know the reasons for doing anything—and usually you need more than one good reason. You are by nature attracted to vocations having to do with new technologies. A career in video or electronics is well suited to your temperament. You could also be an excellent "on-air talent," for example, a television reporter or commentator. You enjoy speaking and expressing yourself, though you are often restrained, holding your opinions in abeyance until expressing them will prove most beneficial to your position. In any sort of power struggle, you retain your confidence and, once you have moved upward or been victorious, you will not abandon your triumph but make use of it for the next step in life.

YOUR DEEP INTUITIVE PERSONALITY

Here you are truly remarkable. Your intuition is of the highest order, well-organized and reliable. You can depend upon it in choosing friends and confidants; and from this side of your nature springs your irresistible beauty and charm, drawing to your circle friends who are all too willing to serve and defer to you. When it comes to your deep, intuitive side, there is something of the enchantress about you.

YOUR INTELLIGENCE

You have an analytic mind and are an excellent observer. Your observations and your analyses run deep, calling your intuitive powers into play when need be. Your memory is astonishing, as is your insatiable curiosity. It is a simple thing for you to get to the heart of any problem and understand it.

YOUR EMOTIONAL NATURE

Impetuousness is as far from your nature as the laurel rose is from the dandelion. Your affections, for the most part, are secret, and you are not that approachable yourself. Heaven help the man who throws himself at you—and many probably do, or would like to. Once you are past your reserve, however, you are a most exquisite lover, and able to express your emotions quite fully. There is a certain fickleness in your heart, so be sure that you do not commit yourself when you do not mean it, lest you leave a trail of broken hearts. Sexually, you are reserved as well, but once you blossom, you enjoy a refined sensuality and are able to receive and give the most when you are the master in your relationship.

YOUR HEALTH AND VITALITY

You have naturally good health, and with it a sixth sense for taking precise and good care of yourself. When all is going well for you in the world, your health is positively dazzling, for it is then that you follow a well-balanced regime. In times of stress and emotional malaise, you might have troubles with your neck and its glands. Pay particular mind to your thyroid glands.

THE SOCIAL YOU

With your grace and charm, you know how to entertain people, and are good at bringing people together. Of course, you are at your best socially when people come together around you, as the center. You enjoy the conventional entertainments more than the avant-garde, and a large sit-down dinner party is among your favorite social gatherings. At a dinner, you have an uncanny ability to arrange the seating so that everyone is nearby someone who will spark his or her dynamism. Often, you enjoy sitting back and watching the outcomes of this sort of casual match-making. With your drive to triumph, you can be assured of success, especially on the social level—as long as you avoid retreating into yourself before the opportunity arises to bring an activity about.

NamePortrait
34
Associated Names

Almeira	Calida	Elsa	Kyrena
Almeria	Calla	Elsbeth	Kyrenia
Almira	Callia	Else	Lasca
Bab	Carnation	Elsie	Lee
Babb	Cass	Elspeth	Leela
Babette	Cassandra	Elspie	Leila
Babie	Cassandre	Elsy	Leilah
Babs	Cassie	Elysa	Leilia
Bathsheba	Cyrena	Elyse	Lela
Bess	Cyrenia	Elysia	Lelah
Bessie	Cythera	Elza	Lelia
Bessy	Cytherea	Erna	Les
Beth	Cytherere	Ernaline	Lesley
Bethany	Cytheria	Ernestine	Lesli
Bethel	Cytherine	Felice	Leslie
Bethesda	Desta	Felicia	Lesly
Bethia	Egberta	Felicidad	Libby
Bethiah	Egberte	Felicie	Lila
Bethseda	Egbertha	Felicite	Lilac
Betina	Egberthe	Felicity	Lilah
Betsy	Egbertina	Felis	Lilais
Betta	Egbertine	Felise	Lili
Bette	Elisa	Fenix	Lilia
Bettina	Elisabeth	Gerardine	Lilian
Betty	Elise	Hera	Liliana
Bliss	Elissa	Ilse	Liliane
Blita	Eliza	Iseult	Lilias
Blitha	Elizabeth	Isoda	Lilika
Blithe	Elma	Isold	Lilith
Blyth	Elmira	Isolda	Lilla
Blythe	Eloise	Isolde	Lilli

Associated Names (cont.)

Lillian	Lizete	Modesty	Sigrid
Lilliana	Lizette	Neda	Sigrud
Lilliane	Lizzie	Nedda	Sigurd
Lillis	Lizzy	Nelda	Solita
Lilly	Lodema	Perpetua	Vala
Lillyan	Lyra	Persis	Verbena
Lily	Lyris	Phoenix	Winema
Lisa	Madora	Rica	Winola
Lisabeta	Medea	Ricadonna	Yseult
Lisbeth	Media	Rickie	Ysolda
Lise	Medora	Roddie	Ysolde
Lisette	Messina	Roddy	Ysolt
Liza	Modesta	Roderica	Zerla
Lizabeta	Modeste	Rodericka	Zerlina
Lizabeth	Modestia	Semira	Zerlinda
Lizbeth	Modestine	Sigrath	Zerline

Name Portrait 35

Solitary Traveler

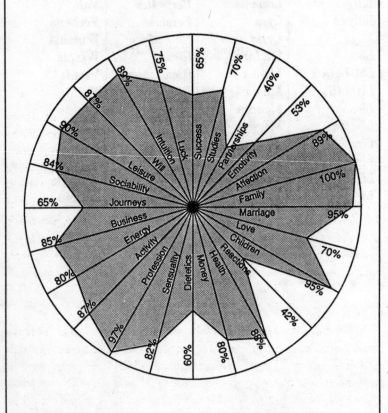

Element : Water

Mineral : Tourmaline

Animal : Crab

Plant : Lilac

Sign : Cancer

Color : Blue

Personality Type:

Solitary Traveler

(Associated names – page 245)

BASIC CHARACTER

You are imaginative but withdrawn; active but unstructured. These apparently contradictory characteristics make you a solitary yet powerful individual, someone who, like your special animal totem the crab, will sidestep rather than walk into anything head-on. But the crab is also a symbol of regeneration and those forces which turn the ephemeral things of life into the elements of growth and rebirth. Your own growth stems from following your fierce individuality, and that individuality is best expressed in your favorite setting—secure, quiet, and alone.

YOUR PSYCHOLOGY

As an introvert, you rely very much on your private world, and this often leads to problems in your dealings with outside reality. There is a certain instability in your psyche, which comes from apprehensions and anxieties about what other people think of you. It is important that you be held in high regard by others, or your own self-esteem is damaged. As such, you are easily persuaded and influenced, mainly for fear of being criticized. Your natural tendency to flee and burrow in, like the crab, can end up in a stubborn denial of the rest of the world, for your will is incredibly strong. But once your self-confidence is established, and your anxieties put to rest by the right—that is, calm and quiet—circumstances, you are a source of inspiration to others, sensed more than seen—like the perfume of the lilac, your plant totem.

HOW YOU ACT AND REACT IN THE WORLD

Discipline and structure are terribly important if you are to be effective in your career or in your social life. You possess a great deal of enthusiasm for things you become involved in and lean to an artistic sort of career. Acting, directing, and lecturing are among the professions most perfectly suited to your character. It is not uncommon for you to take to the road—alone, naturally. But many times you feel this urge only because it is a way of escaping the reality around you at present. Still, you would make a good merchant seaman, even a monk. In whatever you do as a profession, the regimentation—even of the slightest kind—will disturb you. In school, you probably studied what you wanted to, rather than what was being taught, and this pattern follows you throughout life: you will go your own way, and are prone to rejecting the world and starting anew more than once along the road.

YOUR DEEP INTUITIVE PERSONALITY

This is where you can be found most often, listening to your soft inner voice. Your intuition is powerful and apt to make you hesitate in acting in the outer world. But with it comes your galloping imagination which, though it sometimes carries you away, is a source of inspiration and your very best friend.

YOUR INTELLIGENCE

The abstract fascinates you, and with your synthetic, or holistic, mind, you are able to draw far-reaching principles from your astute observations of the world around you. Couple that with a highly reliable memory and an intense curiosity, and you have the picture of a first-rate mind, a broad and deep thinker. Your only problem in this sphere comes from your hesitancy to use your intellectual insights to your profit.

YOUR EMOTIONAL NATURE

You are independent emotionally, as you are in most areas. Though your emotions are rich, there is a certain timidity in expressing them. And woe be to the woman who attempts to intrude herself emotionally on you. Then you will either burrow further into your subterranean world or react with a vicious disdain. You need, on the other hand, tenderness and security, a refuge from the uncaring winds of fate. But any emotional commitment to your refuge must be on your terms. Sensually, you are quiet, and enjoy a tender, fragrant love relationship more than a sexually aggressive one. Your capacity for love is even, and tempered very much by circumstances. Because you tend to idealize love, you may find yourself heading for a mystical, sentimental emotional life.

YOUR HEALTH AND VITALITY

Again, you need a rigorous regimen of proper diet and exercise in order to stay healthy. Your vitality is average and you are prone to exhaustion should you over exercise. Your weak physical point is your digestive system, hence the need to watch your diet.

THE SOCIAL YOU

You are attentive to others, tenderly so, and your sound moral values prevent you from even thinking of harming another's feelings (as you sometimes believe yours have been hurt). Often, you wait for fortune to open doors for you, rather than opening them yourself. Very likely, you head straight home after work, take the phone off the hook, ignore the doorbell, and commune with your private interests—and then wonder why your friend neglected to invite you to his party! People simply have a hard time getting hold of you, though your company is most enjoyable. You need the support and understanding of a partner, someone to manage your social affairs, lest your own solitary independence leads you to a monastic life against your will. Success in life does not swoop down on you, nor do you go out and whisk it up. Rather, it comes slowly but surely, despite your occasional worries over it, and because of your efforts and those of your loved ones.

———————

NamePortrait
35
Associated Names

Alasdair	Burne	Hale	Rambert
Alastair	Byrd	Haley	Riston
Alaster	Byrne	Holcomb	Romney
Aldis	Cadby	Holcombe	Roslin
Aldous	Cain	Holecomb	Roslyn
Aldus	Cato	Holecombe	Ross
Alec	Chelton	Homer	Rosselin
Aleck	Chilton	Homere	Rosslyn
Alex	Claiborn	Howell	Roswald
Alexander	Clay	Hy	Roswall
Alexandre	Clayborne	Hyman	Roswell
Alexios	Claybourne	Hymen	Sacha
Alexis	Clayton	Hymie	Safford
Alick	Clinton	Hywel	Samborn
Alistair	Dag	Hywell	Sanborn
Alister	Dagan	Jynx	Sander
Allister	Dagon	Keenan	Sanders
Alsandair	Dagwood	Kinnell	Sanderson
Ammon	Deems	Lane	Sandie
Barr	Denman	Manton	Sandy
Beal	Doane	Mayer	Saunders
Beale	Durwin	Meyer	Saunderson
Beall	Elme	Milward	Sawny
Beau	Emil	Modred	Schuyler
Blade	Emile	Morgan	Shelby
Bourne	Emilien	Morgen	Whitcomb
Bramwell	Emilio	Murphy	Whitcombe
Bruno	Emlyn	Myer	Wooster
Burbank	Grady	Quinlan	Worcester

Name Portrait 36

Enchanting Adventuress

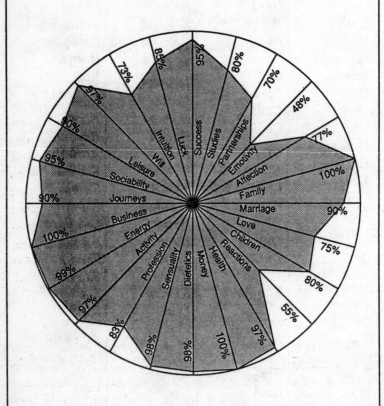

Element : Fire   **Plant** : Hawthorne

Mineral : Tungsten   **Sign** : Aries

Animal : Hippopotamus   **Color** : Blue

Personality Type:

Enchanting Adventuress

(Associated names – page 251)

BASIC CHARACTER

Both irresistible and unstoppable, you are one of those rare, exciting spirits who, like your plant totem, the hawthorn, is as prickly as you are attractive. You have a natural tendency to drive ever forward and most often are a bustle of activity. You possess an awesome will and an independent as well as commanding nature. Despite your wanderlust, you are steady and ambitious, able to commit yourself to learning and preparing for your adventures, as long as that preparation has a feeling of motion. Your animal totem is the hippopotamus, or, as it once was called, the river horse; and that is where you are most at home—galloping up the river and, preferably, taking your friends with you.

YOUR PSYCHOLOGY

Everything that you do has to be directed outward; you need extensive contact with the world. Any withdrawal is seen as a defeat, and for this reason, you sometimes do not carry through your projects to the end, especially if they require any sort of germination period. Despite your extroversion, you tend to be a bit too subjective, which, when combined with your formidable pride, leads you to blame others for your own shortfalls. Your adventuresome spirit might tend to get you into complicated situations, and since withdrawing is so aversive to you, you find yourself getting pricked by your own thorny situations. Yes, you have quite a temper, but as long as you remain well-directed in your activity, and unthwarted, it will have no reason to rear itself.

HOW YOU ACT AND REACT IN THE WORLD

When things are going your way—which means, you're moving forward and at the head of the throng—you are happy and so is everyone around you. But if things are not going that way, you can react with the ferocity of Mount St. Helen's. Most often, however, you are moving along at a pace that suits you—and leaves the rest of the world out of breath. Things just have to be in motion. You are perfectly suited for a vocation that involves a lot of travel; you would make an excellent explorer, pilot, navigator, or doctor—as long as you can make housecalls, that is. You are at your best when you are in a position to give rather than receive orders, or to work independently. You do need to impose some structure and discipline on yourself in order that your undertakings come to bear fruit.

YOUR DEEP INTUITIVE PERSONALITY

Though much that is attractive about you is your inner self, you tend not to heed it too much for guidance, except in your feelings about other people. It might seem to you that you either hit it off with someone or you don't—and so what—but it is your oft unheeded intuition that is probably the deciding voice in these matters. You do have remarkable insight and are able to anticipate problems with great accuracy, but it is doubtful whether this comes so much from intuition as it does from your practical intelligence.

YOUR INTELLIGENCE

Your holistic mind enables you to grasp situations very quickly, without having to waste precious time over details. You use your intellect directly; it is at the service of your projects, your travel, your profession, and rarely do you employ your very active curiosity on idle diversions. Also, your memory is reliable, and you can count on it when you find yourself in one of those prickly situations that attract you so.

YOUR EMOTIONAL NATURE

What a curious mixture your affections are! A "gather-ye-rosebuds-while-ye-may" sort of whimsy rules your emotions, and your affections are a concoction of friendship, sensuality, and sex, gathered on the wing but rarely held for long. Oh, you're apt to embrace your lovers with a heartfelt intensity, but very soon, it's off to other pastures. You're likely to run into your past loves quite often in the course of your adventures, and old flames will be rekindled from time to time. Though you are quite passionate, you can become irritable if someone makes emotional demands upon you, and are often driven by near violent impulses when it comes to tasting life's sensations. It is impossible for your emotions as it is for anything else to hold you down in one place for very long.

YOUR HEALTH AND VITALITY

You have an incredible stamina and your health, in general, is quite good. But you are bound to be affected by the speedy pace of your life, and your diet irregularities and lack of sleep can over time have adverse effects on your hearty constitution. Your weak points are your lungs and general respiratory system, especially when you are young. Beware of accidents in your head-long quests in life.

THE SOCIAL YOU

You are engaging and the center of the action. People are drawn to you, because wherever you are, something is going on. Though at times your friends might find your impetuousness frightening, they stick to you. It is a simple thing for you to organize a lively get-together, and a dinner party with you will likely be a moveable feast—appetizers in one part of town, soup in another, the main course on the train, dessert across the state line, and cognac and coffee somewhere in the Pyrenees. It is not only your swiftness that makes it difficult for your friends and associates to keep up with you, however—it's also your social disorderliness. You're not one to send out invitations. Still, people around you are devoted, for in your company, there's rarely a dull moment.

———————————

NamePortrait
36
Associated Names

Acantha	Brunehilde	Cypressa	Liesse
Adonia	Brunella	Cypris	Lotus
Aleria	Brunelle	Desma	Marjolaine
Amena	Brunetta	Easter	Mona
Amina	Brunhild	Eastre	Octavia
Amine	Brunhilda	Ena	Octavie
Ariadna	Brunhilde	Enid	Ottavia
Ariadne	Cal	Enya	Ottavie
Ariana	Calandra	Eostre	Radella
Ariane	Calandre	Euclea	Rama
Aritha	Calandria	Eugenia	Rami
Arlana	Callie	Eugenie	Ramona
Avena	Cally	Fleta	Ramonda
Avene	Capriccia	Fleur	Ray
Azalee	Caprice	Fleurette	Raymonda
Azalia	Caressa	Garland	Raymonde
Azaliea	Caresse	Gen	Sapphira
Azelia	Carissa	Gena	Serhilda
Balbina	Carisse	Gene	Serhilde
Balbine	Carressa	Genie	Serilda
Balbinia	Chloe	Gina	Serilde
Bertrada	Cipressa	Hagar	Tavi
Bertrade	Clio	Helma	Tavia
Bruella	Clo	Hilma	Tavie
Bruelle	Cloe	Kerri	Tavy
Brundhild	Comfort	Kerry	Topaz
Brunehilda	Cypres	Kloe	

Name Portrait 37

Master of the Waves

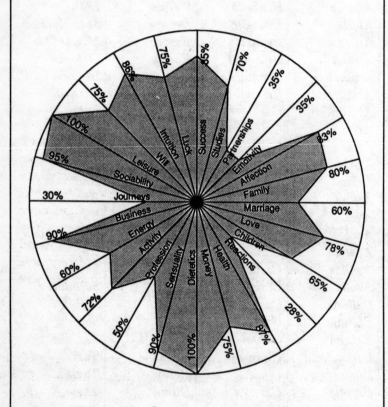

Element : Air

Mineral : Opal

Animal : Tuna

Plant : Beech tree

Sign : Aquarius

Color : Orange

Personality Type:

Master of the Waves

(Associated names – page 257)

BASIC CHARACTER

You possess a dual nature and at times it seems as if you have two complete personalities. There is the tranquil man, like the beech tree, your plant totem, spreading its branches over the stream, watchful, recumbent, peaceful. Then there is the mobile man, like your animal totem the tuna—"one of the gamest of fighting fish." But in general, you are more sentimental than active, out of a natural preference. You tend to see life as a grand play and can most often be found front row center. You love freedom, and if your freedom is threatened, you can become mobilized into swift and effective action.

YOUR PSYCHOLOGY

It isn't unusual to hear you say, "Perhaps today, but then again, perhaps tomorrow." Procrastination is a problem for you. It stems from your tendency toward introversion and often leads you into states of anxiety and worry over little things. Your will is strong but very seldom does it come into action. It's as if you were guided by the idea, "Suppose it's my will not to have any will?" A paradox, to be sure. You're an inveterate daydreamer, which can hold you back in the world, especially when your daydreaming substitutes for action.

253

HOW YOU ACT AND REACT IN THE WORLD

You hurry slowly, acting with discretion and holding your reactions in check. You're not one to leap before you've looked the situation over thoroughly. At times, you can become very involved in your work or studies, but at other times, you simply lose interest. Your accomplishments in the world are nevertheless respectable, as you are able to persevere when something interests you. Though you probably have had a bit of a problem in choosing a profession, once you do make a choice you can be quite successful. You would make a very good musician, though in your less adventuresome moods, will more likely opt for a more secure and comfortable vocation as, say, a civil servant. You do not have exaggerated illusions about what you can and cannot do. Friendship is sacred to you, and you find in it a sort of refuge, especially after one of those adventures which you are forced into from time to time.

YOUR DEEP INTUITIVE PERSONALITY

Your intuition is most highly developed. You can feel the storms of life coming better than the ocean albatross. When you follow your remarkable inner voice, you are able to navigate with the ease of the tuna, expending only the energy you must to get through any adventure. Though your intuition leads you toward a subjective sort of introversion, very often it is a faithful and sure guide to your actions and reactions.

YOUR INTELLIGENCE

Despite your great sense of intuition, you have an analytical mind. Often, you become burdened down by trivial details and have a propensity to mull everything over, no matter how small. This makes you a bit slow to react to your mental insights and hesitant to take a firm intellectual stand. But your attention to detail is an aid in many ways, in that you are able to see everything that goes into a situation and precisely how each detail fits in with the others. Working in combination with your intuition, your analytic mind gives you the potential for a powerful intellect.

YOUR EMOTIONAL NATURE

You're a tender tyrant; as long as you are comfortable, you are happy and return your happiness. Though you tend to be possessive, you rarely assert yourself or impose your will on your loved ones. You prefer an uncomplicated life, where the pleasures are many and the strife is rare. You enjoy good food and wine, and in choosing your beloved are apt to take these things into consideration. In general, your affections are a combination of the sensual, of a quiet and possessive love, and of mutual, reassuring comfort. Still, your sex life is rather irregular and can entangle you in complicated situations; since your first inclination is to act on your emotions only in ways that protect your personal comfort, you have a tendency to send out signals that can be greatly misunderstood. You enjoy sex, but will flee from a sexual liaison that threatens your easy-going side. It is that side of yourself of which you are the most possessive, and woe be unto the querulous lover who asks that you give it up for love's sake alone.

YOUR HEALTH AND VITALITY

In general, you enjoy a strong constitution and good health. But you tend to overindulge in food and drink, and this can lead to weight problems and exhaustion. You must get enough exercise, lest your robust body round out to butterball proportions. Your weak points are your mouth and your teeth, so along with regular exercise, plan regular visits to the dentist!

THE SOCIAL YOU

Like your totem, the tuna, you are at your best in the warmth of the crowd. You enjoy mixing good friendship with good food, and are often entertaining at your home.

Among your friends, you will remain subdued; you would perish before you would impose yourself on anyone—but give you the right occasion, and you spring to the fore. You have marvelously good fortune, especially where friendship is concerned, and often find yourself surrounded by charming women and devoted allies. It is only when these parts of your life are threatened that you become a fierce and fighting fish.

NamePortrait
37
Associated Names

Ackerley	Cary	Halford	Sayer
Ackley	Cleveland	Houghton	Sayers
Algar	Felice	Millard	Sayre
Alger	Felicien	Montagne	Sayres
Amand	Felix	Montagu	Topaz
Andoche	Fife	Montague	Truesdale
Armel	Fyfe	Monte	Trusdale
Bogart	Fyffe	Monty	Wyman
Brodie	Gorman	Pitt	Wymer
Brody	Greeley	Putnam	
Carey	Grover	Remi	

Name Portrait 38

Woman of Quiet Force

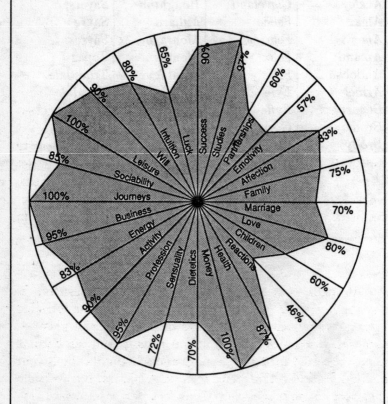

Element : Earth
Mineral : Seleniate
Animal : Sole

Plant : Fern
Sign : Capricorn
Color: Red

Personality Type:

Woman of Quiet Force

(Associated names – page 262)

BASIC CHARACTER

Your strong emotions and positive morality, in combination with your will, make you a resourceful and goal-directed person. You tend to be scrupulous and self-effacing, despite your high level of activity. Though you often appear quiet and sober on the outside, you are motivated by a forceful combination of intellect, principles, and purpose. You're a faithful, dedicated worker and friend with an unobtrusive charm and high ideals.

YOUR PSYCHOLOGY

At times, your scruples give way to punctiliousness, especially if you feel your morals or privacy are being intruded upon. You have an inclination toward anxiety and nervousness when too much is asked of you socially, and can become almost obsessed with guilt feelings and self-doubts about your abilities. Much of this stems from your natural introversion. Like your totem plant, the retiring fern, you lean toward shyness and the shadows of others. Still, you are perfectly capable of lashing out with the ferocity of your totem animal, the sole, should your personal universe be threatened; you are quick to anger over emotional issues. Your will is strong, even if you don't always apply it when you could. Although you are sensitive to failure, you are not easily discouraged from pursuing a course which you've chosen.

HOW YOU ACT AND REACT IN THE WORLD

Because you are meticulous and well-organized, you enjoy work which makes use of these administrative skills. It takes you a little while to adapt to a new situation, though once you have made the adjustment, you become dedicated to the job. You are drawn to demanding work, into which you can throw yourself and your great powers of concentration. The best career choices are those that do not involve too much contact with the public. Managerial work and professions dealing with law and medicine are naturals for you. You could also be an excellent masseuse or beauty consultant, a technician, chemist, or researcher. A writing career is also a very likely choice.

YOUR DEEP INTUITIVE PERSONALITY

There is something captivating about your intuition—all the more pity that you do not heed your inner voice more often than you do. It is penetrating and effective, but you tend not to put much faith in it.

YOUR INTELLIGENCE

Your mind works systematically and methodically, and yet it is lively. Intellectually, you tend to be analytical and require a thorough understanding of details in order to decide precisely how you should act on any problem or in any situation. Your memory, like your intellect, is well-structured and vast.

YOUR EMOTIONAL NATURE

You tend to restrain yourself when it comes to expressing your feelings, partly because of a natural distrust of others' affections. Great declarations of love are downright distasteful to you—too theatrical and pretentious to be real. Still, you can be a most endearing and faithful lover, and you require a lot of understanding and considerable attention and affection. Sexually and sensually, you are soft and shy, and your sexuality is often inhibited by considerations of the status quo. You're able to turn off your sexuality in the name of good taste and are more apt to be seduced than to do the seducing.

YOUR HEALTH AND VITALITY

Although you tire easily and your health can suffer from nervous strain, you enjoy generally good vitality and health. You need fresh air and some sort of regular exercise in order to keep from succumbing to mental exhaustion. Your weak areas are the intestines and nervous system.

THE SOCIAL YOU

You have a small circle of faithful friends whom you entertain with a quiet charm. You do not like to be intruded upon—a surprise party is a horror to you. Often you become upset by the superficiality of large gatherings and tend to shy away from a demanding social schedule. You need the softness and sincerity of special friends in small gatherings, not the loud and frightfully boisterous clamor of anonymous crowds. The intimate setting of trusted and proven friends helps you to bring out your pleasant sensibilities and, at the same time, to act in your natural, slightly reserved way.

———

NamePortrait
38
Associated Names

Allegra	Earley	Hildy	Noelie
Aria	Earlie	Hollie	Noella
Bertie	Earline	Holly	Noelle
Billie	Edouardine	Iona	Nola
Billy	Edwardina	Ione	Nolana
Bobbie	Edwardine	Jerusha	Noleta
Bobby	Erin	Joccoaa	Nolita
Bobette	Erlene	Kara	Novella
Bobina	Erline	Karell	Paquita
Briana	Fan	Karen	Rheta
Brina	Fanchon	Karena	Roberta
Bryna	Fanny	Karin	Roberte
Cadena	Fran	Karina	Robertha
Cadence	France	Karine	Roberthe
Cadenza	Franceline	Karyn	Robertine
Caltha	Frances	Keziah	Robina
Cara	Francesca	Levana	Robinette
Cariad	Francette	Levania	Robinia
Carina	Francine	Lola	Ruberta
Carine	Francisca	Melantha	Ruperta
Carita	Francoise	Melanthe	Samantha
Cedena	Francy	Merl	Thada
Charissa	Francyne	Merla	Thadda
Charita	Frankie	Merle	Thaddea
Charity	Gitana	Merlina	Thee
Charris	Hedy	Merline	Theo
Charry	Heidi	Merola	Theola
Cherry	Hild	Meryl	Tizane
Dara	Hilda	Mireille	Velvet
Disa	Hilde	Myrlene	Vevay
Earlene	Hildie	Noel	Viv

262

Associated Names (cont.)

Vivette	Vivie	Warda	Zea
Vivi	Vivien	Willa	Zenia
Vivia	Viviene	Xena	Zezili
Vivian	Vivienna	Xene	Zippora
Viviana	Vivyan	Xenia	Zipporah
Viviane	Vyvyan	Yerusha	

Name Portrait 39

Worthy Teacher

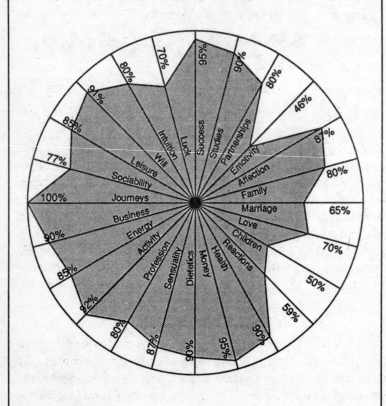

Element : Air   **Plant** : Lemon tree

Mineral : Chrome   **Sign** : Gemini

Animal : Cock & Albatross   **Color** : Blue

Personality Type:

Worthy Teacher

(Associated names – page 269)

BASIC CHARACTER

You are both reserved and aggressive, materialistic and mysterious, cool on the surface, but aflame inside. The paradoxes of your nature are expressed in a number of ways, and it is not surprising that someone with such apparently opposite sides has a dual animal totem, the cock and the albatross. Like the cock, the bird of the dawn and a symbol of vigilance as well as activity, you are keenly aware of the world around you and know how to express yourself according to your perceptions. And like the albatross, symbol of the mysterious, the hidden, and the inevitability of fate, you are secretive, guarded, and tend toward a passionate mysticism.

YOUR PSYCHOLOGY

Despite—or perhaps because of—your strong dual nature, you are often troubled with a deep inner conflict. An introvert by nature, you are nonetheless open-minded. Still, you tend toward a sort of egoism, and often interpret things according to your own self-interest. It is difficult for you to express your needs, and as a consequence, you can become irritable or excitable. Like your plant totem, the lemon tree, there is a propensity in you to give way to acidic statements. Often, when perturbed, you can go from caustic irony to rage. It is a lifelong problem for you to keep your calm and hold your tongue. But it is best that you develop acceptable ways of expressing yourself, as these inner conflicts between materialism and mysticism, action and reservation, can lead to inhibitions, and if you allow inhibitions to rule your life, you might well find yourself growing old and sour, rather than with the balanced grace of wisdom which can also be yours.

HOW YOU ACT AND REACT IN THE WORLD

It is sometimes difficult, even for you, to tell if you are acting out of your naturally strong will or out of just plain stubbornness. You have a remarkable ability to persevere at a task, though that perseverance sometimes degenerates into obstinacy. It is your natural assertiveness, though, that is the most notable thing about you. You are able to impart your ideas and your unusual insights with a great ease and persuasion, which makes you an ideal teacher. Not so easy, however, is your capacity to learn from others. You seem to know it all, and in a way, you're right. Occasionally, you act impetuously, but most often are able to think things through very concisely before you decide what sort of action a situation calls for. You are able, despite your tendency not to give too much heed to others' teachings, to apply yourself to long courses of study with an astonishing conscientiousness. If teaching is not your choice, you are also given to a career as a high government official, or an acute industrial manager. In whatever you do, however, it is important for you that others learn from your novel perceptions and that the fire inside can be drawn upon.

YOUR DEEP INTUITIVE PERSONALITY

You have a refined and sensitive inner awareness and are able to draw upon your intuition in your understanding of the world. Your intuitive nature is the source of your attractiveness as well as of your most subtle insights and understandings. You often speak or act directly from intuition, as if you had a spiritual guide inside you, and for this reason, you are often misunderstood in the world at large. But have hope, for your inner voice never fails you.

YOUR INTELLIGENCE

With your incisively analytic mind, you are able to understand the logic of things. Coupled with your remarkable intuitive powers, it lends your intellect an endearing but sometimes caustic sense of irony and dry wit. You are able to draw on your analysis of any situation or problem quickly and precisely. You are a decision-maker, even though you are a bit low on the energy side—though you know what needs to be done, you often are not driven to do it. But the power of your intellect is best shown in the ways you can impart your analysis and insights to others verbally.

YOUR EMOTIONAL NATURE

Your dual nature shows itself in your emotional life quite often. At one moment, you are all giving and surrendering to some burning passion; and the next, you are withdrawing, denying, and taking it all back. You're just never quite sure how you should express yourself emotionally, and this is in part due to those inner conflicts between the introverted, cool man and the passionate, driven man. Usually, you will wait until another has proven her devotion before you give any sign that you have an interest. Another reason for your hesitancy to respond is your sense of propriety: at all costs, appearances must be preserved. Sexually, you're a fascinating mixture of aggression and evasiveness, apathy and action; and your sex life is far from simple. With mood swings like yours, you are bound to entangle yourself in liaisons and affairs of the most baroque character.

YOUR HEALTH AND VITALITY

With your superior stamina and generally strong constitution, it is a wonder that you aren't a picture of health. But your tendency to abuse stimulants and alcohol, and to ignore such "commonplace" concerns as a good diet and regular exercise can lead to nervous ailments, especially to headaches. You tend to be accident-prone when you are either nervous

or excited—so learning to concentrate, perhaps to meditate,
is important for your well-being.

THE SOCIAL YOU

Although you have a natural tendency to hold yourself
aloof, your relations with other people are quite good. Your
friends or associates may have the impression that you are
bearing the sins of the world on your shoulders but, martyr-
complex aside, you do enjoy the company of others from time
to time. You are at your best socially in a conventional setting. You entertain, it seems, because it is proper to entertain. But in truth, you enjoy opening up your private life to
your close friends, introducing them to your family or lover.
It is important to you, as well, to be able to escape from the
rigors of city life into the country. One of your fantasies is to
own a retreat in the woods, preferably near a stream. You
possess great fortune, and your natural aggressiveness goes
far to abetting Lady Luck in your behalf. Rarely will you
give the Lady credit, however, for among the dearest things
to you is that your worth is known abroad.

NamePortrait
39
Associated Names

Bec	Francklyn	Lazare	Searl
Beck	Frank	Lazarus	Searle
Blair	Frantz	Litton	Seth
Boniface	Franz	Marien	Seton
Bridger	Fremont	Marin	Severn
Cecil	Galen	Mario	Sherlock
Chandler	Gideon	Marion	Sherwood
Darcie	Gladwin	Marius	Siegfrid
Darcy	Gontran	Nelson	Siegfried
Darsey	Hal	Paco	Sigfrid
Darsy	Harailt	Paquito	Sissil
Digby	Harald	Pell	Somerset
Eleazar	Harold	Pelton	Somerton
Elizer	Harris	Porcia	Stockley
Fran	Harrison	Porsha	Stockton
Francelin	Harry	Portia	Stockwell
Francesco	Herald	Prescot	Taggart
Franchot	Hereld	Prescott	Torr
Francis	Herold	Remus	Vallis
Francisque	Herrick	Risley	Wainwright
Franck	Kleber	Sabin	Ward
Francklin	Lazar	Scully	

Name Portrait 40

Proud Messenger

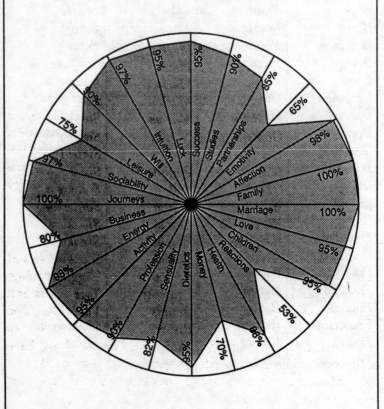

Element : Water   **Plant** : Nettle
Mineral : Mercury   **Sign** : Cancer
Animal : Horse   **Color**: Blue

Personality Type:

Proud Messenger

(Associated names – page 274)

BASIC CHARACTER

You are active, energetic, restless and have a hair-trigger response to the influences that surround you. Your dynamic nature and drive for importance could easily make you the leader of some social movement. Like your animal totem, the horse, you are a messenger of the masses and an authority figure to be recognized.

YOUR PSYCHOLOGY

Basically you are an extrovert who needs to feel involved in the activities of the world. When you're not busy advising, arranging, and controlling situations, you're both restless and discontented. The key to your psyche is your pride. The most profound part of you seeks the approval that comes from making a noteworthy appearance. Because you have such overwhelming ego needs, at times your personality can be oppressing. Your nature is deeply emotional and your emotions press the buttons of your will.

HOW YOU ACT AND REACT IN THE WORLD

Because your emotions are so strong, you are quick to anger and sometimes let loose before you know all the details. Fortunately you can summon a certain semblance of calm before the situation is totally out of control. Since you possess many egocentrical tendencies, your friendships require a certain amount of patience and understanding. Since many people bore you over prolonged periods, your desire is for them to disappear and be replaced by different faces. You demonstrate an extraordinary devotion to your work, perhaps because you are so sensitive to the idea of failure. You abhor being treated as just an ordinary person. In your mind that's about as bad as being nothing at all.

YOUR DEEP INTUITIVE PERSONALITY

Your intuitions are sometimes confused with your emotions, and your hypersensitivity to your own feelings can easily influence what you sense might be happening.

YOUR INTELLIGENCE

You have an exceptional intelligence and a rapid speed of comprehension. Not only are you a master of detail, but you're also skillful at controlling larger issues. Your memory is good and your curiosity inexhaustible. However, because you tend to overdramatize so many issues, you need to develop emotional discipline. At times your histrionics create a crowd around you. Since this is your deepest desire, you'd be particularly suited for a career in the theater, staging, music, and dance programs. However, other areas of the arts and fashion are also attractive. Because you have such excellent taste and pleasure-loving proclivities, you could also excel in such diverse areas as restoring buildings, working with furniture, or running a restaurant. Travel could also be tantalizing since it appeals to your love of change, as well as to your need to escape.

YOUR EMOTIONAL NATURE

You tend to be possessive at the same time that you want the freedom to do whatever moves you. Emotionally, you can be capricious, egocentrical, and concerned with having your desires gratified. Your egocentricity can descend to the level of juvenile selfishness if you do not try to be more objective in your thinking. Essentially, you are on a search for pleasure and happiness. Wherever it will take you is where you want to turn. You could easily make this your primary goal in life since it seems to be the thread of your existence. Taken to the limit, your explosive sensuality can take you in many directions.

YOUR HEALTH AND VITALITY

Your health problems are minor and have a psychological origin. Be careful that your mental stress doesn't lead to high blood pressure and that your food indulgence doesn't bring on obesity. Another area of weakness is the eyes due to your tendency to overstrain them.

THE SOCIAL YOU

Although you have something of a tyrannical nature, in social situations you know how to turn on the charm. You adore formal receptions, dinner parties with interesting people, and being in the center of things. Despite the fact that in private your temper may change like the weather, in public you project the kind of charisma that makes you a highly memorable person.

———————

NamePortrait
40
Associated Names

Ahren	Elihu	Kelsey	Seely
Archambaud	Elijah	Knut	Taffy
Ariel	Elinot	Knute	Thurlow
Bastien	Elisha	Langley	Valere
Bliss	Ellice	Lawford	Valerian
Brant	Elliot	Malin	Valerius
Canut	Elliott	Mansfield	Vali
Canute	Ellis	Marl	Vere
Carter	Ellison	Marlen	Verge
Cedric	Elson	Marlin	Vergil
Cheney	Ely	Marlon	Virge
Cheyney	Enoch	Maslen	Virgie
Crepin	Fred	Maslin	Virgil
Crisp	Freddie	Maslon	Virgile
Crispen	Freddy	Merl	Virgy
Crispin	Gabbie	Merle	Welford
Dante	Gabby	Merlin	Wharton
Dave	Gabe	Morison	Wilfred
David	Gabie	Morrison	Wilfrid
Davie	Gabin	Platt	Wilfried
Davin	Gable	Renton	Wolfgang
Davis	Gabriel	Sanford	Zach
Davy	Gaby	Sealey	Zachariah
Durand	Gannon	Seb	Zacharias
Durant	Hedley	Seba	Zacharie
Eli	Illias	Sebastian	Zachary
Elias	Jaoven	Sebastien	Zack
Elie	Joachim	Seeley	

Name Portrait 41

Tenacious Contestant

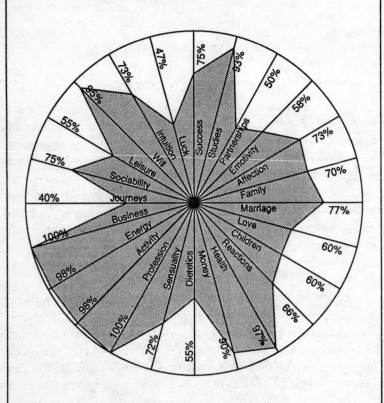

Element : Earth   **Plant** : Pear tree
Mineral : Quartz   **Sign** : Taurus
Animal : Leopard   **Color** : Red

Personality Type:

Tenacious Contestant

(Associated names – page 280)

BASIC CHARACTER

You are independent, exceptionally active, and have strong yet inscrutable emotions. Like your animal totem, the leopard, you are at once valorous and ferocious, as aggressive as you have to be to get what you want in the world. Once you have attained a goal, almost nothing in the universe can make you give it up. Underneath your outwardly assertive nature, however, there is a sweetness and tenderness, not unlike your totem plant, the sturdy pear tree, whose fruit is soft and nourishing.

YOUR PSYCHOLOGY

In spite of your tenacity, you are an introvert by nature, difficult to get close to and somewhat explosive of temperament. Though you make judgments with thoughtfulness and perspicacity, you give no quarter and show little clemency once you've decided that someone is an enemy. You can become fearfully obstinate, which is a consequence of your powerful will. Your natural activism can turn to fanaticism. You tend to oppose other people at times simply for the sake of it, and with that tendency comes a propensity to project your own explosiveness onto other people.

HOW YOU ACT AND REACT IN THE WORLD

Whatever you do, you do it passionately. You enjoy competition and if there's no one else to compete with, then you'll find a way to surpass your own last achievement. You assume an excellent attitude toward your work, and have a great sense of responsibility and authority. You are especially drawn to careers that involve conflict: medicine or medical research, pharmacy, politics, labor organizing, business management, or the military. If there is a feminist organization nearby, you are undoubtedly active in it, if for no other reason than to prove your own worth.

YOUR DEEP INTUITIVE PERSONALITY

Since the straight and narrow path is yours, you put little faith in your good intuition. You rely on sturdy calculation rather than the savory fruits of your inner voice. Still, it is there, to be heeded, if and when you feel you need it.

YOUR INTELLIGENCE

You have a broad and direct perspective of things that is holistic rather than analytic. Still, at times it seems that your intellect works in an analytic mode, because you can be frightfully calculating. You can be dryly witty in your observations; your mind is like an arrow, precise and sure of its target.

YOUR EMOTIONAL NATURE

No one would ever accuse you of being a maudlin sentimentalist. You keep your strong emotions under control until the proper moment, and you are not very free with your sexual charms. You tend to scorn the "animal nature" of man and are very discreet in your shows of affection and desire. Propriety plays a big part in your emotional life, though at times it leads you to serious inhibitions sexually. Once a lover lives up to your often incredibly high standards, he will receive your affection, but you will never be possessed. Most likely, you will dominate any relationship; if you do not have at least equal standing, you tend to become pessimistic and depressed or frustrated.

TENACIOUS CONTESTANT

YOUR HEALTH AND VITALITY

You simply will not give in to sickness or fatigue. Still, you have to recognize that your physical well-being cannot be controlled by your will, and though you have considerable stamina, you tend to push yourself beyond your limits. When you don't know when to stop and rest, you can be subject to fevers. Your weak points are your liver and your genitals.

THE SOCIAL YOU

The company you keep is composed of people with artistic or literary talents and ambitions—you seem to be drawn to such people naturally. Most likely, your social gatherings also include people of political convictions as well as co-workers. In short, yours are lively, intellectually stimulating parties, much like the nineteenth-century salons at which all manner of artistic and political subjects are mulled over at length. You tend to keep a firm hand over the proceedings, however, and see to it that no one gets out of hand. You can be very supportive of those in whom you have faith—and one glance or tilt of the head can let someone else know that he or she is no longer welcome in your refined circle. Still, to those whom you do admire and appreciate, you are a warm and gracious hostess, a steady admirer, and an arch defender.

NamePortrait
41
Associated Names

Adar	Delicia	Guenevere	Michaella
Adina	Di	Guenna	Michel
Aimee	Dian	Guinevere	Michele
Amabel	Diana	Guinivere	Micheline
Amabella	Diane	Gwenhwyvar	Michella
Amabelle	Dianna	Hebe	Michelle
Amecia	Dinah	Helga	Michelline
Ami	Dyana	Hope	Mikaela
Amice	Dyane	Imperia	Nichola
Amicia	Dyanna	Imperial	Nicholina
Amie	Effie	Iunis	Nicky
Amy	Effy	Jarvia	Nicol
Armilla	Elga	Jennifer	Nicola
Aymee	Eppie	Juna	Nicole
Aziza	Euphemia	June	Nicoletta
Azizah	Euphemie	Junella	Nicolina
Clem	Filana	Junette	Nicoline
Clematis	Freda	Junia	Nike
Clemence	Freddie	Juniata	Nikki
Clemency	Freddy	Junine	Nikky
Clementia	Geneva	Juno	Nikola
Clementina	Genevieve	Lala	Nissa
Clementine	Genevra	Lalita	Olga
Cordelia	Genevre	Maura	Olva
Cordelie	Genvra	Maureen	Oola
Cordella	Geromina	Maurine	Pasha
Cordie	Ginerva	Micada	Phemie
Dayana	Ginette	Micaela	Philana
Deanna	Goda	Michaela	Roma
Dee	Guda	Michaelina	Sabra
Delia	Guenever	Michaeline	Soledad

Associated Names (cont.)

Ula	Vanora	Vicenta	Wilf
Ultima	Veda	Vincencia	Wilfreda
Urielle	Vedis	Vincentia	Wilfreida
Valida	Velda	Vinciane	Wilfrieda

Name Portrait 42

Sentimental Sermonizer

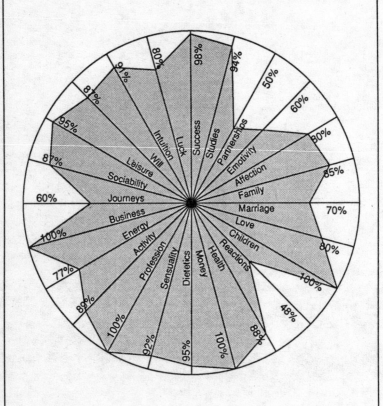

Element : Fire

Mineral : Uranium

Animal : Bison

Plant : Olive tree

Sign : Aries

Color : Yellow

Personality Type:

Sentimental Sermonizer

(Associated names – page 287)

BASIC CHARACTER

Above all, you are a man of profound sentiments. There is the great romantic in you, and you are keenly attuned to human suffering. But though you would like to, you do not always act on your romantic beliefs. The spirit is willing, as they say, but the flesh is weak. Instead, you express your overpowering emotions with your lively tongue. Always quick to deliver your opinions and convictions verbally, your speechifying often takes the place of action. You are also prone, by nature, to extremes of beliefs, best symbolized by your two totems: the sturdy and powerful bison, capable of violent passion; and the olive tree, the Roman symbol of peace, consecrated to Jupiter and Minerva.

YOUR PSYCHOLOGY

Despite the refinement of your character, you have a tendency toward self-destructive behavior, which is a symptom, really, of your inner combat between extremes. You are a man of combat, but rarely do you take it outside yourself. You tend to become exhausted from this inner strife between "war" and "peace" and can become drained by emotional tension. But your will is strong and often sees you through emotionally charged events or ideas.

HOW YOU ACT AND REACT IN THE WORLD

Your reactions to situations are subdued or delayed. Oftentimes, you will speak your piece rather than act. For you, everything begins with a proclamation of your high principles, though this is not always followed by action. But with your refined and powerful emotions, you often find yourself in the thick of things. Your profession must call upon your verbal abilities, and for this reason you would make an excellent psychologist, lawyer, or even a church leader. A career in journalism, education, sales, politics, or in a top executive spot is also a possibility for you. Whatever your vocation, however, you will probably choose it not so much out of a direct and thoughtful decision, but as events in your life dictate. The temptation to find "the ideal" profession, one which will fit all your principles and sentimental ideas of perfection, will arise from time to time, for there is in you a dichotomy between what is actually possible for you to do and a sort of utopian dream wherein you can abolish all suffering and injustice by one swift stroke. As a consequence, you do not always act pragmatically, but in general, once you are in a profession, your work will go smoothly and you will not in reality want very seriously to leave it.

YOUR DEEP INTUITIVE PERSONALITY

You possess an astonishing intuition, with a direct, seemingly magical vision of the world. Your attractiveness finds its source here, in your deeper self—in your sensitive and romantic soul. The way that you sense suffering, for instance, so immediately and keenly, leaves others feeling at times as if you have taken on the troubles of the world; but this awareness comes from within and can be a very dynamic source of inspiration for you in the world.

YOUR INTELLIGENCE

With your simultaneously synthetic and analytic mind, you have the capacity for pure intellectualism. Not only can you grasp a problem as a whole, but you also analyze its details, and can separate cause and effect with great speed. Your memory, especially of emotionally charged events, is very good; and your curiosity has, naturally, a romantic bent.

YOUR EMOTIONAL NATURE

Though you need an enormous amount of love and understanding, it is not so easy for you to demonstrate your own feelings. But they are there, powerful and passionate at one moment, and soothing and calm the next. With the right person, that is, someone whose admiration you have, and whom you trust, you can open and blossom and return her affections. There is, on the other hand, another duality to your emotional nature: should you run away from or should you leap into love? Sometimes you may feel at odds with yourself emotionally for not demonstrating your passion; and at other times, you berate yourself inwardly for falling prey to the flesh. Still, when this duality can be reconciled, you are the best of lovers, able to offer and receive the peacefulness which love brings, as well as its thundering passions.

YOUR HEALTH AND VITALITY

Your health is at its best when you are leading a more or less sedentary life. It is extremely important that you establish a nutritious diet and get enough sleep and fresh air, lest you become troubled by mild depressions and frequent minor illnesses. Your vocal chords are especially delicate—oddly enough, perhaps—and can also be affected by a faulty regimen.

THE SOCIAL YOU

Here again, you are a man of extremes. You can be assertive one day and too timid to leave the house the next. Your subjectivity leads you to interpreting social situations as if you were the central attraction, so if you're not feeling up to that next big party, your shy side will come out. But when you are out, you're in the crowd, declaiming most likely, on such things as crime and punishment, war and peace. You're not exactly a sea of calm, and often your turbulence makes waves at the stodgiest of social functions. Your belief in your own words is contagious, however, and you can stir up an audience to action and passion. At the same time, you are really only looking for your own peace in your dealings with others, so though you may have a lot of friends and acquaintances, most likely there is only a small and devoted circle with whom you are at your relaxed best.

———————

NamePortrait
42
Associated Names

Alaric	Corbin	Jeff	Porter
Alarick	Corby	Jeffers	Ransley
Aleric	Darren	Jefferson	Rich
Alerick	Darrick	Jeffery	Richie
Arsene	Desmond	Jeffrey	Rick
Botolf	Eloi	Jeffry	Rickward
Botolph	Fleming	Jordan	Rickwood
Botolphe	Frewen	Jordane	Ricky
Bowie	Frewin	Jordon	Ricy
Boyce	Galloway	Jorge	Stacey
Brainard	Gallway	Jorin	Stacy
Brainerd	Galway	Joris	Takis
Broc	Geof	Jourdain	Teagan
Brock	Geoff	Jurgen	Tiegan
Brockie	Geoffrey	Kedar	Tormey
Brockley	Geoffroy	Maerwine	Tormy
Brok	Geordie	Marvin	Ulric
Cash	Georg	Marwood	Ulrich
Cassius	George	Merv	Ulrick
Colier	Georges	Mervin	Van
Colis	Georgie	Mervyn	Wayland
Collier	Georgy	Merwin	Woodrow
Collyer	Godfrey	Merwyn	Woodruff
Colyer	Gordie	Pepi	Woodward
Corbet	Gordy	Pepin	Youri
Corbett	Holmes	Peppi	Yuri
Corbie	Igor	Peppin	Yurie

Name Portrait 43

Patient Atlas

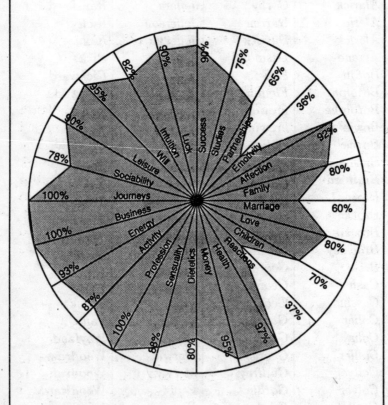

Element : Earth   **Plant** : Honeysuckle
Mineral : Lapis lazuli   **Sign** : Taurus
Animal : Zebu ox   **Color**: Orange

Personality Type:

Patient Atlas

(Associated names – page 293)

BASIC CHARACTER

You are a man of great will and equal patience. Truth and justice are important to you, and in your own calm and unhurried way you see to it that they reign in your world. You are an observer more than a philosopher and cautiously weigh the elements of situations before rendering your judgment or decision. You possess a keen sense of altruism and tend to shun those who are driven by egoism. Your own thoughtful quietness and often lengthy considerations of the world around you makes you a source of inspiration and confidence for others, a role which you gladly accept.

YOUR PSYCHOLOGY

You need structure, or your powerful will can lead to pendulum shifts between obstinacy and impulsiveness. In spite of your rather goal-directed life, you have a tendency to brood and worry about whether all will turn out all right. It will, but only if you can pull yourself away from fretting and get to work on the problem at hand. It is difficult for you to admit your errors, and seldom will you say that you might be wrong about a decision. This is where the obstinacy comes in. Like your animal totem, the ox, you tend to push on in the face of odds to the contrary, until you have proven that you are right. And the energy that you expend in doing this is astronomical!

HOW YOU ACT AND REACT IN THE WORLD

Something might inspire you to action on Monday, and by Thursday, maybe Friday, when everyone else has forgotten it, you're beginning to do something about it. It takes a while to get the ox into the yoke, but once he's there, he'll persevere to the end of the last furrow. Most of the projects you undertake turn out well—you are extremely effective, even if you wouldn't win any speed contests! You excel at tests of strength, both physical strength and strength of the will. Sports is important to you, and it would not at all be surprising to find you on an Olympic team. Professionally, you are drawn to medicine, engineering, agronomy, or livestock breeding—any sort of area where you can apply your practical good sense. You also have an interest in ad hoc philanthropic organizations—as long as they get results—and other socially beneficial activities in which your natural altruism can be put to good use.

YOUR DEEP INTUITIVE PERSONALITY

Your inner voice is strong and guides you especially in detecting the slightest fallacy in an argument and the merest falsity in action. You tend to act on your intuition, which can take you into some rather bizarre situations and encounters.

YOUR INTELLIGENCE

Despite your strong intuition, you do not always see the whole picture at once, for you have a very analytic mind. It is part wild and part disciplined, so the more discipline you exercise intellectually, the more effective your analyses of situations are. Essentially, yours is a practical mind, taking things one step at a time instead of by leaps and bounds. You tend to enlist your memory of past experiences before you make a decision on any matter.

YOUR EMOTIONAL NATURE

You're not exactly a ball of fire, but like your plant totem, the amorous honeysuckle, you can be outward-going in your affections. One question you probably ask yourself a lot where emotions are concerned is: "Will my love help set things right in the world?" You are the axle of any love relationship, though you are slow to show your affections. Yet in spite of your often well concealed emotions, you do need a lot of tenderness and understanding yourself before you can express yourself with confidence and freedom. Your sense of duty impels you to respect your lovers and your few close friends. Discretion is the word that guides your love affairs, though at times they may become impulsive and physically passionate. When you feel that it's all right, you can be the most ardent of lovers, never with a long string of affairs, but with deep and meaningful, selective relationships.

YOUR HEALTH AND VITALITY

With the physical and moral energy you are usually expending, it is a good thing that you are as naturally healthy as you are. Your constitution is strong and your vitality excellent. As long as you get enough fresh air and sleep, relaxation and exercise, you will remain in good health. Your weakness is in your bone structure, especially the spinal column, so exercises should be guided with this in mind.

THE SOCIAL YOU

The conventional social relationships are your favorite rather than the big party or the impromptu celebration. After all, what's to celebrate, when so much in the world needs righting? It would not be surprising to hear you speak of "social obligations," for in a way, that is what your social life is—a debt to be paid out of politeness. You're at your best when you are with your beloved family or your few close friends. Much of your social life revolves around them—and a number of philanthropic organizations to which you no doubt belong. If you're not up on the latest social etiquette, that's no problem, for what you are up on is the right way to make the world a better place, and as long as that is the concern, you will throw yourself into things and forget about that big party—the height of idle folly!—down the street.

———————

NamePortrait
43
Associated Names

Annibal	Frazier	Gerardin	Magnus
Arundel	Gaetan	Gerhardt	Ridge
Baldemar	Gail	Gerhart	Ridgeway
Bing	Gale	Gerrard	Ridgley
Brook	Garett	Gerry	Romeo
Brooke	Garey	Glen	Sampsi
Brooks	Gari	Glendon	Samsi
Byram	Garrard	Glenn	Sancho
Byrom	Garret	Glyn	Selwin
Cavell	Garrett	Glynn	Selwyn
Elsdon	Garrick	Grant	Skeat
Elston	Garrie	Harman	Skeet
Ermin	Garritt	Harmon	Skeeter
Florent	Garroth	Herm	Skeets
Florentin	Garry	Herman	Varian
Florian	Garth	Hermann	Whitman
Flory	Gary	Hermie	Whitmore
Fraser	Gayle	Hermon	Wilmer
Frasier	Gearard	Judicael	Wilmot
Frazer	Gerard	Lilian	Wilmur

Name Portrait 44

Soul of the Winds

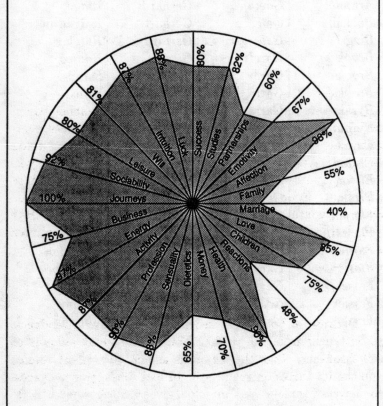

Element : Air **Plant** : Aspen

Mineral : Platinum **Sign** : Gemini

Animal : Sea gull **Color** : Violet

Personality Type:

Soul of the Winds

(Associated names – page 299)

BASIC CHARACTER

You have intense emotions and a keen imagination, which are not always reflected in your actions. Like your totem animal, the sea gull, you would just as soon allow the winds to take you where they will. And also like the gull, you will not land unless you know that there is something stable underfoot. Your high level of energy often results in a sensitive nervousness, as you are not the quickest to act. But your lofty morality and sometimes almost painful sensitivity see you through the worst of times—and those come to you rarely enough.

YOUR PSYCHOLOGY

Because of your great sensitivity, you have a tendency to withdraw from the world. You need a great amount of self-assurance. Like the timorous aspen, your plant totem, you cannot thrive on rough soil. In bad times, you are prone to nervous anxiety and may be given to following others' propositions against your own better judgment. It's not that you are not assertive; it's just that it is easier, when your self-confidence is low, to follow the current rather than to put up a good struggle. But as long as you have structure and purpose in your life, your psychological problems will be at a minimum, and your otherwise fluctuating will can show itself strongly as a guiding force.

HOW YOU ACT AND REACT IN THE WORLD

Such changeability! You can adapt to a new situation most readily—especially when the old one becomes too intolerable to stand any more. You will probably have a history of careers by midlife—musician to salesman, international delegate to missionary. You like to move around, to have your outer life reflect your rich imagination. Rare is the Guy who owns his own home; you are more likely to be a renter, and a hotel is going to be your residence more than once in life. Your interests are continually moving; and you probably have several circles of old friends. In general, you get very good results from jobs which you enjoy doing; you are very capable of committing yourself heart and soul to a carefully selected project. But it must suit your easily shifted temperament and your fine sensitivity. If it does not, you do not hesitate to say a very polite but quite firm "no," and let the winds carry you to the next port of call.

YOUR DEEP INTUITIVE PERSONALITY

Your fertile imagination and attractive inner self are the source of much of your energy and inspiration. It is to your intuition that you turn, rather than to any authority figure, for advice and guidance. In this way, you are your own best friend. Still, your active intuition can at times reinforce your anxieties when it comes to questions about your own self-worth. Sometimes it is telling you to go when outward circumstances suggest that you should stay, or to withdraw when others are telling you to be aggressive. In general, of course, you can rely on your intuition as long as you do not fall into the trap of dwelling solely in it.

YOUR INTELLIGENCE

Because you have a holistic intellect, you are resilient, able to see at a glance the full extent of any situation or problem. You rarely trouble yourself with details—why bother, when the picture is there, complete, before you? Much of your intense energy is spent here, in your intellect, and you carefully consider everything before you decide whether it is worth your while to participate. You have an engaging way of expressing your ideas and an uncanny ability to generalize and abstract whole ideological worlds from the merest of facts. Your ideas are fluid and can be applied in many directions at once; and, thanks to your clever imagination, you are able to do just that, in words if not always in deeds.

YOUR EMOTIONAL NATURE

You seem sometimes to be two different people. One moment, you are the ardent, expressive lover, and the next, the shy, quiet type. You need a lot of reassurance. You are prone to make compromises when it comes to your emotions, but if the winds shift, you are bound to be following their drift. For a man of such strong emotions, you have trouble making up your mind about love, even when it's staring you in the face. But no real problem: during one of those bursts of sexuality and affection, the breeze is most likely to bring the right ship your way, and you can perch there safely, despite all the intervening if's, and's, and but's while you circle her deck as she lays anchor. In other words, you're more likely to be seduced than to seduce.

YOUR HEALTH AND VITALITY

You have a robust constitution and good health—as long as you go easy on the alcohol and stimulants. If you are bored and disillusion has set in, you may be stricken with a variety of ailments and fatigue. Since you are always reaching for the heights of sensitive experiences, you may be prone to using hallucinogens: beware of abusing them, as they may tempt you away from the quiet and calm regimen which is a necessity for maintaining your health. Especially sensitive are your eyes and nervous system.

THE SOCIAL YOU

Here, as in most areas, you tend to vacillate. You might be open to a big fete one day and closed to it the next. In general, you like entertainment that is in style. The most recent club, the latest fashion can draw you out. You tend to be a bit possessive about your friends—whether it's the "old crowd" or the newest one—and like to plan parties to which all your friends can come and mingle. (You, of course, might take it into your head to split before the evening is out!) Generally, you have remarkable success socially, despite your neither-here-nor-there attitude. Your closest friends are those who are aware of and attentive to your great sensitivity and feelings.

NamePortrait
44
Associated Names

Ashby	Cody	Gustave	Summer
Athanase	Corwen	Gustavos	Sumner
Athanasius	Corwin	Gustavus	Tanguy
Barrie	Cosimo	Gustof	Tudal
Barris	Cosme	Guy	Upton
Barry	Cosmo	Guyon	Valdemar
Baruch	Doyle	Howland	Valdimar
Bo	Enguerran	Langworth	Walcott
Brough	Gatien	Morley	Waldemar
Brougher	Guido	Osgood	Waldemer
Burr	Gus	Quillan	Wiatt
Clark	Gustaf	Quillon	Wyatt
Clarke	Gustav	Ralston	

Name Portrait 45

Perfect Beauty

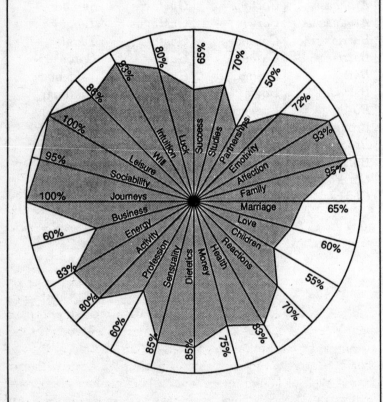

Element : Air   **Plant** : Orchid

Mineral : Jade   **Sign** : Gemini

Animal : Codfish   **Color** : Yellow

Personality Type:

Perfect Beauty

(Associated names – page 304)

BASIC CHARACTER

It is almost as if you are ruled by your emotions, so sentimental as you get over the flowering of a rose, the brushstroke on a Renaissance painting, a sweet musical refrain. You are a very emotional person at heart, though you have the capacity to distance yourself from the world and assume a mask of regality. Still, everything touches you and affects you. You have an innate sense of poetry, of beauty and elegance. Like your totem plant, the orchid, you are fragile and need to have your tenderness returned in order to thrive.

YOUR PSYCHOLOGY

Though you often and justifiably rely upon your beauty and charm to get you through, you have a tendency to postpone things. Your highly sentimental nature runs you the risk of carrying you into fantasy instead of into action in the real world. You're a contrary sort of person who can withdraw into a shell of haughtiness, especially if you are threatened by failure. Basically, you are an introvert and view the world subjectively, hence your tendency to make hasty decisions. But, even withdrawn and viewing the world from your private tower, you can rely on your astonishing will power to overcome adverse situations. Even so, you had better keep an eye on that powerful will, or it can turn to stubbornness, not allowing you to forget another's transgression. You are as slow to forgive as you are quick to anger.

HOW YOU ACT AND REACT IN THE WORLD

You have a need for discipline which, for you, just doesn't come with all the other gifts nature gives you. But once you have established a structure, you can be a good student, especially if your studies have to do with tradition—the classics, art, or history. You have a great appreciation for wealth and luxury, and tend to prefer careers in which there is a side of glamor. You would be well suited to a career in the arts or in the beauty trade. Public relations or fashion design are other areas compatible to your nature. You're certainly not the sort of woman who will be content on the assembly line; independence is very important for you and such routine work would be offensive to your fine sensibilities. But again, those very sensibilities are prone to take you into fantasy, and you may find that you've chosen a career not so much out of interest in the work itself as out of the glamorous world which it conjured for you in your daydreams.

YOUR DEEP INTUITIVE PERSONALITY

What makes you so enchantingly beautiful is your powerful intuition. It is so effective that it seems at times as if you have the gift of prophecy. This is the seat of your inspiration and, many times, of the way you act in the world. Your inner self lends you a sort of other-worldliness which people find charming and irresistibly attractive.

YOUR INTELLIGENCE

The last thing you're going to bother yourself with is details. Your mind is synthetic—that is, holistic. You see a situation or a problem all at once, as a complete picture. Your intellect functions in tandem with your intuition, so you really don't have much use for analysis; in fact, that sort of intellectualism bores you no end. But it also means that you need to work extra hard to establish an inner discipline for following through on projects and studies. Your curiosity is intense, and your verbal gifts splendid.

YOUR EMOTIONAL NATURE

Your emotions are boundless. Affection and love are the highest on your list of life's priorities, though this side of life might be a bit tumultuous for you. It's sort of like riding a roller coaster, going through your ups and downs of emotions. You need a lot of tenderness and affection, which you can return twofold. You also need a certain amount of security, at least ultimately, for like your animal totem, the codfish, you may like the deep water but you stay close to shore. This, plus your taste for comfort, might lead you to a permanent relationship with an older man—someone who can give you the stability you so need. In the meantime (and, perhaps, even after) you will be about, flirting and charming hosts of male admirers, not exactly flitting from one affair to the next, but waxing and waning through them.

YOUR HEALTH AND VITALITY

You have a fragile constitution, and a strict regimen is essential for your good health. Without it, you might be plagued by a variety of minor stomach ailments. Your acute sensitivity makes you prone to certain psychosomatic illnesses, but nothing major. You must watch your sugar intake and your posture. Daily walks should be part of your regimen in order to prevent possible trouble with your spine.

THE SOCIAL YOU

Charming and graceful, you enjoy the company of others and often consider your friends as an indispensable part of your life. You can be a dazzling hostess, especially at a ceremonious affair. There is something in you that craves ritual and ceremony; most of your entertaining is likely to be rather formal and traditional. Undoubtedly, there are more men than women in your close circle of friends. You can keep a conversation going with wit and the most evocative questions, plus a dash of sexual innuendo if need be. You are at your social best when you are at your husband's or lover's side, but even alone your beauty lights up the room and draws others out.

Ab	*Blanchette*	*Ela*	*Gale*
Abbey	*Blandine*	*Elaine*	*Gayl*
Abbie	*Blanka*	*Elane*	*Gayle*
Abby	*Blasia*	*Elani*	*Gelasia*
Abella	*Blinne*	*Elanie*	*Gelasie*
Abigail	*Blinnie*	*Eleanor*	*Gisela*
Aileen	*Bluinse*	*Eleanore*	*Gisele*
Aisleen	*Bona*	*Elena*	*Gisella*
Aleen	*Bonita*	*Elene*	*Giselle*
Alene	*Bonne*	*Eleni*	*Guida*
Alina	*Bonnie*	*Elenie*	*Helen*
Aline	*Branca*	*Elenor*	*Helena*
Amedee	*Buena*	*Elenora*	*Helene*
Anjali	*Buona*	*Elenore*	*Heliena*
Annonciade	*Cherida*	*Elina*	*Ileana*
Annunciata	*Cleo*	*Elinor*	*Ileane*
Bab	*Cleopatra*	*Elinora*	*Ilena*
Babb	*Delcine*	*Elinore*	*Ilene*
Babette	*Docie*	*Ella*	*Iline*
Bar	*Doxie*	*Ellen*	*Illeana*
Barbara	*Doxy*	*Ellene*	*Illene*
Barberine	*Dulce*	*Ellenita*	*Illona*
Barbette	*Dulcea*	*Ellie*	*Illone*
Barbie	*Dulcia*	*Ellyn*	*Ilona*
Barbra	*Dulciana*	*Elna*	*Isleen*
Bas	*Dulcibella*	*Elnna*	*Laini*
Bellance	*Dulcibelle*	*Eudocia*	*Lainie*
Bianca	*Dulcie*	*Eudosia*	*Lana*
Blanca	*Dulcine*	*Eudoxia*	*Lena*
Blanch	*Dulcinea*	*Gael*	*Lenora*
Blanche	*Eileen*	*Gail*	*Leona*

Associated Names (cont.)

Leonora	Mahalia	Nellwyn	Pythia
Leonore	Mathurine	Nelly	Querida
Leora	Milene	Nila	Quiterie
Lesbia	Mylene	Nita	Samara
Lina	Nela	Nora	Spring
Lora	Nell	Norah	Venetia
Mahala	Nella	Novak	
Mahalah	Nellie	Pythea	

Name Portrait 46

Faithful Queen

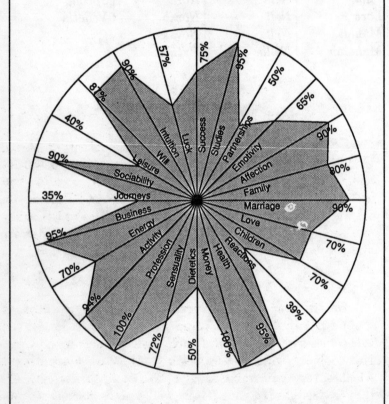

Element : Air   **Plant** : Grapevine

Mineral : Sapphire   **Sign** : Libra

Animal : Reindeer   **Color** : Red

Personality Type:

Faithful Queen

(Associated names – page 310)

BASIC CHARACTER

Like your animal totem, the regal reindeer, symbol of purity and elevation, you possess a quiet, unimposing dignity. Graceful and attractive, your often intense activity is guided by your firm moral code which also lends you a refinement and a modesty which are rare qualities in today's world. You are loyal to friends and expect loyalty in return. Though you are very emotional and sensitive, you tend toward timidity and secretiveness, which add to the impression of majesty and aristocracy.

YOUR PSYCHOLOGY

Despite your self-confidence, you tend to become anxious if you are forced to get involved with people and situations; this comes from your natural introversion. You assume a surface coolness, which oftentimes is a protective mask behind which a very vulnerable spirit is trembling like a leaf. Although you have a strong will, you tend to conceal it; you would rather perish than impose yourself on anyone. Vulgar people and disloyal friends are anathema to you and will feel the icy wind of your contempt. Your own emotional nature is very strong but sometimes conflicts with your stern moral code, and you may tend to sublimate your sexual desires into an aristocratic aloofness. You need support in order to flourish—like your totem plant the grapevine.

HOW YOU ACT AND REACT IN THE WORLD

Because of your sense of duty, you have a practical approach to the world. Most likely, you undertake to study something not so much out of an intellectual drive as out of your need to know the why's and wherefore's of something so that you can apply it to your life. You can be either a very loyal and contributing wife and mother, or a dedicated professional in a career which demands a certain cool-headedness and high principles. Law and psychiatry are two fields to which you are very well suited; you would also find fulfillment in any of the service industries. You can throw yourself into your work, and at times it might seem as if work overwhelms you. You are not the sort of person who leaves the job at five and picks it up again in the morning.

YOUR DEEP INTUITIVE PERSONALITY

You have a powerful intuition, which borders on foresight, especially when it comes to anticipating the pattern of your life. Your premonitory gifts can be somewhat intimidating. With so highly refined an inner voice, it is no wonder that people find you as attractive as they do. There is a possibility that your gifts in this realm can lead to mysticism or religious endeavors.

YOUR INTELLIGENCE

With your quick mind, you are able to see the whole of a problem or situation immediately and maintain a broad perspective. Rather than deal with things by details, you see the whole picture. You are excellent at drawing up plans for projects, but because of your way of overlooking details, do not like to be troubled putting plans into action. It is necessary for you to exert extra intellectual discipline to follow things through.

YOUR EMOTIONAL NATURE

Prudence and faithfulness rule your otherwise highly charged emotions. You are slow to acknowledge your emotions, but once you do, you form long-lasting attachments. Though you are a very sensual woman, you are selective. Far be it from you to have a string of lovers! Instead, you will spend your time deciding which qualities are essential to your lover and then measure all potential mates by this very strict portrait. It's not that you idealize a perfect lover; but long before you meet the man who can capture your heart, you will know what sort of traits he must have, and your decision will be clear-headed and based on the future. Once in a relationship, you are loyal to the end; your faith in your love is deep and rich, and once it is established you feel free to express your great sensuality.

YOUR HEALTH AND VITALITY

Normally, your health is excellent. You possess great stamina and are able to go about the business of life without physical complaints. However, it is important that you get enough sleep, as you do not resist fatigue very well. Your weaknesses are in your blood system and in the endocrine glands.

THE SOCIAL YOU

Friendships are precious to you, and you entertain your friends with style. The more popular amusements put you off; your way of entertaining is more formal—the large sit-down dinner, for example, or the theatre or concerts. You are very attractive socially, and people tend to be drawn to you. As in your love relationship, you are a faithful friend, able to sacrifice for someone close to you. There is nothing vulgar in your social life; loud and ostentatious people turn you off. The last thing you would do would be to impose your opinions on anyone else. With your strong will and your high moral standards, you are able to overcome social difficulties. These qualities also prevent you from becoming egotistical. In all, your quiet dignity and abiding trust in your friends provide you with a rich and rewarding social life.

NamePortrait
46
Associated Names

Adamina	Carlotta	Etty	Josette
Addie	Caro	Eurica	Josiane
Addy	Carol	Fifi	Josie
Amber	Carola	Githa	Juli
Ambrosia	Carole	Gytha	Julia
Ambrosina	Carolina	Harriet	Juliana
Ambrosine	Caroline	Harriette	Juliane
Beula	Carrie	Harriot	Julianna
Beulah	Charla	Harriotte	Julianne
Biddie	Charleen	Hattie	Julie
Biddy	Charlene	Hatty	Julienne
Breita	Charlie	Henrietta	Juliet
Bride	Charline	Henriette	Julietta
Bridey	Charlotta	Henrika	Juliette
Bridget	Charlotte	Hester	Julina
Bridie	Charyl	Hesther	Juline
Brie	Cher	Hettie	Karla
'Brieta	Cheri	Hetty	Kjersti
Brietta	Cherida	Hildemar	Kjerstie
Brigette	Cherie	Idonia	Levina
Brigid	Cherry	Idonie	Lina
Brigida	Cheryl	Iduna	Line
Brigit	Durene	Jill	Lotta
Brigitte	Eiric	Jo	Lotti
Brita	Eister	Joette	Lottie
Brydie	Enrica	Joletta	Lotty
Capucine	Essa	Josepha	Lupe
Carla	Essie	Josephe	Mina
Carlie	Esther	Josephina	Mosella
Carline	Etta	Josephine	Moselle
Carlita	Ettie	Josetta	Mozel

Associated Names (cont.)

Mozella	Sadey	Sibbie	Velika
Mozelle	Sadie	Sibby	Win
Nada	Sadye	Sibel	Winifred
Nadege	Sal	Sibell	Winifreida
Nadette	Salaidh	Sibella	Winifrid
Nadia	Sallie	Sibie	Winifrida
Nadine	Sally	Sibilla	Winifrieda
Netta	Sara	Sibille	Winnie
Nima	Sarah	Sibyl	Winny
Nina	Sarene	Sibylle	Wyne
Nineta	Sarette	Sile	Wynne
Ninetta	Sari	Sileas	Yosepha
Ninette	Sarine	Sorcha	Yusepha
Ninon	Sarita	Sybella	Zada
Oprah	Sharie	Sybil	Zara
Ordelia	Sharleen	Sybille	Zarah
Ordella	Sharlene	Sybyl	Zaria
Pepita	Sharline	Tabbie	Zona
Porcia	Sheree	Tabby	Zora
Portia	Sherri	Tabitha	Zorah
Rilla	Sherrie	Tabithe	Zorana
Rille	Sherry	Tacita	Zorina
Rillete	Sheryl	Tacitah	Zorine
Sadella	Sib	Velica	

Name Portrait 47

Ardent Lover

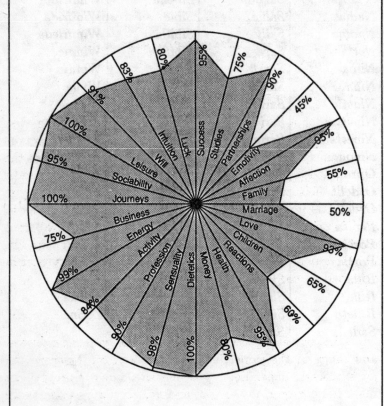

Element : Earth **Plant** : Orange tree
Mineral : Alabaster **Sign** : Capricorn
Animal : Mountain goat **Color** : Violet

Personality Type:

Ardent Lover

(Associated names – page 317)

BASIC CHARACTER

Even though your feet are usually on the ground, you prefer the higher places, much like your animal totem, the mountain goat. At once stable and quick to act, you're the sure-footed type, ready to leap to the next height or after the next of life's opportunities. There's almost no keeping you down! You possess a remarkable self-confidence which allows you, in spite of your traditional values, to be quite tolerant of others' lifestyles. Though you are by nature a bit secretive about your life, there is the speechifier and the storyteller in you, and an engaging, warm sense of humor.

YOUR PSYCHOLOGY

Like your plant totem, the orange tree, you can be sweet and tangy at the same time. You're both an introvert and an extrovert, depending upon the situation. Your private inner life is important to you, and unless you have the space to enjoy it, you can become quite irascible and headstrong. Anxieties about other people tend to put you into a protective shell of irony. You possess a powerful, dominating will, but at times it can degenerate into stubbornness or flare up into a quick temper. In all, though, you are an even-tempered sort of person as long as the plateaus of life are always taking you higher.

HOW YOU ACT AND REACT IN THE WORLD

You have a quick wit, and a penchant for giving long, flowery speeches. There is an ardent manner about you, especially around potential lovers, and it can carry over into your work. But though you are quick to make career choices, you are not as quick to act on those decisions. You can be wary of "traps" and therefore tend to act cautiously. Still, your reactions are very strong and very quick. You can be the provocateur in a sensitive situation as often as not. Your independence is important to you, and in general you dislike working for other people. You would do well in a business which you owned, or as a mining engineer or a farmer. Careers that offer you contact with the earth are the best. As a doctor with a small country practice or as a veterinarian, you could also develop your potentials. Your good nature and your natural story-telling talent go far toward smoothing over any problems with people, both on the job and in general.

YOUR DEEP INTUITIVE PERSONALITY

Your intuition takes the form of common sense, and is finely attuned to people and situations. This is the source of your self-confidence and your occasional aggressiveness with members of the opposite sex. A good love to you is good sense, after all.

YOUR INTELLIGENCE

With your quick, synthetic mind, you can look at any problem and see its solution at once. You do not focus on details but view things holistically, seeing the major lines, as it were, instead of the individual points. Your memory is good and your curiosity alert, both of which add useful dimensions to your intellect.

YOUR EMOTIONAL NATURE

It might strike your many lovers as odd, but you are rather possessive. But it's a one-way possession: "You are mine," but not "I am yours"! You need a lot of love and affection, both of which help establish your sense of security, and with the right person, you can return it in abundance. Though there is certainly the playboy in you, you hate to live alone; and even if you do have your own hideaway to retreat to, you no doubt share living quarters with at least one lover. At any rate, you're not the type to slip out of your lover's house before morning. Your sex life probably began quite early and will remain high on your list of priorities. You are a demanding lover as well and do not conceal your sexual aims nearly as much as you sometimes do your deeper emotions. Because you are, at heart, a sensitive and, ironically, somewhat shy fellow emotionally, you sometimes withdraw from serious emotional commitments. Nonetheless, your needs for physical comfort and emotional security will eventually lead you to a stable home life, where the sharper edges of those peaks and valleys will be somewhat refined.

YOUR HEALTH AND VITALITY

You have remarkably good stamina and, in general, excellent health. It seems as if you have some secret pact with the earth which furnishes you your great vitality. But you do need plenty of sleep—afternoon naps are a good idea. You have a tendency to indulge a bit too much in food and drink which may cause liver problems or trouble in your digestive system. You should be especially wary of taking too many antibiotics.

THE SOCIAL YOU

You are witty, charming, and a pleasant companion. One of your favorite ways to pass an evening is to have dinner with a group of friends. Though your love life is not lacking, you can at times be a bit overaggressive when it comes to women, but there is something engaging and irresistible in the way you say, "Hi, will you go home with me, and by the way, what's your name?" That's probably because you have an uncanny ability to work your way out of the thorniest situations. You have very good luck socially, especially in your middle years. And in all, you manage to achieve the modest comforting success you desire and usually have the wisdom to avoid any exhausting pursuit for professional glory. Comfort, a good love life, and a circle of mutually devoted friends are the most important things to you.

NamePortrait
47
Associated Names

Adalbert	Eanruig	Henri	Syd
Adelbert	Enrique	Henrik	Sydney
Amasa	Farold	Henry	Symphorien
Anscom	Farr	Hercule	Tarik
Anscomb	Farrell	Hercules	Tristam
Ari	Farris	Meredith	Tristan
Arnald	Ferris	Meredydd	Tristen
Arnaud	Hal	Meredyth	Tristin
Arne	Hamlin	Merideth	Webb
Arnie	Hank	Meridith	Webber
Arno	Hanraoi	Meridyth	Weber
Arnold	Harry	Merrie	Webley
Arnould	Heinrich	Merry	Webster
Birtle	Heinrick	Sid	Zadok
Dylan	Hendrick	Sidney	Zaloc

Name Portrait 48

Virile Charmer

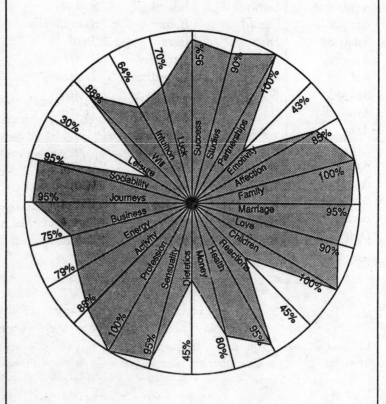

Element : Earth   **Plant** : Ivy

Mineral : Turquoise   **Sign** : Capricorn

Animal : Cobra   **Color** : Violet

Personality Type:

Virile Charmer

(Associated names – page 322)

BASIC CHARACTER

It is important for you to have broad contact with the world. There is much of the adventurer in you but without the impulsiveness that usually comes with a man of adventure. Your sound principles and respect for tradition, as well as your natural prudence and refinement, prevent you from taking too many risks in the world. You are stable but excitable, charming, and assertive. Like your animal totem, the cobra, you dwell in security, but climb up and out to take a look at the world—usually enchanting those you meet in the process.

YOUR PSYCHOLOGY

Despite your high principles you do not always act according to them, and this at times causes you problems. Your natural extroversion can then lead you into turbulence and anxiety. There is a combative side to you, which shows itself in the way that you sometimes say what you think with no regard for the feelings of others. Still, you are quite objective in the way you see things. But your possessiveness sometimes results in your entwining yourself around an idea and not letting go—holding on out of stubbornness as if its acceptance by the world meant your life—not unlike your totem plant, the ivy. Though you have a great deal of natural self-confidence, you are terribly sensitive to failure, and may tend to brood over minor failings when the best thing to do is to get on with things. Your will power is good, even if it isn't a dynamo; you tend to become lethargic if you're not clinging to one of your opinions in the face of odds.

HOW YOU ACT AND REACT IN THE WORLD

It is easy for you to make friends; indeed, you probably have more friends than most people, and rarely do you make a distinction between business associates and friends. You have to live in an animated environment, one which will allow you to tell and play your jokes. Success is important to you, and your choice of career is one of the biggest decisions in your life. It must not only meet your needs for gregariousness and activity, but must assure you some success, a comfortable life, and interesting social connections. But because of your natural prudency, you will be most attracted to stable positions. As a director of a government agency, or as a businessman, all these variables would be covered. Chances are, too, that you might choose a military career. Retirement benefits will weigh heavily in making job choices.

YOUR DEEP INTUITIVE PERSONALITY

You have a fertile imagination, and this is the source of much of your vitality and your fabulous sense of humor. Although you do not always heed your inner voices, it is your intuition that is the source of much of your attractiveness and virility, drawing people to you. It might be difficult for you to admit to this softer side of yourself, but it is there, as your keen imagination shows.

YOUR INTELLIGENCE

One of your most important assets is your analytic mind. With amazing speed, you can analyze and grasp the importance of details in any situation. Aided by your strong curiosity and your sense of directedness, your intellectual powers can at times be awesome.

YOUR EMOTIONAL NATURE

You're a charmer emotionally and sexually. In fact, sometimes you might even be a bit too aggressive when it comes to expressing how you feel about someone. Your passions must be translated immediately into actions—it seems that this is where you expend a great part of your energy. When we said, "expressing how you feel," we did not mean verbal expression. You're not one to write love sonnets on the backs of dance programs; you'll act them out instead. Once married, you have a great loyalty to your mate and family, emotionally and sensually.

YOUR HEALTH AND VITALITY

Vitality like yours is rare; you have an inner compulsion to be physically active. It would be a good idea to plan some sort of exercise regimen to make up for what is very likely a rather sedentary professional life. Some sort of outdoor life is necessary for the continuance of your naturally good health, or you might tend to become nervous. Your weak point is in your bone structure; posture must be watched. With your sometimes turbulent disposition, you will have to be careful of accidents.

THE SOCIAL YOU

You are extremely sociable, and to hear people talk, you would think you had guests every evening. Your way of entertaining is to have everyone over on Sunday. You like hunting, dancing, and especially, unannounced parties. These kinds of social activities go with your life style, as do social affairs connected with your career. You have very strong likes and dislikes, though your morality adjusts to the event. You feel a great love and closeness for your family, and enjoy doing things with them, though you do not let a close family life interfere with your independence. Your combination of luck and shrewdness makes you a social success.

NamePortrait
48
Associated Names

Adriel	Chaunceller	Garnock	Kelley
Ahearn	Chauncey	Hearn	Kelly
Aherin	Denton	Hearne	Leal
Ahern	Denver	Hugh	Loyal
Aherne	Desire	Hughie	Noah
Borden	Ebbie	Hughy	Noe
Boyne	Eben	Hugo	Wendel
Chance	Ebenezer	Hugues	Wendell
Chanceller	Elwood	Jess	Wetherall
Chancellor	Fitzhugh	Jesse	Wetherell
Chancey	Flinn	Josue	Wetherill
Chaunce	Flint	Kell	Wetherly
Chaunceler	Flynn	Keller	Yancy

Name Portrait 49

Dazzling Seductress

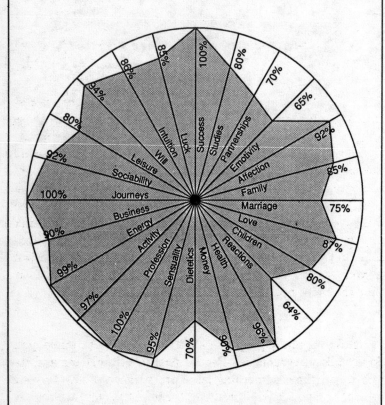

Element : Fire **Plant** : Rose bush

Mineral : Tin **Sign** : Aries

Animal : Magpie **Color** : Blue

Personality Type:

Dazzling Seductress

(Associated names – page 329)

BASIC CHARACTER

You are energetic, idealistic, and captivatingly expressive. Both in word and deed you are able to mesmerize those around you; and like your plant totem, the rose bush, your attractiveness is not vulnerable but protected by much-needed thorns of reality. But despite your sense of realism you are a very emotional woman, easily stimulated to action when your feelings are at stake. Your special animal totem is the talkative magpie: you are able to put what you feel and think into words with no effort. This quality is one of the main reasons that you are the center of your world. Others are drawn to you—and if you want them in your circle you'll see to it that they join up!

YOUR PSYCHOLOGY

However many people would like to be in your circle, you do not allow everyone in. People must be stimulating and interesting or have something fascinating to contribute to your own life or you can do without them. Still, you are an extrovert by nature, and an active one, able to churn up the air around you. At times, you may be a bit too active for your own good. You are tremendously goal-oriented in all you do, and have a penchant for collecting things—not unlike the magpie's habit of hoarding sometimes useless objects. You might occasionally suffer from inner conflicts which arise from your paradoxical idealistic and materialistic sides. But usually, as long as everything you are doing is aimed at a goal, your remarkably strong will can overcome your inner strife.

HOW YOU ACT AND REACT IN THE WORLD

You like to be in control of situations, which means that you make a better boss than you do a worker. There is in you a marvelous ability to master problems, and you are at your best when you are working toward a visible end. You were probably a very good student and not at all a "partying coed." Education is a means to an end, and you undoubtedly identified just what those ends were quite early on in life. You would make an excellent politician or courtroom lawyer, or a chief executive officer in a large corporation. Journalism and acting are two other career choices for which you are very well suited. Whatever your occupation, it absorbs you, and you're just not going to be a happy person unless you feel that you are being successful in your career. You act and react on a level of intensity that is positively stunning. There is a lot of the performer in you. Combine all those qualities, and it wouldn't be at all surprising to find you at the lead of a social or political cause—for your drive and will to succeed and surpass others makes you a natural.

YOUR DEEP INTUITIVE PERSONALITY

Your refined intuitive sense is a very powerful part of your dazzling charm. You are able to use your inner voice to great effect and can rely upon it in understanding other people. At times, you might be tempted to listen to your own intuition more than to the opinions of your friends.

YOUR INTELLIGENCE

With your powerful intuition and your analytic mind, you have a very effective intellect. Nothing gets past you. You can see the most minute details of any situation and then know, almost at once, just how it fits in and what part it is playing. You are witty and fascinating when you speak and use your mind in clever ways. You love to plan things from beginning to end, and with your wit and verbal gifts, you can get up an army of volunteers to carry out a project.

YOUR EMOTIONAL NATURE

Along with your high-powered energy and wit comes a supercharged emotional nature, but one that is protective. You are possessive, and not inclined to offer your affections unless you are sure that they will be returned twofold. Still, you are adaptable emotionally and able to adjust yourself to what is probably a rather tumultuous love life. You can also adjust your lifestyle to your current lover, even though it is yourself and not him whom you believe in ultimately. You are charming and irresistible to most men and bound to have a trail of admirers. You adore flirting—it's one of your best ways of relating to the opposite sex. Sexually, you're something of a volcano—able to remain dormant for long periods but most unstoppable once you do erupt. Don't be amazed at yourself if you find that, as life goes on, you have more than one love affair going. It's only natural for you with your sparkling seductiveness and charms.

YOUR HEALTH AND VITALITY

As long as life is going well for you, and you are doing well in your social and professional life, you will have no problems with your health. You have a remarkably sturdy constitution. But in bad times your health can be affected. Both your heart and your hands are potential trouble areas, so regular checkups are a necessity for you.

THE SOCIAL YOU

You have the uncanny ability to transform the most casual of get-togethers into a grand occasion. You're a natural hostess, with your vitality and enthusiasm, and can draw out the most wilting of wall flowers. It's almost impossible to refuse an invitation from you, so persuasive and intriguing are your ways of getting a party together. You have a wonderful sense of friendship, though at times it borders on the over idealistic; you are this or that cause or ideal. Still, you are unflinchingly loyal. It's astonishing how courageous you can be in the face of life's worst odds; you're rarely thwarted by disappointments. With your good luck and your knack for knowing how to use it and make the best of it, you have a splendid chance of success in whatever you do.

NamePortrait
49
Associated Names

Alberga	Elrica	Jacquine	Mabel
Areta	Gazella	Jacquotte	Maeve
Arete	Geranium	Jamesina	Mave
Aretta	Gill	Jamie	Mavis
Arette	Gillian	Jill	Maybelle
Bathilda	Gillie	Jillian	Meave
Bathilde	Heather	Jillie	Mitra
Batilda	Hedda	Kalypso	Page
Batilde	Hildreta	Kelda	Paige
Callula	Hildreth	Kelly	Pyrena
Calypso	Hildretha	Kelvina	Pyrenia
Cindy	Jackeline	Kevin	Septima
Clytie	Jackelyn	Lene	Tangerine
Cyn	Jacketta	Leneta	Thordia
Cynth	Jackie	Lenetta	Thordie
Cynthia	Jacky	Lenis	Thordis
Cynthie	Jacoba	Lenita	Ulrica
Darcie	Jacobina	Lenos	Volante
Eadwina	Jacobine	Lenta	Win
Eadwine	Jacqueleine	Loella	Wina
Edina	Jacqueline	Louella	Winne
Edine	Jacquelyn	Luella	Winnie
Edwina	Jacquetta	Luelle	Winny
Edwine	Jacquette	Mab	

Name Portrait 50

The Firebrand

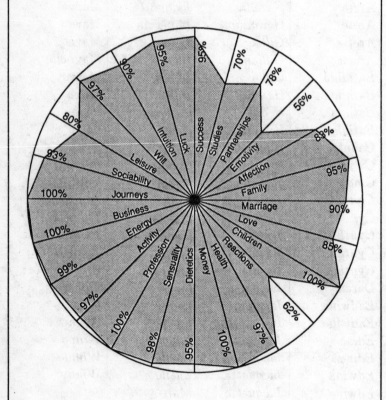

Element : Fire

Mineral : Carbuncle

Animal : Stag

Plant : Box-wood tree

Sign : Aries

Color : Red

Personality Type:

The Firebrand

(Associated names – page 334)

BASIC CHARACTER

You have a noble nature and a character of strength and substance. You tend to be a man of judgment with a sense of purpose that can sometimes be too ideal. At moments you are impatient and determined to move forward, regardless of the cost to others. Your sensibilities often favor group interests far more than individual needs.

YOUR PSYCHOLOGY

You are an extrovert who like the stag, your totem animal, is very much at home in the outside world. You are clever, highly confident, and determined to impress your personal power on everyone around you. Your expectations and perspectives are subjective and, in the extreme, entirely idiosyncratic. Because of your stubborn nature, it is usually easier to manipulate you than to convince you. At the same time, you can influence people persuasively and for the good of all lead a group of the most intelligent thinkers. Your personal position is usually that of a protestor, and your opponents are problems that are not philosophically ideal. You believe both in possibility and in the convictions far beyond the conceptual, and frustration only heightens the challenge of the chase.

HOW YOU ACT AND REACT IN THE WORLD

Ceaseless activity flows from you and it seems that the more you take on, the greater your well-being. Most likely even as a student you were a group leader. You set very high goals and tirelessly pursue your ideals. You tend to listen only to your own voice and seldom take advice, even when it is constructive. You are the sort of self-made man who likes to live life precisely as it suits you. In regard to your freedom you cannot be limited or confined. Yet at the same time, you can easily adapt to conditions of all kinds and it is one of your particularly strong points.

YOUR DEEP INTUITIVE PERSONALITY

You have a fertile imagination and a strong intuition on which you often depend. Because of these qualities your leadership is often inspired and your appeal persuasive, powerful, and very convincing.

YOUR INTELLIGENCE

You have an incisive intelligence that penetrates to the point and puts people in their places quite remarkably. You can synthesize situations and comprehend conditions at a glance. Your memory is good and your desire to understand, exceptional. In terms of career, you are strongly suited for such professions as politics, radio and television, piloting, salesmanship, or athletics.

YOUR EMOTIONAL NATURE

You are strongly possessive and tend to have an all-or-nothing personality. You especially like to dedicate yourself to a worthy cause that will enhance your own particular moral values. You embrace the highest standards for your friends and impose your expectations on everyone around you. Your nature is profoundly sensual and your emotional need for conquest vast. When you want something, you take it without trifling with the consequences. Your assertiveness usually serves you well even though it can be problematic for the people who get caught in between.

YOUR HEALTH AND VITALITY

Because you are usually so overwrought, you need more sleep and should always avoid stimulants. Your energy is inexhaustible and your capacity for driving yourself immeasurable. However, if you don't develop prudence, your drive can lead to eventual loss. Special areas to watch out for are the nervous system, the liver, and the eyes.

THE SOCIAL YOU

Although at times you are difficult to get along with, you're also capable of turning the earth into a heavenly retreat. You tend to wear your heart on your sleeve and open your doors to all who knock. At the same time, you're not in the least shy when it comes to informing people of their limits. You have a strong need for family and desire a home from which to spring to new adventures. In general, your success with life, love, people, and the pursuit of your principles is both dazzling and admirable.

NamePortrait
50
Associated Names

Absalom	Currie	Grandville	Jas
Absolom	Curry	Grantland	Jed
Ainsley	Damen	Granvil	Jeddy
Argyle	Damian	Granville	Jedediah
Avit	Damien	Gunar	Jedidiah
Bert	Darius	Gunnar	Jem
Bertie	Dempster	Gunner	Jemmie
Berton	Dermot	Guntar	Jemmy
Beverley	Diego	Gunter	Jerome
Beverly	Domnin	Gunthar	Jervis
Boyd	Earl	Gunther	Jim
Broughton	Earle	Hamilton	Jimmie
Burt	Early	Hamish	Jimmy
Burton	Ellard	Hastings	Jock
Caldwell	Elton	Hewe	Jocko
Cannon	Erl	Hewett	Laidley
Chan	Erle	Hildebrand	Lennon
Channing	Errol	Ishmael	Miller
Cleeve	Faber	Jack	Milo
Cleve	Fabre	Jackie	Myrddin
Clif	Fabrice	Jackson	Naldo
Cliff	Fabron	Jacme	Omar
Clifford	Gardener	Jacob	Omer
Clive	Gardiner	Jacobus	Parsefal
Clyve	Gardner	Jacques	Parsifal
Cobb	Garner	Jake	Perc
Coop	Ger	James	Perce
Cooper	Gerome	Jamie	Perceval
Curran	Geronimo	Jarv	Percival
Curren	Gervais	Jarvey	Percy
Currey	Gervase	Jarvis	Purcell

Associated Names (cont.)

Rainer	Roc	Sherborne	Vivian
Raini	Rock	Sherbourn	Vivien
Rainier	Rockley	Sherbourne	Wake
Raynold	Rockly	Sherburn	Wakefield
Raynor	Rockwell	Sherburne	Wakeley
Reg	Rocky	Stew	Wakeman
Reggie	Ron	Steward	Washburn
Reggy	Ronald	Stewart	Wickham
Reginald	Ronnie	Stu	Wickley
Regis	Ronny	Stuart	Wykeham
Reinhold	Ronson	Sullie	Zeke
Rene	Seamus	Sullivan	
Reynold	Shamus	Sully	

Name Portrait 51

Passionate Unveiler

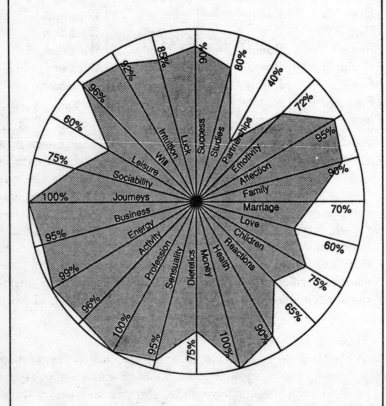

Element : Fire

Mineral : Crystal

Animal : Termite

Plant : Broom shrub

Sign : Leo

Color : Yellow

Personality Type:

Passionate Unveiler

(Associated names – page 341)

BASIC CHARACTER

You have one of those dual natures which, when evenly balanced, gives you the strength and insight you need to meet your high ideals. You like to get to the heart of a matter and with your unusual intuitive powers are usually able to see right through a situation. You are, on the one hand, emotional and explosive; and on the other, logical and cool-headed. You have a great capacity for self-mastery, and though you are able to give thoughtful consideration to problems and situations, you are a bustle of activity once you do decide to act. You're a natural leader, an idealist; and your emotional side might well lead you into revolutionary situations, not unlike your namesake Jeanne d'Arc (Joan of Arc).

YOUR PSYCHOLOGY

With those two sides to your nature, you are prone to a certain amount of inner conflict, most of which can easily be resolved once you apply your considerable logic and natural adaptability. You can be both objective and subjective, and though you are primarily an extrovert, you do enjoy your own quiet time alone. You have a strong propensity to give too much of yourself. It becomes a matter of pride to you—and your pride can get in your way at times. You can also be combative, but this is usually a positive trait, as you seldom become discouraged over a bad turn of events, but take it as a challenge. Your will sees you through time and again; it's not unlike forged steel. Your dealings with others are firm, and you are not afraid to let your will be known. At the same time, you know the value of compromising and making concessions when you must.

HOW YOU ACT AND REACT IN THE WORLD

You want to get things done. It's not the doing so much as it is your need to accomplish things that keeps you so busy. You're an ambitious woman, but your ambitions are usually directed in a crusade-like way; you go right through a situation, effective and expeditious as your special animal totem, the termite. The energy you put into your undertakings is astonishing, and you need it, in order to carry out your mission in life—for that is what life often seems to you—a mission. Precisely what career you choose makes little difference. You're open to a lot of things and probably had a bit of trouble making up your mind. But if you did, you did so early in life, and from then on it was nothing but keeping busy on the road to accomplishment! You could excel in engineering, politics, labor organizing, or medicine—or just about anything that would somehow better the lot of humanity. You seem to be driven by your vision of a better world, and yet you have the resistance and perseverance of your plant totem, the broom shrub, to overcome any stumbling blocks along the way. Like the broom, you can thrive and flower on the sandiest of soil.

YOUR DEEP INTUITIVE PERSONALITY

For you, intuition is a sort of clairvoyance. Truly, it is a sixth sense, and the source of your beauty and charm. It is not only your own best guide, but can and probably often does tell you much about the inner lives of others about you.

YOUR INTELLIGENCE

You have one of those rare minds which is both analytical and holistic. You can see things at once, and yet are able to understand all the details. This gives you a powerful intellect. You are able to keep a good perspective on any problem. And with your fine memory and unquenchable curiosity little can come your way in life that you are unable to understand and pursue.

YOUR EMOTIONAL NATURE

When you're in love, you can move mountains. Your emotions are very important to you and your overall well-being, though at times they may tend to become exaggerated in the big picture. For you, it's all or nothing. There is no such thing as a kind-of love affair—it's unequivocal dedication, devotion, and commitment, or forget the whole thing. Sexually, it's the same. You have a very earthy sensuality and enjoy the pleasures of loving. But there is an inclination in you to turn your back on the senses and devote yourself to mystical endeavors. If this is so, then it is the same as if your ideals and mystical quest were a lover—you devote yourself fully. All or nothing at all. The only thing you have to be on guard against in either case is giving too much of yourself. As in every other thing, your emotions and sensuality are of downright heroic proportions—and your love life can probably get pretty exhausting at times!

YOUR HEALTH AND VITALITY

Even though you have favorable health in general and a very strong constitution, you do have to be extra careful to take care of yourself. It's that high energy level, coupled with your powerful emotions. You tend to overexert yourself, and this can lead to stomach troubles. You must be sure that you are eating nutritional meals, and eat regularly, and make an effort to stay away from stimulants, tobacco, and alcohol.

THE SOCIAL YOU

You must have the trust and confidence of your friends and associates before you can warm up to people and be truly as socially engaging as you can be. Your social life is not nearly as important to you as your crusades and your work, but toward those few close friends you do have, you are wonderfully loyal and indulgent—overindulgent at times. There is something reserved in your social manners, but maybe that is only because you are usually under so much other pressure from work and love that you feel you don't have time to let go. Of course, idle amusements are simply not your thing. Yours is a vision without a lot of time for a frivolous night on the town. Rather, you are inspired to action and exploits by your work and any of a number of social causes in which you might be involved.

———————

NamePortrait
51
Associated Names

Armande	Clorinde	Dorothy	Hetty
Armandine	Cornela	Dorris	Hitty
Bel	Cornelia	Dorthea	Ilka
Bell	Cornelie	Dorthy	Irena
Bella	Cornelle	Dory	Irene
Belle	Cornie	Dot	Irenee
Belva	Cunegonde	Dotty	Irenna
Belvia	Dawn	Eir	Irina
Binga	Dee	Eirena	Isa
Calligenia	Deel	Eirene	Isabeau
Canace	Delma	Erena	Isabel
Carma	Delmar	Eudora	Isabella
Carmel	Delmare	Eudore	Isabelle
Carmela	Deva	Ferdinanda	Isadora
Carmelina	Devani	Fernanda	Isadore
Carmeline	Dodo	Fernande	Isbel
Carmelita	Doll	Fernandina	Ishbel
Carmella	Dolley	Freya	Isidora
Carmie	Dollie	Georgana	Isidore
Cele	Dolly	Georgene	Isobel
Celesta	Dora	Georgetta	Isobella
Celeste	Dore	Georgette	Issie
Celestin	Doretta	Georgia	Issy
Celestina	Dori	Georgiana	Izzy
Celestine	Doria	Georgie	Jan
Chantal	Dorice	Georgina	Jana
Chlorinda	Doris	Georgine	Jane
Chlorinde	Dorise	Georgy	Janean
Clarinda	Dorothe	Giorgia	Janet
Clarinde	Dorothea	Halcyon	Janetta
Clorinda	Dorothi	Halcyone	Janette

Associated Names (cont.)

Janice	Mathilde	Parnella	Sheena
Janina	Matilda	Parnelle	Shena
Janine	Matilde	Parthenia	Sine
Janna	Mattea	Penta	Sinead
Jayne	Matthea	Penthea	Sita
Jean	Matthia	Penthia	Theona
Jeanette	Mattie	Pernella	Theone
Jeanine	Maud	Pernelle	Tilda
Jeanne	Maude	Perrette	Valborga
Jeannette	Mehetabel	Perrine	Valburga
Jehanne	Mehetabelle	Petra	Vanina
Jenette	Mehetabie	Petrina	Vedetta
Jennifer	Mehitabel	Petronella	Vedette
Jenny	Mehitabelle	Petronelle	Voleta
Joan	Mehitable	Petronia	Voletta
Joana	Melina	Petronilla	Walborga
Joanna	Mercedes	Petronille	Walburga
Joanne	Merci	Petula	Wenona
Johanna	Mercia	Pierette	Wenonah
Johanne	Mercy	Pierrette	Winona
Jordana	Metabel	Pulcherie	Winonah
Juana	Naiada	Reini	Ysabeau
Juanita	Naida	Remata	Ysabel
Kanaka	Nairne	Rena	Ysabella
Kanake	Nebula	Renata	Ysabelle
Ketura	Nela	Rene	Ysobella
Lassie	Nelie	Rennie	Ysobelle
Maitilde	Nelli	Renny	Ysolbel
Matelda	Nita	Sean	Zaneta
Mathea	Odette	Seon	Zareta
Mathia	Panthea	Seonaid	Zuleika
Mathilda	Panthia	Shane	

Name Portrait 52

Warrior Monk

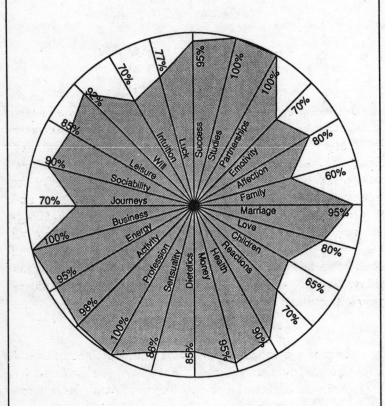

Element : Fire   **Plant** : Truffle
Mineral : Porphyry   **Sign** : Aries
Animal : Dolphin   **Color** : Yellow

Personality Type:

Warrior Monk

(Associated names – page 349)

BASIC CHARACTER

You seem to run on your exceptional intelligence, which is the backbone of your life. Your alert mind is complemented by a high, sturdy morality and a prodigious adaptability. Both a thinker and a doer, you are active and independent-minded. You question everything and have little time for the established way of doing things unless you've tried it out and it works the best for you. You're quite able to do ten things at once and, what's even more impressive, to do them all very well. Like your animal totem, the dolphin, symbol of both prudence and productive action, you are able to think things through and come to a firm decision before you throw yourself into any situation.

YOUR PSYCHOLOGY

There is a nervous energy about you, which comes most often from a dualism in your nature. You're both an introvert and an extrovert—at once the monk and the warrior. Your inner life is as intense as your outer life. Like your plant totem, the truffle, your most delicate insights come after long and quiet reflection, underground, as it were. But at times you tend to become anxious and nervous as a consequence of this dual nature—wanting to act when you are not yet in a position to. Your main problems with other people stem from your vanity. It seems to you that no one can possibly know more than you do, and if anyone hints that he might, you're ready for an argument which of course only you can win. Your temper can flare up, and you can become stubborn in your beliefs. As long as you remember that your somewhat nervous temperament comes from the very sensitive balance between your extroversion and objectivity and your introversion and subjectivity, you can avoid those antagonistic forays. Your will is strong, but tends to get absorbed by your intellect and your tremendous curiosity over every idea, thought, and happening in the world.

HOW YOU ACT AND REACT IN THE WORLD

You absolutely must be occupied. Nothing is more horrible for you than an idle moment. As a consequence, you sometimes throw yourself into activities only to pass the time. You can get sidetracked if you don't allow enough time for thoughtful consideration of your enterprises. You probably decided what you wanted to do—generally, anyway—very early in life; the rest is a race to get things done. With your ability to both think things out and act, you would make a marvelous inventor. Any profession that involves stirring up ideas, people, and things, and which allows you to be your own boss most of the time, is suited to your nature. You would make a fine engineer or an exceptional industrial manager. The ins and outs of complex finance attract you to a career in banking. You would also make an excellent teacher—but your students probably wouldn't get too many A's. You're a very demanding person. You are at your best when you can act alone and without supervision; you can plan the most delicate of operations and then carry them out. But you're not the sort who will easily give responsibility over to others. You're a very capable organizer, however, despite your penchant for believing that only you can run things.

YOUR DEEP INTUITIVE PERSONALITY

It's unusual that someone with such a sharp intuition should heed it so little, but that's most likely what you do.

You like visible proof, the kind that can be measured with a slide rule. Still, it is your deep, inner self which carries such charm for others and is the source of your attractiveness.

YOUR INTELLIGENCE

Not enough can be said here. You have both an analytic and a synthetic mind, which means that you can see things all at once and are still able to analyze all the details. This makes you able to solve problems very quickly with a cold, calculated reasoning as well as a compassionate understanding. You tend to ponder things, to question everything, and not to be satisfied unless you have discovered the root of all problems. It's sort of like you invent the wheel anew every day. It is your brilliant intellect which is the most conspicuous thing about you—by your mind, you stand out from the crowd.

YOUR EMOTIONAL NATURE

Although you have very strong emotions, you tend to hold them in check—with your intellect, naturally. The last thing you'd feel comfortable about is the possibility of "losing control." Rare is the hour when you blurt out your affection or go off on a whim. But your exquisite tenderness, once you no longer conceal it, leads you to a love life of great selflessness and devotion. If you do not express your emotions to a loved one, they may well go into a rich and mystical faith—inward instead of outward. You are a dedicated friend and lover, once you do express yourself, and your strong and romantic sensuality is a delight to the few who have known it.

YOUR HEALTH AND VITALITY

In general, your health is very good, though your sensitive character, inclined as you are to anxieties, may lead you to some psychosomatic strain. You tend to think of yourself as a superman, and this produces nervous tension. You have to keep a regular regimen which includes some sort of meditation, outdoor exercise, and plenty of sleep.

Name Portrait 52

THE SOCIAL YOU

You have a circle of faithful friends, and your own dedication to them is usually reciprocated. Your social life is overall, quite scintillating. You're a brilliant conversationalist—if somewhat opinionated at times—and you enjoy a good party. But it's the best when you're throwing it. You like to bring together family, friends, and professional associates, and in fact often don't make a distinction between your professional and personal life. You can be generous to a fault, especially when you're in one of your outgoing moods. With your exceptionally good luck and your solid personality, you can be seen in the highest of places; and with your amazing adaptability, you rarely lose faith when one of life's little reversals takes you by surprise. You seem to know by instinct that ultimately, you will distinguish yourself in society.

NamePortrait
52
Associated Names

Axel	Humfry	Nathaniel	Vale
Caddock	Hump	Nattie	Valle
Celestin	Humph	Ned	Vaughan
Clifton	Iaian	Newton	Vaughn
Crosbey	Iain	Ogilvie	Vawn
Crosbie	Ian	Osred	Ware
Crosby	Ivan	Osric	Warfield
Dalziel	Jan	Othis	Warford
Dalziell	Jean	Otis	Waring
Ed	Jehan	Radnor	Warren
Eddie	Jerry	Richman	West
Eddy	Jevon	Richmond	Westbrook
Edgar	Jock	Seain	Westby
Edgard	Johan	Sean	Wetherby
Elmo	Johann	Seann	Wheeler
Elmore	John	Shan	Win
Eoin	Johnnie	Shane	Windham
Esmond	Johnny	Shannon	Winne
Ezekiel	Jon	Shawn	Wyn
Fraine	Jonah	Shipley	Wyndham
Frayne	Jonas	Shipton	Wyndhann
Frean	Jonathan	Spence	Wynn
Freen	Jotham	Spencer	Yann
Frey	Lonny	Spenser	Yannick
Freyne	Nat	Standish	Yoann
Gian	Nataniel	Tanton	Zane
Gino	Nate	Trevelyan	Zeb
Hans	Nathan	Twyford	Zebulon
Humfrey	Nathanael	Vail	

Name Portrait 53

Bringer of Hope

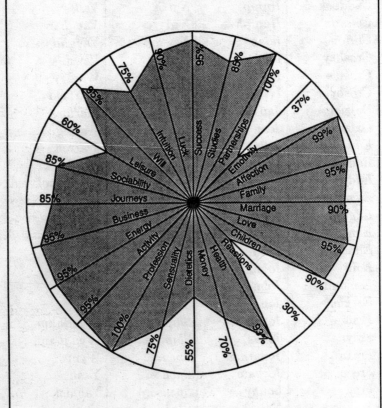

Element : Fire

Mineral : Antimony

Animal : Turtle dove

Plant : Chestnut tree

Sign : Sagittarius

Color : Red

Personality Type:

Bringer of Hope

(Associated names – page 355)

BASIC CHARACTER

Although you seem unfathomable to most people who know you, there is a firm direction in your life. You know what you want and are guided there by a combination of high morals, a self-assurance that comes from your unabiding faith, and your capacity for self-denial in order to reach your goals. You are able to dedicate yourself to your community or to a cause, and even though you can be convincingly enthusiastic, you are essentially reserved. Your totem animal, the turtle dove, is the quiet herald of springtime.

YOUR PSYCHOLOGY

Like your totem plant, the chestnut, your rich inner life is concealed by a strong and sometimes thorny front. You are both an extrovert and an introvert, and sometimes it is difficult to tell which is more important to you—your need to be active in the world, or your need to protect your private life. Because you are so convinced of your mission in life, you sometimes tend to overlook what you consider emotional frivolities, and so seem rather cold. This can cause some anxieties, but in general, you remain very well balanced. You have a very strong will, but you tend to conceal it so that your reactions to situations are somewhat restrained and understated. The only real problem you may have psychologically is in your tendency to withdraw too much, for although you do rely on your inner life to guide you, you also do need an involved, active outward life.

HOW YOU ACT AND REACT IN THE WORLD

In every way, you are a man of deeds and not words. You get things done, and in doing them, you influence others. Maybe this is because you go about things so selflessly. You're not interested in establishing your own reputation or a great name for yourself, but in doing things well. With your sense of devotion and dedication to a job, you are bound to distinguish yourself in a career. Most likely, you decided early on in life what it was that you wanted to do. To you, the value of a job is not measured by its prestige or its salary as much as it is by the service it offers your fellow man. You could be an inspired lawyer, a fair and honest judge, or a courageous labor leader—any profession where your natural humanitarianism can come into play. If you are not self-employed, you are a devoted employee. You are able to devote yourself to a cause as well, body and soul, but without becoming fanatical. You can be so objective that, time and again, you will forget your own interests. You are slow to anger, and rare is the day that you find reason to let go with a biting word or an angry outburst.

YOUR DEEP INTUITIVE PERSONALITY

You have a very good intuition, but it is so well integrated in your whole personality that it doesn't seem like intuition. You already know where you are going, and nothing else is important. Your imagination is rich and well-disciplined, and your subdued attractiveness is captivating.

YOUR INTELLIGENCE

It's not a simple matter to describe your intelligence. It is more holistic than it is analytic. You are able to keep a comprehensive perspective on people and situations. And yet, your astonishing memory retains not only great moments, but the details of things. You tend to be selective in what you want to learn, though you were or are a marvelous student. In all, you probably use your intellect toward practical ends.

YOUR EMOTIONAL NATURE

You are a warm and gentle lover, but you hardly ever allow your emotions to get out of control. There is something virile and self-assured about you which attracts people to you, and because you are not at all possessive, you allow others to express their affections openly. The problem is, with your selflessness and your subdued sensuality, you're not very apt to take the love that is given to you. In fact, it wouldn't be surprising if in later years you turned your emotions more and more toward a religious quest of sorts. You are capable of great devotion. Or, your devotion, given to a wife or lover, can be so great as to set her apart from all others, on a pedestal, if you will.

YOUR HEALTH AND VITALITY

In general, your health is excellent, and you have the vitality to do what you must do. You don't seem to have the time to be sick—it's just not in your game plan! You rarely tire and are at your healthy best when you take the time every day to walk in the fresh air. Your weak spots are in your gall bladder and respiratory system.

THE SOCIAL YOU

There is something about your genuine friendliness that makes people think they've been taken into your family once they meet you. Much of that is the special gift you have for communicating your warmth; and part of it is that it would never cross your mind to belittle another person for any reason. Even if you have experienced a failure at something, your good will and firm convictions remain intact, and this self-confidence is exuded in your dealings with other people.

You are a gracious, giving host, and though perhaps not the life of the party, you're certainly its soul. When you do take time to relax among a gathering of friends, you give off a warm, secure feeling—a feeling of peacefulness, and hope for tomorrow.

NamePortrait
53
Associated Names

Abner	Hackett	Medard	Rube
Anael	Hargrave	Mort	Ruben
Baird	Hargreave	Mortemer	Rubey
Bard	Hargreaves	Mortie	Ruby
Cadda	Hargrove	Mortimer	Rutland
Cadmus	Ike	Odell	Rutledge
Carrick	Ikey	Odin	Ryton
Chad	Ikie	Odo	Sam
Chadda	Iosep	Odolf	Sammie
Ches	Isaac	Orton	Sammy
Chester	Isaak	Payton	Samuel
Cheston	Izaak	Peyton	Samy
Chet	Jo	Prewet	Seigneur
Demas	Job	Prewett	Senior
Diggory	Joe	Prewit	Seosaidh
Eldrid	Joey	Prewitt	Sol
Eldridge	Jose	Pruitt	Taillefer
Eldwin	Joseph	Reuben	Telfer
Eldwyn	Josephin	Rex	Telfor
Elstone	Josiah	Rexford	Telford
Everley	Lennard	Rey	Telfour
Everly	Macaire	Routledge	
Garwood	Manleich	Roy	
Hacket	Manley	Royal	

Name Portrait 54

Man of the Sun

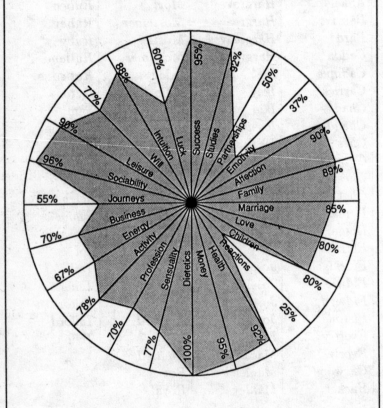

Element : Air

Mineral : Calcium

Animal : Sable

Plant : Apple tree

Sign : Libra

Color : Green

Personality Type:

Man of the Sun

(Associated names – page 360)

BASIC CHARACTER

You're a very calm and relaxed person with a sunny disposition, a sort of devil-may-care approach to life. It seems sometimes that you're just waiting for time to pass by and plucking from it the tastier fruits. Like your plant totem, the apple tree, symbol of earthly desires, you have a well-defined love of pleasures, even though the way you choose to go after them is quite casual. Yet you are a man of clever imagination and rare talents underneath all your laid-back ways, and like the rare and exquisite sable, your animal totem, those talents may one day lead to fine distinction.

YOUR PSYCHOLOGY

Underneath your facade of nonchalance lies an incurable need to be around other people. You also have a tendency not to mean what you say, especially when you're called upon to agree or disagree with someone else's opinions. It's easier to say yes, so you agree, even though inside you hold your own opposed point of view. In work and sometimes socially, this can get you into some serious troubles. You need to develop some sort of discipline in order to develop your latent talents, lest your undisciplined nature lead you only into a hedonistic life. Structure is difficult for you to come by, however, which is due in part to your tendency to hide your own will; you're not at all the aggressive type and wouldn't dream of imposing your will on someone else, or even on yourself!

HOW YOU ACT AND REACT IN THE WORLD

Though you would probably rather do nothing at all than something, you are an excellent student and are drawn to classical or technological subjects. Once you overcome the idea that doing too much of anything is criminal, you can become a distinguished artist or writer, as you have a flair with words; or, due to your love of the finer things in life, you could be an excellent wine merchant. With your casual air, you could make a good salesman or merchant. Whatever it is you choose to undertake, you do it in a minor key, and never would you disrupt the harmony of those around you. Everything you do reflects the basic calmness of your nature, your sense of humor, and your ability to casually dismiss any disruptions or failures.

YOUR DEEP INTUITIVE PERSONALITY

You possess a remarkable insight. Usually, you act with your inner voice as a guide—and it is this part of yourself which keeps you subdued and subdues the more excitable people around you. It is from your intuition that your attractiveness and sense of humor come.

YOUR INTELLIGENCE

Your mind is analytical; you have a penchant for getting involved in the details of something. Most of all, you have a specialist's mind and are at your intellectual best when you are using your insights in order to tell someone else how to do something. You enjoy busying yourself in one specific area, analyzing all the details, and fitting everything together in your mind—and then finding someone to put it all together in fact.

YOUR EMOTIONAL NATURE

Love makes your world go 'round. You love to love, and you love to be loved, and as a consequence, you're always falling in love, and not always with the perfect woman. You're strongly attracted to beauty, including beautiful women, and it is beauty which is the first thing you see. Undoubtedly, there has been more than one great romance in your life. But then, you're a marvelous romancer! You have an endless capacity to love and to show affection, which extends to children. It would not at all be surprising if you were to have a large family—as long as a lot of children wouldn't upset your little paradise of the senses.

YOUR HEALTH AND VITALITY

You have excellent health and are full of stamina, but you need to watch your eating habits and to get enough exercise, for your relaxed nature can lead to weight problems. Also watch the drinking—the wines may be superb, but they can become a habit! As in every other realm of life, you need to discipline yourself here. Your vulnerable spots are in your stomach, intestines, and genitals.

THE SOCIAL YOU

With your bright disposition and your calming nature, you are a magnet to other people. To be in your company is nothing short of superb. You speak well and are an entertaining, uplifting conversationalist. You seem to be able to make other people happy just by your presence. To you, friendship is sacred, and your friends seem to know this intuitively. You're able to offer the right word to ease someone's tension or anxiety, and you instinctively avoid asking embarrassing questions. Most likely you have a real cult feeling for your closest friends, and they are many. You will defend a friend to the end, but you're able to do it with such good humor that no one feels slighted. Your social life reflects your good taste and casualness, and those are also the qualities which ensure you success in life.

NamePortrait
54
Associated Names

Atherton	Clarence	Lee	Morvan
Bellamy	Clavance	Len	Morven
Brad	Cleary	Lenard	Nickson
Bradley	Conroy	Lennie	Nixon
Bradly	Diomede	Lenny	Radcliff
Brady	Eaton	Leo	Radcliffe
Briac	Edric	Leon	Redcliff
Brian	Ewald	Leonard	Redcliffe
Briant	Ewert	Leonce	Skip
Brien	Ewing	Leoner	Skipp
Brieux	Fourier	Leonhard	Skipper
Brion	Grayson	Leonilde	Skippy
Bryan	Hagley	Lion	Skipton
Bryant	Hezekiah	Lionel	Timon
Bryon	Humbert	Llewellyn	Umberto
Burdett	Humbie	Lon	Wilbur
Calliope	Ignatia	Maddison	
Clair	Iniga	Madison	
Clare	Keefe	Morfin	

Name Portrait 55

The Singer and the Dancer

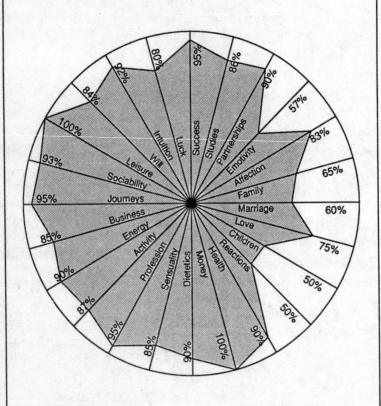

Element : Water   **Plant** : Wheat

Mineral : Sardonyx   **Sign** : Cancer

Animal : Nightingale   **Color** : Red

Personality Type:

The Singer and the Dancer

(Associated names – page 367)

BASIC CHARACTER

You have strong emotions, extraordinary intuition, and a highly creative imagination. There is a dual nature to your character, and either one side or the other—and sometimes both—can predominate. On the one hand, you are the thinker. You can come up with remarkable ideas and insights. On the other, you are the doer, the one who executes the ideas. Like your totem animal, the nightingale, your "song" is usually sweet, an inspiration and the harbinger of the dawn. Like your totem plant, wheat, symbol of power and fertility, you have a practical side to your poetic character which can allow you to get things done.

YOUR PSYCHOLOGY

It's not all that easy to get along with you, despite your sensitive nature, or maybe it's because of your acute sensitivity. You do not take criticism very well, especially if it is criticism of your ideas. You're much less touchy about criticism of your actual work, however, and though you are always full of wonderful ideas, you're a bit of a procrastinator when it comes to carrying things through. You're a starter, but it's a good idea if you have a team with you so that your projects can be carried through. It's also important to you to make a distinction between power and authority. Authority is in the mind, and power is held by people in the world. It sometimes becomes a matter of much importance to you that you are holding both. As long as you are able to keep a balance of authority and power in your life—which is connected with the balance between your ideas and your actions—you are at peace, and your charming, poetic nature comes out and inspires those around you.

HOW YOU ACT AND REACT IN THE WORLD

As long as you're not worrying that your creativity will be slighted if you give substance to your ideas, you are able to remain very effective in your dealings. You were probably a brilliant student, able to get by in classes with little effort. And it's that "getting by" which could become a habit. You need a certain amount of discipline in order to apply yourself to most things, and can get the most done when you are working with others who will add the final touches to any project after you've tired of it and are thinking up the next one. Still, when you have made that transition from thinker to doer, you can throw yourself into your work. You're attracted to work which requires careful planning. A career in science or in business, or as an actor, a writer, or a director would suit that qualification. You would also make a good manager, since you are able to comprehend problems at a single glance. A profession in law or in government is also a possibility. You possess a naturally poetic mind—but unless you have someone following you around with a tape recorder, chances are, much of your verse will never see the dawn!

YOUR DEEP INTUITIVE PERSONALITY

It's as if you have invisible antennae which allow you to anticipate events and understand people in one flashing instant. Your intuition is exceptional, the seat of your inspirational nature and your highly tuned sensitivity. You have the imagination of a great artist or a great inventor, and it is very important to your general well-being that you remain in touch with it.

YOUR INTELLIGENCE

You are able to shift from the general to the specific, or from the specific to the general, with lightning speed and as much ease. Your mind is both analytic and synthetic, or holistic. You possess a great intellectual elasticity, which is especially useful to you when you are confronting complex problems. Your intellect reflects the dual nature of your character—the ability to invent and the ability to bring those inventions to life.

YOUR EMOTIONAL NATURE

Even though you lead your life passionately, you are more responsive to your imagination of the perfect love than you are to the perfect love herself when she stands in front of you! At least that's the way it sometimes appears. The truth is that although you are a warmly affectionate man, you cannot tolerate emotions to interfere in your work; and the perfect love would stand aside when your passions turn to a new idea or project. At times you may be a very sexual person, but your sexuality is usually attached to your emotions. When you love, you love with your whole being—even though you are able to turn off your personal passions and invest them in your work when the creative urge strikes.

YOUR HEALTH AND VITALITY

Your health is quite good, but you tend to tire easily and become nervous without ample sleep. You need a good deal of calm in your life, as well as a regular diet. Of course, too much calm is not a good thing either, or you risk giving way to the sedentary, totally thought-filled side of your nature at the expense of your action side. Your weak points are in your nerves and urinary system.

THE SOCIAL YOU

It is rather easy for you to adjust to different social situations, but you prefer a certain amount of pomp and dignity at your own parties. You dress with great care, most likely, and are concerned to a degree with appearances. Still, there is nothing staid about you. Your parties are bound to be more like Louis the Sun King's than afternoon tea with the college dean. Socially, as in other realms of life, you're probably guided very much by your prodigious intuition. You have a great insight into other people's needs and, if you're in the mood, will meet them. You're a source of inspiration, not only to yourself, but to others. Your own lust to live seems to spill over, influencing and enlightening those around you. It's almost as if you sing the tune to which you—and everyone around you—can't help but dance.

———————

NamePortrait
55
Associated Names

Adney	Gage	Ludo	Sargie
Alabhaois	Galton	Ludovic	Serge
Alois	Gillmore	Ludovick	Sergeant
Aloys	Gilmer	Ludwig	Sergent
Aloysius	Gilmore	Lugaidh	Seymour
Ambert	Gilmour	Luthais	Sloan
Aymar	Halton	Padget	Sloane
Brent	Holbrook	Padgett	Tait
Cadell	Lawler	Page	Tate
Caley	Lawley	Paget	Teyte
Carswell	Levi	Proctor	Tierman
Castor	Lew	Rider	Tiernan
Crosley	Lewes	Rodge	Tierney
Cuthbert	Lewis	Rodger	Wade
Damase	Loic	Rog	Wadley
Dean	Lou	Roger	Zaide
Deane	Louis	Ryder	
Dene	Louison	Sarge	
Deverell	Loulou	Sargent	

Name Portrait 56

Earth Mother

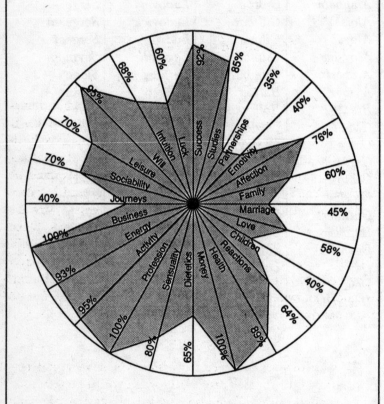

Element : Earth   **Plant** : Lavender

Mineral : Sun stone   **Sign** : Virgo

Animal : Kangaroo   **Color** : Green

Personality Type:

Earth Mother

(Associated names – page 372)

BASIC CHARACTER

You are strong-willed and practical, with a wholesomeness and a highly moral sensibility which sometimes makes it seem as if the earth itself were your invention. You have both feet on the ground, and although you are capable of great activity and rapid reactions, you are somewhat restrained or reserved. You like to be in control, emotionally and intellectually. And although you are scrupulous and efficient, you are sometimes driven to any length to get what you want. Once you have what you want, you hold onto it; there is a certain possessiveness, an inborn sense of ownership, to you. You enjoy beauty, but also useful things—like your plant totem, lavender, known both for its fragrant perfume and for its medicinal qualities.

YOUR PSYCHOLOGY

Because of your natural introversion, you have a tendency to withdraw into yourself, especially when you are confronted with disappointments. You also have a tendency to take on a martyr's role, which is only an exaggeration of your genuine capacity for self-sacrifice. It's sometimes difficult to get close to you, because you have a natural shyness which in bad times can seem like an inferiority complex. Because you are reserved, you tend to become inhibited. You're not one to go out on a great adventure alone. But with a loved one, or with good friends awaiting you in port, you are able to apply your considerable will and make some astonishing moves. Like the kangaroo, your totem animal, you are at your best when you're "leaping" or grazing in a group.

HOW YOU ACT AND REACT IN THE WORLD

Being active is very important to you. Throwing yourself into hard work is your way of overcoming your inhibitions. Though you hesitate and beat around the bush, you ultimately choose a career, either in the home, for you make a marvelous and fair mother, or in a field that can use your prodigious intensity and firm sense of morality. You would make an excellent teacher, for instance, or a fine researcher. You are attracted to tradition and may find a career connected with the classics. As a religious official, you would be able to use your high morality and scruples to the benefit of others. There is a certain desire for conquest in you which drives you to work very hard at whatever you do; and it is important to you that the fruits of your work are seen as your possessions.

YOUR DEEP INTUITIVE PERSONALITY

Although your intuition is good, you tend to distrust it, just as you distrust the power of your considerable charm. You prefer the visible, the logical, and the pragmatic. Still, there is an irrepressible attractiveness—an imperial sort of beauty—which emanates from your deep, inner self.

YOUR INTELLIGENCE

You have a practical mind, which is analytical. It gives you a refined ability to deal with details. With your formidable memory and your sense for logic and pragmatism, you are able to apply your considerable intellect to your work and daily life with good results.

YOUR EMOTIONAL NATURE

Here, you tend to be guarded. Underneath your determined, practical, active exterior is a very vulnerable person who is afraid of being hurt. When someone says he loves you, the first thing you probably ask yourself is, "Why? What does he really want?" Still, you need a secure emotional life; and when you are feeling confident, you are able to receive the love that comes your way—and there is bound to be a lot of it, for there is an irresistible attractiveness about you. Most likely, you will not have a long string of lovers, but one true and proven love—someone who's gone and gotten the grail for you, scaled mountains, battled dragons, and so forth. You might just tell him afterward, "You didn't have to do all that for me," but once he has, you are able to open up to him emotionally and sexually and overcome your inhibitions.

YOUR HEALTH AND VITALITY

In view of the intensity with which you lead your life, you are very fortunate to have excellent stamina. You need plenty of rest, however, and should be careful of overeating or indulging in alcohol. Your intestines and liver are delicate. It is also important to your good health that you avoid chills.

THE SOCIAL YOU

You are at your best socially when you are the hostess. Your parties are likely to be along traditional lines, though you are a perfectly charming hostess as well for an impromptu dinner. You like your guests to feel comfortable in your home, though you do not always feel so comfortable in other people's homes, especially if you believe someone is not up to your standards. Socially, as emotionally, you like to be in control of things. You don't trust your life to luck, but to your own efforts. Whether you are giving a dinner party, or organizing a group of friends to go to a concert, you feel duty-bound to make the evening a success, and usually you do.

NamePortrait
56
Associated Names

Aelda	Fae	Ingrid	Luwanna
Aeldra	Faith	Ingunna	Luwanne
Aeldrida	Fay	Koren	Madra
Aldora	Fayanne	La Roux	Meda
Aloisa	Faye	Labhaoise	Melodia
Aloisia	Gai	Larousse	Melodie
Aloysia	Gay	Laveda	Melody
Berenia	Gilda	Lavetta	Meredeth
Berenice	Gloire	Lavette	Meredith
Bernice	Glori	Leoda	Meredydd
Berny	Gloria	Leola	Meredyth
Bibiane	Gloriana	Leota	Merideth
Bunny	Gloriane	Liusade	Meridith
Burnia	Glorianna	Lodie	Meridyth
Burnice	Glorianne	Lois	Merrie
Candace	Glory	Loise	Merry
Candice	Haley	Lou	Minetta
Candida	Hali	Louane	Minette
Candie	Halie	Louanna	Missy
Candy	Halimeda	Louanne	Nuala
Delight	Hallie	Louisa	Odelia
Donia	Heloise	Louise	Odelie
Druella	Hypatia	Louisette	Odella
Druilla	Inga	Louisitte	Odila
Duena	Ingaberg	Loulou	Odile
Duenna	Ingabert	Loyce	Odilia
Edma	Ingar	Luana	Odilla
Edmee	Ingebiorg	Luane	Otha
Eloisa	Ingeborg	Luise	Othilla
Eloise	Inger	Lulu	Ottilie
Eunice	Ingibiorg	Luwana	Pelagia

EARTH MOTHER

Associated Names (cont.)

Pomona	Rohana	Sera	Thirza
Prospera	Rohane	Serafina	Thyrza
Queena	Rohanna	Serafine	Tiberia
Queenie	Rohanne	Seraphina	Tirza
Radmilla	Roux	Seraphine	Villette
Roanna	Rula	Talitha	

Name Portrait 57

Man of Reason

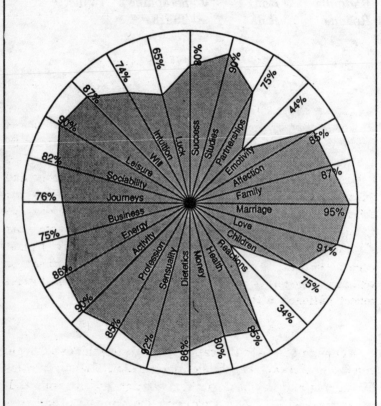

Element : Fire

Mineral : Bronze

Animal : Camel

Plant : Pine tree

Sign : Leo

Color: Orange

Personality Type:

Man of Reason

(Associated names – page 379)

BASIC CHARACTER

You have a refined sensitivity and an inquisitive nature which lends your personality depth and charm. You have a very generous and gracious side to you which is balanced by a certain restraint; you tend to take a long time to reflect before you do anything. Still, you are open to challenge and once you get moving, can be downright courageous in your endurance. Like your animal totem, the camel, you are able to undertake the most arduous journey and by your own inner stamina and resolve, to see it through to the end. Your plant totem, the pine tree, is likewise a symbol of sturdiness, as well as of regeneration and immortality. Both of these totems reflect patience in the face of difficult tasks.

YOUR PSYCHOLOGY

Though you have the capacity for seeing things through, you do not always believe in yourself, and tend to become highstrung and nervous. You're a worrier, despite your ability to deal with other people with determination and conviction. You have a very strong will, which is not only intense but of high quality. So it might strike some as strange that you tend to be submissive at times. But your submission to circumstances or other people's opinions comes about only when you're feeling withdrawn or perhaps inferior. It's a thoroughly unjustified feeling, usually, and eventually you will come to realize that. Then, you can react in one of two ways: either you'll become overaggressive, or you'll tend to repress your feelings and turn them against yourself.

HOW YOU ACT AND REACT IN THE WORLD

Your level of activity is equal to your strong will, so you tend to take on projects that you will see through. You're drawn to language study, and would make an excellent translator or interpreter. Subjects having to do with technology and science are also attractive to you; careers in engineering, scientific research, or technological development are also good choices. Whatever you do professionally, you like to be fully informed about all aspects of a career before you make your choice. It's very unlikely that, once you have begun a career, you will leave it to start on another; you like to finish what you've begun, and finish it to the very end. You're very objective about your actions, and rarely do things to exaggerate your own importance. You're tactful, if a bit timid at times. Still, you resent failure, and in the face of disappointments, may fall back on your psychological defenses to get through. But normally, when your self-confidence is high, you are a devoted worker, and your good efforts bring you success and honest achievements.

YOUR DEEP INTUITIVE PERSONALITY

Although you have remarkable insight, you do not put much faith in your intuition. Your insight is more concrete and relies upon tangible observations. This accounts for your restraint and your reservations about jumping into things.

YOUR INTELLIGENCE

You love to dip down through all the details until you get to the heart of a problem. Then you'll make your evaluations which will be firm and reliable. Your analytic mind is enhanced by your exceptional memory and your unstoppable inquisitiveness. You like to pry into everything and to understand how everything works. When you were a boy, you probably took apart all the clocks in your house and, of course, put them back together again.

YOUR EMOTIONAL NATURE

Because you are so sensitive, it is difficult for you to express your affections. It seems as if whatever you might do or say would appear either too dramatic or too banal. But your deep emotions are very strong, even if you don't always show them. You have a tremendous respect for love and for the one you love. In fact, you tend sometimes to put the one you love high on a pedestal, and this can affect your attitude toward sex. It wouldn't be surprising to hear you say something about a woman's "inviolable nature." But you have a strong sensuality, which needs expression. You can be an affectionate, soothing lover, both emotionally and sexually, as long as you learn to strike a balance between what's properly chivalrous and necessarily cavalier where love is concerned.

YOUR HEALTH AND VITALITY

Your health is very much affected by your state of mind. Because it's difficult for you to "let yourself go," you tend to waste energy and this can lead to minor physical ailments. In general, however, your health is good. You normally keep a well-balanced regimen. You have to be careful of accidents. Your weak point is your back, especially your spinal column.

THE SOCIAL YOU

You're not exactly a social gadabout; you just don't have the time. A good time for you consists of a quiet evening with your family or a few close and trusted friends. You probably have a place to which you can escape and collect your energies in solitude. Though at times you feel duty-bound to submit to big parties, you don't let such activities consume you and are most likely the last to arrive and the first to leave. There is a seriousness, a sobriety, about you which keeps your energies focused on your work and perseverance, rather than on social life. Still, you are a gracious host and a generous friend, willing to give of yourself and to put others at their ease.

_____

NamePortrait
57
Associated Names

Alcott	Colomban	Maxence	Murray
Alford	Diamond	Maxey	Onslow
Aurele	Elder	Maxi	Rufe
Bainbridge	Este	Maxie	Ruff
Blain	Esteban	Maxim	Rufin
Blaine	Estes	Maxime	Rufus
Blane	Gautier	Maximilian	Severin
Blayn	Kanoa	Maximilien	Tripp
Blayne	Lennox	Maximilienne	Wilford
Cal	Lucian	Maximillian	Winchell
Calvert	Lucien	Maximin	Worrall
Calvin	Lucius	Maxwell	Worrell
Calvino	Max	Maxy	Worrill

Name Portrait 58
Impassioned Madonna

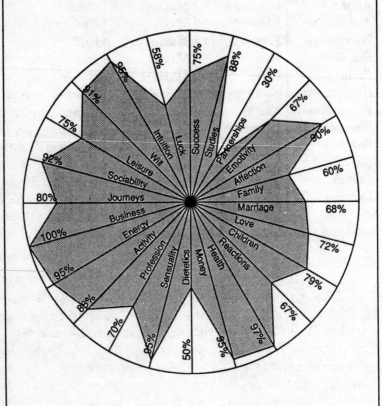

Element : Air

Mineral : Meteorite

Animal : Rooster

Plant : Mistletoe

Sign : Libra

Color : Violet

Personality Type:

Impassioned Madonna

(Associated names – page 384)

BASIC CHARACTER

Emotions seem to rule your life, influencing all you do. You are attracted to beautiful, brilliant, and elegant people and things, and your energetic activity usually helps you to get the best and the brightest that life has to offer. You are terribly big-hearted and capable of great fellowship and devotion; and though you are sometimes fanatically ambitious, your natural charm makes you irresistible to others. Like your totem animal, the rooster, symbol of vigilance and activity, you are strong-willed and always in the middle of the action—usually as the instigator!

YOUR PSYCHOLOGY

Like the mistletoe, your totem plant, you are at once lovely to behold and difficult to hold, at least without getting pricked. You have a tendency to become irritable and explosive when things aren't going your way. Your changeableness from easy-going activity to proud, stubborn intensity can be off-putting at times. Whatever you're involved in, you're involved to the utmost, and are given to excesses in just about every realm of life. But your powerful will is up to the many responsibilities you take on, and your natural extroversion will always keep you in the thick of things.

HOW YOU ACT AND REACT IN THE WORLD

Wherever you go, there is bound to be a lot of turbulence. You're not the sort to make one simple career choice and then set down to a life of routine work. The timeclock is your worst nightmare! You enjoy competition, for it brings out your healthy aggressiveness. With your natural attraction to beautiful things, a career in the luxury trades would be well-suited to your temperament. You could do well as a fashion designer, a cosmetician, or in the theater. With your drive for success, you could be a notable doctor or painter or sculptress, but these sorts of career choices would demand that you harness your over-eagerness to succeed so quickly and get down to long and arduous studies. You tend to over-act to problems that confront you professionally and, instead of sorting things through, you simply explode. But once you can rein in these urges, you are assured of success in your undertakings. Holding them in control, of course, means keeping a hold on your consuming emotions, which, as we've seen, dominate so much of your life.

YOUR DEEP INTUITIVE PERSONALITY

Your intuition is so intense, it overflows into the rest of your life. You have a rare and astonishing ability for psychic insight, especially into physical problems. As long as your equally powerful emotions don't get in the way of your "third eye," you can depend on your strong inner voice for guidance.

YOUR INTELLIGENCE

Surprisingly for someone with such a powerful intuition, your intellect is analytic. This makes for a finely tuned and elastic mind. You can see the details of things and understand how everything fits into the picture—and you can see the whole picture at once. However, because you like to do things so quickly, you tend to overestimate your analytic abilities, which can sometimes get you into trouble. Be careful not to be too hasty in your evaluations and judgments. You have to learn discipline where the intellect is concerned.

YOUR EMOTIONAL NATURE

This is the source of much of your vitality. You are an impassioned woman for whom love comes first. It is as if you invented the art of seduction—perhaps you did! Not only do you love with your whole being, but you expect your passion to be returned in kind. With your charm and your enchanting personality, men are naturally drawn to you like moths to the flame. It's very important that your lover(s) is faithful to you. But whether or not you'll reciprocate is another question entirely. You require a lot of emotional indulgence in your hectic, exciting life, and the one who is able to give it will not only be your "personal property," but will possess you, as well. You probably don't have the calmest of lovelives, but surely yours is the most vital and intense.

YOUR HEALTH AND VITALITY

Fortunately for your busy schedule, you have the constitution of an Amazon, and an astonishing vitality. You're the last one to tire, able to fight back fatigue and catch sleep when you can. You have no idea what regular habits mean. Still, you must avoid using stimulants to excess; your circulatory system, especially in your legs, is delicate.

THE SOCIAL YOU

You are very sociable—too sociable, sometimes. You lead a somewhat disorderly life, but your luck is unusually good and you don't really have to keep a planned social life—things just seem to happen around you. You enjoy a good time with a crowd of good, active friends. A night at home in front of the television is rare for you. Rather, you'll be out dancing, dressed to kill (and seduce), and your delightful ways will soon draw a crowd of admirers, enchanted by your magnetism. You are a devoted friend and have an almost reverential attitude toward your closest circle. You are willing to do just about anything for them, especially to enliven their lives with your own special sparkle.

———

NamePortrait
58
Associated Names

Aleka	Eddie	Lewanna	Mala
Alfonsine	Edna	Linda	Malena
Aloha	Edny	Luanna	Malina
Alonza	Engelbert	Ludmila	Marva
Alphonsina	Engelberta	Ludmilla	Marvel
Alphonsine	Engelbertha	Lynda	Marvela
Aubierge	Engelberthe	Mada	Marvella
Ava	Fawn	Madalaine	Marvelle
Avi	Fonda	Madaleine	Mauricette
Avice	Gardenia	Madalena	Mina
Avis	Glenda	Madaline	Naoma
Avisa	Glenn	Maddalena	Naomi
Avvy	Glenna	Maddalene	Noami
Bambi	Glynis	Maddie	Nomi
Berengaria	Gussie	Maddy	Nomie
Berengere	Gussy	Madel	Norberta
Birdie	Gustava	Madelaine	Norberte
Caledonia	Gustave	Madeleine	Norbertha
Caledonie	Hadwisa	Madelia	Norberthe
Connie	Hibiscus	Madeline	Orel
Conrada	Huetta	Madella	Orela
Conradina	Huette	Madelle	Sue
Conradine	Hugete	Madelon	Sukey
Dahlia	Hugette	Madlin	Suki
Dale	Huguette	Magda	Suky
Dalhia	Jemie	Magdala	Susan
Dalia	Jemima	Magdalane	Susana
Damita	Jemina	Magdalen	Susanna
Desiree	Jeminah	Magdalena	Susannah
Drusilla	Jemmie	Magdalene	Susanne
Ed	Jewel	Magdalyn	Susel

Associated Names (cont.)

Susette	Suzel	Syne	Uda
Susi	Suzetta	Thelma	Udella
Susie	Suzette	Thyra	Udelle
Susy	Suzie	Tourmalina	Zsa-Zsa
Suzanna	Suzy	Tourmaline	
Suzanne	Syna	Trista	

Name Portrait 59

Man of the Moment

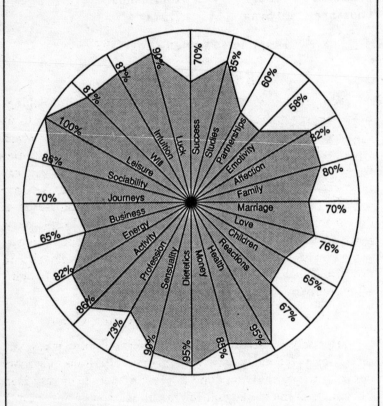

Element : Fire   **Plant** : Ash tree

Mineral : Molybdenum   **Sign** : Sagittarius

Animal : Mink   **Color** : Orange

Personality Type:

Man of the Moment

(Associated names – page 391)

BASIC CHARACTER

You are a man of practical convictions. You do things
to get things done, and the things that get done have to fit
into the scheme of your life. You have a compulsive concern
for success, and, in general, are confident in your abilities
to succeed. Like your totem plant, the ash tree, you are
both elastic and resistant in the face of difficulties. You are
decisive in your actions, and possess a spontaneous sense of
diplomacy with other people. With your natural diplomacy,
and your ability to be a good listener, you are something of
a born salesman. There is also the performer's flourish in
everything you do, which makes you attractive and sought-
after company.

YOUR PSYCHOLOGY

Despite your attractiveness and your outgoing ways, you
often don't get along well with people. Perhaps it's more
accurate to say that you don't hold many people in very high
esteem. Like the mink, your totem animal, you have a smooth
exterior but keep your own habits. Still, you are a natural
extrovert and very objective. You have a very high sense
of personal honor; in other times, you might have been out
dueling every other week to defend it. You have a tendency
to become over-upset if you think someone is stepping on
your toes. And you can become very touchy about money
matters. This is all because, deep down inside, like the mink,

you are a somewhat timid fellow. You need success in order to keep your poise and self-confidence. Though you appear to be quite willful, your will is not as strong as it seems and you sometimes are troubled by doubts about whether your "act" is as convincing as it should be.

HOW YOU ACT AND REACT IN THE WORLD

Although you do things with gusto and an actor's brandish, you essentially have your feet on the ground. Chances are, you're a self-taught, self-made man. What you need for success is not taught in universities but in the college of life. You're always able to get by on your wits, but your work must be interesting to you and each job must promise to advance you in life. With your natural talents for diplomacy and salesmanship, you would make an excellent public relations professional or a diplomat. You could also become a front-line business or government negotiator; a good theater manager; or a reliable legislator who knows just how to pull the right strings to get things done. Anything that involves mass communications or that teaches and entertains fascinates you.

YOUR DEEP INTUITIVE PERSONALITY

It's not so much intuition as it is insight that allows you to sniff things out. Your marvelous spontaneity—your ability to live thoroughly in the present moment—is responsible for this remarkable near-intuition. You seem to know by instinct precisely what is about to happen, and how you can affect the next moment.

YOUR INTELLIGENCE

You have a very elastic mind, which is reinforced by a fine imagination and an uncanny memory for events and details. Though you tend to use your sharp intellect for practical ends, you sometimes become fascinated by more abstract ideas but usually only when those ideas can be translated into useful action. Your curiosity is alert and alive and, coupled with your keen sense of humor, makes you a charming wit.

YOUR EMOTIONAL NATURE

Even though you don't like your affections to weigh heavily on you, you have strong emotions which are influenced by a number of things: your family interests, which are always your first concern; your work, which absorbs so much of your time; and your drive for success. You tend to be possessive where love is concerned and, more than likely, your lovers are less outgoing than you and perhaps even a bit submissive to your needs. You have a great sensual nature, and as well as sex, you enjoy good food, good drink, and good music. Sexually, you tend to be quite steady—not the Don Juan at all, but a practical, down-to-earth, and often passionate husband.

YOUR HEALTH AND VITALITY

You have a strong constitution and excellent health, as long as you are in a dynamic environment. A stultifying office job can affect your good health and might lead you to taking stimulants in order to compensate for your sedentary surroundings. You do need enough sleep and a lot of fresh air and exercise. Your vulnerable spots are your kidneys and urinary system, and your prostate gland.

THE SOCIAL YOU

People feel very much at ease around you—comfortable and free to be themselves. That's probably what they call the "mirror effect"—you're without airs and completely yourself, so others, sensing this, automatically drop their airs and pretentions around you. You enjoy simple entertainments—an easy-going card game perhaps, or a good movie with a few friends. You are quite dedicated to your close friends and cordial to your acquaintances. You do have a streak of the bon vivant in you, which comes out when you are riding the crest of success. Still, even in bad times you keep on an even keel and don't take your own disappointments out on friends and loved ones.

NamePortrait
59
Associated Names

Atworth	Douggie	Hardwyn	Marcello
Carvel	Douggy	Harwin	Marcellus
Carvell	Douglas	Harwyn	Moreland
Cavan	Dugal	Judas	Oxford
Conway	Dugald	Jude	Rhett
Crawford	Duggie	Kavan	Varden
Crowford	Duggy	Keegan	Vardon
Damon	Duglass	Marceau	Verden
Delphin	Einar	Marcel	Verdon
Doug	Hadwin	Marcelin	
Dougal	Hardwin	Marcellin	

Name Portrait 60

Tender Nurturer

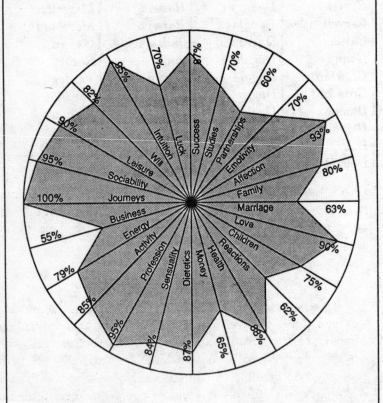

Element : Water   **Plant** : Maple tree

Mineral : Chalcedony   **Sign** : Pisces

Animal : Trout   **Color**: Green

Personality Type:

Tender Nurturer

(Associated names – page 397)

BASIC CHARACTER

You go with the currents, like your totem animal, the trout. This might make you appear flighty at times, but in general, you are rather subdued and withdrawn. You have a very refined moral code, fragile sensibilities, and tend to be rather sensitive. But despite your essentially quiet nature, you are very emotional and quite charming, with high ideals and a sense of dedication to the higher qualities of life and to friends who fit those qualities.

YOUR PSYCHOLOGY

Because you are an introvert by nature and somewhat shy, you sometimes tend to let other people take advantage of your good will and charming personality. You can over-commit yourself and find that you have planned far more than you are capable of doing. Then you might withdraw completely—or else become nervous and anxious, doubting yourself. You need a lot of support to keep up your self-confidence and to keep you away from the habit of simply resigning yourself to a bad situation. Still, there is a stubborn streak in you that says, "Don't let go, no matter what!" Your will can be impressively strong—and then it can flag, especially in situations where your strong emotions are concerned.

HOW YOU ACT AND REACT IN THE WORLD

You tend to react more intensely than you initiate action, and your reactions aren't always very predictable. There is a flightiness about them. You can either flee from a threatening situation or face it with a stubborn resignation. As long as you are occupied with a career that has to do with nourishing or healing others, you can be very effective in your actions. Pediatrics, child care, physical therapy, gynecology, or herbal medicine are fields which allow you to express yourself fully. You would also make a warm and tender, if a bit too permissive, parent. As a mother, you tend to be a total parent, devoting all of yourself to childrearing. Whatever it is you choose to do, you bring to it your very refined, very delicate touch. You're not one to stir up the waters—that would be distasteful and vulgar to you. Rather, you apply yourself softly and knowingly, always following your sensitive emotions.

YOUR DEEP INTUITIVE PERSONALITY

With your finely developed intuition, you are like your plant totem, the maple tree—quiet and almost secretive, taking your modest place deep in the forest, where your sweet syrup overflows in the spring. You're a virtual fountain of instinctive knowledge, and are drawn naturally to the feminine sciences of astrology, synchronicity, and the other precognitive disciplines. You do have a tendency, however, to rely too much on your "inner voice" at the expense of your effectiveness and well-being in the social world.

YOUR INTELLIGENCE

Your mind is holistic—synthetic. You can see things at a single glance, comprehend a situation immediately, and keep a good perspective without wasting your time on details. Though your intellect is good, you sometimes tend to hurry things and may make errors in judgment as a consequence. Sometimes, too, your memory of things is affected too much by your emotions, and it seems as if you're absent-minded. But most likely, it's just that you are pondering the nature of things, consulting your powerful intuition. What you need is intellectual discipline so that your keen intellect can be most effective in your life.

YOUR EMOTIONAL NATURE

With your emotions so high on the scale of forces ruling your life, it isn't at all surprising that you are as affectionate as you are. There is nothing ostentatious about your affections, however. You express yourself in a warm and quiet way which is irresistibly charming. Much of what you feel is spoken silently, in your eyes, or the way you look at someone. Sex is a very delicate area for you. First, you find it absolutely reprehensible that anyone would think to talk about sex. To you, it is a private, tender, meaningful expression of love. Still, you are quite sensual, with strong desires that make themselves known. The only trouble is—will you feel confident enough to express them to the person who is evoking them? Because of your shyness, you might end up settling for a lover who is not worthy of your high ideals and sensibilities—who cannot return your quiet but intense love.

YOUR HEALTH AND VITALITY

Your vitality is very good, but your health, as everything else, is often affected by your emotional moods. You need a very strict diet that is absolutely devoid of stimulants. You must also take care to avoid tranquilizers and depressants. Your weak points are your digestive system and genitals.

THE SOCIAL YOU

Despite your bouts with shyness, you hate being alone and are very sociable. You're attached to your family and a few close friends. Your social life sometimes becomes a bit too hectic for you, however, and you might find you've adopted a life style that is not compatible with your sensibilities simply in order to please someone else. You're a compelling person with a quiet, magnetic attraction, although at times you are flighty and contradictory in your social behavior. You can have a good time at a large, modish party, or with a few quiet friends at home, according to your moods. But wherever you find yourself, you are charming to be around and exude a quiet, inner sturdiness, as if you have many secrets which you might reveal all of a sudden. People stay around; they want to learn your mystery.

NamePortrait
60
Associated Names

Aberah	Constancy	Larraine	Lorelei
Adolfa	Constanta	Laura	Lorelia
Adolfina	Constantia	Laure	Lorelie
Adolpha	Constantina	Laureen	Loren
Adolphina	Constantine	Laurel	Lorena
Adolphine	Constanza	Lauren	Lorenza
Amadea	Consuela	Laurena	Loretta
April	Consuelo	Laurene	Lorette
Avera	Daffy	Laurentine	Lori
Averil	Daisy	Lauretta	Lorie
Averilia	Davida	Laurette	Lorinda
Averill	Davina	Laurie	Lorine
Averilla	Eldora	Lawrence	Lorita
Averyl	Greta	Lennie	Lorna
Avril	Gretchen	Lenny	Lorraine
Avyril	Grete	Leona	Lorrie
Ayril	Gretel	Leonarda	Lorry
Blessin	Grethe	Leonarde	Lura
Blessing	Haralda	Leonardina	Lurleen
Cal	Haraldina	Leonardine	Lurlene
Calantha	Harolda	Leone	Lurlette
Calanthe	Haroldina	Leoni	Lurlina
Callie	Hectorine	Leonie	Lurline
Cally	Ierne	Leontina	Madge
Cleantha	Kalantha	Leontine	Mady
Cleanthe	Kalanthe	Leontyne	Mag
Cliantha	La Reina	Lora	Maggi
Clianthe	Lani	Loraine	Maggie
Con	Lanna	Loralie	Maggy
Connie	Laraine	Lore	Magnhilda
Constance	Larayne	Loree	Magnhilde

Associated Names (cont.)

Magnilda	Margette	Nillie	Roland
Magnilde	Margharita	Nola	Rolande
Magnolia	Margo	Nolie	Rowena
Maida	Margorie	Ondine	Rowenna
Maidel	Margory	Orlanda	Servane
Maidie	Margot	Orlande	Siegfride
Maisie	Marguerita	Orlena	Sigfreda
Marfot	Marguerite	Pearl	Sigfrieda
Margalo	Margueritta	Pearle	Theafania
Margao	Marjery	Pearlie	Theaphania
Margaret	Marjorie	Peggy	Theofanie
Margareta	Mayda	Perl	Theofila
Margaretha	Mayde	Perle	Theofilia
Margarethe	Maydena	Perlette	Theophania
Margaretta	Meg	Perlie	Theophanie
Margarita	Merna	Perlina	Theophila
Marge	Meta	Perline	Theophilia
Margerie	Mirna	Peroline	Valeska
Margerita	Moina	Rabi	Waleska
Margery	Morna	Risa	Zuria
Marget	Moyna	Rita	
Margethe	Myrna	Ro	
Margetta	Nilda	Rola	

Name Portrait 61

Eager Huntress

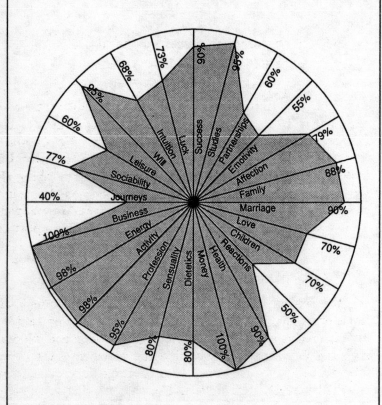

Element : Fire   **Plant** : Tulip

Mineral : Jet   **Sign** : Sagittarius

Animal : Lark   **Color** : Blue

Personality Type:

Eager Huntress

(Associated names – page 404)

BASIC CHARACTER

With your straight-shooting, goal-oriented character, you seem like a force of nature, sure to reach your target quickly and bravely. You are imperturbable in your flight toward success, not unlike the lark, your special animal totem, which mounts to the sky early in the morning and keeps flying after the sun has risen. You have well-balanced reactions and strong emotions, and tend to influence those around you. Your traditional moral code is a source of much comfort to you, as is your work and activities with your family.

YOUR PSYCHOLOGY

You are an extrovert, able to move about through all levels of society. Very likely you matured rapidly as an adolescent. Your plant totem, the tulip, reflects as much, blooming early in spring, its bulbs ripening way before the other flowers begin to bud. Despite your outgoing nature and your clearly defined sense of yourself, however, you do occasionally suffer nervous anxiety over your emotional life. You tend to get irritable and possessive and might distrust other people. Your powerful will can make you become stubborn at times, or else contradictory in your attitudes toward those around you. You are hypersensitive to criticism, gossip, and frustration, and may develop eccentric behavior to compensate for your intractable sensitivities.

HOW YOU ACT AND REACT IN THE WORLD

You have a strong desire to succeed and to learn and are very active in life, but not everything comes easily to you. You want authority and at the same time are influenced by your emotions to a great degree. Your success comes from steady application, and you are certainly up to that. Once you have set a goal for yourself, you follow through, doing everything in your power and sometimes a little bit beyond to reach it. It's like you're stalking a prey, the way you go after things. Possible career choices include pharmacy or medicine, science, language, teaching, and corporate management. Because you have a natural "feel" for the earth and earth sciences, you would also make an efficient and effective agronomist, rancher or even a restauranteur. You tend to be something of a loner where career is concerned, happier in a head-to-head competition than with cooperation among fellow-workers.

YOUR DEEP INTUITIVE PERSONALITY

"Old wives' tales," is probably your reply when someone brings up the subject of intuition. Though your "inner voice" is active in its own unheeded way, you tend not to pay much attention to it, preferring cold logic and visible results instead.

YOUR INTELLIGENCE

You are able to grasp the slightest detail of any problem and put it in place. Your intellect is analytic, keenly so. You have an excellent memory, which is powered as much by your sense for the logical as it is by your emotions, and you're able to call upon it in helping you to solve any problem that confronts you.

YOUR EMOTIONAL NATURE

There is a secret element to your emotions. You rarely approach others with warmth and confidence, waiting instead until they come forward and you are able to trust them. You rely upon traditional ways of expressing your affections, and although partnership and marriage is important to you, you tend not to be very open sexually. Most likely, you are happiest in a love affair if you have the upper hand. You do not like emotional demands to be placed upon you, though you are perfectly willing to make your own demands for security and comfort. Though your emotions are strong, they are very often repressed in favor of career and security.

YOUR HEALTH AND VITALITY

You seem to stock up your health, going through periods of strict obedience to a healthy lifestyle, then depleting your vitality in bursts of intense activity that doesn't have any room for a regular regimen. It is important that you maintain some sort of schedule for a good diet and exercise. You have a tendency toward weight problems if you do not. You need the out of doors—swimming, country hikes, and, if possible, time at the beach—to refresh and reinvigorate yourself. It is important to have iodine in your diet. Your weak points are your stomach and genitals.

THE SOCIAL YOU

As long as your social life doesn't interfere with your professional life, you are a most gracious hostess or guest. You have your own defined social interests, and most likely, a well-structured social life which meets most interests. You have a tendency to adopt the attitudes of friends, but very often that is only a surface reaction in order to avoid a confrontation. You just don't like public squabbles and many times agree just so as not to disagree for the moment. Your friends are a source of comfort and security, as are the traditional entertainments. Though you're far from a gadabout, you're certainly not a recluse when it comes to keeping good and entertaining company.

———————

NamePortrait
61
Associated Names

Alima	Fortuna	Marty	Renita
Arda	Fortune	Matty	Rennie
Ardath	Gartred	Mona	Rhea
Ardatha	Gert	Monca	Ronalda
Ardeen	Gertie	Monica	Ronalde
Ardelis	Gertrud	Monique	Ronnie
Ardella	Gertruda	Natene	Ronny
Ardelle	Gertrude	Nathanaelle	Siobahn
Ardene	Gertrudis	Nathane	Siuban
Ardere	Gerty	Nathania	Truda
Ardine	Gunhilda	Nathene	Trudey
Ardis	Gunhilde	Nerice	Trudi
Ardra	Jodie	Nerima	Trudie
Aridatha	Jody	Nerine	Trudy
Arselma	Judie	Nerissa	True
Arva	Judith	Nerita	Urania
Bernadene	Juditha	Ora	Ursa
Bernadette	Judy	Orsa	Ursel
Bernadina	Latonia	Orsola	Ursie
Bernadine	Lucrece	Quenby	Ursola
Bernardina	Lucrecia	Rana	Ursula
Bernardine	Lucretia	Ranee	Ursule
Berney	Lucrezia	Rani	Ursulette
Bernia	Marta	Rea	Ursuline
Bernie	Martella	Renata	Ursy
Bernita	Martha	Renate	Vespera
Desdemona	Marthe	Rence	
Desmona	Martie	Rene	
Eden	Martita	Renee	

Name Portrait 62

Radiant Lily

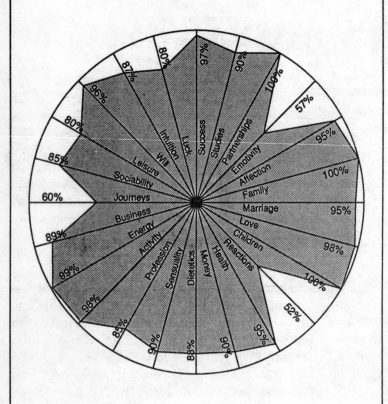

Element : Earth   **Plant** : Lily
Mineral : Emerald   **Sign** : Virgo
Animal : Dove   **Color** : Blue

Personality Type:

Radiant Lily

(Associated names – page 411)

BASIC CHARACTER

You have finely tuned emotions, a high moral code, and a great capacity to act and react. You're not given to following the styles and fashions of the day; your determination and strength comes from within. Your totem animal, the dove, and your totem plant, the lily, reflect the power of your inner life, its beauty and purity which radiate from you in warmth and a seemingly endless capacity for love. You set rigorous standards for yourself and then surround yourself with a protective strength which sees you through to your goals.

YOUR PSYCHOLOGY

Even though there is a sort of magnetic glow around you, you are by nature an introvert. You tend to withdraw into your own world and don't always consider it a very good idea to express your emotions. You can be secretive and jealous and tend to become irritable and short-tempered. There is a lot about you that is contradictory. For instance, despite your essential selflessness, you have an inclination to set yourself up in opposition to certain other people, to observe their behavior closely and become downright annoyed at them. You can be surprisingly harsh at times, especially when someone does something that you consider out of place or unbecoming. You have a fully developed will and can be rather intimidating from time to time. Still, you rarely try to impress others with your own brilliance. You suffer awfully from failure but rarely get discouraged; you're usually ready to plunge in and try again.

HOW YOU ACT AND REACT IN THE WORLD

Although you are a bit explosive and often stubborn, reacting strongly to adverse situations and those whom you consider to be your "natural enemies," you are a very generous person whose actions belie a great amount of tenderness and altruism. You're a remarkable activist, and your busy life is easily sustained because you have the energy to match it. You were most likely a very good student, drawn to classical studies and careers that involve a deep personal commitment. Motherhood is well suited to your firm but tender temperament, as is any profession that brings you into contact with children. You would do well in a career in medicine, education, pediatrics, or religion. You're also attracted to professions that involve social commitment, and for this reason would make an effective union activist or a social commentator in the tradition of Mary Wollstonecraft. It is also possible that you might pursue an artistic career, but most likely, your art would be an expression of your morality and social justice.

YOUR DEEP INTUITIVE PERSONALITY

It might seem ironic that someone with such rich and profound inner convictions puts so little faith in her intuition as you do, but this is most certainly the case. Still, your "inner voice" is strong and your intuition the source of much of your attractiveness, even though you would rather follow the more familiar paths of experience for your insight.

YOUR INTELLIGENCE

You have an analytic mind, which enables you to piece together the details of a problem, rather than to see it all at once. Your memory is astonishingly cast; you forget nothing. With your indefatigable energy, you are able to use your well-focused intellect to great effect in the world.

YOUR EMOTIONAL NATURE

There is a duality about your emotional character which often baffles people. You can be vulnerable and sensitive one day, and harsh and demanding the next. This is probably, at least in part, due to your inclination to be possessive, though your possessiveness is not motivated by a sense of ownership per se, as much as it is by self-protectiveness. You want a faithful lover, yet someone who will not take over your life. This attitude extends to your closest friends. More than anything, you receive great joy in giving. Sexually, you tend to be quite demanding, but you're usually able to keep a rein on your demands. So many of your sensual pleasures are tied to love, that it is difficult to imagine you with a long string of casual affairs. Love for you is to be understood in the loftiest sense of the word, as well as for its more pleasure-giving aspects. With the dove and the lily as your totems, this is not unusual—the powers of heaven and the pure emotions of earth symbolize your emotional life very well.

YOUR HEALTH AND VITALITY

What marvelous vitality! What robust good health! As long as you can develop ways to prevent your powerful emotions from creating stress in your life, you will continue to enjoy the good health that you need to keep up your busy life. Your lungs and skin may present some minor health problems; and your intestines are your most vulnerable spot.

THE SOCIAL YOU

You entertain with simplicity and dignity. Faithfulness, thrift, and courage are your bywords in social life. You're perfectly at ease with other people, but you do not need to be around others, as you're perfectly happy with solitude. Your great inner radiance draws others to you, as does your well of strength and dedication. Your most enjoyable time socially is passed with your close circle of friends, whom you trust and who trust you. You like everything to be in its place, and this includes people, which probably means that you don't mingle well with people out of your social or professional class. But you maintain an even, prudent, and emotionally stimulating social life, however great or small you decide to establish your circle of friends.

———————

NamePortrait
62
Associated Names

Alpha	Consolata	Gracia	Lallie
Anselma	Consolation	Gracie	Lawrie
Artemesia	Deidre	Grayce	Lee
Anselme	Deirdre	Grazia	Leilani
Asta	Derdre	Graziella	Lillani
Astra	Diantha	Griselda	Lullani
Astrid	Dianthe	Griselde	Mae
Astrita	Dianthia	Griseldi	Maia
Athena	Ebba	Grishelda	Maire
Athene	Ella	Grishelde	Mairi
Athenee	Elodie	Grishilda	Maite
Aveline	Engracia	Grishilde	Mamie
Azura	Eula	Grisolde	Manette
Bea	Eulalia	Grizel	Manon
Beata	Eulalie	Grizelda	Mara
Beatrice	Eva	Grizzell	Maraline
Beatrix	Evangelina	Guilla	Maretta
Beattie	Evangeline	Gwenn	Marette
Bee	Eve	Helma	Mari
Beitris	Eveleen	Humphrey	Maria
Billie	Evelina	Isis	Mariam
Billy	Eveline	Isol	Marian
Carma	Evelyn	Isola	Mariana
Cilla	Evie	Isolabella	Marianna
Cinderella	Evita	Isolabelle	Marianne
Cindie	Evonne	Jeremia	Maribelle
Cindy	Eysllt	Jeremiah	Marie
Concordia	Filma	Jeri	Marielle
Concordie	Girosal	Jerrie	Mariette
Concordina	Gorgene	Jerry	Marigold
Concordy	Grace	Jery	Marilla

Associated Names (cont.)

Marilyn	Merrit	Muriel	Tom
Marina	Merritt	Murielle	Tomasa
Marinette	Merritta	Myra	Tomase
Mariom	Merry	Myriam	Tomasina
Marion	Mia	Noemie	Tomasine
Marla	Mimi	Norma	Tommie
Marleen	Mina	Normi	Tommy
Marlena	Minda	Normie	Trix
Marlene	Mindy	Peace	Trixie
Marline	Minerva	Petunia	Trixy
Mary	Minetta	Philmen	Val
Marya	Minna	Philomela	Valeda
Maryann	Minnie	Philomena	Valencia
Maryanne	Minny	Philomene	Valentia
Marygold	Minta	Pholma	Valentina
Marylin	Mintha	Polly	Valentine
Maryline	Minthe	Pollyanna	Valida
Marylise	Mira	Randa	Vallie
Marylou	Mirabel	Randi	Van
Marylyn	Mirabella	Randy	Vancy
Maryruth	Mirabelle	Ronnie	Vanessa
Maryse	Miranda	Ronny	Vangie
Maryvonne	Mirella	Rue	Vania
Maureen	Miriam	Ruella	Vanna
May	Mirilla	Ruth	Vanni
Mearr	Mitzi	Ruthie	Vannie
Mendi	Moira	Selda	Vanny
Mendy	Moire	Selma	Vanya
Meri	Molly	Thetis	Velma
Meriel	Morgan	Thetys	Vera
Merit	Morgana	Thomasa	Verane
Meritta	Moria	Thomase	Verda
Merri	Moya	Thomasina	Verde
Merrie	Muire	Thomasine	Vere

Associated Names (cont.)

Verena	Veta	Willabelle	Zelma
Verene	Virgilia	Willie	Zera
Verina	Vita	Willy	Zeta
Verine	Vitia	Wilma	Zetta
Verla	Vonnie	Zelda	Zeva
Vernona	Vonny	Zele	Zita
Verona	Welma	Zelia	Zitao
Veronica	Wilhelmina	Zelie	
Veronique	Willa	Zelina	

Name Portrait 63

Watchful Thinker

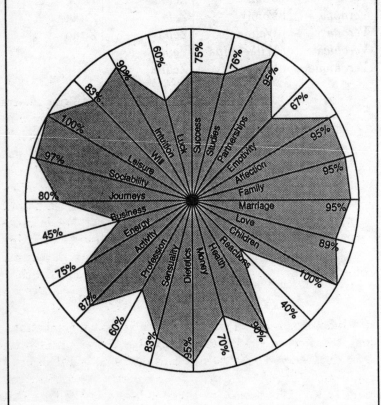

Element : Fire   **Plant** : Birch tree

Mineral : Cornelian   **Sign** : Sagittarius

Animal : Condor   **Color**: Violet

Personality Type:

Watchful Thinker

(Associated names – page 419)

BASIC CHARACTER

You are brilliant, with a contemplative, alluring charm that comes from a refinement and tact in your dealings with the world and people. With your strong emotions, one might expect you to be more expressive about your desires, but you tend to be somewhat secretive about yourself, and your reactions are rather subdued. You need activity, but often would rather wait and watch and hope that all turns out for the best. You can be very convincing once you do make up your mind on the best way to act, and this is probably because of your high moral standards, which, though they are sometimes obtrusive, give you reassurance and confidence.

YOUR PSYCHOLOGY

Indecision is one of your most troublesome mental states, and it can cause you no end of anxiety. You're an introvert by nature, so you tend to withdraw into your world, becoming overcautious. Like your totem animal, the condor, you tend to watch and wait, to circle endlessly in the air. This difficulty of getting out of your contemplative moods and into actions is abetted by your fluctuating will, and your inaction often conceals an inner turbulence. You're acutely sensitive to failure and prone to daydream of great feats, which only aggravates your anxiety. Still, you can be pulled out of your inner world by some great event or challenge, and then you show a fearsome precision and efficiency. Like your totem plant, the birch, you are both tough and tender—you can be flexible and smooth like the birch with its strong yet bending trunk and its slender, delicate branches.

HOW YOU ACT AND REACT IN THE WORLD

You're a very active person, but you have your own way of going about things and don't always understand the more normal ways of getting things accomplished. You might have to adopt some external structure or discipline in order to follow through on your projects. You enjoy school, but for you it is a means to an end, a preparation for a specific goal. Although you are goal-oriented, you do not care for the "knocks" of a struggle, and you have trouble adjusting or changing careers. You tend to specialize in your career, and most likely are attracted to such professions as acting, finance, medicine, or drama. You could also be an excellent novelist, as you're a natural story-teller, and when you don't have a professional outlet for that particular gift, you'll tend to be a great and entertaining talker.

YOUR DEEP INTUITIVE PERSONALITY

It isn't surprising that someone as contemplative as you are possesses such a prodigious intuition. You might experience premonitions quite often in your life; and your intuition helps you to bring many fertile ideas into the world. However, you tend to rely too much on your good luck, and though your intuition is the source of so much of your charm and allure, it often keeps you standing in one place, trusting solely in it.

YOUR INTELLIGENCE

You have a keen intellect and can understand things quickly and totally. However, at times you tend to ramble your way to conclusions and apply your holistic mind to your own life story more than to the problems that are confronting you at the moment. You are able to ponder things at length, and sometimes will think about them for years before you decide what you'll do or if you'll do anything at all.

416

YOUR EMOTIONAL NATURE

Love—and that's with a capital L—and only Love makes the world go 'round. At least, to hear you talk, that's the case. You can make some grand abstractions about the marvels of Love, and at the same time wish to be the one and only ever of your beloved. You can be warm and sensitive in your affections as long as you believe your lover understands you and that you possess her thoroughly. Sensually, you lean to conventional expressions and at times appear a little old-fashioned. You're not exactly a playboy, but when you are in a secure emotional situation, you show your sexuality openly and exquisitely, with an endearing tenderness and charm. Wounded in love, you retreat. You're not sexually aggressive, and your retreat from physical love might result in pursuing some kind of mysticism, for which your sensitive emotions are well suited.

YOUR HEALTH AND VITALITY

Although you have a very strong vitality, your general health reflects your psychic state. You tire easily and are inclined to overtax your system. One cannot say that you plan your diet—more likely, you guess at it, ignore it, or eat on whims. You have to watch your digestive system carefully because of these tendencies. Further, you are prone to asthma, so attention has to be given to the environment you choose to live in.

THE SOCIAL YOU

You're a devoted, faithful, and helpful friend; and you pursue a non-stop social life. You simply must have the company of other people, despite your essential introversion. You delight in giving parties and are wild about big social gatherings. You tend to join fraternal organizations, partly because you want to be useful and help others, and partly because they afford a good outlet for your social energies. Even though you tend to reject others' opinions at first hearing, you are intelligent, tactful, and refined in your dealings in society.

Your high morals and your codified view of people often leads you to believe that other people are morally deficient and therefore need your good judgment desperately—but aside from this usually unexpressed opinion, you are entertaining company and your contemplative nature is a source of guidance and calm to your friends and companions.

———

NamePortrait
63
Associated Names

Amaury	Eb	Kendal	Morel
Amery	Eberhard	Kendall	Morice
Amory	Eberhart	Kendell	Morrell
Con	Ebner	Kendrick	Morrice
Connie	Eurard	Konrad	Morrie
Conrad	Ev	Kort	Morris
Cort	Everard	Kurt	Morry
Corydon	Evered	Maurey	Saturnin
Curt	Everett	Maurice	Vladimir
Dale	Gaynor	Maury	Wladimir
Dalton	Janvier	Meriadec	
Daly	Ken	Mo	

Name Portrait 64

Honest Judge

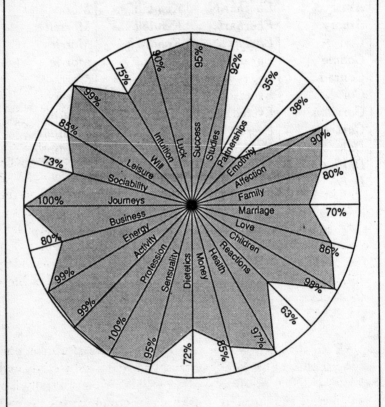

Element : Earth

Mineral : Sulphur

Animal : Tiger

Plant : Elm tree

Sign : Virgo

Color : Red

Personality Type:

Honest Judge

(Associated names – page 425)

BASIC CHARACTER

Strength, valor, and justice are the three words which people commonly think of when you're around. There is something cool-headedly courageous about you which literally exudes an aura of confidence and power. You're logical and straightforward, and very proud of it. But much of your personal power comes from an instinctive way of seeing and dealing with things, much like your totem animal, the tiger, symbol of natural strength and valor. Your total self-confidence leads you to clear-cut decisions from which you will not budge. You have powerful reactions, a consuming will, and prodigious energy to see you through most of life's situations.

YOUR PSYCHOLOGY

Even though you possess all the qualities of a man who is the master of his fate, you tend to be very subjective, and unable to put yourself in another's place. Your normally fair and honest judgment of others can become irrational and influenced by your subjectivity, and thence, too harsh. You do not adjust well to change, and your immense pride often stands in your way and causes you nervous tension and grief. Under an appearance of irritability, you hold your intense reactions under control—abetted by your iron will—and often have consequent trouble sleeping at night; insomnia is the most prevalent symptom of your inner anxiety. You are more introverted and withdrawn than you appear to be and have a tendency to isolate yourself from the world—the world with which you actually do need so much contact.

HOW YOU ACT AND REACT IN THE WORLD

Seeing you in action makes everyone realize that they're dealing with someone in "championship class." You like to set records, always aspiring to better your last accomplishment. You are attentive to events around you, well-disciplined, and logical in your approach to people and things. You always work toward a precise goal and seem to thrive on hard work even though it never seems you're getting much pleasure out of it. You simply will not take "the line of least resistance," and often make things downright difficult for yourself by finding ever new challenges to take up. You demand the same precision and thoroughness from your subordinates that you yourself give to any task and tend to be a perfectionist. Defeat upsets you but does not stop you; it becomes transmogrified into a new challenge. Careers in medicine and surgery or business and the military are particularly attractive to one of your temperament.

YOUR DEEP INTUITIVE PERSONALITY

Why is it that you distrust your intuition so, when it is the source of so much of your insight and understanding? Perhaps it's because of your undying faith in reason and logic—but whatever it is, you have a well-developed, sometimes oracular inner voice to which you respond more or less unconsciously. It is not refined, but it is strong.

YOUR INTELLIGENCE

How lively, how analytically brilliant—and at the same time, how cool and logical! Your intellect is pitilessly logical and allows you to dissect any situation honestly and often from an aloof, emotionless standpoint. Yet, you have an unrelenting memory for emotionally charged events. That, with your immense capacity for contemplation, gives you a mind to reckon with.

YOUR EMOTIONAL NATURE

You are warmly affectionate, even if your emotions rise to the surface with hesitancy. Emotions just aren't logical, and it takes a while before you will recognize that they are there. Once you do, you can be tender, giving, and faithful. You never forget the affections you have received—any more than you do any emotional hurt you've gotten—and return in kind what you are given. You tend to be possessive and like to be dominant in a relationship. Where you might be hesitant about expressing your emotions, however, you are downright impulsive sexually. Most likely, you began your sexual explorations at an early age. Your seductive powers lie not so much in a suave and sophisticated line, but in an instinctive, usually unconscious sexuality which you simply cannot help but exude.

YOUR HEALTH AND VITALITY

You have the longevity of the elm tree, your plant totem, which survives over the centuries with a cool reassurance. You have a good understanding of your physical limits and are able to resist most illnesses—sometimes by pure stubbornness of will! Your logical nature helps you to retain a healthy regimen, despite occasional lapses. You have to keep an eye on your circulatory system, especially your heart.

THE SOCIAL YOU

You choose friends very intelligently and tend to have a few exclusive friendships which are very important to you. You're a loyal friend, and your friends often adopt your attitudes toward friendship, taking your attitudes as an example. Still, you're not all that easy to get close to because of your lack of diplomacy and your sometimes terrifying straightforwardness. Still, you enjoy big social events not so much for themselves as for the diversion they offer. People trust you—even when you don't trust them—and luck favors you even though you do not rely upon it for success. Success comes to you, not necessarily early in life, but firmly and lastingly.

———

NamePortrait
64
Associated Names

Adam	Dicky	Mariel	Richard
Adan	Dimitri	Micah	Richerd
Addison	Dixon	Mich	Rick
Adin	Dmitri	Michael	Rickert
Aenas	Eden	Michel	Rickie
Aeneas	Egan	Mickie	Ricky
Ahmed	Elery	Micky	Riocard
Aickin	Ellerey	Miguel	Ritch
Aidan	Ellery	Mikael	Ritchie
Aiken	Eneas	Mike	Roch
Aikin	Fairley	Mischa	Sigwald
Aric	Fairlie	Misha	Vital
Bradburn	Fairly	Mitch	Vito
Carmichael	Farl	Mitchell	Welborne
Ciprian	Farley	Napoleon	Welbourne
Cyprian	Fox	Parish	Welby
Cyprien	Genest	Parr	Winfield
Demetrius	Hardey	Parrish	Winfred
Demmy	Hardi	Parry	Wingate
Diccon	Hardie	Rab	Winifred
Dick	Hardy	Rabbie	Winifrid
Dickie	Hartwood	Rabby	Zeus
Dickon	Harwood	Ricard	
Dickson	Knight	Rich	

Name Portrait 65
Triumphant Builder

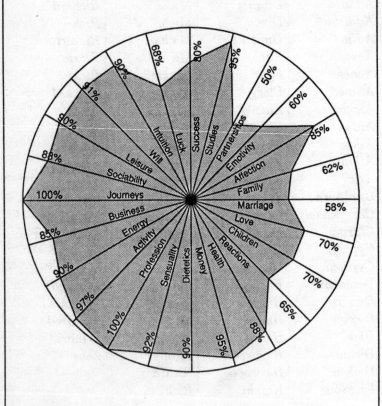

Element : Fire   **Plant** : Hemlock

Mineral : Sandstone   **Sign** : Sagittarius

Animal : Beaver   **Color** : Red

Personality Type:

Triumphant Builder

(Associated names – page 431)

BASIC CHARACTER

Whether it's your love life, your business life, or a weekend outing to the mountains, you're organizing things into a perfect structure. Like your totem animal, the beaver, you are a natural builder, constructing all aspects of your life. Though you are emotional and rather excitable, you're not quick on the trigger. And though you've got to keep busy to keep happy, you approach things with a combination of go-getter enthusiasm and practical patience. You are precise, intelligent, and effective, capable of great achievements. Your totem plant, the hemlock, is the symbol of sturdy purpose, which is reflected in your approach towards your many involvements.

YOUR PSYCHOLOGY

You tend to be a perfectionist, and this can cause you anxieties and inner turbulence when all is not up to your very high standards. Because you are subjective, your perception of the world is colored by your own sensitivities. You are keenly sensitive to moral defeat and become irritable over both your own and those which you perceive in other people. You can hold a grudge to the end of time. You need a bit more emotional discipline in order to keep your occasionally hot temper in check; though you can be angelically patient most times, you explode when your frightfully high standards are not being met. Your will is very strong and effective, but can become stubbornness or lead you into bitterness if things aren't going your way. Your natural caution, by the same token, can turn into inhibition and keep you from acting—which results in a lot of nervous tension, as it is important for you to keep busy.

HOW YOU ACT AND REACT IN THE WORLD

You do not react quickly, but you do react with such a great intensity and so emotionally that at times a hurricane would be calmer company. There's something of the revolutionary in you, but as a rule, that urge to do everything over is held in constructive check by the finely tuned structure you've given your life. It is willful application to tasks that leads to your success. You are a good student, attracted both to the classics and science and math. You would make an excellent administrator or lawyer, or else a legislator because you know how to wait for the opportune moment before pitching in and getting involved in issues. The manufacturing industry might interest you if you had an active role in designing and planning both products and their sale. Everything that arouses society interests you, and it would not be surprising to find you in a career in radio or television. Your controlled and precise way of dealing would also make you a fine policeman.

YOUR DEEP INTUITIVE PERSONALITY

Your intuition is profound and spontaneous. It offers you keen and rapid insights, which you are not afraid to use in your busy life. Sometimes, you merely talk about your intuitively divined understandings—a sort of intellectual exhibitionism which gives you a lot of self-satisfied pleasure.

YOUR INTELLIGENCE

You possess a deeply perceptive and practical intellect, which is far more subdued than you let on. To hear you talk, you are the quickest wit around, and although there is a lot of truth to that, you are at your intellectual best when you let your mind work at its own level. You depend on your insights and should not draw conclusions before you've taken the time to mull things over a while. Your curiosity is intense and active; you need time to digest everything you take in.

YOUR EMOTIONAL NATURE

Despite your highly emotional nature, your affections are often very controlled. You are passionate and loving, but the structure you impose on yourself doesn't always allow you to express yourself with ease. But love is important to you, and once you are confident that you won't be betrayed, you are a fine and concerned lover. Sexually, you tend to be a bit aggressive and undoubtedly lead a rather complicated sex life. Your desires are intense, even though you're the last one to admit it, so it's an on-again-off-again approach you take. Whenever you do let yourself go, however, you bring a lot of happiness and pleasure to others.

YOUR HEALTH AND VITALITY

Your vitality is marvelous, even though you do tend to overeat. Very often, your health is dependent on your moods. As long as you're caught up in enthusiasm over a project, you're in good health. But if you allow your pessimism to take over, you are troubled by minor ailments. Your weaknesses lie in your hearing and your sense of balance.

THE SOCIAL YOU

Friendship is very important to you, and your social life revolves around your carefully chosen friends. Still, you can take off on an occasional bout of Dionysian partying, no matter how selective and discriminating you normally are about your company. You are pleasing company, attentive to everything—and such a fine conversationalist. You never lose track of what someone is saying and can take up the line of discussion with someone hours after you were interrupted—a marvelous gift to have at one of those crowded parties. You have a great love for family and children and like to include them in your exciting social life. You're not afraid to criticize someone or to let someone know how to do something better and more efficiently. "If I were you..." is probably one of your favorite expressions. Success comes to you, not out of any quirk of fate, but from your own hard work.

———————————

NamePortrait
65
Associated Names

Aaron	Hartford	Newland	Pol
Ace	Hertford	Newlands	Pollock
Acey	Hi	Newlin	Powell
Achille	Hiram	Newlyn	Sigismond
Aron	Huxford	Noel	Sigismund
Brice	Hy	Nowell	Sigmond
Bryce	Hyram	Orlan	Sigmund
Cowan	Jarman	Pablo	Thorbert
Drew	Jerman	Paley	Torbert
Druce	Jermyn	Paolo	Verner
Dunstan	Kai	Paul	Warner
Edsel	Kenrick	Pauley	Werner
Ford	Natale	Paulie	Yale
Haroun	Nello	Paulin	

Name Portrait 66

Generous Heart

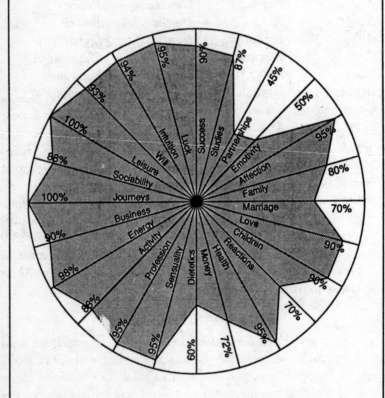

Element : Fire   **Plant** : Oak tree
Mineral : Cobalt   **Sign** : Aries
Animal : Ram   **Color** : Yellow

Personality Type:

Generous Heart

(Associated names – page 436)

BASIC CHARACTER

You're as effervescent as fine champagne and scintillating as a diamond, with a natural exuberance and sense of humor that delight your friends and associates. You tend to be very active and sometimes high-strung and nervous, with an inclination to overreact and get involved in numerous protest movements. Your totem animal is the ram, symbol of creativity. But like the ram, you can become belligerent when your good sense of humor cannot sustain you or convince others that you must do what you want to do. You're fiercely independent and when all is well, you can be big-hearted to a fault. There's a touch of the performer in you, which is sparked by your strong emotions.

YOUR PSYCHOLOGY

Your sparkling personality has many facets, and you tend to be pulled—or to push—in a number of directions at once, which can result in a certain amount of dissembling. Even though you're an extrovert and need an audience, you are very subjective. You do not adjust easily and can become irritable. Your strong emotions often work against you and lead you into escapist daydreams. Failure upsets you but does not discourage you from trying the next task on the horizon—or the next twelve all at once. Your will tends to fluctuate and sometimes translates into pure stubbornness. Angered, you react swiftly and sometimes violently, which is

433

confusing to people for you usually present a facade of great self-confidence; but you are secretly less self-assured than you appear, and you depend on your wit and charming humor to substitute for a depth of real confidence.

HOW YOU ACT AND REACT IN THE WORLD

If it were physically possible, you would live out all your fantasies; but you tend to be a little more realistic than that. You need to take time to reflect before acting, otherwise you tend to take on too many tasks at once and to forget about some of them before they're halfway finished. You seem to work by fits and starts, even though you are devoted to your work. There's something of a circus pitchman in you—you need an audience and can be manipulative if it's necessary. Most likely, you're plagued by financial woes because you simply don't know how to manage money. Money is to spend, and if you have any extra cash on hand it's because there's nothing to buy at the moment. Your creative and acting talents combined might send you to a career on the stage, and your intellectual abilities, combined with those, could lead you to a career in writing or investigative journalism. But whatever your profession, you bring your own special sparkle to it and leave your own big-hearted mark.

YOUR DEEP INTUITIVE PERSONALITY

With such remarkable intuition, it would not be surprising to find you in a little shop telling fortunes or reading the stars. You put your incredibly spontaneous perceptions to clever and effective use; and they are part of your alluring, sometimes entrancing charm.

YOUR INTELLIGENCE

Though you have a brilliant intellect, you prefer to rely upon your imagination. Your creative insights do not come from plowing through the mundane details of any problem, but from swift and sudden realizations—or else they do not come at all. Your mind works best when you're able to share your insights with others—part of the showman sentiment.

YOUR EMOTIONAL NATURE

You have a thirst for warmth and affection, but you cringe if someone is imposing or too aggressive toward you emotionally. Then you take flight with superhuman speed. Paradoxically, if someone you care about withholds her affections altogether, you'll also run away. Balance is what you need. And though your own emotions run deep, you are restrained in expressing affection. Once the proper setting is established though, you are charming, attractive, and amazingly generous in giving your love. Your sexual desires are strong, though you don't always admit to them, and this is bound to take you into many a complicated love affair. But because you are so ruled by your heart, you always find a way to enjoy a satisfying love life.

YOUR HEALTH AND VITALITY

Your strength and stamina and your physical resistance to ailments is very well typified by your totem plant, the sturdy oak. You must pay special attention to your eyes and bones. Your inclination toward escapism may lead you into abusing drugs and alcohol.

THE SOCIAL YOU

There are two sides to you here—the man who loves a parade, and the man who rains on it. When you're feeling good, you're the life of the party, full of charm and showmanship, bringing a diplomacy and charm that are absolutely angelic. But in a cloudy mood, your cleverness can be caustic. It is important for you to choose your company well and to avoid people who get on your nerves, lest your better side drown in your own downpour. In all, you are a lucky person, and your good luck plays an important role in your success, especially during middle age when you've learned how to control some of your more impulsive sparkles.

NamePortrait
66
Associated Names

Aldo	Fagon	Manfried	Raf
Aldrich	Fred	Oram	Rafael
Alric	Freddie	Oran	Rafaello
Arledge	Freddy	Oren	Rafe
Attwood	Frederic	Orin	Raff
Atwood	Frederick	Orran	Raffaello
Atwoode	Frederik	Orren	Ralf
Audric	Frederique	Orrin	Ralph
Bardolf	Fredric	Parkin	Ramsden
Bardolph	Fredrick	Parnell	Ramsey
Bardolphe	Friedrich	Peadar	Rand
Bardulf	Fritz	Pearce	Randal
Bardulph	Hap	Pedro	Randall
Bonaventure	Huntley	Perkin	Randell
Bordolphe	Huntly	Pernell	Randolf
Bourdolph	Ignace	Perrin	Randolph
Braden	Ignacio	Pete	Randy
Cal	Ignate	Peter	Raphael
Cale	Ignatius	Peterkin	Ripley
Caleb	Iniss	Petria	Rolf
Caradoc	Innes	Petrie	Rolfe
Caradock	Inness	Petter	Rolph
Chadwick	Innis	Pierce	Seager
Cordell	Ker	Piere	Segar
Craddock	Kerby	Piero	Seger
Derry	Kerr	Pierre	Skelly
Didier	Kirby	Pierrick	Skerry
Eldric	Kjetil	Pierro	Stancliff
Eldrich	Latham	Pierrot	Stancliffe
Fagan	Macbeth	Piers	Standcliff
Fagin	Manfred	Pietro	Standcliffe

436

Associated Names (cont.)

Storm	Thorndyke	Tormond	Warley
Tavis	Thorne	Tormund	Wellington
Tavish	Thorneley	Turner	Weston
Tevis	Thornely	Upwood	Whistler
Thaine	Thornley	Vance	Windsor
Thane	Thornly	Vladislav	Worth
Thayne	Thorton	Wardell	Worton
Thormond	Thurmond	Warden	Wyborn
Thormund	Toland	Wardley	Wyborne

Name Portrait 67

Guiding Light

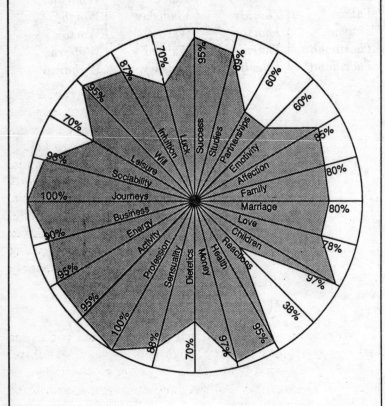

Element : Fire   **Plant** : Acacia

Mineral : Aluminum   **Sign** : Leo

Animal : Ibis   **Color** : Green

Personality Type:

Guiding Light

(Associated names – page 442)

BASIC CHARACTER

With your many enviable talents, your self-confidence, and your well-developed sense of humanitarianism, you're a born leader. Though you're a bit eccentric and often inscrutable, you are sure of yourself and have enough energy to pursue your often crusading goals. Your totem animal is the ibis, symbol of wisdom, and the bird associated with the Egyptian god Thoth; and your plant totem, the acacia, stands for initiation and deep knowledge. Those are powerful associations and account for the fact that you are usually in the center of things, the sun in your own galaxy, influencing others and lighting the way with your brilliant personality and refined sensitivities.

YOUR PSYCHOLOGY

You are an extrovert, at your very best when you're out and doing among people. Though you are open to others' opinions, you have a tendency to be rather close-minded, or to seem to know it all. It's not unusual for someone with so powerful a personality to become as domineering as you often do, but on occasion you can be downright tyrannical, in spite of your great sense of altruism. Failure doesn't affect you in the least, and you are able to control your reactions with your great patience. But there are times when you lose your temper, sometimes violently, especially if your strong will has been crossed by what you see as an evil or morally wrong act

439

or person. There's a disorderly streak in you, which comes from your tendency not to be practical and your belief that your powerful will can see you through absolutely everything.

HOW YOU ACT AND REACT IN THE WORLD

You're a dynamo, and your all-consuming activity takes you into diverse and often bizarre situations. You need to learn discipline early on in order to make the best of your many talents—and in order that you can be in control of things, for you are at your best when you're in charge. You adapt easily to new environments and are apt to change careers often. Any position of leadership attracts you, and you are drawn to a number of endeavors: stage and film directing; writing; politics or the military; research, science, and technology; and business and industry. You could also make an excellent doctor or a great religious leader. And your creativity would make you a first-rate inventor.

YOUR DEEP INTUITIVE PERSONALITY

Much of your charm and inspiring confidence comes from your active intuition. It seems as if someone is passing you all the right answers—and in a way, someone is. Your inner voice is strong and refined, and your imagination, fertile. Heeding your intuition aids you immeasurably in your many pursuits, and keeps you from getting sidetracked with useless speculation.

YOUR INTELLIGENCE

Your mind works with great precision and clarity; you are able to understand things totally and quickly, for your intellect is both analytic and synthetic. This affords you astonishing mental agility because you have both an overall perspective on problems as well as the ability to focus on details. Your memory is remarkable, and you have a finely tuned curiosity.

YOUR EMOTIONAL NATURE

There's poetry in your affections, at least in the way you express your emotions. It's not a flowery phrase, but an intense act of love which is so inspirational to your lovers. You are very sensual, with pronounced desires which made themselves felt early on in your life. You're more of a Romeo than a Don Juan—able to integrate your marvelous sensuality into your emotional life. But though love and sex often go together for you, your sexual affairs are often apt to outdistance your emotional commitments. You're not averse to sexual dalliances, as long as they are kept refined and romantic.

YOUR HEALTH AND VITALITY

In spite of your irregular schedule, you keep your good health. You have prodigious stamina and, as a rule, are physically up to your intensely active lifestyle. You need the out of doors; your health is greatly helped by the salt air of the beach—one of your favorite vacation spots. Your weak spot is your endocrine system, which might cause you some problems later in life.

THE SOCIAL YOU

Because of your magnetism and your elegant manners, you put other people at ease. You are an extremely social being, able to adjust to just about any social setting. There's so much refinement in your dealing with others that people tend to seek you out, and when they leave you, they leave with an indelible impression of your bright, inspiring personality. Your self-mastery is reflected in the sort of parties you give—relaxed yet exciting affairs at which you are the main attraction. People enjoy your wit and charm, and you are apt to have a good number of people orbiting around you and looking to you for guidance. Your luck is good, and success most likely comes to you early in your career.

NamePortrait
67
Associated Names

Ad	Farnell	Montgomery	Romford
Adolf	Felips	Nemo	Rumford
Adolfus	Fellips	Olney	Rye
Adolph	Fernald	Orman	Seabert
Adolphe	Fernall	Ormand	Seabright
Adolphus	Filbert	Ormen	Seabrook
Adolpus	Filip	Ormin	Sebert
Ardley	Fillip	Ormond	Sebrook
Argus	Fridolf	Pembroke	Shadwell
Arne	Fulton	Phelips	Smedley
Arney	Gaston	Phellipps	Smedly
Arnie	Godefroy	Phellips	Southwell
Asa	Harden	Phellips	Stearn
Boden	Harding	Phelps	Stearne
Boswell	Heck	Phil	Stern
Bosworth	Hector	Philbert	Sterne
Chapman	Kay	Philemon	Strothers
Churchill	Konstantin	Philibert	Struthers
Conn	Konstantine	Philip	Tad
Constant	Kyle	Philipp	Tadd
Constantin	Langford	Philippe	Taddy
Constantine	Leo	Philips	Terell
Devin	Leopold	Phillie	Terence
Devlin	Lepp	Phillip	Terrel
Dolf	Linus	Phillipp	Terrell
Dolph	Mal	Phillipps	Terrence
Duffy	Malvin	Phillips	Terrill
Edolf	Mel	Philly	Terris
Ephrem	Melvil	Philo	Terry
Farnall	Melville	Phineas	Thad
Farnel	Melvin	Pip	Thaddee
		Preston	

Associated Names (cont.)

Thaddeus	*Tirrell*	*Treherne*	*Ulmar*
Thady	*Torley*	*Tyrell*	*Ulmer*
Theophane	*Torrance*	*Tyrrel*	*Val*
Theophile	*Trahearn*	*Tyrrell*	*Wain*
Theophilus	*Trahearne*	*Udolf*	*Waine*
Thorley	*Trahern*	*Ulfred*	*Waite*
Tirell	*Trehearn*	*Ulger*	*Wayne*
Tirrel	*Trehern*	*Ullock*	*Xylon*

Name Portrait 68

Persevering Achiever

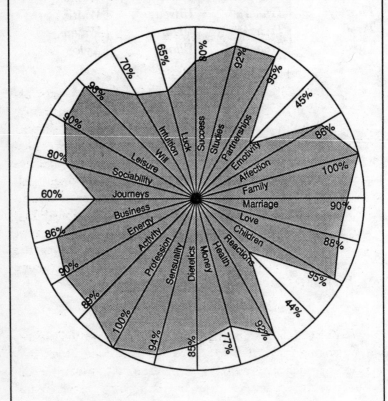

Element : Earth   **Plant** : Hemp

Mineral : Bromine   **Sign** : Taurus

Animal : Ox   **Color** : Blue

Personality Type:

Persevering Achiever

(Associated names – page 448)

BASIC CHARACTER

It seems as if nothing could stand in your way—not because of any hyperactivity, but out of patience, endurance, and a loyal kind of stick-to-itiveness—all attributes of your animal totem, the laboring, self-sacrificing ox. You are guided by high principles and uncompromising moral sensibilities and are thrifty and cautious in all your undertakings. Although you are not acquisitive, you have a sense of ownership which reflects an attitude of concern and responsibility, appreciation and love, for the things you do own. In your resolve, in the way you dig in and give no quarter, you are effective in all you do. Your perseverance and faithfulness reveal a highly developed sense of diplomacy and tact.

YOUR PSYCHOLOGY

With such an astonishingly strong will—a "willful" will—it's surprising how often you allow yourself to drift off into situations which you cannot control. Your totem plant is the hemp, a sturdy practical plant, but it is part terrestrial and part aquatic, and like it, you tend to get washed away at times, despite your sturdy self-reliance. You are an extrovert and view the world quite objectively. This lends you a lot of self-confidence, but there is a duality at work here too, for at times you tend to become timid to the point of shyness. Your powerful will can lead you into immovable stubbornness when all is not going smoothly for you; and your angelic patience can become devilish obstinacy. Failures rarely affect you, and you forge ahead, no matter what.

HOW YOU ACT AND REACT IN THE WORLD

Though you sometimes set more goals for yourself than even you can possibly accomplish, you rarely take on any project until you've studied it from all angles and are sure of all possible ramifications of your actions. Your reactions are similarly subdued; you never plunge into something mindlessly. It would not be unusual for you to take up the trade or profession of your father. You are attracted to careers that require your kind of self-assured perseverance and bring visible rewards. Agronomy, the crafts, architecture, and physical engineering are some of the fields which might be inviting to you. You could also be an effective, first-rate industrial or business manager or a dedicated soldier. Whatever you do, you give it your all as a devoted, loyal, and admirably just worker.

YOUR DEEP INTUITIVE PERSONALITY

Though you have an inner voice worth heeding, you would rarely admit to it. For you, understanding the pros and cons of the world is far too important to take much time listening to an intuition you're not even sure you believe in. Still it is the source of much of your deep charm.

YOUR INTELLIGENCE

You have a finely tuned analytic intellect, which you tend to apply to your work and goals more than for the sake of intellectual meanderings. You are able to break down a situation into all its details, study each, and then put them all together again with a deep understanding of how everything works. You are contemplative and studious, and the idea of going about trying to dazzle anyone by your quiet intelligence is appalling to you, as intellectually, you tend to be a bit shy.

YOUR EMOTIONAL NATURE

Love comes to you slowly, discreetly; and your own expressions of affection are as restrained as they are deep. Bold and flashy declarations or cliches are in the worst of taste to you. Instead, you express yourself with an endearing and indestructible attachment and devotion. Your sexual desires are not always attached to your emotions, however, and because you are a very sensual man, with early developed sex drives, you are not averse to some wide and far-flung affairs from time to time. When love does come to you, it is magnificent and lasting, and though you require a lot of understanding, you return it with tenderness and an almost unheard-of steadfastness of heart.

YOUR HEALTH AND VITALITY

To say you have the stamina of an ox might be pressing the point a bit too far, but your vitality and health are very solid, and it's almost impossible to keep pace with you. However, you must be careful not to overestimate your own physical strength. You need a lot of fresh air and exercise and have to take extra pains not to overindulge in alcohol or food. Your weak points are your shoulders, your kidneys, and your liver.

THE SOCIAL YOU

Friends are sacred to you; there's absolutely no length to which you wouldn't go for the benefit of those close to you. Most of your social life revolves around your close-knit group, almost religiously, but from time to time you cannot resist a big bash in an unusual setting filled with strangers. You entertain with a natural grace and with such good will that your guests cannot help but feel relaxed and at home with you. Your own self-assurance is infectious in social situations, and if most people you know can't keep up with you, they surely try to, for the sake of staying close to you.

NamePortrait
68
Associated Names

Adrian	Englebert	Milbourne	Renaud
Adrien	Habib	Milburn	Renault
Aodh	Hadrian	Milburne	Rennard
Aoidh	Hadrien	Norvel	Reynard
Artemas	Hobart	Norvie	Salvadore
Artemis	Hoyt	Norvil	Salvator
Aylmer	Hubbard	Norville	Salvatore
Aymeric	Hube	Norvin	Shep
Bandric	Hubert	Norvyn	Shepard
Beaumont	Huey	Norward	Shepherd
Burl	Hurley	Norwell	Shepp
Burleigh	Huxley	Norwin	Sheppard
Burley	Inglebert	Norwood	Shepperd
Byrle	Kenley	Norwyn	Sheppy
Cort	Kenward	Oswald	Slade
Cortie	Kenway	Quincy	Stanhope
Corty	Kenyon	Radmund	Stoddard
Court	Kurt	Raimond	Strahan
Courtenay	Lammond	Ramon	Stratford
Courtland	Lammont	Ramuntcho	Suffield
Courtney	Lamond	Ray	Tancred
Curt	Lamont	Rayburn	Tanner
Curtis	Leverett	Raymon	Thierry
Dedrick	Mael	Raymond	Trevor
Dolan	Maynard	Raymund	Tuxford
Drake	Melaine	Raynard	Tyrone
Dud	Melbourne	Reamonn	Wadsworth
Duddie	Melburn	Redman	Willoughby
Duddy	Melburne	Redmond	Yorick
Dudley	Meldon	Redmund	York
Dudly	Menard	Rehard	Yorke
Engelbert	Milbourn	Reinhard	Zeeman

Name Portrait 69

Cavalier Prophet

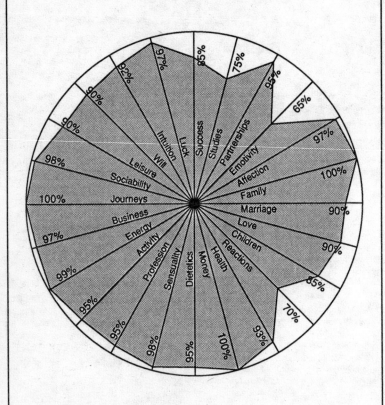

Element : Earth   **Plant** : Walnut tree
Mineral : Moonstone   **Sign** : Capricorn
Animal : Panther   **Color** : Red

Personality Type:

Cavalier Prophet

(Associated names – page 454)

BASIC CHARACTER

You're an excitable person, mostly because you have such strong emotions and are always ready to burst into action. But there's another aspect which prevents you from jumping into things impulsively: your tendency to reflect first. You have astonishing energy and are goal-oriented, so once you do take action, it's usually very effective. You have a very imposing presence, not unlike your plant totem, the walnut tree. It is also reflected in your animal totem, the panther, which, when it leaps out of the shadows and into light, brings all of its strength and cunning into a sudden and fierce battle.

YOUR PSYCHOLOGY

Even though you are an impressive character, you tend to hide your fragile side from people. You have a good will, but often you operate on pure nerves, if you don't simply become stubborn and heedlessly aggressive. Still, you tend to be open-minded and self-confident, and though you are very emotional, your emotions are usually under control. Your great intuition can guide you around the worst pitfalls when you're in action. When you feel exposed and your fragile side is laid bare, you become irritable; you have a hot and flash-fire temper which can lead you into all sorts of turmoil once it is unleashed; and it's unleashed, usually, for an audience.

HOW YOU ACT AND REACT IN THE WORLD

"Self-starter" might have been coined with you in mind. Though you can be patient, diplomatic, and reflective, you most often are out there taking advantage of every opportunity that comes along. You're a marvelously enterprising spirit, committed to your work and confident that you can do it well. You are very persuasive with others through your facility of convincing rhetoric. You're always sure you'll get by and don't always rely on school and study as necessary to success. You are clever with your hands and can develop marketable manual skills. You could be a first-rate engineer or technician. Your keen imagination might be put to practical use in finance or the stock market. Though you are not the most structured of people, you can impose an amazing discipline on yourself once you are involved in a career.

YOUR DEEP INTUITIVE PERSONALITY

Your intuition is so strong and effective that you come close to possessing the qualities of a prophet. Because it is well integrated into your personality, you rely upon it and may acquire a reputation for giving infallible predictions. It's also of great aid to you in your day-to-day active life, allowing you to see things clearly and rapidly.

YOUR INTELLIGENCE

Intellectually, you are practical more than speculative. You have an active and untiring curiosity and a reliable sense of analysis. You tend to use your keen intellect toward your own ends—that is with a goal in mind. Your memory for facts in the employ of some goal-directed motive is often frighteningly uncanny.

YOUR EMOTIONAL NATURE

You need to be loved, and you need to be reassured of love by constant affections, which makes you highly susceptible to flattery. Though you return affections with great charm and an ineffably rough tenderness, you tend to be possessive and at times can be downright tyrannical with the one you love. The family is sacred to you, even though you act a bit cavalierly with your loved ones at times. Sexually, you're a real dynamo, and your life is undoubtedly written in long lines of love affairs. Sensual pleasures are important to you— so important that it doesn't matter in the least if the hearts you break along the way could populate a small village. In short, it's a case of the sacred and the profane when it comes to love—and you'll take both.

YOUR HEALTH AND VITALITY

Your stamina is prodigious and your resistance to fatigue often heroic. But because you tend to be nervous and high-strung, you have to be careful of psychosomatic ailments, such as headaches and stomach upsets. You need considerable sleep to maintain your high level of nervous and willful energy.

THE SOCIAL YOU

Without a big social life, what would you do? You seem to swim down rapids of crowded receptions, parties, and drinking halls. But they're not just any receptions, etc., because you are drawn to the accoutrements of money and worldly success. The beautiful people, people with luxuries and status, are your crowd. If you meet someone you like at a party who does not seem to like you so much, you'll end up convincing him or her in the end, and walk away with a new friend. You'll clutch first those who seem to be resisting you, and they won't resist for long; you are charming and entertaining company, a pleasure to be with and a constant source of enlightenment and confidence.

_____

NamePortrait
69
Associated Names

Anson	Gearey	Rick	True
Ashley	Geary	Ricky	Trueman
Ballard	Gery	Rob	Truman
Beagan	Haakon	Robbie	Trumane
Beagen	Hako	Robby	Wallace
Bob	Hakon	Robert	Wallache
Bobbie	Kadir	Roberto	Waller
Bobby	Laibrook	Robin	Wallie
Brewster	Landry	Romuald	Wallis
Bundy	Latimer	Roparz	Wally
Burell	Lealand	Rupert	Walsh
Clyde	Lee	Ruprecht	Warton
Cullan	Leigh	Scanlon	Welch
Cullen	Leland	Selden	Welsh
Cullin	Leyland	Septimus	Whitby
Dallas	Leyman	Sexton	Whitelaw
Doran	Lyman	Sextus	Whitfield
Dorian	Marmion	Spalding	Whitford
Ennea	Ogden	Spaulding	Whitley
Ennis	Orvil	Sutherland	Wolcott
Eric	Orville	Thorald	Wulcott
Erich	Orvin	Thorold	Wythe
Erick	Pomeroy	Torald	
Erik	Rama	Tremaine	
Fletcher	Rami	Tremayne	

Name Portrait 70

Joyful Seeker

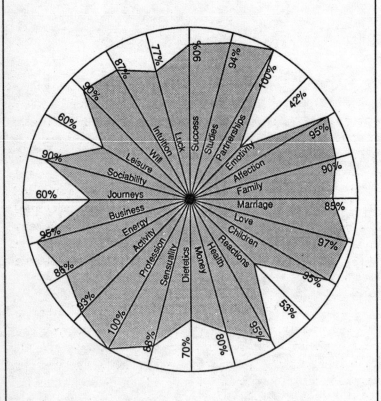

Element : Fire   **Plant** : Laurel
Mineral : Beryl   **Sign** : Aries
Animal : Vampire   **Color** : Green

Personality Type:

Joyful Seeker

(Associated names – page 461)

BASIC CHARACTER

You are an active man with a vital presence and a *joie de vivre* that leaves a remarkable impact on all you meet, at work or at play. There is an almost perfect balance between your strong will and your level of activity, and you employ your energy in mastering your fate. Part of that mastery depends upon understanding—a total understanding in your search for the higher, the "universal" man. Dedicated, principled, and strong, you are capable of throwing yourself into a cause or your work and of having a lasting effect. Like your plant totem, the laurel, which is Apollo's tree, there is an element of conquest, or victory, in all you undertake.

YOUR PSYCHOLOGY

You possess a powerful will, but never would you consider imposing it on others. Instead, you always give the impression of being spontaneous and facile, though you may have thought through many of your actions before you undertake them. By nature you are an extrovert, and your outward turning reaches as far as the extents of the universe. It seems, at times, that you are under a compulsion to find the truth at any cost, and this can result in one of two difficulties: either you can be misled; or you can appear overaggressive to people around you. This is not so much aggression as it is your astonishing energy level, with which few others could ever compete. You are a compassionate sort of person, whose own happiness is often dependent upon the happiness of those around you.

HOW YOU ACT AND REACT IN THE WORLD

Most often you go about things without worry, rarely becoming angry or excited—and why should you, when you've most likely got everything in hand. Like the ancient alchemists would have liked to do, you transform all that you invest your energy in, into gold. Very probably, you spend your life studying, learning—mulling over your vast experiences and readings in your never-ending search for the universal truths. You have an astounding adaptability, which, when coupled with your fertile mind and multifarious experiences, makes you well suited for a profession that has to do with perception and the human condition. You would make an excellent humanistic psychologist or medical doctor, a well-heeded teacher, union leader, or a far-seeing politician. As a writer, you would pass along your ideas of "what is to be done" with great clarity of insight and with precision. In all, you act rather than react; if someone comes to you with an argument, you will be open to it, of course, but if it is foolhardy, you will likely ignore it and go on about your business.

YOUR DEEP INTUITIVE PERSONALITY

Though your intuition is of the highest quality, you do not depend upon it as your starting point. Rather, you turn to your inner voice in order to confirm your rational conclusions. In this way, your intuition is an accessory to your overall intelligence and personality and not a source of inspiration so much as confirmation.

YOUR INTELLIGENCE

Yours is an incisive, highly analytical mind. You possess the ability to unravel the knottiest of problems and do not hesitate to apply your analyses to the world around you. With your intense and active curiosity, you are bound to show up where the action is; and with your vast and particular memory, you often appear to be a walking encyclopedia. You're a born investigator and a real source of information.

YOUR EMOTIONAL NATURE

Emotionally, you are very stable, though your emotions lie dormant until you are touched by another. Then, awakened, you are a most compassionate person, able to give precisely what the other needs. Do not be alarmed to learn that your animal totem is the much misunderstood vampire; contrary to the common wisdom, the vampire is a symbol of this sort of "contact passion"; aroused by the emotional needs of another, you can enter a mutually nourishing relationship. You act on the feelings of your heart more than you do on sexual attraction, and, in fact, sex very often takes a second and sometimes ignored part in your love relationships. Still, in all, your sexuality is very healthy and expressed openly.

YOUR HEALTH AND VITALITY

Like your basic character, your vitality is well-balanced. In general, you enjoy good health and great vigor as long as you respect your physical limits, which you are sometimes wont to ignore. In times of high nervous energy—if you are inactive or frustrated—you might suffer minor nervous ailments which a return to your natural balance can correct.

THE SOCIAL YOU

You are open and ready to assume a position of responsibility for your friends. As long as you do not spread yourself too thin—which you tend to do—you enjoy a balanced, active, and joyful social life. You like to choose your own friends rather than having them choose you, and you are not the sort who is going to wait around to see what happens; you'll make it happen. Your exuberance is infectious, and your friends are most likely to be intelligent, witty, and as active as you are. Still, you are a seeker, and at the drop of a hat are apt to follow a calling or take up a cause if it might bring you a step closer to a total understanding of your universe.

———————

NamePortrait
70
Associated Names

Aguistin	Cesar	Flavius	Sheffield
Aime	Cesare	Guerin	Stefan
Ame	Dewey	Guerric	Steffen
Amerigo	Emeric	Gus	Stephan
Augie	Emerson	Gussy	Stephen
August	Emery	Hanno	Stephenson
Auguste	Emmerich	Haven	Steve
Augustin	Emmery	Ira	Steven
Augustine	Emory	Llew	Stevenson
Augustus	Erasme	Mayhew	Stevie
Austen	Erasmus	Merrick	Tiffany
Austin	Erastus	Ras	Todd
Bentley	Etienne	Rasmus	Wesleigh
Bently	Fay	Red	Wesley
Brander	Fayette	Seraph	Westleigh
Caesar	Flavian	Seraphim	
Cesaire	Flavien	Seraphin	

Name Portrait 71

Bearer of Good Fortune

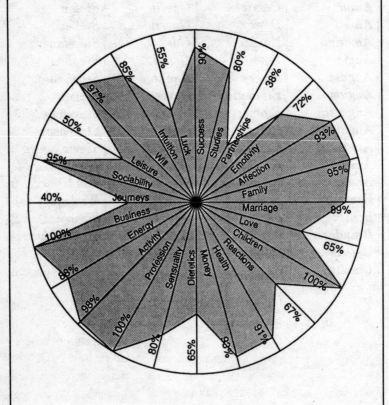

Element : Air   **Plant** : Linden tree

Mineral : Marble   **Sign** : Aquarius

Animal : Doe   **Color** : Orange

Personality Type:

Bearer of Good Fortune

(Associated names – page 466)

BASIC CHARACTER

You are a fascinating woman with an illuminating tenderness and a deep dedication to the higher qualities of life. Anything selfish and false in the world offends you to the core. You live by rigorous principles and possess a sense of honor that comes from the heart. Though you have strong emotions, you tend to keep them channeled in useful activity that is of service to other people and by your own code of conduct. Your occasional anxieties and distress are usually offset by your sense of a mission and your soothing reassurance which is also a symbolic attribute of your plant totem, the linden tree. You tend to be self-sacrificing and self-effacing in all you do.

YOUR PSYCHOLOGY

There are times when you carry your self-effacement to extremes; you tend to excuse others' behavior and make too many demands on yourself. Under such a self-imposed rule, your emotions become taxed, and you become excitable and your temper can flare up and explode. You have a terrible fear of being betrayed, and any infringement on your principles can incite your anger. Still, you are usually in control, a natural extrovert; you act with great self-confidence when you have a mission to perform, but otherwise, you tend to be as timid as your totem animal, the doe. Your will is astonishing, not so much for its intensity, but for its quality—you tend to have a great influence on people, transforming their attitudes and evoking their humanity and responsiveness to the ills of their fellow man.

HOW YOU ACT AND REACT IN THE WORLD

You are happiest when you are sharing and giving of yourself. Your attentiveness to the needs of others takes you into community life where you pursue a number of activities, mostly in service to humanity. You are well-disciplined and dedicated to your work, always ready to sacrifice your own comfort to lend a helping hand or offer a soothing word. You plan well for your career and are not afraid of lengthy study or apprenticeship. You are an admirable mother, understanding and nurturing. You would also be an excellent doctor or nurse, a pediatrician, or a field worker for social service agencies. Whatever you do, you seem to bring light and better awareness to all those around you.

YOUR DEEP INTUITIVE PERSONALITY

For someone with so much empathy, you put little trust in your inner voice. It is there, guiding you quietly whether you heed it or not, but you put your faith in reason and your own code of conduct.

YOUR INTELLIGENCE

Your mind is quick and alert; you are able to get a broad perspective on a problem quickly and can confront complex situations which might stymie others. Your intellect is holistic instead of analytic. You have a fine memory, especially for events that have some emotional charge to them. Your curiosity is active but never invades the privacy of others.

YOUR EMOTIONAL NATURE

Emotional gamesmen, Casanovas, and philanderers turn you off so quickly, they don't even have a chance to get in the second word of their famous lines before you've fled from them. You need a tender, sensitive love which will match your own. You are very emotional by nature, but your morals do not allow you to be flippant about your affections; they're delivered from the heart. You are as discreet and fragile sexually as you are emotionally. You are the faithful, dedicated lover and wife and tend to express your affections with a maternal regard for your lover.

YOUR HEALTH AND VITALITY

Usually your vitality is excellent, you have the stamina you need to resist fatigue and overwork. Your zest for life helps you overcome illness. You have to pay attention to your sympathetic nervous system, however, for upsets tend to harm you severely. Also, your kidneys and genitals are delicate.

THE SOCIAL YOU

Your radiant personality shines on those around you, charming them quietly and giving everyone a buoyant cheerfulness. You are an excellent and discreet hostess, always sure to see that everyone is happy and has what he needs. Loud or brassy parties usually appall you, as does anything that is superficial and insincere. You are happiest with a small group of loving friends who can share your warmth and generosity of spirit with genuine appreciation.

———————————

NamePortrait
71
Associated Names

Abra	Eleonor	Hertha	Lucie
Ada	Eleonora	Honey	Lucienne
Adda	Eleonore	Honor	Lucile
Addie	Elinor	Honora	Lucilla
Addy	Elinora	Honoria	Lucille
Aida	Elinore	Honorine	Lucinda
Alloula	Elnora	Honour	Lucy
Allula	Elnore	Kyna	Lysandra
Aloula	Ema	Lea	Manuela
Alula	Emlyn	Leah	Manuella
Armida	Emlyne	Leala	Manuelle
Aurora	Emma	Leana	Marcela
Aurore	Emmaline	Leane	Marcelia
Aveline	Emmanuelle	Leanna	Marceline
Brook	Emmie	Leanor	Marcella
Brooke	Emmott	Leatrice	Marcelle
Clover	Emmy	Leatrix	Marcellia
Clovie	Erda	Lee	Marcelline
Daffodil	Ertha	Leigh	Marchella
Deana	Gaetane	Lenora	Marchelle
Deane	Gilberta	Lenore	Marchita
Delcine	Gilberte	Leonora	Marcia
Dena	Gilbertha	Leonore	Marcie
Diamanta	Gilberthe	Lia	Marcile
Dorcas	Gilbertina	Liana	Marcille
Eartha	Gilbertine	Liane	Marcy
Eda	Gillie	Lianna	Marilda
Edda	Gilly	Lianne	Marquita
Eleanor	Haldana	Lucette	Marsha
Eleanora	Hazel	Lucia	Mignon
Eleanore	Herta	Lucianna	Mignonette

Associated Names (cont.)

Muguette	Raoghnailt	Severine	Theresa
Nora	Raquel	Shelley	Therese
Norah	Ray	Tara	Tobe
Noreen	Rexana	Terencia	Tobey
Norine	Rexanna	Terentia	Tobi
Norrey	Rochalla	Teresa	Toby
Norrie	Rochalle	Terese	Toireasa
Norry	Rochella	Teresita	Tracey
Pamphila	Rochelle	Teressa	Tracie
Pamphile	Rochette	Teri	Tracy
Pascale	Rufin	Terri	Trilby
Pascaline	Rufina	Terrie	Tullia
Rachel	Samella	Terry	Ulima
Rachele	Samelle	Tertia	Ulva
Rachelle	Samuela	Tess	Wanetta
Rachilde	Samuella	Tessa	Wanette
Rae	Samuelle	Tessie	Zebeda
Rahel	Segolene	Tessy	Zita

Name Portrait 72

The Sower and the Reaper

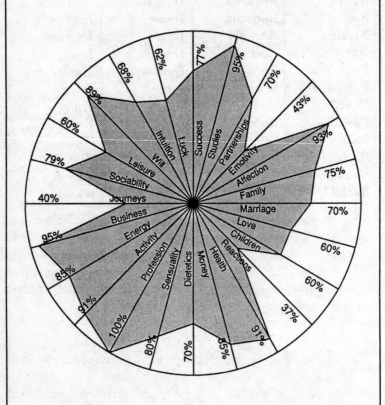

Element : Air
Mineral : Onyx
Animal : Python

Plant : Juniper tree
Sign : Aquarius
Color : Blue

Personality Type:

The Sower and the Reaper

(Associated names – page 472)

BASIC CHARACTER

Though you are well-intentioned and sincere, you tend to be a man of extremes. You can go from skepticism to burning enthusiasm over the same person or project. You have a reassuring presence and seem to be guided by cool reason; but you also can become excitable and given to excess, especially where your friends and beliefs are concerned. You must have proof—visible proof—of everything, so you rarely act on impulse or speculation, but once the proof is in, you act with dedication and resolve. Essentially, you're a practical man and make use of all your talents to tangible, useful ends. Your plant totem, the juniper tree, is wholly apt as a symbol of your character—every bit of it, from fruit to root, is used to some productive end.

YOUR PSYCHOLOGY

At times, your cool reason becomes downright frigid, and it seems as if you are without any emotions. This is bound to be the case, especially, if you feel you are under emotional pressures—from self-doubts—your naturally doubting nature going to an extreme and turning in on you. Still, you're not afraid of failure and your dedication to work often borders on out and out fanaticism. You tend to measure your self-worth by your actions, and it is on your actions that your self-esteem is built. The one thing that can incite your anger is betrayal, and then you are capable of reacting violently.

HOW YOU ACT AND REACT IN THE WORLD

Your quiet charm lies in the firmness of your character, in the way you take things one progressive step at a time. You opt for the long term and follow your plans through to the end. But your work must have tangible results; you must be able to reap what you sow. You would make a good agronomist, soldier, chemist, or explorer; and you can become dedicated to a cause. When you do join in a struggle, you go beyond your own self-interest and make changes that will give greater meaning to human life in general.

YOUR DEEP INTUITIVE PERSONALITY

Just as the mythical python, your totem animal, guarded the oracles, you tend to coil your sense of logic and reason about yourself and ignore even the existence of intuition. You tend to view intuition as impulse and consider that sort of thing as a silly urge.

YOUR INTELLIGENCE

You are in constant pursuit of the verifiable truth, and pass up few opportunities to demonstrate it logically to whoever will lend an ear. You deal in observable realities with the intellect of a logician—analytically and practically. You have no time for abstractions or intellectual gamesmanship.

YOUR EMOTIONAL NATURE

You are faithful and devoted in your love, but you don't show your affections readily, and often you tend to be moody or stand-offish when it comes to your feelings. In this realm, you deal in black and white only. Either you love or you don't, and you won't pursue a halfway relationship. Your sensuality is also ruled by your moods. One day you can suppress your strong sexual desires with your cool reason—and the next, you're indulging your appetite with a hot and fiery affair. Your passion and your love don't always have to be the same. One comes and goes; the other is there, sturdy and firm.

YOUR HEALTH AND VITALITY

Your state of health is subject to your psychological and emotional moods, though you appear to have great vitality and physical strength. You need to follow a strict health regimen; you do not take to excesses well. If possible, avoid too much heavy athletic activity. Your weak spots are your lungs and your liver.

THE SOCIAL YOU

Though you frequently beg off from social engagements—usually claiming that you have too much work to do—you do need to have your views heard by your own friends. A big party, where little serious conversation is possible, is not your sort of do; you would rather spend your leisure with friends whom you know and trust. You can be an engaging talker in such situations. You have a strong respect for family ties, and your ultimate success is assured by your strength, your firmness, and your fine intentions.

———

NamePortrait
72
Associated Names

Adlai	Cranston	Hamal	Rolph
Ailean	Derck	Hamelin	Rolphe
Ailin	Derek	Hamelyn	Rolt
Alain	Derk	Imre	Rudolf
Alan	Derrick	Josh	Rudolph
Aland	Derry	Joshua	Rudy
Alekos	Dirk	Lani	Shay
Alin	Dolf	Lanny	Shea
Allan	Dolph	Leandre	Sheridan
Allen	Dory	Macy	Sutcliff
Allyn	Ellsworth	Massey	Sutcliffe
Alun	Elroy	Nye	Tam
Aneurin	Elsworth	Obadiah	Tammany
Auban	Enos	Obie	Tammie
Aubin	Erskine	Orford	Tammy
Bland	Faroukh	Primo	Tenison
Blandford	Faruch	Radolf	Tennison
Blanford	Faruq	Rankin	Tennyson
Bronson	Galvan	Renald	Thom
Bruce	Galven	Rene	Thomas
Burdon	Galvin	Renny	Tom
Cam	Garraway	Robinson	Tomas
Cameron	Garroway	Rodolf	Tommy
Camm	Garvin	Rodolph	Walker
Coile	Garwin	Rodolphe	Wheatley
Corentin	Graeme	Rolfe	Wheaton
Coyle	Graham	Rollo	

Name Portrait 73

Man of the Hearth

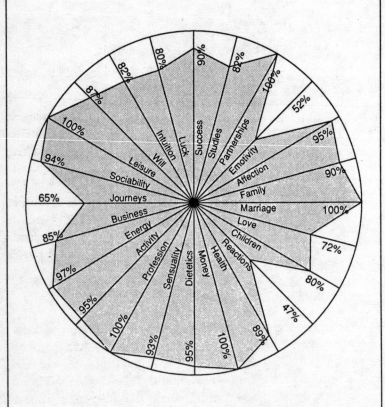

Element : Earth **Plant** : Thistle

Mineral : Silica **Sign** : Virgo

Animal : Cricket **Color** : Green

Personality Type:

Man of the Hearth

(Associated names – page 478)

BASIC CHARACTER

You are an active person with balanced emotions and a good-natured equanimity about you. You tend to be sensitive to anything concerning humanity or human happiness. This is expressed primarily in your love of the home. Your totem animal, the cricket, is a symbol of the hearth, and like it, you are dedicated to family and domestic life. You are very eager to please people, sometimes too eager, and in general are happy with your lot in life. Your sensitivities tend to lead you into humanitarian causes to which you dedicate yourself whole-heartedly.

YOUR PSYCHOLOGY

There are times when your eagerness to please can lead you astray, taking you into positions and actions that actually betray your own moral code. This is in part due to a certain lack of self-confidence and your doubts about your abilities to meet your goals. Your emotions are painfully close to the surface; when you are annoyed, you become like your totem plant, the thistle, angry and prickly. Either you blow up in a temper, or you retreat, withdrawing from the world for a while. One thing you hate is to be asked to justify yourself or your actions. In such an event, you become defensive and often belligerent; but your belligerence is mostly show, and you are easily calmed after your outburst.

HOW YOU ACT AND REACT IN THE WORLD

Oh, to be a country gentleman, a landed squire! But in spite of your favorite daydream, you need a lot of action to stay happy, and the sedate life of a lord of the manor simply isn't your style. At times, you do things just for the sake of keeping busy and often are inclined to take on too much at once. Though your life is not as well-structured as you would like, you are very enterprising, a hard-working student, and a cooperative professional. You are drawn to traditional academic subjects, especially foreign languages. You would be an excellent teacher, government official, or businessman, as long as your business did not mean a lot of personal contact with clients. There is another aspect which your fervent need for activity can take, and that is an inclination to gambling. As a consequence, you may experience a lot of financial ups and downs during your life.

YOUR DEEP INTUITIVE PERSONALITY

You have a refined intuition but are likely to refer to your inner voice as your "luck." You rely on it in games, especially when there is a risk involved. But you rarely heed it for guidance in other aspects of your life.

YOUR INTELLIGENCE

Details are not your thing even though you are able to solve problems readily. Your intellect is brilliant and incisive, synthetic rather than analytic. You would not dream of using your intelligence to dominate others. Your curiosity is insatiable, and your imagination fertile.

YOUR EMOTIONAL NATURE

You are very warm and affectionate, sometimes too affectionate. You tend to be attentive to your lover's needs, and your attentiveness is a form of your own special kind of possessiveness, which is not a drive to control someone but to serve your lover. Your sexuality is strongly tied to your sentiments; you are dedicated to family and home, and your feelings go to the hearth first. Even though you have occasion to shower your affections on some people with ulterior and not necessarily honorable motives, you yourself react strongly and bitterly to emotional disappointments, often taking your wounded heart out of circulation for long periods while it mends in isolation.

YOUR HEALTH AND VITALITY

Because you love good food and good wine, you have a tendency to become overweight. You need a lot of fresh air and sunshine but should avoid excessive sports. Your ribs are especially fragile, and your endocrine system will have to be watched, as it is prone to disorders.

THE SOCIAL YOU

You're a charming and gracious host and probably the chef at your own large and engaging parties. You throw yourself into community life and bring an extra sparkle to your friends. Most of your entertaining revolves around the home. The rest of it may well be taken up with regular poker games, to which you have a near addiction. You know what you want out of life, and your generally practical approaches (poker aside) brings a calming reassurance to your family and friends. You're an excellent, reassuring father; and with your luck and hard work, you can anticipate brilliant success in the world.

NamePortrait
73
Associated Names

Alroy	Harlow	Lawrance	Roddy
Angus	Hippolyte	Lawrence	Roderic
Ashford	Isador	Lawson	Roderick
Bick	Isadore	Lin	Rodhlann
Bickford	Isidor	Linn	Rodi
Bjorn	Isidore	Lon	Rodie
Burchard	Issy	Lonnie	Rodney
Burckhard	Iz	Lonny	Rodric
Burgard	Izzie	Loren	Rodrick
Burkhart	Izzy	Lorenz	Rodrigue
Chalmer	Keelan	Lorenzo	Roe
Chalmers	Keeley	Lori	Roland
Chetwin	Kelvan	Lorin	Roley
Chetwyn	Kelven	Lorrie	Rollin
Chris	Kelvin	Lorry	Rollins
Christian	Kit	Lyn	Rollo
Christie	Kristian	Lynn	Rolly
Christy	Kristin	Ordway	Roly
Colver	Labhras	Orlando	Rorie
Culver	Labhruinn	Othman	Rorry
Cynric	Landon	Otho	Rory
Delano	Langdon	Otto	Rowan
Dietrich	Langston	Oxton	Rowe
Edan	Larrance	Plato	Rowell
Efrem	Larry	Rick	Rowen
Elvis	Lars	Rickie	Rowland
Elvy	Lauren	Ricky	Rurick
Eph	Laurence	Roan	Rurik
Ephraim	Laurent	Rod	Rush
Gouverneur	Laurie	Rodd	Rushford
Hamlet	Lauritz	Roddie	Sproule

478

Associated Names (cont.)

Sprowle	Vic	Victoir	Victorin
Thaw	Vick	Victor	Warrick
Twitchell	Vicky	Victorien	Warwick

Name Portrait 74

Persuasive Leader

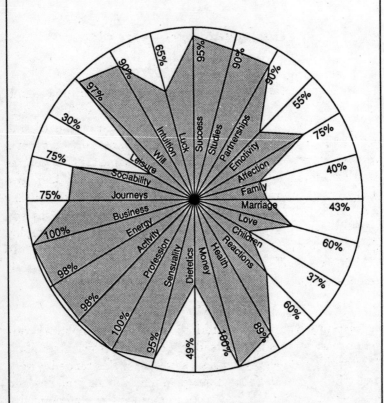

Element : Earth   **Plant** : Cypress tree
Mineral : Lead   **Sign** : Taurus
Animal : Deer   **Color** : Red

Personality Type:

Persuasive Leader

(Associated names – page 484)

BASIC CHARACTER

It is important for you to be in a position of power, but your leadership is usually from behind the scenes or just offstage. You are active and energetic, well-organized and patient—all at the same time—which lends your character a certain awesome quality. Freedom is important to you, as well as influence, and like your totem animal, the deer, you will pursue it even if it means leading a secretive, solitary existence. There is a certain intellectual modesty about you despite your brilliance and even though you often employ your intellect toward convincing and persuading others into action. You have leanings toward mysteries and the occult sciences, which comes from your secretive side.

YOUR PSYCHOLOGY

Despite your calm exterior, you suffer from inner turbulence and can sink into sadness or depression. Your plant totem, the melancholy cypress, symbolizes this tendency very well. Still, you also lean toward Machiavellian schemes and can become stubborn and truly imperious if your persuasive techniques aren't coming to fruit. A personal affront can evoke your sometimes terrifying temper and call up your capacity to hold a silent grudge to the end of time.

HOW YOU ACT AND REACT IN THE WORLD

It seems as if you were once stimulated by an enormous electrical force which has kept you going and going. You are at your best with long-term projects; sometimes they may take years to bear fruit, but when they do, the results are stupefying. You tend to discover your worth through your work and are drawn toward rare and unusual careers and amusements. You want to study what no one else has ever taken up. Though you might be a candidate for a long and arduous initiation into some mystery cult, you also earn distinctions in the practical world. You would make an outstanding secret agent, a many-skilled businessman, or an influential and effective politician, able to persuade a nation to vote for you easily.

YOUR DEEP INTUITIVE PERSONALITY

You have the intuition, insight, and sensitivity of a born sleuth. Your powerful inner voice shows in your eyes like a spark—and sometimes a glint—and you rely upon it in most of your worldly endeavors. It's like an eagle at other times, swooping in on its prey. Your intuition is the source of much of your power of persuasion, and it lends you an almost bewitching quality.

YOUR INTELLIGENCE

Although you tend to be modest about it, your intellect is quick and incisive, holistic rather than analytic. It gives you the ability to "pull strings" with confidence from behind the scenes and can make of you a true leader.

YOUR EMOTIONAL NATURE

Intrigue plays a part in your love life, which is bound to be complex. Though you don't always show it, you are capable of dramatic bursts of affection. Conquest and possession tend to rule your sex life. You have a powerful and magnetic sexuality and a very active sex life. You are a decidedly masculine lover, and though you are capable of real and warm feelings toward a lover who is up to your standards, you tend to lead a complicated emotional life which takes you into a number of bizarre and strongly sensual situations.

YOUR HEALTH AND VITALITY

Even though you push yourself to the limit, you usually maintain a strong enough vitality to see you through. Your diet is pure anarchy, so you have to watch your digestive system. You need plenty of sleep and fresh air; and if you indulge in a lot of contact sports, you will have to be careful of injuries. You are also susceptible to tropical diseases.

THE SOCIAL YOU

You can get along with a variety of people from all different backgrounds and walks of life, but your regular social life is most likely conducted with a few chosen and trusted friends. There is something of a Rasputin in you, which shows in your social dealings. Your persuasiveness, for one thing, can be downright hypnotic, and it would not be surprising if you had a band of secret followers. You communicate by suggestions and demand courage from your friends. Though you are not an avid party-goer, it is important for you to be around people from time to time, and this need may draw you into fraternal societies and clubs. In all, and in spite of your inclination toward secretiveness, you can be charming and cordial and, of course, influential.

———————

NamePortrait
74
Associated Names

Arval	Huntingdon	Talbot	Wat
Arvel	Huntington	Townsend	Wattie
Barnum	Kirk	Vin	Watty
Byford	Kirkley	Vince	Whitney
Ehren	Kirkwood	Vincens	Whitny
Faust	Mather	Vincent	Witney
Godwin	Milton	Vinney	Witny
Godwine	Morton	Vinny	Woodley
Godwyn	Morty	Vinson	Woodly
Golding	Romain	Wally	Woody
Goldwin	Sim	Walt	Wray
Goodwin	Simeon	Walter	Wren
Hannibal	Simon	Walters	Wright
Hosea	Siomann	Walther	Yehudi
Houston	Stinson	Walton	

Name Portrait 75

Moonlit Charmer

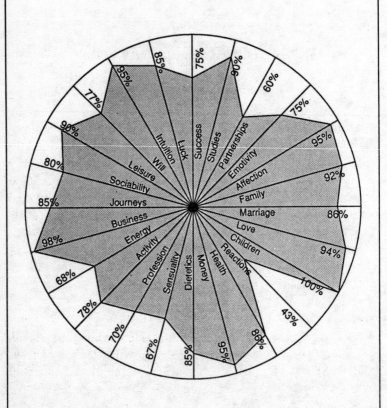

Element : Water

Mineral : Obsidian

Animal : Lizard

Plant : Lily of the valley

Sign : Cancer

Color : Violet

Personality Type:

Moonlit Charmer

(Associated names – page 490)

BASIC CHARACTER

You are a highly emotional person, a romantic, and a dreamer, with a rich, poetic imagination. There is a delicacy about you, like your totem plant, the fragile and subdued lily of the valley. Your deep thoughtfulness often gives way to a nervous restlessness because you tend to reflect the state of the world around you, and can become afflicted by the dark undercurrents that precede millennial transformations. Your totem animal, the lizard, is symbolic of the unconscious intuitive powers which portend vast changes. But you yourself seek stability in your private and often inscrutable life, no matter how high-strung and restless you feel.

YOUR PSYCHOLOGY

Though you tend to be timid, edgy, and your moods are often changeable, you have a strong will which is equal to your emotions. You are a natural introvert and tend to isolate yourself from the world; your self-discipline poses an eternal problem for you. You would rather withdraw than take a gamble on life, and your fear of failure only exacerbates your inhibitions. Still, if you feel threatened, you can be quick to anger, and your changeableness sometimes leads you into self-destructive behavior. It is extremely important for someone with your sensibilities and sensitivities to make prolonged efforts at integrating your very intuitive personality with your actions in the world.

HOW YOU ACT AND REACT IN THE WORLD

Your behavior tends to be rather subdued, though in the face of intractable reality, you often become flighty and distant or indecisive. Because you have a strong attraction to mystery cults, you might join such a group, and your leanings would be more to a Madame Blavatsky than a Robespierre. History interests you and science and math don't seem to exist for you. Though you might spend a lot of your time in search of the ideal protective life, you are open to creative careers. You could be a fine writer or insightful journalist, given the right amount of self-discipline; and you could succeed in a career in acting or fashion design.

YOUR DEEP INTUITIVE PERSONALITY

Your intuition is remarkable, radiant, and alive. It lends you an other-worldly sort of beauty. It is one of the strongest aspects of your whole character and is felt powerfully in everything you do.

YOUR INTELLIGENCE

You have a synthetic mind, and tend to be deeply contemplative. You rely upon your intuition more than upon your intellect, and though this at times leads to some disorderly thinking, you are bright and at times come up with some astonishingly astute observations and insights.

YOUR EMOTIONAL NATURE

Although you are shy and restrained in your affections, once you have discovered love, you can be terribly jealous and possessive. You are inclined to look at love as a retreat from worldly cares, and that escape must be protected at all costs. It seems always as if you are in search of the ideal lover; and the more understanding and compassionate, gentle and caring a lover is, the closer he comes to your ideal. Sexually, you are inclined to lead a rather complex life. At the two extremes are a passionate plunge into sex, often as a means of escape from troubles, and a total withdrawal from any sexuality, which can lead you into a rich mystical life.

YOUR HEALTH AND VITALITY

Overwork and fatigue are your nemeses. Your vitality and good health depend on getting plenty of relaxing sleep. Meditation exercises would benefit you greatly, as would relaxing sports such as swimming and tennis. You suffer from minor illnesses and slight accidents, and you are inclined to resort to stimulants to keep you going. You must be particularly careful to avoid back injuries.

THE SOCIAL YOU

You are at once captivating and disconcerting. You tend to vacillate between an outgoing warmth and a remote coolness which borders on superficiality. You are very guarded about forming friendships one moment and then thrust yourself on a whole party the next. It all depends on your mood and, very likely, the psychology of the world at the moment. But when you are in a social mood and have left your extraterrestriality behind, you can be the life of the party— a brilliant, sparkling guest—as long as you know that you have your own secure nest to return to when the clock strikes twelve, or one, or two.

———————

NamePortrait
75
Associated Names

Acacia	Duna	Oma	Thea
Aeldrida	Dwana	Ona	Theana
Ag	Edmonda	Onawa	Theano
Agata	Edmonde	Oona	Thecla
Agatha	Edmunda	Oonagh	Thecle
Agathe	Eldrida	Pandora	Thekla
Agathy	Eranthe	Pen	Theora
Aggie	Ginger	Penelope	Thera
Aggy	Ginnie	Penn	Thia
Alzena	Ginny	Penna	Traviata
Amethyst	Gipsy	Penny	Una
Angel	Gypsy	Phebe	Ventura
Angela	Hermosa	Phoebe	Verda
Angelica	Hesper	Placida	Verena
Angelina	Hespera	Placidia	Verna
Angeline	Hesperia	Poppaca	Verneta
Angelique	Ian	Poppy	Vernice
Angelita	Iantha	Radinka	Vernis
Angie	Ianthe	Saba	Vernita
Anthea	Ianthina	Sheba	Vevila
Anthia	Janthina	Sid	Vir
Bliss	Janthine	Sidney	Virgi
Blita	Jinny	Sidonia	Virgie
Blitha	Keely	Sidonie	Virginia
Blithe	Kirstie	Svetlana	Virginie
Bluma	Kirstin	Syd	Virgy
Blyth	Kirstina	Sydney	Virina
Blythe	Kirsty	Tai	Virna
Day	Laverna	Taite	Xylia
Duana	Laverne	Tecla	Xylona

Name Portrait 76

Lone Soldier

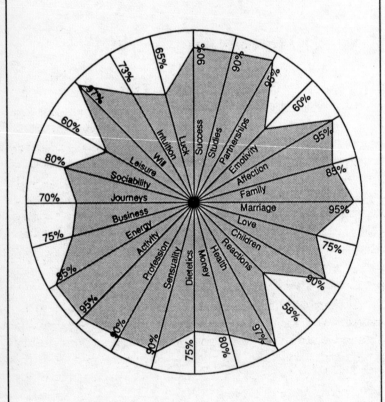

Element : Earth **Plant** : Yew tree

Mineral : Basalt **Sign** : Capricorn

Animal : Wild boar **Color** : Green

Personality Type:

Lone Soldier

(Associated names – page 497)

BASIC CHARACTER

With the wild boar, symbol of intrepidness, as your animal totem, you are a man of courage and powerful intelligence. Everything about you runs deep and at the same time is magnificently expressed in your extraordinary actions. Your intense fearlessness is matched by your expansive heart and high sense of morality. You have about you a joy of living which is the envy of those who know you. You are capable of great deeds, but you must have your unfettered freedom from convention in order to act at your best.

YOUR PSYCHOLOGY

If there is one thing that irks you no end, it is to be judged. You know who you are and what you are capable of, and woe to the person who gives you any sort of contrary assessment. You have a tendency, when provoked, to carry a grudge to the end of time, a trait which is engendered by your terrific pride.

Both introverted when you need to be and extroverted when you are called upon to perform, you follow your own inner voices and rarely heed convention. This makes you somewhat slow to adapt to changing situations and environments, but once you do adapt, you are in there and moving, making changes that must be made, and to the winds with anyone else. It is not only your morality and courage which

493

guide you, but your incredible, sustaining will. Your will provides your impetus for your actions, and you often tend to impose your powerful will on others.

HOW YOU ACT AND REACT IN THE WORLD

By nature you are a loner and therefore follow your own path. There is little timidity in any of your undertakings; and failure at one enterprise challenges you to succeed at the next. You are a whirlwind of activity but a directed whirlwind in that you know where you are going, even though you might make some mistakes along the way. You are not averse to taking risks. Love of nature might well take you into a career in ecology, a field which you will study seriously if not with a scholarly attitude. You are well disciplined and tend to dedicate yourself to your work. A career that requires daring, the expression of your authority, and personal strength will be your choice. You would make an excellent explorer or a superlative soldier, a sailor, a professional athlete, or an effective organizer, as long as you do not have to dwell long with the crowds. You are driven in most of your activities by a sense of justice and right, and have little time for those whose lives fall far from these goals of humanity.

YOUR DEEP INTUITIVE PERSONALITY

Your intuition is highly developed and takes its place among your well evolved instincts. You have a true sixth sense for sniffing things out and being able to anticipate events. It is your inner voice which keeps you on the alert and off the beaten paths.

YOUR INTELLIGENCE

Essentially you have an analytic mind. You observe and dissect events and people, and only after all the data has passed through your razor-sharp mind do you make a decision. Your memory is very reliable—you should depend upon it more than is your habit to do. In all, your intellect is earthy. You have, despite your swift mind, a feet-on-the-ground mentality which, when combined with your intuitive powers, makes you a man of depth as well as of practical and effective action.

YOUR EMOTIONAL NATURE

Though you may go through many love affairs, affection and sex are, for you, a serious matter. You will not tolerate betrayal, and far from your horizon is the insincere or manipulative lover. Oh, many will try to win your affections, but your keen intuition, when you allow it to overspeak your strong sexuality, will set things right and send such lovers packing. Most likely, you experimented with sex very early on and were involved quite seriously in a love affair in your teens. As you grow older, you find that you are at your emotional best in a loyal, permanent, and reciprocally respectful relationship—which does not bar an affair or two on the side, for when the flesh calls, you do find a way of answering. Your emotional and sexual energies are as prodigious as your intellectual and psychological drives. Still, as far as choosing a lasting partner, you are as particular as you are in everything else. She must allow you your independence and return your loyalty, which does not always include sexual loyalty, but a steel-hard emotional commitment.

YOUR HEALTH AND VITALITY

As in every other realm, your vitality is infused with a great, sustaining energy. Sometimes, it seems as if you are a pillar of strength, able to eat anything and go without rest for days on end. Still, you are human and do run the risk of overdoing it. You have a habit, when a cold or a fever strikes, of saying, "Oh, so what. It'll pass." But such minor illnesses, especially when they're ignored, can wear you down and make you less effective. You must go out of your way to watch your eating habits. Regular outdoor exercise should also be part of your daily regimen.

THE SOCIAL YOU

Concerning society, you have a take-it-or-leave-it attitude. A difficult man to get close to, you do, all the same, have your close circle of friends who have won your respect. You are a generous father and a supportive husband, though you must be treated with a certain tact and diffidence. Any social activity that binds you is repulsive—heaven forbid the annual office Christmas party; you'll no doubt have some good excuse for not being there! Though you are a much admired man, you are at the same time a much feared man. No one wants to get on the wrong side of you, and if someone is so foolish as to end up there—well, you may not say anything at once, but years later, at this or that social gathering, you just might charge. Afterward, like your plant totem the yew, symbol of sadness, you will feel just lousy. Above all, you enjoy yourself around others whom you love as energetically as they love you, which generally keeps your social world rather small but intense and active.

———————————

NamePortrait
76
Associated Names

Abe	Brendon	Guillaume	Rule
Abie	Burnett	Hartman	Scot
Abraham	Burney	Hartmann	Scott
Abram	Calliste	Hayward	Scottie
Aby	Clodomir	Haywood	Scotty
Adalard	Colter	Heyward	Servan
Adelard	Colton	Heywood	Sherwin
Adhelard	Cormac	Ingar	Uilleam
Anastase	Cormack	Inger	Uilliam
Anastasius	Cormick	Ingvar	Wiley
Anatholia	Corrie	Kadin	Wilhelm
Anthelme	Deck	Kenelm	Wilhem
Anyon	Dex	Kev	Wilkes
Bancroft	Dexter	Kevan	Wilkie
Bill	Eidrich	Keven	Will
Billie	Elwell	Kevin	Willard
Billy	Erland	Lacy	Willet
Black	Erling	Leger	William
Blake	Garfield	Liam	Williamson
Blakeley	Gil	Mac	Willie
Blakey	Giles	Martial	Willis
Bram	Gilles	Martian	Willy
Bran	Gillet	Narcisse	Wilson
Brandan	Gillett	Prosper	
Brendan	Gresham	Ruelle	

Name Portrait 77

Just and Earnest Striver

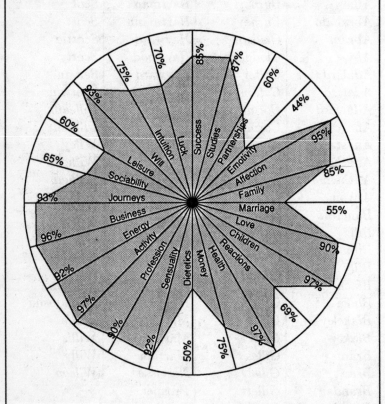

Element : Earth   **Plant** : Wild rose

Mineral : Zinc   **Sign** : Taurus

Animal : Ladybug   **Color**: Orange

Personality Type:

Just and Earnest Striver

(Associated names – page 502)

BASIC CHARACTER

Underneath what appears to be a layer of skepticism, your great love of mankind and innate sense of justice lend you a rare and solid strength of character. You are highly principled and operate from an exalted morality. Though you are inclined to become irascible at times, that is only because your moral sense has been offended in some way. You are strong-headed about your beliefs and sensibilities, among which is loyalty. In the face of betrayal, you can become explosive, though you prefer to react without any warning whatever. You reach for perfection, and in this respect your totem plant, the wild rose, is an apt symbol: it is the plant of the garden of Eros and the paradise of Dante.

YOUR PSYCHOLOGY

In spite of your general love of mankind, you're not very easy to get close to. You tend toward introversion and withdrawal, and you have a volatile temperament. Where justice is concerned, you can muster up amazing aggressiveness—but where you are concerned, you tend to be rather indecisive like your totem animal, the ladybug, which never quite knows whether to walk or to fly. Your indecisiveness is usually over what might be the appropriate action to take in a situation, and you positively cringe if anyone comments on it while you're in the process of deciding. Though you are inclined to be influenced by other people's opinions, your will is strong, and you cling to it, like a ladybug to a leaf in a storm.

HOW YOU ACT AND REACT IN THE WORLD

You are conscientious, dedicated, and loyal in all your pursuits, whether professional or social. Though at times you get it into your head that you might not be up to the goals you've set, you usually are; and your honesty and commitment to a project will invariably see you through to its completion. You are inclined to stick to one line of work and do not adjust very easily to career change—or any vast change in your life, for that matter. You could become an excellent technician or engineer, as you tend to be good with your hands. By the same token, you could be a productive and hard-working farmer or an admirable sailor who will literally get to know all the ropes.

YOUR DEEP INTUITIVE PERSONALITY

There is something about the idea of intuition that turns you off. You select the visible world over the darker, more shadowy one, which is the way you view your inner self. Still, your intuition is strong and reliable, however often you prefer the senses to its insistent whisper.

YOUR INTELLIGENCE

Your intellect is deep and honest; you tend to mull things over before you choose a side of an issue or decide which course of action is best. Because of your introverted tendencies, you often dwell deep in your mind, where you are able to come up with some rarefied insights. It is important to you to be able to express your intellectual illuminations with your friends, and you can become irritable and feisty if you don't have that opportunity.

YOUR EMOTIONAL NATURE

Love plays an important and vital part in your life. Without it and the understanding that is part of love, you tend to

pale and lose faith in yourself. But it should not be a possessive sort of love—it should be an indulgent tenderness. You
are perfectly willing to return such love in kind, as long as you
do not feel that your giving is contingent upon your receiving.
You can be an exquisitely powerful lover with your strong yet
refined sexuality. Ultimately, and in spite of a certain sexual and sensual adventurousness, you seek a long and lasting
affair, inclining toward monogamy more than polygamy. If
ever you feel emotionally betrayed, your fierce anger bursts
into the open, and a love affair can shatter irreparably.

YOUR HEALTH AND VITALITY

Even though you have a marvelous vitality, you tend to
jeopardize your health with a chaotic schedule. You do not
eat regularly and tend to push yourself to your physical limit
at times. You have to be especially careful of muscle strain
and injuries to the spinal column.

THE SOCIAL YOU

You're not going to allow yourself to become tied to a
demanding social schedule; freedom is just too important to
you. But your versatile nature leaves you open for a wide
array of social encounters, and usually your high qualities
are a source of charm and attraction to people. You would
not be caught dead or alive among a party of opportunists
or superficial crowd-pleasers; it's not only out of your style,
but offensive to your principles. You have a firm sense of
friendship, and your own small circle is likely to be made up
of people who share your morality and goals in life.

NamePortrait
77
Associated Names

Ashton	Israel	Luc	Reagen
Ashur	Issie	Lucas	Regan
Craig	Ivan	Luck	Regen
Crayton	Ivar	Lukas	Rick
Creighton	Iven	Luke	Roden
Denley	Iver	Lukey	Rowsan
Dustin	Ives	Lute	Rowson
Dwight	Ivo	Luther	Roxbury
Eldon	Ivon	Mannie	Sonny
Emanuel	Ivor	Manny	Stein
Emmanuel	Izzie	Manoel	Stowe
Erwin	Jared	Manuel	Swain
Esau	Jay	Manus	Swayne
Evan	Ken	Mayo	Sweeney
Ewan	Keneth	Nahum	Sweyn
Ewen	Kenn	Odilon	Symington
Foy	Kennard	Oglesby	Tiler
Girvan	Kennedy	Owain	Ty
Girven	Kennet	Owen	Tye
Girvin	Kenneth	Paddy	Tyler
Herwin	Kenny	Padraic	Tyson
Howard	Kenton	Padraig	Uillioc
Howe	Keren	Pat	Ulises
Howie	Kern	Patric	Ulysses
Hyde	Killian	Patrice	Wagner
Immanuel	Layton	Patrick	Watford
Irvin	Leighton	Patsy	Watkins
Irvine	Lothair	Patton	Watson
Irving	Lothaire	Paxton	Wells
Irwin	Lothar	Peyton	Wolfram
Isaie	Lothario	Reagan	Wolseley

502

Associated Names (cont.)

Wolsey	Yvain	Yves
Woolsey	Yvan	Yvon

Name Portrait 78

Sensual Singer

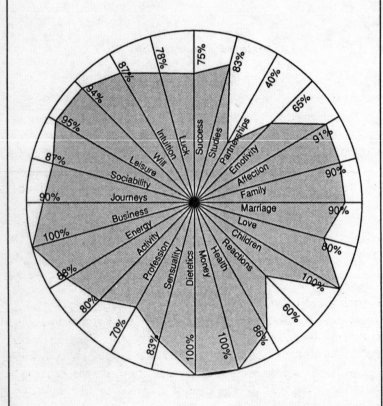

Element : Fire   **Plant** : Cherry tree

Mineral : Coral   **Sign** : Leo

Animal : Cicada   **Color**: Blue

Personality Type:

Sensual Singer

(Associated names – page 508)

BASIC CHARACTER

At heart you are an emotionalist who can soar to the heights of rapture or plummet into a gloom of depression at the slightest provocation. Though nobody else seems to understand what sends you up or brings you down, to you it is all quite clear. You are highly sensitive to the world around you, and this sensitivity also lends you an alluring beauty and charm as irresistible as the blossoms of your totem plant, the cherry tree. Alongside your strong emotions is a firm moral sense of the right and wrong ways of the world.

YOUR PSYCHOLOGY

In spite of your often carefree approach to things, which is symbolized by your animal totem, the cicada, your feelings are so close to the surface that you tend to overreact to problems and obstacles. Your temper is fiery and, once aroused, can come under the influence of your considerable will and lead you into authoritarian attitudes. You are an extrovert by nature and tend to get deeply involved in life, but this tendency often conflicts with your inclination toward indecision; you become easily afflicted with instability and lack of balance in your life if you do not have a secure environment which helps you realize your creative potentials.

HOW YOU ACT AND REACT IN THE WORLD

In general, you are more interested in your home life than in your career and will most likely change jobs and professions often—always in search of the romantic ideal. You need structure and discipline in order to keep your powerful reactions from overtaking your best efforts. You are a good student, with a lively curiosity, and are drawn to subjects that involve public life. Among the professional areas to which you are attracted are restoration work, business, and early childhood education. You are very seldom discouraged by failure and are capable of extraordinarily courageous dedication to your work or to an emotionally inspired social cause.

YOUR DEEP INTUITIVE PERSONALITY

You have a rarefied sort of charm, which comes from the depth of your astonishing intuition. It is difficult to distinguish your acute sensitivities from your swift intuitive insights, or whether your keen emotions are being pricked into life from the events around you or the song of your inner voice.

YOUR INTELLIGENCE

Your lively intellect is full of fantasy and good humor, fed by your prodigious memory of emotionally important events and your imaginative curiosity. Your mind is synthetic rather than analytic; you are able to comprehend at a glance all the forces at work in any situation or problem. Instead of mulling over each detail in a problem, you sense how they interact with each other and come together to form the whole picture.

YOUR EMOTIONAL NATURE

Although you often appear cool and distant at first meeting, you are the most affectionate of people. Your sensuality and sentiments often rule you in the extreme. There is no way to control your emotional possessiveness, which nonetheless has a sweetness to it which most people find irresistible. Normally, you are more faithful than you would like to let on, but your sexuality is powerful, and whether it is preserved for one loyal lover or not, it demands expression. In many ways, you are a person of the senses, oblivious to social taboos and restrictions when it comes to pursuing your sensual nature. Most likely, you will have many loves and a lively, if sometimes complicated, sex life.

YOUR HEALTH AND VITALITY

Diet is especially important to your good health, for although you are vigorous and can resist disease very well, you have a tendency to overeat and tax yourself physically. You need outdoor exercise, especially swimming. It is possible that you will experience troubles in your urinary tract, your kidneys, or your genitals. You should also be especially careful about taking tranquilizers of any kind.

THE SOCIAL YOU

You have an almost religious dedication to friendship that is at once warm, tender, and firm. Your family and close friends are the focus of your social life, but you are also very sociable outside these groups and can feel at home just about anywhere. You are a gracious hostess, radiating warmth with your infectious joy in living. You add a sparkle to any party and lead a successful, very fortunate social life. The good things of life for you are in your social goings on, and your spirited, sensitive presence is often like a song, enlivening even the most staid gathering.

NamePortrait
78
Associated Names

Adabel	Aubine	Jade	Melvine
Adabela	Chiquita	Joelle	Menzies
Adabella	Dela	Jovita	Nomida
Adabelle	Della	Jyoti	Numidia
Adalia	Delora	Lana	Orea
Adaline	Delores	Lane	Primmie
Adela	Deloris	Lanetta	Primrose
Adelaide	Delorita	Lanette	Primula
Adele	Dione	Leya	Prunella
Adelia	Dolly	Linetta	Prunelle
Adelina	Dolores	Linette	Rasia
Adelind	Echo	Linnet	Rhoda
Adeline	Edelina	Linnetta	Rhodantha
Adelle	Edeline	Linnette	Rhode
Adila	Edlyn	Lola	Rhodes
Alain	Erwina	Loleta	Rhodia
Alana	Fabiola	Lolita	Rohesia
Alanna	Galatea	Lollie	Romhilda
Alarica	Garnet	Lolly	Romhilde
Alarice	Garnette	Lynette	Romilda
Alarise	Greer	Lynn	Romilde
Alayne	Gregoria	Lynne	Ros
Albina	Harmonia	Lynnette	Rosa
Albine	Harmonie	Malva	Rosabel
Albinia	Harmony	Malvie	Rosabella
Alina	Irvetta	Malvina	Rosabelle
Allene	Irvette	Mauve	Rosalee
Allyn	Iva	Melba	Rosaleen
Alma	Ivana	Melva	Rosalyn
Alvina	Ivanna	Melville	Rosalynd
Aubina	Ivanne	Melvina	Rosamond

Associated Names (cont.)

Rosamonda	Rosemarie	Rosine	Rozina
Rosamund	Rosemary	Rosita	Sheridan
Rosamunda	Rosemond	Roslyn	Vega
Rosanna	Rosemonde	Rosmunda	Vida
Rosanne	Rosemund	Rosy	Vidonia
Rose	Rosena	Roz	Vigilia
Rosel	Rosene	Rozalind	Yevetta
Roseline	Rosetta	Rozaline	Yevette
Rosella	Rosette	Rozamond	Yvetta
Roselle	Rosia	Rozelin	Yvette
Rosellen	Rosie	Rozello	Zita
Roselyn	Rosina	Rozenn	Zoe

Name Portrait 79

Enterprising Intriguer

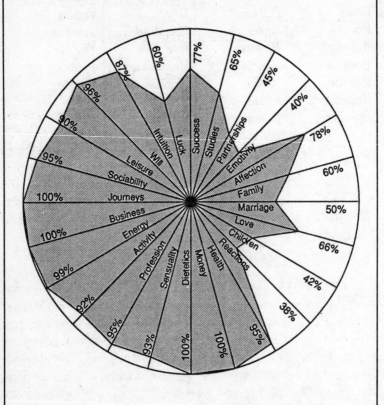

Element : Air   **Plant** : Valerian

Mineral : Pitchblende   **Sign** : Libra

Animal : Hedgehog   **Color** : Blue

Personality Type:

Enterprising Intriguer

(Associated names – page 514)

BASIC CHARACTER

You are highly moral, assertive, and courageously determined to pursue success. The accoutrements of a successful life are important to you; you enjoy expensive things, the fine luxuries that bespeak a refined lifestyle. There is a touch of intrigue in your soul, which is reflected in your innate sense of politics. Much of your life is directed toward climbing the ladder of profession and career; your self-confidence is unshakable in that pursuit because it is abetted by a powerful will and strong emotions.

YOUR PSYCHOLOGY

As assertive as you are, you have a strong tendency toward introversion when things are not going your way. Rather than turning your assertiveness into stubborn aggression, you will curl up into a ball and hide under the bushes, like your totem animal, the shy hedgehog. Fortunately, this doesn't happen very often, for you are not easily convinced that events might not portend success for you. Though you are emotional, you control your feelings, to the extent sometimes, that you appear callous and unfeeling. This, too, is a protective measure, and goes hand-in-hand with your propensity for settling accounts with anyone who you feel has done you a disservice: you never forget anything. You have a tendency toward distrust and inflexibility, which comes from your steel-like willpower. Failure, to you, is a personal affront.

HOW YOU ACT AND REACT IN THE WORLD

You have a strong impulse to contradict both other people's opinions and the general flow of events. This gives you a certain dynamism which is almost impossible to resist. Much of your exceptionally intense activity is directed toward career and success. You are capable, competent, and competitive, with a natural devotion to your profession. You can plan the most complex projects, as well as take over any job that has some ticklish political elements to it, and resolve it with tact and caution. Life will very likely lead you into some unusual careers and projects. You can be a marvelous actress or an excellent museum curator, archivist, archeologist, or historian. Professions that involve refined sensibilities and knowledge are especially attractive to you. It would not be at all surprising, either, if you were to become a secret agent, applying your natural bent for intrigue.

YOUR DEEP INTUITIVE PERSONALITY

All you need is a crystal ball and the picture would be complete. Your intuitive sense is so highly developed and strong, that you seem able to anticipate events. This lends you a marvelous charm which is sometimes overwhelming. Your sharp imagination comes from your intuition, as does your ability to devise and solve projects of vast complexity.

YOUR INTELLIGENCE

Despite your powerful intuition, your intellect is practical. You approach things in a concrete way, and can think problems through rather than trying to rely on your inner vision for a quick and speedy solution. Yet, in conjunction with your intuition, your mind becomes a force to reckon with.

YOUR EMOTIONAL NATURE

You are very seductive, but you are also highly selective about whom you're going to seduce. At heart, you are monandrous; exquisitely sensual but refined in the way you express yourself. Although you are, for the most part, able to love selflessly and sincerely, your love is somewhat restrained; and if the opportunity presents itself, you are perfectly capable of using your affections toward professional success: you are well aware of the power of the heart and know how to use it to advantage. Still, once you have met someone who meets your high standards, you give your all to him somewhat possessively but with enduring, finely tuned ardor.

YOUR HEALTH AND VITALITY

With your tendency to lead a balanced life, you maintain excellent health and great vitality. You resist diseases well because you know how to protect yourself from them. Your weak spot is your respiratory system, and you should avoid smoking at all costs.

THE SOCIAL YOU

Your home is an open and welcome place for your select group of intimates, and there you are able to entertain with grace and style. You know how to start up an interesting and intellectually stimulating conversation, and your own fascinating life is a source of much interest to your friends. Your plant totem, the valerian, symbolizes the ease with which you can calm and soothe your guests with your attractiveness and fine sensibilities.

Adria	Corentine	Ivonne	Myrtille
Adriana	Crescent	Jasmin	Myrtis
Adriane	Crescenta	Jasmina	Myrtle
Adrianna	Crescente	Jasmine	Nata
Adrianne	Crescentia	Jessamie	Natacha
Adrienne	Devona	Jessamine	Natala
Alda	Eadie	Jessamy	Natale
Aleda	Eadith	Jessamyn	Natalia
Aleta	Eady	Kama	Natalie
Alida	Eaidie	Lavina	Natasha
Alita	Eala	Lavinia	Nathalie
Aminta	Eda	Leda	Natica
Amintha	Ede	Lena	Natika
Aminthe	Edie	Lind	Natividad
Amity	Edith	Linda	Nattie
Atlancia	Editha	Linde	Netie
Atlantia	Edithe	Lindie	Netta
Belinda	Ediva	Lindy	Nettie
Bella	Edythe	Lita	Netty
Bellanca	Eglantina	Lynd	Noelle
Belle	Eglantine	Lynda	Ombeline
Bina	Eglentyne	Mertle	Paquerette
Binnie	Eglintyne	Mildred	Primavera
Brina	Eglyntine	Mildrid	Prud
Celene	Elata	Milli	Prudence
Celie	Elda	Millie	Prudentia
Celina	Hadria	Milly	Prudie
Celinda	Holda	Mirle	Prudy
Celine	Holde	Myrta	Prue
Chelsea	Holle	Myrtia	Raisa
Cleva	Hulda	Myrtilla	Raissa

Associated Names (cont.)

Raisse	Savina	Sena	Venita
Ria	Sebastiana	Thalia	Venus
Royale	Sebastiane	Tia	Vina
Rubetta	Sebastianna	Trissie	Vinia
Rubette	Sebastianne	Trissy	Vinita
Rubia	Sebastienna	Val	Vinnie
Rubie	Sebastienne	Valeria	Vinny
Rubina	Sela	Valerie	Von
Ruby	Selena	Valery	Vonnie
Sabina	Selene	Vallie	Yasmin
Sabine	Selia	Valona	Yasmina
Sabrin	Selie	Valonia	Yasmine
Sabrina	Selina	Valora	Yvona
Sabrine	Selinda	Valorey	Yvonne
Salene	Semele	Valorie	
Savanna	Semelia	Valory	

Part III

Index of Names

INDEX OF GIRLS' NAMES

GIRLS' NAMES

GIRLS' NAMES

GIRLS' NAMES

GIRLS' NAMES

GIRLS' NAMES

GIRLS' NAMES

GIRLS' NAMES

GIRLS' NAMES

GIRLS' NAMES

GIRLS' NAMES

GIRLS' NAMES

GIRLS' NAMES

GIRLS' NAMES

34 Cyrena, *pp.* 234–239
34 Cyrenia, *pp.* 234–239
9 Cyrilla, *pp.* 80–84
34 Cythera, *pp.* 234–239
34 Cytherea, *pp.* 234–239
34 Cytherere, *pp.* 234–239
34 Cytheria, *pp.* 234–239
34 Cytherine, *pp.* 234–239
28 Dacia, *pp.* 196–201
71 Daffodil, *pp.* 462–467
60 Daffy, *pp.* 392–398
14 Dagmar, *pp.* 112–117
58 Dahlia, *pp.* 380–385
60 Daisy, *pp.* 392–398
58 Dale, *pp.* 380–385
58 Dalhia, *pp.* 380–385
58 Dalia, *pp.* 380–385
17 Dalila, *pp.* 130–134
58 Damita, *pp.* 380–385
27 Danella, *pp.* 190–195
27 Danelle, *pp.* 190–195
27 Dania, *pp.* 190–195
27 Danica, *pp.* 190–195
27 Daniela, *pp.* 190–195
27 Danielea, *pp.* 190–195
27 Danielle, *pp.* 190–195
27 Danitza, *pp.* 190–195
19 Daphne, *pp.* 142–146
38 Dara, *pp.* 258–263
49 Darcie, *pp.* 324–329
31 Darel, *pp.* 214–220
31 Darelle, *pp.* 214–220
23 Daria, *pp.* 166–170
31 Darleen, *pp.* 214–220
31 Darlene, *pp.* 214–220

31 Darline, *pp.* 214–220
31 Darrelle, *pp.* 214–220
31 Darry, *pp.* 214–220
31 Daryl, *pp.* 214–220
60 Davida, *pp.* 392–398
60 Davina, *pp.* 392–398
51 Dawn, *pp.* 336–342
75 Day, *pp.* 486–490
41 Dayana, *pp.* 276–281
71 Deana, *pp.* 462–467
71 Deane, *pp.* 462–467
41 Deanna, *pp.* 276–281
14 Deb, *pp.* 112–117
14 Debbie, *pp.* 112–117
14 Debby, *pp.* 112–117
14 Debora, *pp.* 112–117
14 Deborah, *pp.* 112–117
14 Debra, *pp.* 112–117
14 Decima, *pp.* 112–117
16 Dee, *pp.* 124–129
41 Dee, *pp.* 276–281
51 Dee, *pp.* 336–342
51 Deel, *pp.* 336–342
62 Deidre, *pp.* 406–413
62 Deirdre, *pp.* 406–413
78 Dela, *pp.* 504–509
45 Delcine, *pp.* 300–305
71 Delcine, *pp.* 462–467
14 Delfine, *pp.* 112–117
14 Delia, *pp.* 112–117
41 Delia, *pp.* 276–281
41 Delicia, *pp.* 276–281
56 Delight, *pp.* 368–373
17 Delila, *pp.* 130–134
17 Delilah, *pp.* 130–134

GIRLS' NAMES

GIRLS' NAMES

45 Elena, pp. 300–305

45 Elene, pp. 300–305

45 Eleni, pp. 300–305

45 Elenor, pp. 300–305

45 Elenora, pp. 300–305

45 Elenore, pp. 300–305

71 Eleonor, pp. 462–467

71 Eleonora, pp. 462–467

71 Eleonore, pp. 462–467

14 Elfie, pp. 112–117

27 Elfreda, pp. 190–195

27 Elfreida, pp. 190–195

27 Elfrida, pp. 190–195

27 Elfried, pp. 190–195

27 Elfrieda, pp. 190–195

27 Elga, pp. 190–195

41 Elga, pp. 276–281

17 Eliane, pp. 130–134

17 Eliette, pp. 130–134

45 Elina, pp. 300–305

45 Elinor, pp. 300–305

71 Elinor, pp. 462–467

45 Elinora, pp. 300–305

71 Elinora, pp. 462–467

45 Elinore, pp. 300–305

71 Elinore, pp. 462–467

31 Elisa, pp. 214–220

34 Elisa, pp. 234–239

34 Elisabeth, pp. 234–239

34 Elise, pp. 234–239

31 Elissa, pp. 214–220

34 Elissa, pp. 234–239

34 Eliza, pp. 234–239

34 Elizabeth, pp. 234–239

45 Ella, pp. 300–305

62 Ella, pp. 406–413

45 Ellen, pp. 300–305

45 Ellene, pp. 300–305

45 Ellenita, pp. 300–305

21 Ellice, pp. 154–158

45 Ellie, pp. 300–305

21 Ellis, pp. 154–158

45 Ellyn, pp. 300–305

34 Elma, pp. 234–239

34 Elmira, pp. 234–239

45 Elna, pp. 300–305

45 Elnna, pp. 300–305

71 Elnora, pp. 462–467

71 Elnore, pp. 462–467

62 Elodie, pp. 406–413

56 Eloisa, pp. 368–373

17 Eloise, pp. 130–134

34 Eloise, pp. 234–239

56 Eloise, pp. 368–373

49 Elrica, pp. 324–329

34 Elsa, pp. 234–239

34 Elsbeth, pp. 234–239

34 Else, pp. 234–239

34 Elsie, pp. 234–239

34 Elspeth, pp. 234–239

34 Elspie, pp. 234–239

34 Elsy, pp. 234–239

14 Elva, pp. 112–117

27 Elva, pp. 190–195

14 Elvia, pp. 112–117

14 Elvie, pp. 112–117

14 Elvina, pp. 112–117

17 Elyette, pp. 130–134

34 Elysa, pp. 234–239

34 Elyse, pp. 234–239

GIRLS' NAMES

GIRLS' NAMES

GIRLS' NAMES

GIRLS' NAMES

GIRLS' NAMES

GIRLS' NAMES

GIRLS' NAMES

GIRLS' NAMES

GIRLS' NAMES

GIRLS' NAMES

GIRLS' NAMES

GIRLS' NAMES

GIRLS' NAMES

79 Kama, *pp.* 510–515

51 Kanaka, *pp.* 336–342

51 Kanake, *pp.* 336–342

38 Kara, *pp.* 258–263

38 Karell, *pp.* 258–263

38 Karen, *pp.* 258–263

38 Karena, *pp.* 258–263

38 Karin, *pp.* 258–263

38 Karina, *pp.* 258–263

38 Karine, *pp.* 258–263

46 Karla, *pp.* 306–311

38 Karyn, *pp.* 258–263

16 Kasmira, *pp.* 124–129

16 Kate, *pp.* 124–129

16 Katel, *pp.* 124–129

16 Katerine, *pp.* 124–129

16 Kateryn, *pp.* 124–129

16 Kath, *pp.* 124–129

16 Katharina, *pp.* 124–129

16 Katharine, *pp.* 124–129

16 Katherina, *pp.* 124–129

16 Katherine, *pp.* 124–129

16 Katheryn, *pp.* 124–129

16 Kathie, *pp.* 124–129

16 Kathleen, *pp.* 124–129

16 Kathlene, *pp.* 124–129

16 Kathryn, *pp.* 124–129

16 Kathy, *pp.* 124–129

16 Katia, *pp.* 124–129

16 Katie, *pp.* 124–129

16 Katrin, *pp.* 124–129

16 Katrina, *pp.* 124–129

16 Katrine, *pp.* 124–129

16 Katryn, *pp.* 124–129

16 Katty, *pp.* 124–129

16 Katy, *pp.* 124–129

16 Kay, *pp.* 124–129

16 Kaye, *pp.* 124–129

27 Kayla, *pp.* 190–195

75 Keely, *pp.* 486–490

49 Kelda, *pp.* 324–329

49 Kelly, *pp.* 324–329

27 Kelosia, *pp.* 190–195

49 Kelvina, *pp.* 324–329

36 Kerri, *pp.* 246–251

36 Kerry, *pp.* 246–251

16 Ketti, *pp.* 124–129

16 Ketty, *pp.* 124–129

51 Ketura, *pp.* 336–342

49 Kevin, *pp.* 324–329

38 Keziah, *pp.* 258–263

5 Kim, *pp.* 56–60

14 Kimberley, *pp.* 112–117

14 Kimberly, *pp.* 112–117

27 Kineta, *pp.* 190–195

75 Kirsten, *pp.* 486–490

75 Kirstie, *pp.* 486–490

75 Kirstin, *pp.* 486–490

75 Kirstina, *pp.* 486–490

75 Kirsty, *pp.* 486–490

16 Kit, *pp.* 124–129

16 Kitty, *pp.* 124–129

46 Kjersti, *pp.* 306–311

46 Kjerstie, *pp.* 306–311

21 Klara, *pp.* 154–158

36 Kloe, *pp.* 246–251

16 Kora, *pp.* 124–129

56 Koren, *pp.* 368–373

19 Krista, *pp.* 142–146

19 Kristabel, *pp.* 142–146

GIRLS' NAMES

GIRLS' NAMES

71 Lee, pp. 462–467
34 Leela, pp. 234–239
71 Leigh, pp. 462–467
34 Leila, pp. 234–239
34 Leilah, pp. 234–239
62 Leilani, pp. 406–413
34 Leilia, pp. 234–239
25 Leithia, pp. 178–182
34 Lela, pp. 234–239
34 Lelah, pp. 234–239
34 Lelia, pp. 234–239
31 Lemuela, pp. 214–220
31 Lemuella, pp. 214–220
9 Lena, pp. 80–84
45 Lena, pp. 300–305
79 Lena, pp. 510–515
9 Lene, pp. 80–84
49 Lene, pp. 324–329
49 Leneta, pp. 324–329
49 Lenetta, pp. 324–329
49 Lenis, pp. 324–329
49 Lenita, pp. 324–329
60 Lennie, pp. 392–398
60 Lenny, pp. 392–398
45 Lenora, pp. 300–305
71 Lenora, pp. 462–467
71 Lenore, pp. 462–467
49 Lenos, pp. 324–329
49 Lenta, pp. 324–329
1 Leocadie, pp. 32–36
56 Leoda, pp. 368–373
56 Leola, pp. 368–373
19 Leoma, pp. 142–146
45 Leona, pp. 300–305
60 Leona, pp. 392–398

60 Leonarda, pp. 392–398
60 Leonarde, pp. 392–398
60 Leonardina, pp. 392–398
60 Leonardine, pp. 392–398
60 Leone, pp. 392–398
60 Leoni, pp. 392–398
60 Leonie, pp. 392–398
45 Leonora, pp. 300–305
71 Leonora, pp. 462–467
45 Leonore, pp. 300–305
71 Leonore, pp. 462–467
60 Leontina, pp. 392–398
60 Leontine, pp. 392–398
60 Leontyne, pp. 392–398
1 Leopolda, pp. 32–36
1 Leopoldina, pp. 32–36
1 Leopoldine, pp. 32–36
45 Leora, pp. 300–305
56 Leota, pp. 368–373
34 Les, pp. 234–239
45 Lesbia, pp. 300–305
34 Lesley, pp. 234–239
34 Lesli, pp. 234–239
34 Leslie, pp. 234–239
34 Lesly, pp. 234–239
25 Leta, pp. 178–182
25 Letha, pp. 178–182
25 Lethia, pp. 178–182
25 Lethita, pp. 178–182
25 Leticia, pp. 178–182
25 Letitia, pp. 178–182
25 Letizia, pp. 178–182
25 Lettia, pp. 178–182
25 Lettice, pp. 178–182
25 Lettie, pp. 178–182

GIRLS' NAMES

GIRLS' NAMES

62 Mae, *pp.* 406–413
17 Maelle, *pp.* 130–134
49 Maeve, *pp.* 324–329
60 Mag, *pp.* 392–398
58 Magda, *pp.* 380–385
58 Magdala, *pp.* 380–385
58 Magdalane, *pp.* 380–385
58 Magdalen, *pp.* 380–385
58 Magdalena, *pp.* 380–385
58 Magdalene, *pp.* 380–385
58 Magdalyn, *pp.* 380–385
60 Maggi, *pp.* 392–398
60 Maggie, *pp.* 392–398
60 Maggy, *pp.* 392–398
60 Magnhilda, *pp.* 392–398
60 Magnhilde, *pp.* 392–398
60 Magnilda, *pp.* 392–398
60 Magnilde, *pp.* 392–398
60 Magnolia, *pp.* 392–398
45 Mahala, *pp.* 300–305
45 Mahalah, *pp.* 300–305
45 Mahalia, *pp.* 300–305
62 Maia, *pp.* 406–413
60 Maida, *pp.* 392–398
60 Maidel, *pp.* 392–398
60 Maidie, *pp.* 392–398
62 Maire, *pp.* 406–413
62 Mairi, *pp.* 406–413
60 Maisie, *pp.* 392–398
62 Maite, *pp.* 406–413
51 Maitilde, *pp.* 336–342
5 Majesta, *pp.* 56–60
58 Mala, *pp.* 380–385
14 Malan, *pp.* 112–117
58 Malena, *pp.* 380–385

58 Malina, *pp.* 380–385
14 Malinda, *pp.* 112–117
78 Malva, *pp.* 504–509
78 Malvie, *pp.* 504–509
78 Malvina, *pp.* 504–509
62 Mamie, *pp.* 406–413
14 Manda, *pp.* 112–117
14 Mandie, *pp.* 112–117
14 Mandy, *pp.* 112–117
62 Manette, *pp.* 406–413
62 Manon, *pp.* 406–413
71 Manuela, *pp.* 462–467
71 Manuella, *pp.* 462–467
71 Manuelle, *pp.* 462–467
62 Mara, *pp.* 406–413
62 Maraline, *pp.* 406–413
71 Marcela, *pp.* 462–467
71 Marcelia, *pp.* 462–467
71 Marceline, *pp.* 462–467
71 Marcella, *pp.* 462–467
71 Marcelle, *pp.* 462–467
71 Marcellia, *pp.* 462–467
71 Marcelline, *pp.* 462–467
71 Marchella, *pp.* 462–467
71 Marchelle, *pp.* 462–467
71 Marchita, *pp.* 462–467
71 Marcia, *pp.* 462–467
71 Marcie, *pp.* 462–467
71 Marcile, *pp.* 462–467
71 Marcille, *pp.* 462–467
71 Marcy, *pp.* 462–467
31 Marelda, *pp.* 214–220
31 Marella, *pp.* 214–220
62 Maretta, *pp.* 406–413
62 Marette, *pp.* 406–413

GIRLS' NAMES

60 Marfot, *pp.* 392–398

60 Margalo, *pp.* 392–398

60 Margao, *pp.* 392–398

60 Margaret, *pp.* 392–398

60 Margareta, *pp.* 392–398

60 Margaretha, *pp.* 392–398

60 Margarethe, *pp.* 392–398

60 Margaretta, *pp.* 392–398

60 Margarita, *pp.* 392–398

60 Marge, *pp.* 392–398

60 Margerie, *pp.* 392–398

60 Margerita, *pp.* 392–398

60 Margery, *pp.* 392–398

60 Marget, *pp.* 392–398

60 Margethe, *pp.* 392–398

60 Margetta, *pp.* 392–398

60 Margette, *pp.* 392–398

60 Margharita, *pp.* 392–398

60 Margo, *pp.* 392–398

60 Margorie, *pp.* 392–398

60 Margory, *pp.* 392–398

60 Margot, *pp.* 392–398

60 Marguerita, *pp.* 392–398

60 Marguerite, *pp.* 392–398

60 Margueritta, *pp.* 392–398

62 Mari, *pp.* 406–413

62 Maria, *pp.* 406–413

62 Mariam, *pp.* 406–413

62 Marian, *pp.* 406–413

62 Mariana, *pp.* 406–413

62 Marianna, *pp.* 406–413

62 Marianne, *pp.* 406–413

62 Maribelle, *pp.* 406–413

62 Marie, *pp.* 406–413

62 Marielle, *pp.* 406–413

62 Mariette, *pp.* 406–413

62 Marigold, *pp.* 406–413

71 Marilda, *pp.* 462–467

62 Marilla, *pp.* 406–413

62 Marilyn, *pp.* 406–413

62 Marina, *pp.* 406–413

62 Marinette, *pp.* 406–413

62 Mariom, *pp.* 406–413

62 Marion, *pp.* 406–413

60 Marjery, *pp.* 392–398

36 Marjolaine, *pp.* 246–251

60 Marjorie, *pp.* 392–398

62 Marla, *pp.* 406–413

62 Marleen, *pp.* 406–413

62 Marlena, *pp.* 406–413

62 Marlene, *pp.* 406–413

62 Marline, *pp.* 406–413

71 Marquita, *pp.* 462–467

71 Marsha, *pp.* 462–467

31 Marta, *pp.* 214–220

61 Marta, *pp.* 400–404

61 Martella, *pp.* 400–404

61 Martha, *pp.* 400–404

61 Marthe, *pp.* 400–404

61 Martie, *pp.* 400–404

31 Martina, *pp.* 214–220

31 Martine, *pp.* 214–220

61 Martita, *pp.* 400–404

61 Marty, *pp.* 400–404

58 Marva, *pp.* 380–385

58 Marvel, *pp.* 380–385

58 Marvela, *pp.* 380–385

58 Marvella, *pp.* 380–385

58 Marvelle, *pp.* 380–385

62 Mary, *pp.* 406–413

62 Marya, *pp.* 406–413
62 Maryann, *pp.* 406–413
62 Maryanne, *pp.* 406–413
62 Marygold, *pp.* 406–413
62 Marylin, *pp.* 406–413
62 Maryline, *pp.* 406–413
62 Marylise, *pp.* 406–413
62 Marylou, *pp.* 406–413
62 Marylyn, *pp.* 406–413
62 Maryruth, *pp.* 406–413
62 Maryse, *pp.* 406–413
62 Maryvonne, *pp.* 406–413
51 Matelda, *pp.* 336–342
51 Mathea, *pp.* 336–342
51 Mathia, *pp.* 336–342
51 Mathilda, *pp.* 336–342
51 Mathilde, *pp.* 336–342
45 Mathurine, *pp.* 300–305
51 Matilda, *pp.* 336–342
51 Matilde, *pp.* 336–342
51 Mattea, *pp.* 336–342
51 Matthea, *pp.* 336–342
51 Matthia, *pp.* 336–342
51 Mattie, *pp.* 336–342
61 Matty, *pp.* 400–404
51 Maud, *pp.* 336–342
51 Maude, *pp.* 336–342
41 Maura, *pp.* 276–281
41 Maureen, *pp.* 276–281
62 Maureen, *pp.* 406–413
58 Mauricette, *pp.* 380–385
41 Maurine, *pp.* 276–281
78 Mauve, *pp.* 504–509
49 Mave, *pp.* 324–329
49 Mavis, *pp.* 324–329

5 Maxene, *pp.* 56–60
5 Maxie, *pp.* 56–60
5 Maxima, *pp.* 56–60
5 Maxine, *pp.* 56–60
62 May, *pp.* 406–413
49 Maybelle, *pp.* 324–329
60 Mayda, *pp.* 392–398
60 Mayde, *pp.* 392–398
60 Maydena, *pp.* 392–398
31 Meara, *pp.* 214–220
62 Mearr, *pp.* 406–413
49 Meave, *pp.* 324–329
56 Meda, *pp.* 368–373
34 Medea, *pp.* 234–239
34 Media, *pp.* 234–239
34 Medora, *pp.* 234–239
60 Meg, *pp.* 392–398
5 Megan, *pp.* 56–60
5 Meghan, *pp.* 56–60
51 Mehetabel, *pp.* 336–342
51 Mehetabelle, *pp.* 336–342
51 Mehetabie, *pp.* 336–342
51 Mehitabel, *pp.* 336–342
51 Mehitabelle, *pp.* 336–342
51 Mehitable, *pp.* 336–342
7 Mel, *pp.* 68–73
14 Mel, *pp.* 112–117
14 Melan, *pp.* 112–117
14 Melane, *pp.* 112–117
14 Melania, *pp.* 112–117
14 Melanie, *pp.* 112–117
38 Melantha, *pp.* 258–263
38 Melanthe, *pp.* 258–263
14 Melany, *pp.* 112–117
78 Melba, *pp.* 504–509

GIRLS' NAMES

41 Micaela, *pp.* 276–281

41 Michaela, *pp.* 276–281

41 Michaelina, *pp.* 276–281

41 Michaeline, *pp.* 276–281

41 Michaella, *pp.* 276–281

41 Michel, *pp.* 276–281

41 Michele, *pp.* 276–281

41 Micheline, *pp.* 276–281

41 Michella, *pp.* 276–281

41 Michelle, *pp.* 276–281

41 Michelline, *pp.* 276–281

71 Mignon, *pp.* 462–467

71 Mignonette, *pp.* 462–467

41 Mikaela, *pp.* 276–281

79 Mildred, *pp.* 510–515

79 Mildrid, *pp.* 510–515

45 Milene, *pp.* 300–305

14 Milia, *pp.* 112–117

14 Milicent, *pp.* 112–117

14 Milisent, *pp.* 112–117

14 Milissent, *pp.* 112–117

7 Mill, *pp.* 68–73

14 Milli, *pp.* 112–117

79 Milli, *pp.* 510–515

14 Millicent, *pp.* 112–117

7 Millie, *pp.* 68–73

14 Millie, *pp.* 112–117

31 Millie, *pp.* 214–220

79 Millie, *pp.* 510–515

14 Milly, *pp.* 112–117

31 Milly, *pp.* 214–220

79 Milly, *pp.* 510–515

62 Mimi, *pp.* 406–413

46 Mina, *pp.* 306–311

58 Mina, *pp.* 380–385

62 Mina, *pp.* 406–413

62 Minda, *pp.* 406–413

62 Mindy, *pp.* 406–413

62 Minerva, *pp.* 406–413

56 Minetta, *pp.* 368–373

62 Minetta, *pp.* 406–413

56 Minette, *pp.* 368–373

62 Minna, *pp.* 406–413

62 Minnie, *pp.* 406–413

62 Minny, *pp.* 406–413

62 Minta, *pp.* 406–413

62 Mintha, *pp.* 406–413

62 Minthe, *pp.* 406–413

62 Mira, *pp.* 406–413

62 Mirabel, *pp.* 406–413

62 Mirabella, *pp.* 406–413

62 Mirabelle, *pp.* 406–413

62 Miranda, *pp.* 406–413

38 Mireille, *pp.* 258–263

62 Mirella, *pp.* 406–413

62 Miriam, *pp.* 406–413

62 Mirilla, *pp.* 406–413

79 Mirle, *pp.* 510–515

60 Mirna, *pp.* 392–398

56 Missy, *pp.* 368–373

49 Mitra, *pp.* 324–329

62 Mitzi, *pp.* 406–413

34 Modesta, *pp.* 234–239

34 Modeste, *pp.* 234–239

34 Modestia, *pp.* 234–239

34 Modestine, *pp.* 234–239

34 Modesty, *pp.* 234–239

60 Moina, *pp.* 392–398

62 Moira, *pp.* 406–413

62 Moire, *pp.* 406–413

GIRLS' NAMES

GIRLS' NAMES

61	Nathane, pp. 400–404	46	Netta, pp. 306–311

61 Nathane, pp. 400–404
61 Nathania, pp. 400–404
61 Nathene, pp. 400–404
79 Natica, pp. 510–515
79 Natika, pp. 510–515
79 Natividad, pp. 510–515
79 Nattie, pp. 510–515
7 Neala, pp. 68–73
7 Neale, pp. 68–73
51 Nebula, pp. 336–342
34 Neda, pp. 234–239
34 Nedda, pp. 234–239
45 Nela, pp. 300–305
51 Nela, pp. 336–342
34 Nelda, pp. 234–239
51 Nelie, pp. 336–342
45 Nell, pp. 300–305
45 Nella, pp. 300–305
51 Nelli, pp. 336–342
45 Nellie, pp. 300–305
45 Nellwyn, pp. 300–305
45 Nelly, pp. 300–305
28 Neola, pp. 196–201
28 Neoma, pp. 196–201
61 Nerice, pp. 400–404
61 Nerima, pp. 400–404
61 Nerine, pp. 400–404
61 Nerissa, pp. 400–404
61 Nerita, pp. 400–404
1 Nessa, pp. 32–36
1 Nessie, pp. 32–36
1 Nessy, pp. 32–36
1 Nesta, pp. 32–36
79 Netie, pp. 510–515
9 Netta, pp. 80–84

46 Netta, pp. 306–311
79 Netta, pp. 510–515
9 Nettie, pp. 80–84
79 Nettie, pp. 510–515
9 Netty, pp. 80–84
79 Netty, pp. 510–515
27 Neva, pp. 190–195
27 Nevada, pp. 190–195
1 Neysa, pp. 32–36
41 Nichola, pp. 276–281
41 Nicholina, pp. 276–281
41 Nicky, pp. 276–281
41 Nicol, pp. 276–281
41 Nicola, pp. 276–281
41 Nicole, pp. 276–281
41 Nicoletta, pp. 276–281
41 Nicolette, pp. 276–281
41 Nicolina, pp. 276–281
41 Nicoline, pp. 276–281
41 Nike, pp. 276–281
41 Nikki, pp. 276–281
41 Nikky, pp. 276–281
41 Nikola, pp. 276–281
45 Nila, pp. 300–305
60 Nilda, pp. 392–398
60 Nillie, pp. 392–398
46 Nima, pp. 306–311
7 Nina, pp. 68–73
46 Nina, pp. 306–311
46 Nineta, pp. 306–311
46 Ninetta, pp. 306–311
7 Ninette, pp. 68–73
46 Ninette, pp. 306–311
7 Ninon, pp. 68–73
46 Ninon, pp. 306–311

GIRLS' NAMES

56 Odilia, *pp.* 368–373

56 Odilla, *pp.* 368–373

17 Ofelia, *pp.* 130–134

17 Ofilia, *pp.* 130–134

19 Ola, *pp.* 142–146

41 Olga, *pp.* 276–281

21 Olimpie, *pp.* 154–158

28 Olinda, *pp.* 196–201

31 Olive, *pp.* 214–220

31 Olivette, *pp.* 214–220

31 Olivia, *pp.* 214–220

31 Ollie, *pp.* 214–220

31 Olva, *pp.* 214–220

41 Olva, *pp.* 276–281

21 Olympe, *pp.* 154–158

21 Olympia, *pp.* 154–158

21 Olympie, *pp.* 154–158

75 Oma, *pp.* 486–490

79 Ombeline, *pp.* 510–515

75 Ona, *pp.* 486–490

75 Onawa, *pp.* 486–490

60 Ondine, *pp.* 392–398

60 Ondyne, *pp.* 392–398

41 Oola, *pp.* 276–281

75 Oona, *pp.* 486–490

75 Oonagh, *pp.* 486–490

14 Opal, *pp.* 112–117

14 Opalina, *pp.* 112–117

14 Opaline, *pp.* 112–117

17 Ophelia, *pp.* 130–134

17 Ophelie, *pp.* 130–134

46 Oprah, *pp.* 306–311

14 Ora, *pp.* 112–117

61 Ora, *pp.* 400–404

14 Orabel, *pp.* 112–117

14 Orabella, *pp.* 112–117

14 Orabelle, *pp.* 112–117

14 Oralia, *pp.* 112–117

14 Oralie, *pp.* 112–117

46 Ordelia, *pp.* 306–311

46 Ordella, *pp.* 306–311

78 Orea, *pp.* 504–509

58 Orel, *pp.* 380–385

58 Orela, *pp.* 380–385

9 Orenda, *pp.* 80–84

14 Oriana, *pp.* 112–117

14 Orianna, *pp.* 112–117

14 Orianne, *pp.* 112–117

14 Oriel, *pp.* 112–117

60 Orlanda, *pp.* 392–398

60 Orlande, *pp.* 392–398

60 Orlena, *pp.* 392–398

17 Orna, *pp.* 130–134

14 Orpah, *pp.* 112–117

61 Orsa, *pp.* 400–404

61 Orsola, *pp.* 400–404

7 Orva, *pp.* 68–73

56 Otha, *pp.* 368–373

56 Othilla, *pp.* 368–373

36 Ottavia, *pp.* 246–251

36 Ottavie, *pp.* 246–251

56 Ottilie, *pp.* 368–373

5 Ozora, *pp.* 56–60

49 Page, *pp.* 324–329

49 Paige, *pp.* 324–329

31 Pallas, *pp.* 214–220

14 Palma, *pp.* 112–117

14 Paloma, *pp.* 112–117

14 Palometa, *pp.* 112–117

14 Palomita, *pp.* 112–117

GIRLS' NAMES

GIRLS' NAMES

GIRLS' NAMES

GIRLS' NAMES

16 Reine, pp. 124–129

51 Reini, pp. 336–342

16 Rejane, pp. 124–129

51 Remata, pp. 336–342

51 Rena, pp. 336–342

51 Renata, pp. 336–342

61 Renata, pp. 400–404

61 Renate, pp. 400–404

61 Rence, pp. 400–404

51 Rene, pp. 336–342

61 Rene, pp. 400–404

61 Renee, pp. 400–404

61 Renita, pp. 400–404

51 Rennie, pp. 336–342

61 Rennie, pp. 400–404

51 Renny, pp. 336–342

25 Reseda, pp. 178–182

31 Reva, pp. 214–220

71 Rexana, pp. 462–467

71 Rexanna, pp. 462–467

61 Rhea, pp. 400–404

38 Rheta, pp. 258–263

78 Rhoda, pp. 504–509

78 Rhodantha, pp. 504–509

78 Rhode, pp. 504–509

78 Rhodes, pp. 504–509

78 Rhodia, pp. 504–509

19 Rhonda, pp. 142–146

79 Ria, pp. 510–515

5 Riba, pp. 56–60

19 Rica, pp. 142–146

34 Rica, pp. 234–239

34 Ricadonna, pp. 234–239

23 Ricarda, pp. 166–170

23 Richarda, pp. 166–170

23 Richarde, pp. 166–170

34 Rickie, pp. 234–239

23 Ricky, pp. 166–170

46 Rilla, pp. 306–311

46 Rille, pp. 306–311

46 Rillete, pp. 306–311

16 Rina, pp. 124–129

21 Rindi, pp. 154–158

21 Rindy, pp. 154–158

16 Rioghnach, pp. 124–129

60 Risa, pp. 392–398

60 Rita, pp. 392–398

1 Riva, pp. 32–36

5 Riva, pp. 56–60

60 Ro, pp. 392–398

56 Roanna, pp. 368–373

38 Roberta, pp. 258–263

38 Roberte, pp. 258–263

38 Robertha, pp. 258–263

38 Roberthe, pp. 258–263

38 Robertine, pp. 258–263

38 Robina, pp. 258–263

38 Robinette, pp. 258–263

38 Robinia, pp. 258–263

71 Rochalla, pp. 462–467

71 Rochalle, pp. 462–467

71 Rochella, pp. 462–467

71 Rochelle, pp. 462–467

71 Rochette, pp. 462–467

34 Roddie, pp. 234–239

34 Roddy, pp. 234–239

34 Roderica, pp. 234–239

34 Rodericka, pp. 234–239

56 Rohana, pp. 368–373

56 Rohane, pp. 368–373

GIRLS' NAMES

56 Rohanna, *pp.* 368–373

56 Rohanne, *pp.* 368–373

78 Rohesia, *pp.* 504–509

60 Rola, *pp.* 392–398

60 Roland, *pp.* 392–398

60 Rolande, *pp.* 392–398

41 Roma, *pp.* 276–281

31 Romella, *pp.* 214–220

31 Romelle, *pp.* 214–220

78 Romhilda, *pp.* 504–509

78 Romhilde, *pp.* 504–509

78 Romilda, *pp.* 504–509

78 Romilde, *pp.* 504–509

31 Romola, *pp.* 214–220

61 Ronalda, *pp.* 400–404

61 Ronalde, *pp.* 400–404

19 Ronda, *pp.* 142–146

61 Ronnie, *pp.* 400–404

62 Ronnie, *pp.* 406–413

61 Ronny, *pp.* 400–404

62 Ronny, *pp.* 406–413

78 Ros, *pp.* 504–509

78 Rosa, *pp.* 504–509

78 Rosabel, *pp.* 504–509

78 Rosabella, *pp.* 504–509

78 Rosabelle, *pp.* 504–509

78 Rosalee, *pp.* 504–509

78 Rosaleen, *pp.* 504–509

78 Rosalyn, *pp.* 504–509

78 Rosalynd, *pp.* 504–509

78 Rosamond, *pp.* 504–509

78 Rosamonda, *pp.* 504–509

78 Rosamund, *pp.* 504–509

78 Rosamunda, *pp.* 504–509

78 Rosanna, *pp.* 504–509

78 Rosanne, *pp.* 504–509

78 Rose, *pp.* 504–509

78 Rosel, *pp.* 504–509

78 Roseline, *pp.* 504–509

78 Rosella, *pp.* 504–509

78 Roselle, *pp.* 504–509

78 Rosellen, *pp.* 504–509

78 Roselyn, *pp.* 504–509

78 Rosemarie, *pp.* 504–509

78 Rosemary, *pp.* 504–509

78 Rosemond, *pp.* 504–509

78 Rosemonde, *pp.* 504–509

78 Rosemund, *pp.* 504–509

78 Rosena, *pp.* 504–509

78 Rosene, *pp.* 504–509

78 Rosetta, *pp.* 504–509

78 Rosette, *pp.* 504–509

78 Rosia, *pp.* 504–509

78 Rosie, *pp.* 504–509

78 Rosina, *pp.* 504–509

78 Rosine, *pp.* 504–509

78 Rosita, *pp.* 504–509

78 Roslyn, *pp.* 504–509

78 Rosmunda, *pp.* 504–509

78 Rosy, *pp.* 504–509

56 Roux, *pp.* 368–373

60 Rowena, *pp.* 392–398

60 Rowenna, *pp.* 392–398

7 Rox, *pp.* 68–73

7 Roxana, *pp.* 68–73

7 Roxane, *pp.* 68–73

7 Roxanna, *pp.* 68–73

7 Roxanne, *pp.* 68–73

7 Roxie, *pp.* 68–73

7 Roxina, *pp.* 68–73

GIRLS' NAMES

GIRLS' NAMES

51 Shena, *pp.* 336–342

46 Sheree, *pp.* 306–311

17 Sheri, *pp.* 130–134

78 Sheridan, *pp.* 504–509

46 Sherri, *pp.* 306–311

46 Sherrie, *pp.* 306–311

17 Sherry, *pp.* 130–134

46 Sherry, *pp.* 306–311

17 Sheryl, *pp.* 130–134

46 Sheryl, *pp.* 306–311

17 Shir, *pp.* 130–134

17 Shirl, *pp.* 130–134

17 Shirlee, *pp.* 130–134

17 Shirleen, *pp.* 130–134

17 Shirlene, *pp.* 130–134

17 Shirley, *pp.* 130–134

17 Shirlie, *pp.* 130–134

46 Sib, *pp.* 306–311

46 Sibbie, *pp.* 306–311

46 Sibby, *pp.* 306–311

46 Sibel, *pp.* 306–311

46 Sibell, *pp.* 306–311

46 Sibella, *pp.* 306–311

46 Sibie, *pp.* 306–311

46 Sibilla, *pp.* 306–311

46 Sibille, *pp.* 306–311

46 Sibyl, *pp.* 306–311

46 Sibylle, *pp.* 306–311

75 Sid, *pp.* 486–490

75 Sidney, *pp.* 486–490

75 Sidonia, *pp.* 486–490

75 Sidonie, *pp.* 486–490

5 Sidra, *pp.* 56–60

5 Sidria, *pp.* 56–60

60 Siegfride, *pp.* 392–398

60 Sigfreda, *pp.* 392–398

60 Sigfrieda, *pp.* 392–398

1 Signa, *pp.* 32–36

34 Sigrath, *pp.* 234–239

34 Sigrid, *pp.* 234–239

34 Sigrud, *pp.* 234–239

34 Sigurd, *pp.* 234–239

1 Sil, *pp.* 32–36

46 Sile, *pp.* 306–311

17 Sileas, *pp.* 130–134

46 Sileas, *pp.* 306–311

1 Silva, *pp.* 32–36

1 Silvana, *pp.* 32–36

1 Silvia, *pp.* 32–36

1 Silvie, *pp.* 32–36

16 Simona, *pp.* 124–129

16 Simone, *pp.* 124–129

16 Simonetta, *pp.* 124–129

16 Simonette, *pp.* 124–129

51 Sine, *pp.* 336–342

51 Sinead, *pp.* 336–342

61 Siobahn, *pp.* 400–404

9 Sireen, *pp.* 80–84

9 Sirena, *pp.* 80–84

9 Sirene, *pp.* 80–84

17 Sis, *pp.* 130–134

17 Sisile, *pp.* 130–134

17 Sisle, *pp.* 130–134

17 Sisley, *pp.* 130–134

17 Sissie, *pp.* 130–134

17 Sissy, *pp.* 130–134

51 Sita, *pp.* 336–342

61 Siuban, *pp.* 400–404

19 Sofi, *pp.* 142–146

19 Sofia, *pp.* 142–146

GIRLS' NAMES

GIRLS' NAMES

75 Thea, *pp.* 486–490

16 Theadora, *pp.* 124–129

16 Theadosia, *pp.* 124–129

60 Theafania, *pp.* 392–398

75 Theana, *pp.* 486–490

75 Theano, *pp.* 486–490

60 Theaphania, *pp.* 392–398

75 Thecla, *pp.* 486–490

75 Thecle, *pp.* 486–490

16 Theda, *pp.* 124–129

38 Thee, *pp.* 258–263

75 Thekla, *pp.* 486–490

58 Thelma, *pp.* 380–385

16 Theo, *pp.* 124–129

38 Theo, *pp.* 258–263

16 Theodora, *pp.* 124–129

16 Theodore, *pp.* 124–129

16 Theodosia, *pp.* 124–129

60 Theofanie, *pp.* 392–398

60 Theofila, *pp.* 392–398

60 Theofilia, *pp.* 392–398

38 Theola, *pp.* 258–263

51 Theona, *pp.* 336–342

51 Theone, *pp.* 336–342

60 Theophania, *pp.* 392–398

60 Theophanie, *pp.* 392–398

60 Theophila, *pp.* 392–398

60 Theophilia, *pp.* 392–398

75 Theora, *pp.* 486–490

75 Thera, *pp.* 486–490

71 Theresa, *pp.* 462–467

71 Therese, *pp.* 462–467

62 Thetis, *pp.* 406–413

62 Thetys, *pp.* 406–413

75 Thia, *pp.* 486–490

56 Thirza, *pp.* 368–373

62 Thomasa, *pp.* 406–413

62 Thomase, *pp.* 406–413

62 Thomasina, *pp.* 406–413

62 Thomasine, *pp.* 406–413

31 Thora, *pp.* 214–220

31 Thorberta, *pp.* 214–220

31 Thorberte, *pp.* 214–220

31 Thorbertha, *pp.* 214–220

49 Thordia, *pp.* 324–329

49 Thordie, *pp.* 324–329

49 Thordis, *pp.* 324–329

58 Thyra, *pp.* 380–385

56 Thyrza, *pp.* 368–373

79 Tia, *pp.* 510–515

31 Tibelda, *pp.* 214–220

56 Tiberia, *pp.* 368–373

25 Tiffanie, *pp.* 178–182

25 Tiffany, *pp.* 178–182

25 Tiffy, *pp.* 178–182

25 Tiphanie, *pp.* 178–182

25 Tiphany, *pp.* 178–182

51 Tilda, *pp.* 336–342

31 Tilly, *pp.* 214–220

21 Tim, *pp.* 154–158

21 Timmie, *pp.* 154–158

21 Timmy, *pp.* 154–158

21 Timothea, *pp.* 154–158

19 Tina, *pp.* 142–146

21 Tina, *pp.* 154–158

31 Tina, *pp.* 214–220

25 Tiphaine, *pp.* 178–182

56 Tirza, *pp.* 368–373

25 Tish, *pp.* 178–182

25 Tita, *pp.* 178–182

GIRLS' NAMES

GIRLS' NAMES

GIRLS' NAMES

GIRLS' NAMES

38 Vivienna, *pp.* 258–263
38 Vivyan, *pp.* 258–263
23 Volanda, *pp.* 166–170
49 Volante, *pp.* 324–329
51 Voleta, *pp.* 336–342
51 Voletta, *pp.* 336–342
79 Von, *pp.* 510–515
62 Vonnie, *pp.* 406–413
79 Vonnie, *pp.* 510–515
62 Vonny, *pp.* 406–413
38 Vyvyan, *pp.* 258–263
51 Walborga, *pp.* 336–342
51 Walburga, *pp.* 336–342
27 Walda, *pp.* 190–195
60 Waleska, *pp.* 392–398
25 Wallace, *pp.* 178–182
25 Wallie, *pp.* 178–182
25 Wallis, *pp.* 178–182
25 Wally, *pp.* 178–182
16 Wanda, *pp.* 124–129
16 Wandie, *pp.* 124–129
16 Wandis, *pp.* 124–129
71 Wanetta, *pp.* 462–467
71 Wanette, *pp.* 462–467
38 Warda, *pp.* 258–263
27 Welda, *pp.* 190–195
62 Welma, *pp.* 406–413
16 Wenda, *pp.* 124–129
16 Wendeline, *pp.* 124–129
7 Wendy, *pp.* 68–73
16 Wendy, *pp.* 124–129
51 Wenona, *pp.* 336–342
51 Wenonah, *pp.* 336–342
41 Wilf, *pp.* 276–281
41 Wilfreda, *pp.* 276–281

41 Wilfreida, *pp.* 276–281
41 Wilfrieda, *pp.* 276–281
62 Wilhelmina, *pp.* 406–413
38 Willa, *pp.* 258–263
62 Willa, *pp.* 406–413
62 Willabelle, *pp.* 406–413
62 Willie, *pp.* 406–413
62 Willy, *pp.* 406–413
62 Wilma, *pp.* 406–413
46 Win, *pp.* 306–311
49 Win, *pp.* 324–329
49 Wina, *pp.* 324–329
34 Winema, *pp.* 234–239
46 Winifred, *pp.* 306–311
46 Winifreida, *pp.* 306–311
46 Winifrid, *pp.* 306–311
46 Winifrida, *pp.* 306–311
46 Winifrieda, *pp.* 306–311
49 Winne, *pp.* 324–329
46 Winnie, *pp.* 306–311
49 Winnie, *pp.* 324–329
46 Winny, *pp.* 306–311
49 Winny, *pp.* 324–329
34 Winola, *pp.* 234–239
51 Winona, *pp.* 336–342
51 Winonah, *pp.* 336–342
46 Wyne, *pp.* 306–311
46 Wynne, *pp.* 306–311
7 Xanthe, *pp.* 68–73
7 Xaviera, *pp.* 68–73
7 Xaviere, *pp.* 68–73
38 Xena, *pp.* 258–263
38 Xene, *pp.* 258–263
38 Xenia, *pp.* 258–263
75 Xylia, *pp.* 486–490

GIRLS' NAMES

GIRLS' NAMES

INDEX OF BOYS' NAMES

BOYS' NAMES

BOYS' NAMES

72 Allyn, pp. 468–472

30 Almo, pp. 208–213

55 Alois, pp. 362–367

4 Alonso, pp. 50–54

4 Alonzo, pp. 50–54

55 Aloys, pp. 362–367

55 Aloysius, pp. 362–367

4 Alphonse, pp. 50–54

4 Alphonsin, pp. 50–54

4 Alphonso, pp. 50–54

4 Alphonsus, pp. 50–54

29 Alpin, pp. 202–207

11 Alric, pp. 92–96

66 Alric, pp. 432–437

73 Alroy, pp. 474–479

35 Alsandair, pp. 240–245

30 Alston, pp. 208–213

20 Altman, pp. 148–152

33 Alton, pp. 228–233

72 Alun, pp. 468–472

2 Alva, pp. 38–42

2 Alvah, pp. 38–42

12 Alvan, pp. 98–103

2 Alvar, pp. 38–42

12 Alvin, pp. 98–103

12 Alwin, pp. 98–103

12 Alwyn, pp. 98–103

12 Amable, pp. 98–103

8 Amadee, pp. 74–78

37 Amand, pp. 252–257

47 Amasa, pp. 312–317

63 Amaury, pp. 414–419

55 Ambert, pp. 362–367

32 Ambroise, pp. 222–227

32 Ambros, pp. 222–227

32 Ambrose, pp. 222–227

32 Ambrosius, pp. 222–227

70 Ame, pp. 456–461

70 Amerigo, pp. 456–461

63 Amery, pp. 414–419

3 Amhlaoibt, pp. 44–48

35 Ammon, pp. 240–245

63 Amory, pp. 414–419

18 Amos, pp. 136–141

53 Anael, pp. 350–355

76 Anastase, pp. 492–497

76 Anastasius, pp. 492–497

76 Anatholia, pp. 492–497

10 Anatol, pp. 86–90

10 Anatole, pp. 86–90

4 Andeol, pp. 50–54

6 Anders, pp. 62–66

6 Andie, pp. 62–66

6 Andir, pp. 62–66

37 Andoche, pp. 252–257

6 Andre, pp. 62–66

6 Andreas, pp. 62–66

6 Andrew, pp. 62–66

6 Andrien, pp. 62–66

6 Andy, pp. 62–66

72 Aneurin, pp. 468–472

32 Ange, pp. 222–227

32 Angelo, pp. 222–227

73 Angus, pp. 474–479

20 Annan, pp. 148–152

43 Annibal, pp. 288–293

8 Anntoin, pp. 74–78

47 Anscom, pp. 312–317

47 Anscomb, pp. 312–317

4 Anse, pp. 50–54

BOYS' NAMES

4 Ansel, *pp.* 50–54

4 Ansell, *pp.* 50–54

4 Anselm, *pp.* 50–54

4 Anselme, *pp.* 50–54

4 Anshelm, *pp.* 50–54

20 Ansley, *pp.* 148–152

69 Anson, *pp.* 450–454

8 Anstice, *pp.* 74–78

8 Anstiss, *pp.* 74–78

76 Anthelme, *pp.* 492–497

8 Anthony, *pp.* 74–78

8 Antoine, *pp.* 74–78

8 Anton, *pp.* 74–78

8 Antonin, *pp.* 74–78

8 Antonio, *pp.* 74–78

8 Antony, *pp.* 74–78

26 Anwell, *pp.* 184–188

26 Anwyl, *pp.* 184–188

26 Anwyll, *pp.* 184–188

76 Anyon, *pp.* 492–497

68 Aodh, *pp.* 444–448

68 Aoidh, *pp.* 444–448

20 Apollos, *pp.* 148–152

24 Arcadius, *pp.* 172–176

24 Arcady, *pp.* 172–176

10 Arch, *pp.* 86–90

40 Archambaud, *pp.* 270–274

10 Archard, *pp.* 86–90

10 Archer, *pp.* 86–90

10 Archerd, *pp.* 86–90

10 Archibald, *pp.* 86–90

10 Archie, *pp.* 86–90

10 Archimbald, *pp.* 86–90

10 Archy, *pp.* 86–90

26 Arden, *pp.* 184–188

26 Ardin, *pp.* 184–188

67 Ardley, *pp.* 438–443

18 Ardolf, *pp.* 136–141

18 Ardolph, *pp.* 136–141

67 Argus, *pp.* 438–443

50 Argyle, *pp.* 330–335

47 Ari, *pp.* 312–317

64 Aric, *pp.* 420–425

40 Ariel, *pp.* 270–274

20 Aries, *pp.* 148–152

8 Aristide, *pp.* 74–78

8 Aristodemus, *pp.* 74–78

8 Aristotle, *pp.* 74–78

8 Arlay, *pp.* 74–78

66 Arledge, *pp.* 432–437

8 Arlen, *pp.* 74–78

8 Arley, *pp.* 74–78

8 Arlie, *pp.* 74–78

8 Arly, *pp.* 74–78

15 Armand, *pp.* 118–122

37 Armel, *pp.* 252–257

15 Armin, *pp.* 118–122

15 Armond, *pp.* 118–122

18 Armstrong, *pp.* 136–141

15 Armyn, *pp.* 118–122

47 Arnald, *pp.* 312–317

29 Arnall, *pp.* 202–207

30 Arnatt, *pp.* 208–213

47 Arnaud, *pp.* 312–317

47 Arne, *pp.* 312–317

67 Arne, *pp.* 438–443

30 Arnett, *pp.* 208–213

67 Arney, *pp.* 438–443

47 Arnie, *pp.* 312–317

67 Arnie, *pp.* 438–443

BOYS' NAMES

47 Arno, *pp.* 312–317

47 Arnold, *pp.* 312–317

30 Arnot, *pp.* 208–213

30 Arnott, *pp.* 208–213

47 Arnould, *pp.* 312–317

65 Aron, *pp.* 426–431

32 Arpad, *pp.* 222–227

42 Arsene, *pp.* 282–287

13 Art, *pp.* 104–110

13 Artair, *pp.* 104–110

68 Artemas, *pp.* 444–448

68 Artemis, *pp.* 444–448

13 Arthur, *pp.* 104–110

13 Artie, *pp.* 104–110

13 Artur, *pp.* 104–110

13 Artus, *pp.* 104–110

43 Arundel, *pp.* 288–293

32 Arvad, *pp.* 222–227

74 Arval, *pp.* 480–484

74 Arvel, *pp.* 480–484

33 Arvin, *pp.* 228–233

67 Asa, *pp.* 438–443

22 Ascot, *pp.* 160–164

22 Ascott, *pp.* 160–164

29 Ashburn, *pp.* 202–207

44 Ashby, *pp.* 294–299

22 Asher, *pp.* 160–164

73 Ashford, *pp.* 474–479

69 Ashley, *pp.* 450–454

26 Ashlin, *pp.* 184–188

77 Ashton, *pp.* 498–503

77 Ashur, *pp.* 498–503

26 Aswin, *pp.* 184–188

26 Aswine, *pp.* 184–188

44 Athanase, *pp.* 294–299

44 Athanasius, *pp.* 294–299

26 Athelhard, *pp.* 184–188

54 Atherton, *pp.* 356–360

32 Atley, *pp.* 222–227

66 Attwood, *pp.* 432–437

22 Atwater, *pp.* 160–164

30 Atwell, *pp.* 208–213

66 Atwood, *pp.* 432–437

66 Atwoode, *pp.* 432–437

59 Atworth, *pp.* 386–391

72 Auban, *pp.* 468–472

2 Aubert, *pp.* 38–42

2 Aubin, *pp.* 38–42

72 Aubin, *pp.* 468–472

12 Aubrey, *pp.* 98–103

12 Aubry, *pp.* 98–103

66 Audric, *pp.* 432–437

12 Audwin, *pp.* 98–103

70 Augie, *pp.* 456–461

70 August, *pp.* 456–461

70 Auguste, *pp.* 456–461

70 Augustin, *pp.* 456–461

70 Augustine, *pp.* 456–461

70 Augustus, *pp.* 456–461

57 Aurele, *pp.* 374–379

13 Aurthur, *pp.* 104–110

70 Austen, *pp.* 456–461

70 Austin, *pp.* 456–461

29 Avenall, *pp.* 202–207

29 Avenel, *pp.* 202–207

29 Avenell, *pp.* 202–207

29 Averel, *pp.* 202–207

29 Averell, *pp.* 202–207

29 Averil, *pp.* 202–207

29 Averill, *pp.* 202–207

BOYS' NAMES

12 Barth, *pp.* 98–103

12 Barthelemy, *pp.* 98–103

12 Barthelmey, *pp.* 98–103

12 Barthol, *pp.* 98–103

12 Bartholome, *pp.* 98–103

12 Bartholomew, *pp.* 98–103

22 Barthram, *pp.* 160–164

12 Bartie, *pp.* 98–103

12 Bartley, *pp.* 98–103

12 Bartolome, *pp.* 98–103

20 Barton, *pp.* 148–152

22 Bartram, *pp.* 160–164

44 Baruch, *pp.* 294–299

10 Basil, *pp.* 86–90

10 Basile, *pp.* 86–90

10 Basilio, *pp.* 86–90

10 Basilius, *pp.* 86–90

40 Bastien, *pp.* 270–274

12 Bat, *pp.* 98–103

12 Baudoin, *pp.* 98–103

12 Baudouin, *pp.* 98–103

12 Baudric, *pp.* 98–103

30 Bax, *pp.* 208–213

30 Baxter, *pp.* 208–213

10 Bay, *pp.* 86–90

10 Bayard, *pp.* 86–90

20 Bayley, *pp.* 148–152

3 Beach, *pp.* 44–48

3 Beacher, *pp.* 44–48

69 Beagan, *pp.* 450–454

69 Beagen, *pp.* 450–454

35 Beal, *pp.* 240–245

35 Beale, *pp.* 240–245

35 Beall, *pp.* 240–245

4 Beaman, *pp.* 50–54

4 Beamer, *pp.* 50–54

13 Bearnard, *pp.* 104–110

11 Beathan, *pp.* 92–96

11 Beatie, *pp.* 92–96

11 Beattie, *pp.* 92–96

11 Beatty, *pp.* 92–96

11 Beaty, *pp.* 92–96

35 Beau, *pp.* 240–245

6 Beaufort, *pp.* 62–66

68 Beaumont, *pp.* 444–448

22 Beavais, *pp.* 160–164

30 Beavan, *pp.* 208–213

30 Beaven, *pp.* 208–213

39 Bec, *pp.* 264–269

39 Beck, *pp.* 264–269

3 Beech, *pp.* 44–48

3 Beecher, *pp.* 44–48

26 Belden, *pp.* 184–188

26 Beldon, *pp.* 184–188

54 Bellamy, *pp.* 356–360

11 Ben, *pp.* 92–96

15 Ben, *pp.* 118–122

15 Bendix, *pp.* 118–122

15 Benedic, *pp.* 118–122

15 Benedick, *pp.* 118–122

15 Benedict, *pp.* 118–122

15 Benedix, *pp.* 118–122

15 Bengt, *pp.* 118–122

15 Benito, *pp.* 118–122

11 Benjamin, *pp.* 92–96

11 Benjy, *pp.* 92–96

15 Bennet, *pp.* 118–122

15 Bennett, *pp.* 118–122

11 Bennie, *pp.* 92–96

11 Benny, *pp.* 92–96

BOYS' NAMES

15 Benny, *pp.* 118–122
15 Benoit, *pp.* 118–122
11 Benoni, *pp.* 92–96
15 Benot, *pp.* 118–122
11 Benson, *pp.* 92–96
70 Bentley, *pp.* 456–461
70 Bently, *pp.* 456–461
26 Benton, *pp.* 184–188
4 Berenger, *pp.* 50–54
26 Beres, *pp.* 184–188
26 Beresford, *pp.* 184–188
4 Berg, *pp.* 50–54
4 Berger, *pp.* 50–54
4 Bergess, *pp.* 50–54
4 Berk, *pp.* 50–54
13 Berk, *pp.* 104–110
13 Berke, *pp.* 104–110
10 Berkeley, *pp.* 86–90
10 Berkley, *pp.* 86–90
13 Bern, *pp.* 104–110
13 Bernard, *pp.* 104–110
13 Bernardin, *pp.* 104–110
13 Bernhard, *pp.* 104–110
13 Bernie, *pp.* 104–110
13 Berny, *pp.* 104–110
2 Bert, *pp.* 38–42
11 Bert, *pp.* 92–96
12 Bert, *pp.* 98–103
22 Bert, *pp.* 160–164
50 Bert, *pp.* 330–335
12 Berthold, *pp.* 98–103
12 Berthoud, *pp.* 98–103
2 Bertie, *pp.* 38–42
12 Bertie, *pp.* 98–103
50 Bertie, *pp.* 330–335

22 Bertin, *pp.* 160–164
12 Bertold, *pp.* 98–103
50 Berton, *pp.* 330–335
22 Bertram, *pp.* 160–164
22 Bertramd, *pp.* 160–164
22 Bertrand, *pp.* 160–164
2 Berty, *pp.* 38–42
30 Bevan, *pp.* 208–213
30 Beven, *pp.* 208–213
50 Beverley, *pp.* 330–335
50 Beverly, *pp.* 330–335
22 Bevis, *pp.* 160–164
73 Bick, *pp.* 474–479
73 Bickford, *pp.* 474–479
76 Bill, *pp.* 492–497
76 Billie, *pp.* 492–497
76 Billy, *pp.* 492–497
43 Bing, *pp.* 288–293
30 Birch, *pp.* 208–213
13 Birk, *pp.* 104–110
30 Birk, *pp.* 208–213
13 Birke, *pp.* 104–110
30 Birket, *pp.* 208–213
30 Birkett, *pp.* 208–213
30 Birkey, *pp.* 208–213
26 Birley, *pp.* 184–188
26 Birney, *pp.* 184–188
47 Birtle, *pp.* 312–317
18 Bishop, *pp.* 136–141
73 Bjorn, *pp.* 474–479
76 Black, *pp.* 492–497
35 Blade, *pp.* 240–245
22 Blagden, *pp.* 160–164
57 Blain, *pp.* 374–379
57 Blaine, *pp.* 374–379

BOYS' NAMES

39 Blair, *pp.* 264–269
15 Blaise, *pp.* 118–122
76 Blake, *pp.* 492–497
76 Blakeley, *pp.* 492–497
76 Blakey, *pp.* 492–497
72 Bland, *pp.* 468–472
72 Blandford, *pp.* 468–472
57 Blane, *pp.* 374–379
72 Blanford, *pp.* 468–472
15 Blase, *pp.* 118–122
57 Blayn, *pp.* 374–379
57 Blayne, *pp.* 374–379
15 Blayze, *pp.* 118–122
15 Blaze, *pp.* 118–122
40 Bliss, *pp.* 270–274
20 Blyth, *pp.* 148–152
20 Blythe, *pp.* 148–152
44 Bo, *pp.* 294–299
26 Boas, *pp.* 184–188
26 Boase, *pp.* 184–188
26 Boaz, *pp.* 184–188
69 Bob, *pp.* 450–454
69 Bobbie, *pp.* 450–454
69 Bobby, *pp.* 450–454
67 Boden, *pp.* 438–443
37 Bogart, *pp.* 252–257
6 Bonar, *pp.* 62–66
66 Bonaventure, *pp.* 432–437
6 Bonaz, *pp.* 62–66
39 Boniface, *pp.* 264–269
13 Bonne, *pp.* 104–110
13 Boone, *pp.* 104–110
8 Boot, *pp.* 74–78
8 Boote, *pp.* 74–78
8 Booth, *pp.* 74–78

8 Boothe, *pp.* 74–78
48 Borden, *pp.* 318–322
66 Bordolphe, *pp.* 432–437
18 Borg, *pp.* 136–141
13 Boris, *pp.* 104–110
67 Boswell, *pp.* 438–443
67 Bosworth, *pp.* 438–443
8 Both, *pp.* 74–78
42 Botolf, *pp.* 282–287
42 Botolph, *pp.* 282–287
42 Botolphe, *pp.* 282–287
66 Bourdolph, *pp.* 432–437
13 Bourke, *pp.* 104–110
11 Bourn, *pp.* 92–96
11 Bourne, *pp.* 92–96
35 Bourne, *pp.* 240–245
32 Bowen, *pp.* 222–227
42 Bowie, *pp.* 282–287
42 Boyce, *pp.* 282–287
50 Boyd, *pp.* 330–335
48 Boyne, *pp.* 318–322
54 Brad, *pp.* 356–360
64 Bradburn, *pp.* 420–425
66 Braden, *pp.* 432–437
24 Bradford, *pp.* 172–176
54 Bradley, *pp.* 356–360
54 Bradly, *pp.* 356–360
54 Brady, *pp.* 356–360
42 Brainard, *pp.* 282–287
42 Brainerd, *pp.* 282–287
76 Bram, *pp.* 492–497
35 Bramwell, *pp.* 240–245
76 Bran, *pp.* 492–497
20 Brand, *pp.* 148–152
76 Brandan, *pp.* 492–497

70 Brander, *pp.* 456–461

20 Brandon, *pp.* 148–152

40 Brant, *pp.* 270–274

29 Brawley, *pp.* 202–207

76 Brendan, *pp.* 492–497

76 Brendon, *pp.* 492–497

55 Brent, *pp.* 362–367

26 Bret, *pp.* 184–188

26 Brett, *pp.* 184–188

69 Brewster, *pp.* 450–454

54 Briac, *pp.* 356–360

54 Brian, *pp.* 356–360

54 Briant, *pp.* 356–360

65 Brice, *pp.* 426–431

39 Bridger, *pp.* 264–269

54 Brien, *pp.* 356–360

54 Brieux, *pp.* 356–360

33 Brigham, *pp.* 228–233

54 Brion, *pp.* 356–360

42 Broc, *pp.* 282–287

42 Brock, *pp.* 282–287

42 Brockie, *pp.* 282–287

42 Brockley, *pp.* 282–287

6 Broderic, *pp.* 62–66

6 Broderick, *pp.* 62–66

37 Brodie, *pp.* 252–257

6 Brodrick, *pp.* 62–66

37 Brody, *pp.* 252–257

42 Brok, *pp.* 282–287

18 Bromley, *pp.* 136–141

72 Bronson, *pp.* 468–472

43 Brook, *pp.* 288–293

43 Brooke, *pp.* 288–293

43 Brooks, *pp.* 288–293

44 Brough, *pp.* 294–299

44 Brougher, *pp.* 294–299

50 Broughton, *pp.* 330–335

72 Bruce, *pp.* 468–472

35 Bruno, *pp.* 240–245

32 Brush, *pp.* 222–227

54 Bryan, *pp.* 356–360

54 Bryant, *pp.* 356–360

65 Bryce, *pp.* 426–431

54 Bryon, *pp.* 356–360

32 Buck, *pp.* 222–227

32 Buckley, *pp.* 222–227

13 Bud, *pp.* 104–110

13 Budd, *pp.* 104–110

20 Buko, *pp.* 148–152

69 Bundy, *pp.* 450–454

35 Burbank, *pp.* 240–245

30 Burch, *pp.* 208–213

73 Burchard, *pp.* 474–479

73 Burckhard, *pp.* 474–479

54 Burdett, *pp.* 356–360

72 Burdon, *pp.* 468–472

69 Burell, *pp.* 450–454

4 Burford, *pp.* 50–54

4 Burg, *pp.* 50–54

73 Burgard, *pp.* 474–479

4 Burgess, *pp.* 50–54

13 Burk, *pp.* 104–110

4 Burke, *pp.* 50–54

13 Burkett, *pp.* 104–110

73 Burkhart, *pp.* 474–479

68 Burl, *pp.* 444–448

68 Burleigh, *pp.* 444–448

68 Burley, *pp.* 444–448

11 Burn, *pp.* 92–96

11 Burnaby, *pp.* 92–96

BOYS' NAMES

BOYS' NAMES

BOYS' NAMES

18 Collin, *pp.* 136–141

42 Collyer, *pp.* 282–287

18 Colman, *pp.* 136–141

57 Colomban, *pp.* 374–379

76 Colter, *pp.* 492–497

76 Colton, *pp.* 492–497

73 Colver, *pp.* 474–479

2 Colvert, *pp.* 38–42

42 Colyer, *pp.* 282–287

24 Con, *pp.* 172–176

63 Con, *pp.* 414–419

24 Conal, *pp.* 172–176

24 Conan, *pp.* 172–176

24 Conant, *pp.* 172–176

22 Conlan, *pp.* 160–164

22 Conlin, *pp.* 160–164

22 Conlon, *pp.* 160–164

24 Conn, *pp.* 172–176

67 Conn, *pp.* 438–443

24 Connaire, *pp.* 172–176

24 Connall, *pp.* 172–176

24 Connel, *pp.* 172–176

63 Connie, *pp.* 414–419

24 Connor, *pp.* 172–176

63 Conrad, *pp.* 414–419

54 Conroy, *pp.* 356–360

67 Constant, *pp.* 438–443

67 Constantin, *pp.* 438–443

67 Constantine, *pp.* 438–443

59 Conway, *pp.* 386–391

50 Coop, *pp.* 330–335

50 Cooper, *pp.* 330–335

42 Corbet, *pp.* 282–287

42 Corbett, *pp.* 282–287

42 Corbie, *pp.* 282–287

42 Corbin, *pp.* 282–287

42 Corby, *pp.* 282–287

18 Corcoran, *pp.* 136–141

66 Cordell, *pp.* 432–437

72 Corentin, *pp.* 468–472

32 Corey, *pp.* 222–227

18 Corguoran, *pp.* 136–141

76 Cormac, *pp.* 492–497

76 Cormack, *pp.* 492–497

76 Cormick, *pp.* 492–497

10 Cornal, *pp.* 86–90

10 Cornall, *pp.* 86–90

10 Corneille, *pp.* 86–90

10 Cornel, *pp.* 86–90

10 Cornelius, *pp.* 86–90

10 Cornell, *pp.* 86–90

10 Cornille, *pp.* 86–90

18 Corquoran, *pp.* 136–141

76 Corrie, *pp.* 492–497

63 Cort, *pp.* 414–419

68 Cort, *pp.* 444–448

68 Cortie, *pp.* 444–448

68 Corty, *pp.* 444–448

44 Corwen, *pp.* 294–299

44 Corwin, *pp.* 294–299

32 Cory, *pp.* 222–227

63 Corydon, *pp.* 414–419

44 Cosimo, *pp.* 294–299

44 Cosme, *pp.* 294–299

44 Cosmo, *pp.* 294–299

68 Court, *pp.* 444–448

68 Courtenay, *pp.* 444–448

68 Courtland, *pp.* 444–448

68 Courtney, *pp.* 444–448

32 Covell, *pp.* 222–227

BOYS' NAMES

BOYS' NAMES

BOYS' NAMES

BOYS' NAMES

BOYS' NAMES

33 Ed, *pp.* 228–233

52 Ed, *pp.* 344–349

73 Edan, *pp.* 474–479

2 Edbert, *pp.* 38–42

33 Edd, *pp.* 228–233

32 Eddie, *pp.* 222–227

33 Eddie, *pp.* 228–233

52 Eddie, *pp.* 344–349

32 Eddy, *pp.* 222–227

33 Eddy, *pp.* 228–233

52 Eddy, *pp.* 344–349

12 Edel, *pp.* 98–103

12 Edelie, *pp.* 98–103

24 Edelmar, *pp.* 172–176

64 Eden, *pp.* 420–425

52 Edgar, *pp.* 344–349

52 Edgard, *pp.* 344–349

33 Edison, *pp.* 228–233

33 Edlin, *pp.* 228–233

32 Edme, *pp.* 222–227

32 Edmond, *pp.* 222–227

32 Edmund, *pp.* 222–227

67 Edolf, *pp.* 438–443

33 Edouard, *pp.* 228–233

54 Edric, *pp.* 356–360

65 Edsel, *pp.* 426–431

33 Edson, *pp.* 228–233

33 Eduard, *pp.* 228–233

33 Edvard, *pp.* 228–233

20 Edwald, *pp.* 148–152

33 Edward, *pp.* 228–233

33 Edwin, *pp.* 228–233

73 Efrem, *pp.* 474–479

64 Egan, *pp.* 420–425

26 Egbert, *pp.* 184–188

13 Egmont, *pp.* 104–110

74 Ehren, *pp.* 480–484

76 Eidrich, *pp.* 492–497

59 Einar, *pp.* 386–391

2 Elbert, *pp.* 38–42

12 Elden, *pp.* 98–103

57 Elder, *pp.* 374–379

12 Eldin, *pp.* 98–103

77 Eldon, *pp.* 498–503

66 Eldric, *pp.* 432–437

66 Eldrich, *pp.* 432–437

53 Eldrid, *pp.* 350–355

53 Eldridge, *pp.* 350–355

53 Eldwin, *pp.* 350–355

53 Eldwyn, *pp.* 350–355

39 Eleazar, *pp.* 264–269

64 Elery, *pp.* 420–425

40 Eli, *pp.* 270–274

40 Elias, *pp.* 270–274

40 Elie, *pp.* 270–274

40 Elihu, *pp.* 270–274

40 Elijah, *pp.* 270–274

40 Elinot, *pp.* 270–274

40 Elisha, *pp.* 270–274

39 Elizer, *pp.* 264–269

50 Ellard, *pp.* 330–335

64 Ellerey, *pp.* 420–425

64 Ellery, *pp.* 420–425

40 Ellice, *pp.* 270–274

40 Elliot, *pp.* 270–274

40 Elliott, *pp.* 270–274

40 Ellis, *pp.* 270–274

40 Ellison, *pp.* 270–274

72 Ellsworth, *pp.* 468–472

35 Elme, *pp.* 240–245

BOYS' NAMES

BOYS' NAMES

BOYS' NAMES

65 Ford, *pp.* 426–431

15 Forest, *pp.* 118–122

15 Forester, *pp.* 118–122

15 Forrest, *pp.* 118–122

15 Forrester, *pp.* 118–122

15 Forrie, *pp.* 118–122

15 Forster, *pp.* 118–122

20 Fortunat, *pp.* 148–152

20 Fortune, *pp.* 148–152

15 Foss, *pp.* 118–122

15 Foster, *pp.* 118–122

54 Fourier, *pp.* 356–360

33 Fowler, *pp.* 228–233

64 Fox, *pp.* 420–425

77 Foy, *pp.* 498–503

52 Fraine, *pp.* 344–349

39 Fran, *pp.* 264–269

39 Francelin, *pp.* 264–269

39 Francesco, *pp.* 264–269

39 Franchot, *pp.* 264–269

39 Francis, *pp.* 264–269

39 Francisque, *pp.* 264–269

39 Franck, *pp.* 264–269

39 Francklin, *pp.* 264–269

39 Francklyn, *pp.* 264–269

39 Frank, *pp.* 264–269

39 Frantz, *pp.* 264–269

39 Franz, *pp.* 264–269

43 Fraser, *pp.* 288–293

43 Frasier, *pp.* 288–293

52 Frayne, *pp.* 344–349

43 Frazer, *pp.* 288–293

43 Frazier, *pp.* 288–293

52 Frean, *pp.* 344–349

40 Fred, *pp.* 270–274

66 Fred, *pp.* 432–437

40 Freddie, *pp.* 270–274

66 Freddie, *pp.* 432–437

40 Freddy, *pp.* 270–274

66 Freddy, *pp.* 432–437

66 Frederic, *pp.* 432–437

66 Frederick, *pp.* 432–437

66 Frederik, *pp.* 432–437

66 Frederique, *pp.* 432–437

66 Fredric, *pp.* 432–437

66 Fredrick, *pp.* 432–437

18 Freeman, *pp.* 136–141

52 Freen, *pp.* 344–349

39 Fremont, *pp.* 264–269

42 Frewen, *pp.* 282–287

42 Frewin, *pp.* 282–287

52 Frey, *pp.* 344–349

52 Freyne, *pp.* 344–349

4 Frick, *pp.* 50–54

67 Fridolf, *pp.* 438–443

66 Friedrich, *pp.* 432–437

66 Fritz, *pp.* 432–437

8 Fulbert, *pp.* 74–78

6 Fuller, *pp.* 62–66

67 Fulton, *pp.* 438–443

37 Fyfe, *pp.* 252–257

37 Fyffe, *pp.* 252–257

40 Gabbie, *pp.* 270–274

40 Gabby, *pp.* 270–274

40 Gabe, *pp.* 270–274

40 Gabie, *pp.* 270–274

40 Gabin, *pp.* 270–274

40 Gable, *pp.* 270–274

40 Gabriel, *pp.* 270–274

40 Gaby, *pp.* 270–274

BOYS' NAMES

BOYS' NAMES

BOYS' NAMES

77 Girvin, *pp.* 498–503

39 Gladwin, *pp.* 264–269

20 Glanvil, *pp.* 148–152

20 Glanville, *pp.* 148–152

43 Glen, *pp.* 288–293

43 Glendon, *pp.* 288–293

43 Glenn, *pp.* 288–293

43 Glyn, *pp.* 288–293

43 Glynn, *pp.* 288–293

20 Goddard, *pp.* 148–152

67 Godefroy, *pp.* 438–443

42 Godfrey, *pp.* 282–287

74 Godwin, *pp.* 480–484

74 Godwine, *pp.* 480–484

74 Godwyn, *pp.* 480–484

74 Golding, *pp.* 480–484

74 Goldwin, *pp.* 480–484

39 Gontran, *pp.* 264–269

74 Goodwin, *pp.* 480–484

3 Gordan, *pp.* 44–48

3 Gorden, *pp.* 44–48

3 Gordie, *pp.* 44–48

42 Gordie, *pp.* 282–287

3 Gordon, *pp.* 44–48

3 Gordy, *pp.* 44–48

42 Gordy, *pp.* 282–287

37 Gorman, *pp.* 252–257

73 Gouverneur, *pp.* 474–479

22 Gower, *pp.* 160–164

35 Grady, *pp.* 240–245

72 Graeme, *pp.* 468–472

72 Graham, *pp.* 468–472

50 Grandville, *pp.* 330–335

33 Granger, *pp.* 228–233

43 Grant, *pp.* 288–293

50 Grantland, *pp.* 330–335

50 Granvil, *pp.* 330–335

50 Granville, *pp.* 330–335

54 Grayson, *pp.* 356–360

13 Greagoir, *pp.* 104–110

37 Greeley, *pp.* 252–257

13 Greg, *pp.* 104–110

13 Gregg, *pp.* 104–110

13 Gregoire, *pp.* 104–110

13 Gregor, *pp.* 104–110

13 Gregory, *pp.* 104–110

13 Greiogair, *pp.* 104–110

76 Gresham, *pp.* 492–497

2 Griff, *pp.* 38–42

2 Griffin, *pp.* 38–42

2 Griffith, *pp.* 38–42

22 Griswold, *pp.* 160–164

37 Grover, *pp.* 252–257

2 Gruffyd, *pp.* 38–42

20 Guenole, *pp.* 148–152

70 Guerin, *pp.* 456–461

70 Guerric, *pp.* 456–461

44 Guido, *pp.* 294–299

76 Guillaume, *pp.* 492–497

15 Guin, *pp.* 118–122

50 Gunar, *pp.* 330–335

50 Gunnar, *pp.* 330–335

50 Gunner, *pp.* 330–335

50 Guntar, *pp.* 330–335

50 Gunter, *pp.* 330–335

50 Gunthar, *pp.* 330–335

50 Gunther, *pp.* 330–335

44 Gus, *pp.* 294–299

70 Gus, *pp.* 456–461

70 Gussy, *pp.* 456–461

44 Gustaf, *pp.* 294–299

44 Gustav, *pp.* 294–299

44 Gustave, *pp.* 294–299

44 Gustavos, *pp.* 294–299

44 Gustavus, *pp.* 294–299

44 Gustof, *pp.* 294–299

33 Guthnie, *pp.* 228–233

33 Guthrie, *pp.* 228–233

33 Guthry, *pp.* 228–233

44 Guy, *pp.* 294–299

44 Guyon, *pp.* 294–299

20 Gwenola, *pp.* 148–152

15 Gwyn, *pp.* 118–122

15 Gwynn, *pp.* 118–122

69 Haakon, *pp.* 450–454

68 Habib, *pp.* 444–448

53 Hacket, *pp.* 350–355

53 Hackett, *pp.* 350–355

10 Haddan, *pp.* 86–90

10 Hadden, *pp.* 86–90

10 Haddon, *pp.* 86–90

32 Hadley, *pp.* 222–227

68 Hadrian, *pp.* 444–448

68 Hadrien, *pp.* 444–448

59 Hadwin, *pp.* 386–391

3 Hagan, *pp.* 44–48

3 Hagen, *pp.* 44–48

3 Haggan, *pp.* 44–48

3 Haggen, *pp.* 44–48

54 Hagley, *pp.* 356–360

24 Haig, *pp.* 172–176

69 Hako, *pp.* 450–454

69 Hakon, *pp.* 450–454

39 Hal, *pp.* 264–269

47 Hal, *pp.* 312–317

2 Halbert, *pp.* 38–42

18 Haldan, *pp.* 136–141

18 Haldane, *pp.* 136–141

18 Halden, *pp.* 136–141

35 Hale, *pp.* 240–245

35 Haley, *pp.* 240–245

18 Halfdan, *pp.* 136–141

37 Halford, *pp.* 252–257

26 Hall, *pp.* 184–188

26 Hallam, *pp.* 184–188

26 Halley, *pp.* 184–188

12 Halliwell, *pp.* 98–103

29 Hallward, *pp.* 202–207

6 Halsey, *pp.* 62–66

13 Halstead, *pp.* 104–110

13 Halsted, *pp.* 104–110

6 Halsy, *pp.* 62–66

55 Halton, *pp.* 362–367

29 Halward, *pp.* 202–207

72 Hamal, *pp.* 468–472

22 Hamar, *pp.* 160–164

72 Hamelin, *pp.* 468–472

72 Hamelyn, *pp.* 468–472

50 Hamilton, *pp.* 330–335

50 Hamish, *pp.* 330–335

73 Hamlet, *pp.* 474–479

47 Hamlin, *pp.* 312–317

22 Hammar, *pp.* 160–164

15 Handley, *pp.* 118–122

30 Hanford, *pp.* 208–213

47 Hank, *pp.* 312–317

15 Hanley, *pp.* 118–122

74 Hannibal, *pp.* 480–484

70 Hanno, *pp.* 456–461

47 Hanraoi, *pp.* 312–317

BOYS' NAMES

52 Hans, *pp.* 344–349

4 Hansel, *pp.* 50–54

66 Hap, *pp.* 432–437

39 Harailt, *pp.* 264–269

39 Harald, *pp.* 264–269

11 Harbert, *pp.* 92–96

11 Harbin, *pp.* 92–96

6 Harcourt, *pp.* 62–66

8 Harden, *pp.* 74–78

67 Harden, *pp.* 438–443

64 Hardey, *pp.* 420–425

64 Hardi, *pp.* 420–425

64 Hardie, *pp.* 420–425

67 Harding, *pp.* 438–443

59 Hardwin, *pp.* 386–391

59 Hardwyn, *pp.* 386–391

64 Hardy, *pp.* 420–425

15 Hareford, *pp.* 118–122

15 Harford, *pp.* 118–122

53 Hargrave, *pp.* 350–355

53 Hargreave, *pp.* 350–355

53 Hargreaves, *pp.* 350–355

53 Hargrove, *pp.* 350–355

8 Harl, *pp.* 74–78

8 Harlan, *pp.* 74–78

8 Harland, *pp.* 74–78

8 Harleigh, *pp.* 74–78

8 Harley, *pp.* 74–78

8 Harlon, *pp.* 74–78

73 Harlow, *pp.* 474–479

8 Harly, *pp.* 74–78

43 Harman, *pp.* 288–293

43 Harmon, *pp.* 288–293

39 Harold, *pp.* 264–269

65 Haroun, *pp.* 426–431

13 Harper, *pp.* 104–110

39 Harris, *pp.* 264–269

39 Harrison, *pp.* 264–269

39 Harry, *pp.* 264–269

47 Harry, *pp.* 312–317

8 Hart, *pp.* 74–78

13 Hart, *pp.* 104–110

65 Hartford, *pp.* 426–431

8 Hartleigh, *pp.* 74–78

8 Hartley, *pp.* 74–78

76 Hartman, *pp.* 492–497

76 Hartmann, *pp.* 492–497

13 Hartwell, *pp.* 104–110

13 Hartwill, *pp.* 104–110

64 Hartwood, *pp.* 420–425

20 Harv, *pp.* 148–152

20 Harve, *pp.* 148–152

20 Harvey, *pp.* 148–152

13 Harwell, *pp.* 104–110

13 Harwill, *pp.* 104–110

59 Harwin, *pp.* 386–391

64 Harwood, *pp.* 420–425

59 Harwyn, *pp.* 386–391

33 Haslett, *pp.* 228–233

33 Haslitt, *pp.* 228–233

50 Hastings, *pp.* 330–335

18 Havelock, *pp.* 136–141

70 Haven, *pp.* 456–461

18 Havlock, *pp.* 136–141

24 Hawley, *pp.* 172–176

3 Hayden, *pp.* 44–48

3 Haydon, *pp.* 44–48

76 Hayward, *pp.* 492–497

76 Haywood, *pp.* 492–497

33 Hazlett, *pp.* 228–233

BOYS' NAMES

BOYS' NAMES

BOYS' NAMES

BOYS' NAMES

BOYS' NAMES

BOYS' NAMES

48 Kelly, *pp.* 318–322

40 Kelsey, *pp.* 270–274

73 Kelvan, *pp.* 474–479

73 Kelven, *pp.* 474–479

73 Kelvin, *pp.* 474–479

26 Kemble, *pp.* 184–188

29 Kemp, *pp.* 202–207

63 Ken, *pp.* 414–419

77 Ken, *pp.* 498–503

63 Kendal, *pp.* 414–419

63 Kendall, *pp.* 414–419

63 Kendell, *pp.* 414–419

63 Kendrick, *pp.* 414–419

76 Kenelm, *pp.* 492–497

77 Keneth, *pp.* 498–503

68 Kenley, *pp.* 444–448

77 Kenn, *pp.* 498–503

77 Kennard, *pp.* 498–503

77 Kennedy, *pp.* 498–503

77 Kennet, *pp.* 498–503

77 Kenneth, *pp.* 498–503

77 Kenny, *pp.* 498–503

65 Kenrick, *pp.* 426–431

8 Kent, *pp.* 74–78

77 Kenton, *pp.* 498–503

68 Kenward, *pp.* 444–448

68 Kenway, *pp.* 444–448

68 Kenyon, *pp.* 444–448

66 Ker, *pp.* 432–437

66 Kerby, *pp.* 432–437

77 Keren, *pp.* 498–503

18 Kermit, *pp.* 136–141

77 Kern, *pp.* 498–503

18 Kerr, *pp.* 136–141

66 Kerr, *pp.* 432–437

32 Kerrin, *pp.* 222–227

18 Kerry, *pp.* 136–141

32 Kerry, *pp.* 222–227

33 Kerwin, *pp.* 228–233

20 Kester, *pp.* 148–152

76 Kev, *pp.* 492–497

76 Kevan, *pp.* 492–497

76 Keven, *pp.* 492–497

76 Kevin, *pp.* 492–497

18 Key, *pp.* 136–141

32 Kieran, *pp.* 222–227

32 Kieren, *pp.* 222–227

32 Kieron, *pp.* 222–227

77 Killian, *pp.* 498–503

26 Kim, *pp.* 184–188

26 Kimball, *pp.* 184–188

26 Kimbell, *pp.* 184–188

26 Kimble, *pp.* 184–188

8 Kime, *pp.* 74–78

12 King, *pp.* 98–103

12 Kingsley, *pp.* 98–103

12 Kingston, *pp.* 98–103

12 Kingswell, *pp.* 98–103

22 Kinnaird, *pp.* 160–164

22 Kinnard, *pp.* 160–164

35 Kinnell, *pp.* 240–245

12 Kinsey, *pp.* 98–103

13 Kipp, *pp.* 104–110

66 Kirby, *pp.* 432–437

74 Kirk, *pp.* 480–484

74 Kirkley, *pp.* 480–484

74 Kirkwood, *pp.* 480–484

33 Kirwin, *pp.* 228–233

20 Kit, *pp.* 148–152

73 Kit, *pp.* 474–479

BOYS' NAMES

BOYS' NAMES

73 Lauritz, *pp.* 474–479
40 Lawford, *pp.* 270–274
55 Lawler, *pp.* 362–367
55 Lawley, *pp.* 362–367
73 Lawrance, *pp.* 474–479
73 Lawrence, *pp.* 474–479
73 Lawson, *pp.* 474–479
18 Lawton, *pp.* 136–141
77 Layton, *pp.* 498–503
39 Lazar, *pp.* 264–269
39 Lazare, *pp.* 264–269
39 Lazarus, *pp.* 264–269
48 Leal, *pp.* 318–322
69 Lealand, *pp.* 450–454
13 Leander, *pp.* 104–110
72 Leandre, *pp.* 468–472
13 Lee, *pp.* 104–110
30 Lee, *pp.* 208–213
54 Lee, *pp.* 356–360
69 Lee, *pp.* 450–454
76 Leger, *pp.* 492–497
13 Leggett, *pp.* 104–110
13 Leggitt, *pp.* 104–110
18 Leicester, *pp.* 136–141
3 Leif, *pp.* 44–48
69 Leigh, *pp.* 450–454
77 Leighton, *pp.* 498–503
22 Leith, *pp.* 160–164
69 Leland, *pp.* 450–454
8 Lem, *pp.* 74–78
8 Lemmie, *pp.* 74–78
8 Lemuel, *pp.* 74–78
54 Len, *pp.* 356–360
10 Lenaic, *pp.* 86–90
54 Lenard, *pp.* 356–360

53 Lennard, *pp.* 350–355
54 Lennie, *pp.* 356–360
50 Lennon, *pp.* 330–335
57 Lennox, *pp.* 374–379
54 Lenny, *pp.* 356–360
54 Leo, *pp.* 356–360
67 Leo, *pp.* 438–443
54 Leon, *pp.* 356–360
54 Leonard, *pp.* 356–360
54 Leonce, *pp.* 356–360
54 Leoner, *pp.* 356–360
54 Leonhard, *pp.* 356–360
54 Leonilde, *pp.* 356–360
67 Leopold, *pp.* 438–443
67 Lepp, *pp.* 438–443
30 Leroy, *pp.* 208–213
4 Les, *pp.* 50–54
4 Lesley, *pp.* 50–54
4 Leslie, *pp.* 50–54
18 Lester, *pp.* 136–141
68 Leverett, *pp.* 444–448
22 Leverton, *pp.* 160–164
55 Levi, *pp.* 362–367
55 Lew, *pp.* 362–367
55 Lewes, *pp.* 362–367
55 Lewis, *pp.* 362–367
69 Leyland, *pp.* 450–454
69 Leyman, *pp.* 450–454
24 Liall, *pp.* 172–176
76 Liam, *pp.* 492–497
13 Liggett, *pp.* 104–110
43 Lilian, *pp.* 288–293
73 Lin, *pp.* 474–479
30 Lincoln, *pp.* 208–213
24 Lind, *pp.* 172–176

618

BOYS' NAMES

55 Luthais, *pp.* 362–367

77 Luther, *pp.* 498–503

24 Lyall, *pp.* 172–176

24 Lyel, *pp.* 172–176

24 Lyle, *pp.* 172–176

69 Lyman, *pp.* 450–454

73 Lyn, *pp.* 474–479

24 Lyndon, *pp.* 172–176

73 Lynn, *pp.* 474–479

10 Lysander, *pp.* 86–90

76 Mac, *pp.* 492–497

53 Macaire, *pp.* 350–355

66 Macbeth, *pp.* 432–437

72 Macy, *pp.* 468–472

54 Maddison, *pp.* 356–360

13 Maddock, *pp.* 104–110

13 Maddox, *pp.* 104–110

54 Madison, *pp.* 356–360

13 Madoc, *pp.* 104–110

13 Madock, *pp.* 104–110

13 Madog, *pp.* 104–110

68 Mael, *pp.* 444–448

42 Maerwine, *pp.* 282–287

22 Magee, *pp.* 160–164

43 Magnus, *pp.* 288–293

20 Maitland, *pp.* 148–152

32 Maixent, *pp.* 222–227

3 Major, *pp.* 44–48

67 Mal, *pp.* 438–443

30 Malachi, *pp.* 208–213

30 Malachie, *pp.* 208–213

18 Malcolm, *pp.* 136–141

40 Malin, *pp.* 270–274

18 Mallory, *pp.* 136–141

18 Malo, *pp.* 136–141

8 Maloney, *pp.* 74–78

67 Malvin, *pp.* 438–443

22 Mandel, *pp.* 160–164

66 Manfred, *pp.* 432–437

66 Manfried, *pp.* 432–437

53 Manleich, *pp.* 350–355

53 Manley, *pp.* 350–355

77 Mannie, *pp.* 498–503

29 Manning, *pp.* 202–207

77 Manny, *pp.* 498–503

77 Manoel, *pp.* 498–503

40 Mansfield, *pp.* 270–274

35 Manton, *pp.* 240–245

77 Manuel, *pp.* 498–503

77 Manus, *pp.* 498–503

4 Manvil, *pp.* 50–54

4 Manville, *pp.* 50–54

33 Marc, *pp.* 228–233

59 Marceau, *pp.* 386–391

59 Marcel, *pp.* 386–391

59 Marcelin, *pp.* 386–391

59 Marcellin, *pp.* 386–391

59 Marcello, *pp.* 386–391

59 Marcellus, *pp.* 386–391

33 Marcius, *pp.* 228–233

33 Marco, *pp.* 228–233

33 Marcus, *pp.* 228–233

24 Marden, *pp.* 172–176

64 Mariel, *pp.* 420–425

39 Marien, *pp.* 264–269

39 Marin, *pp.* 264–269

39 Mario, *pp.* 264–269

39 Marion, *pp.* 264–269

39 Marius, *pp.* 264–269

33 Mark, *pp.* 228–233

40 Marl, *pp.* 270–274

18 Marland, *pp.* 136–141

40 Marlen, *pp.* 270–274

18 Marley, *pp.* 136–141

40 Marlin, *pp.* 270–274

40 Marlon, *pp.* 270–274

18 Marlow, *pp.* 136–141

18 Marlowe, *pp.* 136–141

18 Marly, *pp.* 136–141

12 Marmaduke, *pp.* 98–103

69 Marmion, *pp.* 450–454

24 Marsden, *pp.* 172–176

24 Marsdon, *pp.* 172–176

26 Marsh, *pp.* 184–188

26 Marshall, *pp.* 184–188

33 Marston, *pp.* 228–233

15 Mart, *pp.* 118–122

15 Marten, *pp.* 118–122

76 Martial, *pp.* 492–497

76 Martian, *pp.* 492–497

15 Martie, *pp.* 118–122

15 Martin, *pp.* 118–122

15 Marton, *pp.* 118–122

15 Marty, *pp.* 118–122

42 Marvin, *pp.* 282–287

42 Marwood, *pp.* 282–287

40 Maslen, *pp.* 270–274

40 Maslin, *pp.* 270–274

40 Maslon, *pp.* 270–274

24 Mason, *pp.* 172–176

72 Massey, *pp.* 468–472

10 Mat, *pp.* 86–90

10 Mata, *pp.* 86–90

74 Mather, *pp.* 480–484

10 Mathew, *pp.* 86–90

10 Mathias, *pp.* 86–90

10 Mathieu, *pp.* 86–90

15 Mathurin, *pp.* 118–122

10 Matt, *pp.* 86–90

10 Matthew, *pp.* 86–90

10 Matthias, *pp.* 86–90

10 Matthieu, *pp.* 86–90

10 Mattias, *pp.* 86–90

10 Mattie, *pp.* 86–90

10 Matty, *pp.* 86–90

63 Maurey, *pp.* 414–419

63 Maurice, *pp.* 414–419

63 Maury, *pp.* 414–419

57 Max, *pp.* 374–379

57 Maxence, *pp.* 374–379

57 Maxey, *pp.* 374–379

57 Maxi, *pp.* 374–379

57 Maxie, *pp.* 374–379

57 Maxim, *pp.* 374–379

57 Maxime, *pp.* 374–379

57 Maximilian, *pp.* 374–379

57 Maximilien, *pp.* 374–379

57 Maximilienne, *pp.* 374–379

57 Maximillian, *pp.* 374–379

57 Maximin, *pp.* 374–379

57 Maxwell, *pp.* 374–379

57 Maxy, *pp.* 374–379

35 Mayer, *pp.* 240–245

32 Mayfield, *pp.* 222–227

70 Mayhew, *pp.* 456–461

68 Maynard, *pp.* 444–448

77 Mayo, *pp.* 498–503

20 Mead, *pp.* 148–152

53 Medard, *pp.* 350–355

20 Medwin, *pp.* 148–152

BOYS' NAMES

67 Mel, *pp.* 438–443

68 Melaine, *pp.* 444–448

68 Melbourne, *pp.* 444–448

68 Melburn, *pp.* 444–448

68 Melburne, *pp.* 444–448

68 Meldon, *pp.* 444–448

67 Melvil, *pp.* 438–443

67 Melville, *pp.* 438–443

67 Melvin, *pp.* 438–443

68 Menard, *pp.* 444–448

22 Mendel, *pp.* 160–164

4 Mercer, *pp.* 50–54

47 Meredith, *pp.* 312–317

47 Meredydd, *pp.* 312–317

47 Meredyth, *pp.* 312–317

63 Meriadec, *pp.* 414–419

47 Merideth, *pp.* 312–317

47 Meridith, *pp.* 312–317

47 Meridyth, *pp.* 312–317

40 Merl, *pp.* 270–274

40 Merle, *pp.* 270–274

40 Merlin, *pp.* 270–274

70 Merrick, *pp.* 456–461

47 Merrie, *pp.* 312–317

20 Merrill, *pp.* 148–152

20 Merritt, *pp.* 148–152

47 Merry, *pp.* 312–317

8 Merton, *pp.* 74–78

42 Merv, *pp.* 282–287

42 Mervin, *pp.* 282–287

42 Mervyn, *pp.* 282–287

42 Merwin, *pp.* 282–287

42 Merwyn, *pp.* 282–287

35 Meyer, *pp.* 240–245

64 Micah, *pp.* 420–425

64 Mich, *pp.* 420–425

64 Michael, *pp.* 420–425

64 Michel, *pp.* 420–425

64 Mickie, *pp.* 420–425

64 Micky, *pp.* 420–425

64 Miguel, *pp.* 420–425

64 Mikael, *pp.* 420–425

64 Mike, *pp.* 420–425

68 Milbourn, *pp.* 444–448

68 Milbourne, *pp.* 444–448

68 Milburn, *pp.* 444–448

68 Milburne, *pp.* 444–448

32 Miles, *pp.* 222–227

4 Milford, *pp.* 50–54

37 Millard, *pp.* 252–257

50 Miller, *pp.* 330–335

4 Millford, *pp.* 50–54

50 Milo, *pp.* 330–335

74 Milton, *pp.* 480–484

35 Milward, *pp.* 240–245

20 Miner, *pp.* 148–152

20 Minor, *pp.* 148–152

64 Mischa, *pp.* 420–425

64 Misha, *pp.* 420–425

64 Mitch, *pp.* 420–425

64 Mitchell, *pp.* 420–425

63 Mo, *pp.* 414–419

35 Modred, *pp.* 240–245

13 Moe, *pp.* 104–110

13 Moise, *pp.* 104–110

18 Monro, *pp.* 136–141

18 Monroe, *pp.* 136–141

37 Montagne, *pp.* 252–257

37 Montagu, *pp.* 252–257

37 Montague, *pp.* 252–257

BOYS' NAMES

BOYS' NAMES

20 Norton, *pp.* 148–152

10 Nortrop, *pp.* 86–90

10 Nortrup, *pp.* 86–90

68 Norvel, *pp.* 444–448

68 Norvie, *pp.* 444–448

68 Norvil, *pp.* 444–448

68 Norville, *pp.* 444–448

68 Norvin, *pp.* 444–448

68 Norvyn, *pp.* 444–448

68 Norward, *pp.* 444–448

68 Norwell, *pp.* 444–448

68 Norwin, *pp.* 444–448

68 Norwood, *pp.* 444–448

68 Norwyn, *pp.* 444–448

65 Nowell, *pp.* 426–431

72 Nye, *pp.* 468–472

33 Oakes, *pp.* 228–233

33 Oakley, *pp.* 228–233

33 Oakly, *pp.* 228–233

72 Obadiah, *pp.* 468–472

2 Obert, *pp.* 38–42

72 Obie, *pp.* 468–472

12 Octave, *pp.* 98–103

12 Octavian, *pp.* 98–103

12 Octavien, *pp.* 98–103

12 Octavius, *pp.* 98–103

12 Octavus, *pp.* 98–103

53 Odell, *pp.* 350–355

77 Odilon, *pp.* 498–503

53 Odin, *pp.* 350–355

53 Odo, *pp.* 350–355

53 Odolf, *pp.* 350–355

69 Ogden, *pp.* 450–454

52 Ogilvie, *pp.* 344–349

77 Oglesby, *pp.* 498–503

33 Okeley, *pp.* 228–233

33 Okely, *pp.* 228–233

3 Olaf, *pp.* 44–48

3 Olar, *pp.* 44–48

3 Olen, *pp.* 44–48

3 Olin, *pp.* 44–48

15 Oliver, *pp.* 118–122

15 Olivier, *pp.* 118–122

15 Ollie, *pp.* 118–122

67 Olney, *pp.* 438–443

50 Omar, *pp.* 330–335

50 Omer, *pp.* 330–335

11 Onesime, *pp.* 92–96

57 Onslow, *pp.* 374–379

66 Oram, *pp.* 432–437

66 Oran, *pp.* 432–437

73 Ordway, *pp.* 474–479

32 Orel, *pp.* 222–227

66 Oren, *pp.* 432–437

26 Orestes, *pp.* 184–188

72 Orford, *pp.* 468–472

66 Orin, *pp.* 432–437

12 Orion, *pp.* 98–103

65 Orlan, *pp.* 426–431

73 Orlando, *pp.* 474–479

67 Orman, *pp.* 438–443

67 Ormand, *pp.* 438–443

67 Ormen, *pp.* 438–443

67 Ormin, *pp.* 438–443

67 Ormond, *pp.* 438–443

2 Oro, *pp.* 38–42

66 Orran, *pp.* 432–437

66 Orren, *pp.* 432–437

11 Orrick, *pp.* 92–96

66 Orrin, *pp.* 432–437

BOYS' NAMES

BOYS' NAMES

BOYS' NAMES

BOYS' NAMES

BOYS' NAMES

42 Rickward, *pp.* 282–287

42 Rickwood, *pp.* 282–287

42 Ricky, *pp.* 282–287

64 Ricky, *pp.* 420–425

69 Ricky, *pp.* 450–454

73 Ricky, *pp.* 474–479

42 Ricy, *pp.* 282–287

29 Riddock, *pp.* 202–207

55 Rider, *pp.* 362–367

43 Ridge, *pp.* 288–293

43 Ridgeway, *pp.* 288–293

43 Ridgley, *pp.* 288–293

13 Ridley, *pp.* 104–110

22 Ridpath, *pp.* 160–164

33 Rigby, *pp.* 228–233

33 Rigg, *pp.* 228–233

24 Riley, *pp.* 172–176

20 Ring, *pp.* 148–152

64 Riocard, *pp.* 420–425

26 Riordan, *pp.* 184–188

66 Ripley, *pp.* 432–437

39 Risley, *pp.* 264–269

35 Riston, *pp.* 240–245

64 Ritch, *pp.* 420–425

64 Ritchie, *pp.* 420–425

3 Ritter, *pp.* 44–48

8 Roald, *pp.* 74–78

73 Roan, *pp.* 474–479

29 Roarke, *pp.* 202–207

69 Rob, *pp.* 450–454

69 Robbie, *pp.* 450–454

69 Robby, *pp.* 450–454

69 Robert, *pp.* 450–454

69 Roberto, *pp.* 450–454

69 Robin, *pp.* 450–454

72 Robinson, *pp.* 468–472

50 Roc, *pp.* 330–335

64 Roch, *pp.* 420–425

18 Rochester, *pp.* 136–141

50 Rock, *pp.* 330–335

50 Rockley, *pp.* 330–335

50 Rockly, *pp.* 330–335

50 Rockwell, *pp.* 330–335

50 Rocky, *pp.* 330–335

73 Rod, *pp.* 474–479

73 Rodd, *pp.* 474–479

73 Roddie, *pp.* 474–479

73 Roddy, *pp.* 474–479

77 Roden, *pp.* 498–503

73 Roderic, *pp.* 474–479

73 Roderick, *pp.* 474–479

55 Rodge, *pp.* 362–367

55 Rodger, *pp.* 362–367

73 Rodhlann, *pp.* 474–479

73 Rodi, *pp.* 474–479

73 Rodie, *pp.* 474–479

22 Rodman, *pp.* 160–164

22 Rodmond, *pp.* 160–164

22 Rodmund, *pp.* 160–164

73 Rodney, *pp.* 474–479

72 Rodolf, *pp.* 468–472

72 Rodolph, *pp.* 468–472

72 Rodolphe, *pp.* 468–472

73 Rodric, *pp.* 474–479

73 Rodrick, *pp.* 474–479

73 Rodrigue, *pp.* 474–479

22 Rodwell, *pp.* 160–164

73 Roe, *pp.* 474–479

55 Rog, *pp.* 362–367

12 Rogan, *pp.* 98–103

BOYS' NAMES

BOYS' NAMES

BOYS' NAMES

BOYS' NAMES

BOYS' NAMES

BOYS' NAMES

BOYS' NAMES

BOYS' NAMES

BOYS' NAMES